New Paradigm in Macroeconomics

"an ambitious attempt to shape the terms of the economic debate over Japan's decade-long post-bubble economic stagnation."

William Grimes, Boston University

"What a wonderful read! ... Werner develops a simple and elegant model based on empirical observations but sufficiently abstract, and one that stands up to empirical testing impressively well. The potential implications are huge. His findings have become influential with those interested in the real world of (Japanese) finance."

Dirk Bezemer, Imperial College, University of London

"Werner has done an excellent job of showing the difficulties and conundrums faced by neoclassical theory when confronted with Japan's recent (and older) performance ... Werner's analysis of banking and credit-money creation, in particular, offers new insights into the enigmas of Japanese capitalism. This is a book that will be read by many more than Japan specialists."

Costas Lapavitsas, SOAS, University of London

Also by Richard Werner:

PRINCES OF THE YEN, JAPAN'S CENTRAL BANKERS AND THE
TRANSFORMATION OF THE ECONOMY

New Paradigm in Macroeconomics

Solving the Riddle of Japanese Macroeconomic Performance

Richard A. Werner

First published in 2005 by
PALGRAVE MACMILLAN
Houndmills, Basingstoke, Hampshire RG21 6XS and
175 Fifth Avenue, New York, N.Y. 10010
Companies and representatives throughout the world.

PALGRAVE MACMILLAN is the global academic imprint of the Palgrave
Macmillan division of St. Martin's Press, LLC and of Palgrave Macmillan Ltd.
Macmillan® is a registered trademark in the United States, United Kingdom
and other countries. Palgrave is a registered trademark in the European
Union and other countries.

ISBN-13: 978–1–4039–2073–7 hardback
ISBN-10: 1–4039–2073–7 hardback
ISBN-13: 978–1–4039–2074–4 paperback
ISBN-10: 1–4039–2074–5 paperback

This book is printed on paper suitable for recycling and made from fully
managed and sustained forest sources.

A catalogue record for this book is available from the British Library.

Library of Congress Cataloging-in-Publication Data

Werner, Richard, 1967–
    New paradigm in macroeconomics : solving the riddle of
Japanese macroeconomic performance / Richard A. Werner.
        p. cm.
    Includes bibliographical references and index.
    ISBN 1–4039–2073–7 (cloth)—ISBN 1–4039–2074–5 (paper)
        1. Japan – Economic conditions – 1989– 2. Neoclassical school of
economics. 3. Macroeconomics. I. Title.

HC462.95. W47 2004
339'.0952—dc22   2004058396

10 9 8 7 6 5 4
14 13 12 11 10 09 08 07 06

Transferred to Digital Printing 2009

Contents

Acknowledgements

I am grateful for the generous advice and support I received during the lengthy gestation period of this book. I have received much advice from my thesis advisers at Oxford, Dr Jenny Corbett and Dr Tim Jenkinson, as well as Mr Nicholas Dimsdale. In addition, I have benefited greatly over the years from many comments by academics and professional economists that are too numerous to mention. Nevertheless, I would like to thank those who provided particularly valuable advice or support during various stages of the research, namely Prof. Robert Z. Aliber, Prof. Jonathan Batten, Dr Joerg Bibow, Prof. Craig Freedman, Prof. Charles A. E. Goodhart, Dr James Gordon, Prof. Harald Hagemann, Prof. Harukiyo Hasegawa, Prof. Walter Hatch, Prof. Declan Hayes, Prof. Glenn Hook, Dr Tobias Hoschka, Dr Tim Jenkinson, Prof. Nobumitsu Kagami, Prof. Keimei Kaizuka, Dr C. H. Kwan, Prof. Paul McNelis, Dr Mark Metzler, Dr Bori Minakovic, Prof. Grayham Mizon, Prof. Stephen Nickell, Prof. Yukio Noguchi, Dr Marcus Noland, Prof. Hirohiko Okumura, Prof. Hugh Patrick, Prof. Hank Pruden, Prof. Ghon Rhee, Prof. Ryuzo Sato, Dr Christopher Scott, Prof. Sir Nicholas Stern, Prof. Joseph E. Stiglitz, Prof. Steve Thomas, Prof. Kazusuke Tsujimura, Dr Peter Warburton and Prof. Kozo Yamamura.

I owe a special thanks to those who have taken it upon themselves to read the entire typescript, namely Hideo Fujiki and Suminori Sakurai of the PHP Research Institute in Tokyo, T. J. C. Cooke, Dr Frank McGroarty, Dr Costas Lapavitsas and especially Dr Dirk Bezemer. Charles Goodhart has also kindly read the book and provided support and much stimulus for improvement, for which I am very grateful. I am also indebted to the many discussants of the relevant papers that I presented at international conferences, especially those most closely resembling chapters in this volume, namely at the 1993 Royal Economic Society Annual Conference, University of York, the 34th Annual Conference of the Money, Macro and Finance Research Group (MMF, 2002) at Warwick University and the 36th Annual Conference of the Money, Macro and Finance Research Group (MMF, 2004) at the Cass Business School. The international conferences in Europe, Japan and the Asia-Pacific region at which parts of this book were presented – and improved thanks to stimulating comments from participants – are unfortunately too numerous to mention. I am also grateful to the anonymous referees of those papers that have been published. The views expressed in this book are, however, mine.

I am also grateful for the research support received during various stages of this research project by the Bank of Japan, the Citicorp Foundation, the Commission for the European Union, the ESRC, the Japan Development Bank, the Japan Foundation, the Japanese Ministry of Education, the Krupp

Foundation, the Ministry of Finance's Institute for Monetary and Fiscal Studies, the Nomura Research Institute and the Profit Research Center Ltd.

The highly supportive environment of Linacre College, the former Institute of Economics and Statistics at Oxford, the University of Tokyo, as well as the collegiate support at Sophia University, Tokyo and the University of Southampton have also furthered the completion of this work.

I would like to thank my editor Amanda Hamilton and her efficient team at Palgrave Macmillan for her professional guidance and enthusiasm for this project. I also would like to thank the publishers of previous versions of parts of this book, usually in the form of articles, for permission to reproduce parts, usually in much modified form, especially Blackwell Publishers Ltd, the East Asian Economic Association, Duncker und Humblot and M. E. Sharpe. Many of the graphics and all of the econometric calculations were produced with the user-friendly PC-Win and PC-Give Version 10.0 software, or its predecessors since Version 7.

Over the years, many research assistants have contributed to this study, foremost among them Yoko Minami and Jenny Alf, whose excellent work deserves particular mention. I have also benefited from the great enthusiasm shown by many of my former and current students at Sophia University and the University of Southampton and would like to thank them for their support. Finally, all insights that I may have contributed I owe to the Lord, who is my Light (Psalm 27).

R. A. W.

Note on the representation of personal names

The ordering of first names and surnames follows the conventions of the English language.

List of Tables and Figures

Tables

Figures

List of Abbreviations and Acronyms

ADL   autoregressive distributed lag
ARCH   autoregressive conditional heteroscedasticity
BIS   Bank for International Settlements
BoJ   Bank of Japan
CD   certificates of deposit
CP   commercial paper
CPI   consumer price index
CY   calendar year
ECB   European Central Bank
FDI   foreign direct investment
FILP   Fiscal Investment and Loan Programme
FY   fiscal year
GDP   gross domestic product
GNP   gross national product
HPM   high powered money (= monetary base, base money, M0)
IBJ   Industrial Bank of Japan
IMF   International Monetary Fund
JGBs   Japanese government bonds
LDP   Liberal Democratic Party
LTCB   Long-term Credit Bank of Japan
LTCBs long-term credit banks (including IBJ and Nippon Credit Bank)
METI   Ministry of Economy, Trade and Industry (formerly MITI)
MoF   Ministry of Finance
NCB   Nippon Credit Bank
Nikkei Nihon Keizai Shinbun
NPO   non-profit organization
ODR   official discount rate
OECD   Organization for Economic Cooperation and Development
o/n   overnight
PSBR   public sector borrowing requirement
Q1   first quarter of the calendar year
s.a.   seasonally adjusted
u/c   uncollateralized
VAR   vector autoregression
WG   window guidance
WPI   wholesale price index
YoY   year-on-year

Part I
Introduction

Prologue: Searching for a New Kind of Economics

The dominant paradigm

In the 1980s and 1990s a school of thought reached the zenith of its power. Its influence had become pervasive. Having been the view of only a minority little more than 20 years earlier, this approach had succeeded in dominating its discipline at all leading universities in the world. Academics that did not adhere to it found it hard to make a career: obtaining jobs or moving up the ladder depended on publications in leading journals – which had been usurped by this particular school of thought.

But dominance in academia was merely the foundation of a much wider-reaching influence. A large number of prominent national and international bureaucrats, journalists, politicians and other 'opinion-makers' had either been trained in the discipline or had otherwise become its followers. As a result, the views proposed by it came to dominate public policy debate by the mid-1980s, permeating the discussion of issues affecting individuals, communities, companies, the nation and the international community. This school of thought is better known by its key tenets than by its name. Its key beliefs are that the pursuit of individual self-interest will lead to a better society, that government intervention beyond the narrow maintenance of law and order should be minimized if not eliminated and that the powers of unfettered markets should be unleashed in virtually every part of society, at home and abroad. For this purpose, structural reforms are recommended to deregulate, liberalize, privatize and open up as many industries and aspects of the economy as possible, as the beneficial forces of the invisible hand, if only allowed to operate freely, would improve people's lives, create wealth, produce prosperity and lead to maximum happiness.

The name of this school is less well-known: neoclassical economics. This may have to do with its somewhat obscure or technical ring. It is also testimony to the extent of its dominance: proponents are often no longer aware that there could be alternative schools of thought. To them, neoclassical economics is synonymous with modern economics *per se*. Most economics

3

programmes at universities consist entirely of neoclassical economics, and students can spend years studying for their degrees without becoming aware that they may have been studying just one particular branch, one of many schools of thought in the discipline of economics.

The financial press cites neoclassical ideas on a daily basis and its followers have entered highest public office. Central bankers are among the first profession to have been closely associated with neoclassical economics. This was followed by financial journalists and civil servants. As a result, the tune of deregulation, liberalization and privatization is being played daily and offered almost as the panacea to many of the world's ills. For instance, in July 2003 we were warned in the *Financial Times* that the German 'economy will stagnate', unless the country does what neoclassical economics recommends, namely to 'accelerate the pace of the economy's structural change ...' What is needed, we are told, is 'privatization, deregulation and liberalization'.[1] State-dominated firms need to be sold off. The labour market needs to become 'more flexible'. This means that employment protection must be abandoned and staff should be laid off, while the remaining ones are made to feel they might be next. 'Reforms of the social security and healthcare systems to reduce ballooning costs' are needed, which often is to say that the lifelong contributors to these systems should be denied the agreed payouts. If such deep structural reforms are not implemented, we are warned, Germany will not be 'fit for the future'.[2] The story is familiar in other countries. In July 2003, neoclassical economist Paul Samuelson, whose textbooks have contributed to the advancement of his school of thought, reaffirmed that 'Free markets [are the] key to prosperity.' Turning to Japan, Samuelson has little trouble identifying the solution to its problems: a recovery is only possible 'by turning away from the old Japanese model' and implementing deep structural reform.[3]

Samuelson's nephew, Lawrence Summers, is another example of a successful neoclassical economist who made it into highest government office. Neoclassical economists have moved beyond being appointed central bank governors, ministers of the economy or treasury secretaries. They have even become prime ministers (such as Spain's former prime minister Aznar) or Presidents (such as Peru's Toledo). In these positions of influence they have done much to advance the policy programme of the neoclassical school of thought.

Anyone who has lived in one of the world's less developed countries – in other words, the vast majority of the world's population – also has ample opportunity to experience the neoclassical policy agenda. Neoclassical economics has dominated the decisions of the large international organizations that deal with economic policy. Among them, regional development banks, the IMF, the World Bank, the BIS, the WTO (and its predecessor), as well as the OECD stand out. Early on, these institutions had focused on hiring and advancing the careers of adherents of the neoclassical school of thought. Already by the late 1970s, they had become bastions of neoclassical economics. Their policy advice duly reflected this. Thanks to the legal, financial and political muscle of these institutions, especially the IMF and the World Bank, the neoclassical free market economics was projected beyond the limitations of a small number of industrialized countries where it had been developed and made its mark on the world by affecting the lives of millions of people in the most far-flung corners of the earth. In over 100 countries, central bank policies, IMF-led structural adjustment programmes and development bank-led reform packages drastically changed fiscal policy, monetary policy, regulatory policy and many aspects of how societies are organized, each time along the neoclassical lines. This could take the form of cutting food subsidies for the financially weak or privatizing the supply of drinking water, thus often pricing the poor out of their water supply. The neoclassical policy agenda was usually supported by the US Treasury, which did much to advance the neoclassical consensus of Washington-based international organizations.

Wherever the World Bank and the IMF became active – most of the developing world – they soon seemed to know the true problems of each country. Little local research was necessary to reach their conclusions. Switching the country name from an earlier study seemed to do much of the job, since the policy advice is highly predictable and appears to apply to all countries: structural reform to implement liberalization, deregulation and privatization, we are told, is the only path to prosperity.

The fall of communism in the late 1980s provided another major boost to the already dominant neoclassical school of thought. Commentators hailed this as evidence that government intervention must be inefficient and only free markets would lead to economic success. There was even talk of the 'end of history', as the paradigm of free market capitalist economies with minimal government intervention now stood unopposed and without rival (Fukuyama, 1992). Free market economists were in great demand as well-paid advisers to the governments of transition economies, where they duly recommended 'shock therapy' – the simultaneous introduction of free markets in almost all industries.

The empirical record

The rise of the neoclassical school of thought to dominance and influence must be considered remarkable, perhaps unprecedented. What, then, has been the result of its dominant influence on the world?

Have the major global economic problems come closer to a solution? Has poverty become less of a problem? Has inequality declined? Has economic growth accelerated and become more stable in the many countries that adopted neoclassical policy advice? Have business cycles receded? Has free market 'shock therapy' delivered the desired results? Has happiness increased?

Since the late 1990s, a growing number of people have become disillusioned with neoclassical economics. They range from students at leading economics departments to established intellectuals in many disciplines, from independent activists to politicians. Many accuse neoclassical economics of failing to deliver on its promises. Often, criticism is targeted against an important aspect of the neoclassical agenda, namely the 'globalization' of the world economy through free trade (mainly for developing countries) and fewer government constraints on large-scale multinational corporations. The neoclassical doctrine, the 'Washington consensus' of unfettered free markets and neoliberalism, has since been labelled 'market fundamentalism', 'market extremism' or even a 'religion'.[4] Experienced civil servant and economist Robert Nelson, for instance, makes the case that economics has become the modern secular religion, complete with a priesthood (economists), a sacred text (Samuelson's *Economics*) and a plan of salvation (material progress and the liberalization agenda will solve the problems of mankind) (Nelson, 2001). The pure free market dogma is still preached by academia and the corporate media, and implemented by central banks, governments and the leading international organizations. However, unease about its results and implications has spread widely over the recent years.

Careful economists had long been aware that the neoclassical paradigm did not offer all the answers. There were many important empirical facts that neoclassical macroeconomics could not explain. However, the dominant school of thought proved adept at distracting attention from its flaws, for instance by labelling inconvenient empirical facts 'puzzles', 'anomalies' or 'paradoxes' – mere curiosities that one need not worry about. Whether the 'mystery of the missing money', the 'puzzle of the velocity decline', the mysterious 'breakdown in the money demand function', a surprising collapse in savings, the inability to explain exchange rates or asset prices, or the problem that interest rates appear to follow economic activity, not lead it as the mainstream proclaims – neoclassical economists have succeeded in keeping a lid on the difficulties that their approach has had in reconciling their theories with reality.

However, just when communism fell and many celebrated the unrivalled supremacy of the neoclassical free market model, a formidable empirical challenge was raised that could not easily be covered up: the East Asian economic success.[5] The stellar economic performance of Japan and the East Asian economies had not been achieved through free markets, liberalization or deregulation policies advanced by neoclassical economics. In 1993, this was reluctantly recognized by the World Bank in its 'East Asian miracle' study. Quite to the contrary, the East Asian success was due to government intervention in the form of clever institutional design and direct intervention in resource allocation, especially in the credit markets.

Until the end of the 1980s, the postwar Japanese economic structure was characterized by restricted and incomplete capital markets, reliance of corporate finance on bank funding, weak shareholder influence, a large number of government regulations, direct government interference in the form of 'guidance', a large number of formal and informal cartels, inflexible labour markets offering full-time staff at large enterprises job security, promotion based on the seniority in terms of years spent with the firm and in-house company unions. In the other East Asian countries there were close similarities, some put in place already under Japanese colonial rule.

Thus according to neoclassical economics, the East Asian economies, foremost among them Japan, should have been economic disaster zones throughout the postwar era: the fundamental theorem of neoclassical welfare economics identifies the particular set of assumptions under which the competitive economy is efficient. These assumptions, which include perfect information, complete markets, perfect competition, no transaction costs, and so forth, define an economy where interventions, such as by the government, cannot but reduce allocative efficiency. The Japanese, as well as key East Asian economies, have at no time during the postwar era resembled such an economy.

Yet instead of low performance, Japan, as well as the main East Asian economies, delivered high economic growth for many decades. The phenomenal growth of the Chinese economy over the past two decades has also occurred without the benefits of the free market model proposed by neoclassical economists.[6] Meanwhile, many of the IMF's free market pupils in Africa and Latin America languished in economic misery. While many neoclassical economists put up a last defence, arguing that East Asia and China have been successful *despite* their different systems, and would have been *even more* successful if they had implemented neoclassical policies, others realized that important lessons for economic theory had to be learned from the East Asian success story. Foremost among them is Joseph Stiglitz, who in the late 1980s turned his eyes towards Japan and East Asia and produced a series of path-breaking articles that profoundly challenged the neoclassical paradigm.[7]

But just when more and more economists and policy-makers were becoming willing to accept that there were serious problems with neoclassical economics and to consider alternative, Asian-inspired approaches, disaster struck the region. Firstly, Japan's economy moved into a decade-long economic downturn beginning in 1992. Then, in 1997, a major financial and economic crisis hit Thailand, Malaysia, Korea and Indonesia, resulting in currency collapses and contracting economies. Proponents of neoclassical economics were quick to place the blame. Ignoring the fact that mainstream economics could not explain the East Asian success, they quickly argued that the economic crises had been inevitable: after all, there was significant government intervention and market regulation in East Asia and the economies had been far removed from the free market paradigm. That, we were told once again, was a recipe for disaster.

Today, many neoclassical economists feel vindicated by the weak economic performance of Japan over the past decade, although they have to admit that most other East Asian economies have returned to their high-growth ways. Japan remains the linchpin around which a major economic argument will be fought: was the extraordinarily long recession of the 1990s really due to Japan's economic structure? If not, what then explains it? Whether a supporter of current mainstream thinking or a proponent of an alternative school of thought, all have to grapple with the realities of Japan. Its economy has become both the stumbling block and also the measuring rod for economic theories.

The Japanese challenge to economics

While there are many empirical facts that neoclassical macroeconomics cannot explain, the concentration of 'puzzles' and 'anomalies' has indeed been largest in the case of Japan – and instead of disappearing alongside with the Japanese recession, the challenge to neoclassical macroeconomics became ever bigger throughout Japan's long downturn. Since Japan is the second largest economy in the world, it is a challenge that mainstream economics cannot easily ignore.

Having puzzled neoclassical economists in the preceding decade through its high growth, during the 1990s Japan sank into an equally inexplicable recession. Unemployment rose to postwar highs, reaching over 3.8 million officially unemployed in the late 1990s.[8] Since 1990, over 210,000 firms have gone bankrupt. This has created much dislocation and bad debts. Every year about 30,000 people have been committing suicide in Japan. According to the National Police Agency, the increase in suicides is connected to corporate failure, unemployment and debt that resulted from the decade-long downturn. In addition, Japan also holds the postwar record for deflation among industrialized countries.

Japan's downturn also lasted longer than what is normally understood as merely cyclical. Most of all, the Japanese economy appears to have confounded every policy response mounted by the authorities. The key policy recommendations of the mainstream schools of economic thought have been implemented over the past decade, yet for years with very little to show for it.

Firstly, the mainstream prescription to reduce interest rates proved to be a disappointment. Most macroeconomic models argue that lower interest rates should result in higher economic growth. This is also the claim made by the world's central banks. In their frequent publications they do not tire of repeating their assertion that the key variable driving the economic cycle is interest rates, and that lower interest rates will stimulate growth. This theory has become so absorbed into modern journalism that the media regularly present it as a well-proven fact.

The Bank of Japan started lowering interest rates as early as 1991. Short-term interest rates have since been reduced from 6% in 1991 to 0.001% in early 2004. Long-term interest rates, as measured by the ten-year benchmark government bond yield, have fallen from over 7% to a record low of 0.4% in early 2003. The most powerful policy tool according to leading theories, central banks and perceived wisdom had been entirely exhausted over the past decade, without having had any noticeable effect on the economy.

The lack of effectiveness of interest rate policy encouraged the implementation of fiscal stimulation. Between 1992 and 1999 over a dozen fiscal spending packages were implemented, amounting to well over ¥120 trillion. Together with these explicit government spending programmes, the 'automatic stabilizer' of recession-induced rises in social support expenditures on the one hand and reductions in corporate, income, capital gains and transaction taxes on the other produced a record amount of national debt. The amount of outstanding central government debt rose to over 150% of annual GDP in 2002. Japan thus embarked on one of the largest fiscal expansion programmes in peacetime history. This also failed to deliver the expected result: whenever government spending increased, private sector economic activity shrank by a similar amount, so that government spending never succeeded in improving economic growth, let alone in 'kick-starting' or 'pump-priming' the economy.

The fact that a decade of record interest rate reductions and vast fiscal expansion failed to help Japan's economy poses a profound challenge to traditional mainstream economics that remains unanswered. While one or two years of incongruence between theory and reality might have been tolerated, over a decade of underperformance despite textbook-style stimulation policies is a sign of a major flaw in mainstream theory.

Instead of weakening the mainstream paradigm, however, the failure of the traditional demand-side theories ironically provided a boost to the more extreme proponents of neoclassical economics, known as 'supply-side' economists. They proposed two arguments, both of which recommended that Japan must respond to the recession by deep structural reform in the form of deregulation, liberalization and privatization: one was based on the assumption that economies always operate at their full employment level. Since demand factors were by assumption excluded in such theories, an economic slump can then only occur when the supply of factors of production restricts the economy. Thus these neoclassical economists argued that a lack of labour (due to demographic problems), insufficient capital, or lagging technology were to blame for Japan's recession. Failing that, Japan's recession must have been due to low productivity, we are told. Since an insufficient supply of production factors or low productivity are seen as the causes of the recession, structural reforms to release more production factors and raise productivity were seen as the answer. Another camp of neoclassical economists cited their theorem of welfare economics, which purports to show that only a deregulated, liberalized and privatized economy with minimal government intervention could be efficient and productive. Since

Japan's economic structure has been characterized by regulations, government intervention and a number of publicly owned companies, such as the post office, these economists also argued that deregulation, liberalization and privatization were the answer.

While both rationales for structural reform are widely supported in the financial press, they turn out to have no foundation in empirical evidence. As will be seen, there is ample evidence of an excess supply of factors of production and significant and sustained downward pressure on factor prices. The argument that insufficient demand has caused Japan's recession remains far better supported by the facts. Given the reality of record unemployment, it appears difficult to justify models that assume full employment. It is also not explained how measures to improve the supply side of the economy should help boost demand. Furthermore, the substantial trade surpluses that Japan accumulated during the 1990s, rivalling the record surpluses of the 1980s, were evidence that Japan's economy was, after all, among the most competitive and productive in the world, even during the 1990s.

Nevertheless, the neoclassical demand for structural reform became mainstream opinion and thus the Japanese government embarked on a major structural reform programme during the 1990s, including several thousand deregulatory measures, administrative reforms and the 'Big Bang' liberalization of financial markets. Yet there is no evidence that these structural reforms boosted economic growth. To the contrary, the empirical relationship between economic performance on the one hand and deregulation, abolition of cartels and greater market reform on the other has been quite the opposite of what neoclassical economics proclaims: when Japan significantly increased the number of cartels in its economy during the 1950s, economic growth accelerated sharply. It is less well-known that structural reforms towards greater market orientation were already started in the 1970s – under US political pressure – resulting in the scrapping of cartels and a steadily growing role for market forces. Thus the number of cartels fell sharply during the 1970s. When the structural reform programme accelerated during the 1980s and 1990s, the number of cartels came down further, finally dropping to zero. However, this shift away from the cartelized Japanese economic structure to a market-oriented economic structure was not accompanied by higher economic growth, as the neoclassical theories had predicted. To the contrary, as the number of cartels fell, so did economic growth. The decade of zero cartels was also when GDP growth dropped to zero.

Since none of the traditional theories could explain events in Japan, some economists became interested in a more fact-based search for possible answers. A group of economists became aware that the state of the Japanese banking system was less than satisfactory during much of the 1990s. It took years for this fairly obvious fact to become acknowledged by most economists, because banks and their role in the economy are greatly neglected in mainstream economics. Strictly speaking, neoclassical economics has no role for money in its models. And those models that grudgingly introduce money make no room for the function of banks. However, since the early 1990s, an increasing number of economists had argued that banks serve a special function in the economy through their activity of lending. This 'lending school' represented a renegade group of empirically-oriented neoclassical economists that hoped to explain some of the 'anomalies' that mainstream models could not deal with. They argued that bank lending was a wrongly neglected variable, which mattered especially in times when banks did not lend sufficiently, for instance due to their own balance sheet problems. Then, they argued, there could be a 'credit crunch' in the economy, as was argued in case of the US downturn of 1990 and 1991, as well as Japan during the 1990s: banks were increasingly suffering from bad debts, which appeared to render them more risk averse, so that they could not lend to those who wished to borrow. The implication was profound, for this explanation relied on the argument that markets were not actually clearing. However, the vast majority of economics textbooks and mainstream theories are based on the assumption that markets clear. Without it, most of neoclassical economics would become irrelevant. There was therefore a great reluctance to accept this 'lending view' and its implication of market rationing.

However the lending view, including its 'credit crunch' variant, also had a problem. While the empirical evidence seemed to suggest that there was something special about banks and their lending, it proved difficult for economists to pinpoint precisely what this was. Theories were proposed that banks serve the function of collecting and administering information on potential borrowers, or of 'monitoring' them. But capital markets do the same thing. Thus the argument ended up focusing on how banks served a special role in 'intermediating' between savers and small-scale borrowers: small and medium-sized enterprises had imperfect access to capital markets (the acknowledgement of which was another move away from the 'efficient market' equilibrium economics of mainstream textbooks).

Yet this lending view also found it very hard to explain the Japanese experience of the 1990s: if indeed a lack of credit supply from Japanese banks had been the cause of Japan's recession, then the incipient credit demand should simply have been met by foreign banks, which apparently had been vying to gain access to the Japanese market. Furthermore, borrowing from capital markets increased throughout the 1990s, a disintermediation process which diminished the reliance on bank funding. The 'bank lending' theories failed to explain why borrowing from these alternative sources did not substitute for a potential lack of bank lending.

The sudden recovery of 2004 once again took economists by surprise and few agree about what caused it. So far, there is no evidence that any of the standard theories explained, let alone predicted, the strong growth rate experienced in this year.

Thus today traditional economics has to face the embarrassing reality that it still has not explained events in Japan. What are the implications of this fact? Most economists have tried to shrug it off as being the fault of Japan – that weird economy that seems to defy theory. Is this response scientifically justified? Any economic theory that claims general validity must also apply to the second-largest economy in the world.

Disillusionment with mainstream economics

It is a good time to revisit Japan, because there is today increasing disillusionment with neoclassical economics on other grounds as well. More and more economists feel that neoclassical economics has simply failed to deliver on too many counts.

Privatization, for instance, was meant to increase the quality of services and reduce their prices. But in many cases this was not achieved. British railways or electricity providers in the US are but two examples from the industrialized world. In many transition and developing countries, privatization was often even more disastrous, appearing akin to a get-rich-quick scheme for a small elite at the expense of everyone else.[9]

Unemployment was said to be the result of 'inflexible labour markets', which result in excessively high and rigid real wages. Cut the wages and unemployment will decline, neoclassical economists assured us. But when real incomes fell – as they did in the US for most middle-class families, or in much of Europe due to the euro-induced inflation – or when real wage growth lagged behind productivity growth – as recently in many countries in the world – there was little sign of an increase in employment, let alone improved standards of living for the majority. Unemployment increased in many cases when real wages fell.

Deregulation, liberalization and other market-oriented structural reforms were meant to bring prosperity to the developing countries. After decades of painful and costly World Bank and IMF programmes, Africa has very little prosperity to show for it. Many Latin-American and Asian developing countries also do not appear any better off as a result of these programmes. There is ample evidence pointing in the opposite direction.

Proponents of neoclassical policies raised hopes that standards of living and the quality of life could be improved all over the world, that poverty and deprivation was going to be a thing of the past. As recent as the 1950s and 1960s, many economists were convinced that, thanks to the advances of economics, an era of stable economic growth and ever-increasing wealth and prosperity had begun and would spread welfare across the world. This is not what happened. There is very little empirical evidence that poverty, destitution, disease and economic inequality have been defeated. To the contrary, many studies seem to indicate that inequality has been increasing.[10] True, the super-rich have done very well from neoclassical policies: in the UK in 2003 their wealth increased by 30%, 15 times as fast as inflation.[11] However, this is true only for the top 0.002% of the population. There is no evidence that the wealth of the majority rose anything like it. The number of people living in urban slums is rising rapidly. Poverty remains an urgent and growing problem. The gap between the well-off and the poor is not closing but widening. While empirical data on this question is interpreted differently (usually depending on one's school of thought), there is little denying that the rich receive more, while the poor are getting less – or that the little they own may even be taken from them. In some countries the concentration of wealth and power that resulted directly from neoclassical policy advice has become so enormous that even an institution such as the World Bank has warned of the 'inefficiency' of such wealth concentration.[12] The fruit of the neoclassical reforms has been increasing inequality, which in turn has triggered new social, political and even military tension in many parts of the world.

According to the neoclassical 'Washington consensus' emanating from the international organizations, there is no need for poor countries to develop indigenous industries, because free markets will ensure that everyone focuses on their comparative advantage, and that will enhance social welfare. This is the famous theory of comparative advantage, proposed by David Ricardo in the nineteenth century and widely cited by the British leadership at the time when dealing with other countries. For the developing countries of the postwar era this argument implied that they had to continue to produce low-value-added and low-priced commodities, whose relative prices are known to decline inexorably, while their consumers must buy finished goods at ever-rising relative prices from abroad – importing them from the largest IMF and World Bank shareholders. Since the well-known long-term trends of falling commodity and rising finished goods prices mean that developing countries will receive ever less for their exports, while having to pay ever more for their imports, they cannot help but become indebted to the rich countries. When debt becomes large, the IMF seems ready to take over the government and arrange for further 'beneficial' market-oriented reforms, such as cutting food subsidies and social welfare, while seizing key domestic assets as collateral for the foreign investors. The outcome has been a significant deterioration of economic performance and standards of living in the Third World.

The free flow of capital was meant to increase prosperity in the Third World. Instead, developing countries have merely become more indebted, spending an increasing amount of their resources on interest and interest-on-interest payments. Often, the interest payments alone are larger than any initial loan received. Furthermore, the liberalization of international capital flows that was strongly urged on developing countries by the US Treasury, the IMF and the other neoliberal international organizations has often produced major economic disasters in the form of balance of payments crises and currency and financial market collapses, as happened during the Asian crisis or many times in Latin America.

The promise of stable economic growth, without cycles, has also not been met. Economic cycles have not disappeared. On the contrary, there is indication that the former business cycles may have turned into larger boom-bust cycles in many countries. There is evidence that over the past 30 years, financial crises have increased in number and become more destructive and menacing in their amplitude. Despite the declared aim of achieving price stability, stability of economic growth and of exchange rates thanks to neo-classical economics, governments and central banks have failed to deliver.

The structural reforms of the labour markets were meant to increase jobs and prosperity. However, it appears that the benefits of labour market reforms have mostly accrued to the employers and large-scale shareholders – a small minority in any country. Employees today generally have less job security, often less pay or less real purchasing power. Meanwhile, the phenomenon of 'jobless recoveries' puzzles observers in many post-reform or post-recession countries, even the US.

The focus of neoclassical economics on the pursuit of self-interest and profits has not helped to protect the environment. The mathematics of compound interest – with interest rates being a key variable in the mainstream representation of an economy – produces pressure constantly to deliver growth. This growth is measured as the gross addition in economic value added as booked in the national income accounts, without netting out the costs of drawing down our (unaccounted) stock of natural assets. Any true cost-benefit analysis must, however, take the environmental destruction and its consequences, including its effect on health and happiness, into consideration. Ever larger parts of the public are becoming aware that the current approach to economics, with minimal government intervention into the workings of large corporations and large-scale shareholders, is producing very costly, often irreparable damage to our most precious asset and the heritage of humankind: our planet.

Neoclassical economics is built on the fundamental axiom that the main motivation and goal of mankind is to accumulate more material wealth. However, scientific studies have demonstrated time and again that this is not what motivates people. The main human motivation is often not economic at all.[13] To spend less time at work and more time with family is usually found to increase happiness. This is not, however, where neoclassical policy advice has been leading the world. As a result, many of the reforms inspired by neoclassical economics have failed to make people happy. Instead, there is evidence that they have become unhappier as a result: many neoclassical structural reforms have implied an increase in working hours required to maintain the standard of living.[14] There is evidence that both parents of middle-income families in the US now have to work, while they did not have to several decades ago. Educational reform, endorsed by neoclassical thinking, has saddled students with substantial debts. Psychologists have found that this is a main source of depression among students.[15] Job stability is a main factor determining happiness, according to empirical research. The increasing job insecurity of neoclassical 'flexible labour markets' has thus left substantial parts of society worse off. There is no evidence that the increasing commercialization of television, cinema and the print media has rendered people happier. On the contrary, companies are attempting – often succeeding – in exploiting human weaknesses for their gain, not seldom leaving people worse off. Studies have found that a stable marital relationship is a main determinant of happiness, and, indeed, of longevity and health. However, the commercialization and trivialization of sex outside marriage – another commodity subject to the free market mechanism, according to neoclassical economics – has not had a salutary effect on marriage and thus has not contributed to making people happier.[16]

Reflecting public dissatisfaction, the British government has recently declared the goal of creating 'sustainable communities'. Disillusionment with the commercialization and draining of local communities has even prompted business lobby groups to abandon the previous emphasis on barebone profit maximization. The president of the CBI employers' body recently lamented in a government-commissioned report that Britain now boasted 'ugly retail parks, isolated schools and hospitals and business parks hermetically sealed from the outside world', where businesses felt no need to provide leadership to the communities they serve.[17] The neoclassical, market-oriented and planning-averse type of policy introduced in Britain since the early 1980s had not taken into consideration the desire of residents to live in a pleasant social setting.

Increased inequality has had an impact on public safety. In some countries, such as the US and the UK, the prison population has increased significantly. The fruits of neoclassical policies have been alienation of long-term unemployed, a feeling of disenfranchisement due to a lack of opportunities to improve one's status and hence a lower level of loyalty to society. Higher crime rates are one outcome, which in turn affects the rest of society negatively – though without showing up as a minus in the national income accounts (greater spending on police, the legal system and prisons, as well as on the military, are recorded as a positive contribution to national income).

Neoclassical economics is built on the premise that individuals care most of all for themselves and act independently of each other. The state of happiness of one is assumed to have no impact on others. Social relationships and the desire of individuals to relate to others and receive respect within social groups are outside the neoclassical model. A growing group of economists, originating in France but quickly spreading across the world's economics campuses, has thus argued that neoclassical economics is 'autistic' – as it has difficulties in recognizing that humans need to relate to others.[18]

Neoclassical economics talks about competition as a key mechanism, but at the same time ignores the reality that most mature industries are highly concentrated and dominated by a small number of firms. Some of these firms have become highly influential and it is not clear that the pursuit of their profits increases overall prosperity. This may be most apparent in the case of the weapons and war services industries. Indeed, in a world where a small number of firms or large-scale shareholders maintain a dominant position, and where the neoclassical agenda has severely limited the restraints that governments can place on corporations, it even becomes questionable whether democracy can be maintained, or whether vested interests will not simply 'buy' the politicians (for instance by funding their election campaigns).

Mainstream consumer theory assumes that individuals know everything and face no time constraints on their activities. According to this theory, consumers cannot be duped easily by unscrupulous corporations. But the reality is different, which is why government intervention is often required. The evidence is that consumers are not perfectly informed, hence even the largest supermarket chains get away with misleading pricing of products that costs consumers dearly and earns their large-scale shareholders nice profits purely due to misinformation.[19]

Military conflicts have not abated. While the causes may be different in each case, there are also common threads: often, economic inequality, rivalry and competition over limited economic resources, ranging from water to oil, other minerals, raw materials and arable land appear to be fundamental causes of conflict. Whether it was Hitler's declared quest for 'living space' in the East, or Japanese efforts to gain economic autarky and establish an independent economic bloc that could not be blackmailed by outside colonial powers, economic motives have never been absent in warfare. The Middle East, including the occupation of Iraq, may be another case in point. Despite its dominant position, neoclassical economics has not been able to make any positive contribution in this important area. To the contrary, its policy prescriptions, by increasing inequality and strengthening oligopolistic large-scale corporations, may have made matters worse.

On a fundamental level, neoclassical economics talks much about market equilibrium – that state of affairs when demand is said to equal supply. Even many critics of neoclassical economics find the neoclassical case plausible that markets tend towards equilibrium and often can be considered in a state of equilibrium, or at least approaching one. However, for market equilibrium, there are many conditions that must necessarily be fulfilled. Neoclassical economics deals with this by simply assuming them to be fulfilled. Foremost among these assumptions is the requirement that everyone has perfect information of all relevant facts. If this is not true, markets will not be in equilibrium. And then the entire edifice of neoclassical economics is irrelevant. In this case, a quite different kind of economics is required.

The fundamental flaw

A different kind of economics is indeed what many are now demanding. A large number of students have lost interest in neoclassical economics, as they recognize that it has become divorced from reality. While high hopes existed in the 1960s about the ability of mathematical models to explain or forecast economic developments, the business world today does not place great store by economic forecasters. Institutional investors prefer to talk to strategists rather than economists. Even major asset management firms have abandoned taking positions on currencies, for instance, as economics has failed to explain exchange rates. Professional economists working at corporations and financial institutions have long realized that they cannot stick to academic economic models if they want to remain relevant. They have long abandoned them, leaving the academic economists as followers of an esoteric science that has little, if anything to do with economic reality.

Could it be, one hardly dare ask, that we got things upside down? Could it be that many of the world's ills are actually *caused* by the drive to create free markets and by the wrong type of economics? Neoclassical economics has had its chance at improving things. It has failed. The time has come for a new kind of economics.

The critics of neoclassical economics agree that economics should be about economic reality and should be demonstrably relevant to it. This will strike the non-economist as obvious. However, it is not obvious in mainstream economic thinking: the neoclassical school of thought is based on the deductive approach. This methodology argues that knowledge is brought about by starting with axioms that are not derived from empirical evidence, to which theoretical assumptions are added (again not empirically backed), and on the basis of which tools of logic (mathematics) are utilized to prove theoretical results.

There is an alternative approach. This approach examines reality, identifies important facts and patterns, and then attempts to explain them, using logic, in the form of theories. These theories are then tested and modified as needed, in order to be most consistent with the facts of reality. This methodology is called inductivism.[20] All the natural sciences and most scientific disciplines use this approach. Inductivism is not only dominant in science, it also describes how we learned as infants about this world. When we touched the hot stove in the kitchen and burnt our fingers we learned inductively that doing so again would also hurt again. When men saw the sun 'rising' in the East several times, they induced that it would continue to do so in the future. Inductivism is not only scientific, it is also common sense. This is why before the arrival of neoclassical economics (and its nearly identical historical predecessor, classical economics), the majority of economists quite naturally followed the inductive approach.[21]

Neoclassical economics turns out to be the one school of thought within the discipline of economics, indeed one of the very few intellectual disciplines in general, that rejects the inductive approach favoured by scientists, and prefers deductivism. It must be considered a unique phenomenon in the history of thought that the originally marginal and eccentric deductive approach to economics has today become the mainstream school of thought.

Unhindered by economic reality, deductive economists can start with their preferred axioms, which do not need to be supported by facts – such as the axiom that individuals only care about the maximization of their own material benefit. Additional unrealistic assumptions produce the theories that are so removed from reality. While this is certainly allowed and may be useful as an exercise in logic, the theories, which are specific to the hypothetical environment created by the assumptions, are then used to advance policy recommendations. By this stage, no further mentioning is made of the assumptions necessary for the validity of the argument. The jump from the theoretical and hypothetical models to actual, supposedly workable policy advice is not usually explained. It is striking how seamlessly neoclassical economists have bridged the gap from their wholly fictional world of unrealistic models to recommendations of policies that actual politicians are supposed to implement in reality.

Obfuscation has certainly played a role: to hide the fact that much of theoretical mainstream economics consists of irrelevant existence theorems and axiomatically asserted 'findings', impenetrable jargon was used. It seems that lack of content was covered up by shrouding models in ever-more advanced mathematics that awes mathematicians and that makes even experts reluctant to criticize.[22] Many observers where blinded by what masqueraded as science, when, by comparison, it would be unthinkable for physicists to suggest that one should assume the laws of physics were suspended – for the sake of argument and to see what type of interesting model one gets – and then proceed to act on these findings in this actual world, where the laws of physics do apply. Political supporters of the conclusions and policy recommendations of neoclassical economics (these are often the economists themselves) are guilty of failing to point out the highly unusual conditions necessary for their theories and recommendations to be valid. Abstract models that rely on unrealistic assumptions and apply only to a theoretical dream world are prone to be usurped by interested parties and thus may simply become excuses for advocating policies preferred by some. Thus deductivism is certainly useful for those who wish to support preconceived ideas with the cloak of being 'scientific'. Yet few scientists would consider purely deductive approaches scientific.

It can be seen that the deductive methodology is the fundamental reason why economics could end up so far removed from reality. If a gap between reality and theory is pointed out (by some pesky inductivist), deductivism does not require neoclassical economists to change their theory. Instead, deductivists are entitled to demand that reality be changed to suit their theory (which is correct by axiom). If the long list of assumptions required for neoclassical models to work – perfect information, complete markets, no government intervention, perfect competition, no increasing returns to scale – does not seem to reflect reality, it is logically consistent for deductivists to suggest that structural changes be implemented so that reality moves closer in line with their models. The deductive approach also explains why the increasing dominance of the neoclassical approach resulted in a relegation to secondary status of those branches of economics that do look at reality, such as applied economics, economic history, political economy and regional economic studies. They dealt with uncomfortable facts and thus their influence had to be reduced so as not to threaten the deductive mainstream.

The main contribution of neoclassical economics

Nevertheless, despite its deductive methodology and unrealistic assumptions, neoclassical economics, like its predecessor, classical economics, has not been useless. To the contrary, interpreted correctly, it can be seen to have provided a valuable service to mankind. To recognize this contribution, it is necessary to recall what neoclassical theories actually say. Many observers, and even many economists, believe that neoclassical economics has proven that only free, unimpeded markets and free trade can lead to economic success, while government intervention is doomed to inefficiency and failure. This is not in fact true. Instead, neoclassical models have demonstrated quite precisely that free markets and free trade *would only then* lead to optimum welfare, and government intervention *would only then* be an inefficient distortion of the economy, *if and only if* we lived in a world where everyone had perfect information about everything, and a number of other stringent conditions (such as zero transaction costs, constant returns to scale, complete markets, perfect competition, and so on) were met. Likewise, neoclassical economics found that liberalization, deregulation and privatization *would only* improve economies in situations where everyone had perfect information (and transaction costs are zero, there are constant returns to scale, complete markets, perfect competition, and so on).

The most familiar diagramme in economics shows a downward-sloping demand curve and an upward-sloping supply curve. It is said that prices adjust so that markets clear at the point where the two curves cross – and thus markets are in equilibrium or a state approaching it. In actual fact the model says no such thing. It has demonstrated that demand will equal supply *if and only if* everyone had perfect information. The string of highly restrictive and unrealistic assumptions on which the neoclassical models are based are like the uncomfortable small print in a contract that gets easily overlooked. But they have far-reaching implications. Thanks to the rigorous neoclassical models we have learned just how stringent and how exceptional the necessary conditions are in order to obtain market equilibrium, or to obtain the result that free markets or free trade produce an optimal resource allocation. The question is now whether these conditions or at least some of them, could ever hold to be true. If not, then neoclassical economics has rigorously proven to us that free markets and free trade *cannot* be expected to result in optimal resource allocation, maximum welfare or even simple market clearing. In this case, neoclassical economics has proven that deregulation, liberalization and privatization *cannot* be expected to improve anything – which may well explain why the numbers of economically disenfranchized has increased and globalization à la Washington consensus is being increasingly opposed. More than that, if markets do not actually clear, economies would function quite differently from what we have been told by the mainstream textbooks for decades. A very different kind of economics would be required to explain economic reality and help us improve it.

Probably the most important of the premises needed by neoclassical economics for its tenets to hold is the assumption of perfect information. It is so crucial, because even simple market clearing – a very fundamental tenet of much of modern economics – requires it. Joseph Stiglitz, who became the most influential economist to turn against mainstream neoclassical economics, started out his research by 'relaxing' just this one assumption that was presented as fairly innocuous by neoclassical models. Many trained economists had become so familiar with the assumption of 'perfect information' that 'relaxing' it seemed an unusual thing for them.

Since the fiction of 'perfect information' is a standard assumption, most economists have become thoroughly hardened to its enormity. To assume perfect information is a monstrous distortion of reality. It creates a fictional world that is not just a little different from reality, but one that is diametrically opposed to what constitutes the very essence of the world we live in. All economic activity is based on the very fact that information is not perfectly and equally distributed. To realize the far-reaching implications of the assumption of perfect information, consider what a world would look like if the neoclassical assumption of 'perfect information' indeed held true.

If there was perfect information ...

- there would not be meetings at companies, government agencies and other institutions. In actual fact, much activity at any organization is taken up by holding meetings in order to inform, communicate, discuss, decide, motivate, and so on;
- there would be no need for firms to exchange information. In actual fact, gathering information is crucial for businesses. Since medieval times, trade fares, product shows, conferences, symposia and events are well-documented as important engines of growth and innovation: such growth depends on information flows, on firms getting to know other firms, meeting customers, and so on;

- there would be no books, no newspapers, no news programmes on TV. Reuters and Bloomberg, even the internet, would not be viable. Customers would not pay to obtain information about what they know already. The large media conglomerates, such as Bertelsmann or AOL Time Warner, would not exist;
- analysts would not have to spend hours poring over corporate figures to analyse the state of a company. All the multitude of data would not only be instantly known, people would also have the requisite knowledge to interpret them correctly;
- there would be no corporate accounting scandals, which surprised investors, regulators and, on occasion, accountants alike and resulted in multibillion-dollar losses for investors. The scandals include Enron, WorldCom, Tyco, Parmalat, and so on;
- there would have been no surprise at former NYSE chairman Richard Grasso's enormous pay cheque, which became a scandal when it became widely 'known'. It had been agreed much earlier and was no secret;
- there would not be any secret services, indeed there would not be any secrets – political, military, commercial or otherwise. Instead, secret services command multibillion-dollar budgets;
- actors would not be able to become politicians. In reality, actors have become governors, even presidents of major countries. The fact that they are known to many people is often sufficient for them to get elected to highest office. This demonstrates the enormous value of information and of being known. It seems to beat any other quality that politicians might have. In a world of perfect information this would be unthinkable;
- all products would be equally well-known and easily available to consumers. In reality, the biggest bottleneck for sellers of new goods and services is to get their product and its availability known to potential buyers. This is why distribution channels are so important and valuable for businesses. Shelf-space in shops is limited. The market for prime shelf-space is rationed. Psychologists are paid to suggest which places are more likely to be spotted and which arrangements in shops are more likely to trigger purchases. None of this would be possible or necessary in a world of perfect information. In bookshops those books for which the publishers have paid large advances appear in prominent places and stay on shelves much longer. Others are in remote corners, with only one copy available for only a limited time, or not in the shop at all. Which book will get bought? Is it really the quality of the book that decides it? Or the advertising and positioning in the bookshop? The internet has not changed this reality: the profusion of websites means that putting up one's product on the internet does not ensure any sales or even hits. The time during one day is limited (rationed). So is the time each computer user sits in front of a screen. Thus only a limited number of websites can appear before the eyes of each computer user. While the supply of

websites is very large, the effective demand for them is much smaller: the market for website watching is rationed, like every other market;

- there would be no need to learn different languages, mathematics or any subject at all – least of all economics. People would know the true economics already! There would be no need for education and training, no need for schools and universities, no need for companies to spend on training their staff and acquire further technical skills. The money spent by India over several decades to achieve a high level of education (government intervention often criticized by neoclassical economists) would have been unnecessary and today African countries would be as much leaders in software development as India. There would be no need to learn local languages and customs for a firm entering a different market. There would be no need for any expertise at all;

- there would be no need to hire anyone except new graduates, since work experience would count for nothing. However, wages as determined by the labour markets indicate that work experience is valued by employers, as inexperienced new graduates command lower wages in the market. Despite being the cheapest offering on the labour market, firms choose to hire only few new graduates, instead relying mostly on more expensive staff;

- there would not be any advertising or the attempt to build brands. The existence of brands is a reflection of imperfect information: consumers cannot be sure whether a product will fulfil its claimed purpose, whether it is faulty or whether it will have a sufficiently long lifespan to make the purchase worthwhile. The only way around this information problem is for producers to build a reputation for high quality, based on the past track record. Once this has happened, consumers will have confidence. This was realized in early medieval times in Europe, where trade guilds were created and implemented strict quality control. Essentially they were cartels that forbid people from engaging in their trade, except with the permit from the guild, which would only be granted after examinations and quality controls. As a result, many European cities developed a high reputation for a specific product, which in turn helped convince customers to buy their products as they inspired confidence. If knives or other steel equipment were stamped as originating from Sheffield, Solingen or Toledo, customers would, based on the reputation built up over the years, have confidence in the product. This means that each product carries a reputation externality with it, which the price does not reflect, and which each individual producer may not even consider. The significant sums spent on advertising by corporations are evidence of how important information imperfections are and how important it is for firms to be known and to have a good reputation;

- there would not be money. Barter proved cumbersome in the absence of the coincidence of wants, if one did not know exactly who might wish to buy which amount of one's produce. Money was an answer and its existence demonstrates that information is not perfect and never has been;

- there would be no technological innovation, and hence there would be no real growth. Empirical studies, including by Solow (1957) have shown that much of economic growth is accounted for by technological innovation. However, such innovation is the result of improved recipes (Romer, 1990) to rearrange already given resources. In other words, growth is due to information. Without new information, there could not be real growth. To assume perfect information means that all information is already available and equally disseminated. There are two levels at which this is relevant: perfect information means that future technology should already be known today. Secondly, if we accept imperfect information of future technologies, then the dissemination of this new technology may occur imperfectly – as indeed patent laws ensure. Either way, imperfect information exists. In reality, one of the most important investments by firms is on research and development of new recipes, that is, new information, about what new products could be made, how new goods and services could be assembled, and so on. Once such new information has been generated, firms will try hard to keep it secret and prevent it from falling into the hands of competitors. Patents represent one way to maintain an information advantage temporarily. Secrecy is another. Anyone who has worked in a firm will know that corporate secrets are important and often protected explicitly in employment contracts;
- there would be no talk about or need for 'technology transfer' to developing countries. All technology would already be known;
- there would be no headhunters: financial sector headhunters usually charge 30% of the first year's pay package of the person they have successfully introduced to a firm. With a modest start-up annual package of US$100,000 base salary and an annual bonus of US$200,000, this would amount to almost US$100,000 just for one deal. There are many headhunting firms, in many countries. None of these could exist if there was perfect information;
- there would be no export/import firms, which capitalize on their knowledge of another country. In reality, knowledge of language, customs, laws, taxes and customs duties is worth money. That's why such firms can charge a commission, which usually continues as long as the goods are exported or imported;
- there would be no literary agents. They know the publishers and the names of the suitable editors, usually because they worked as editors at publishers before. They then sell their knowledge, charge 10% or 15% (for overseas deals, when sub-agents are involved, 20%) of all monies. There is also the reputation aspect, another result of imperfect information: agents act as a screening device and try to build up a good track record of books, so that editors at publishing houses will trust their recommendations. If there was perfect information, editors would not need that service, neither would authors;

- no activity could exist, which is based on an information advantage or the provision of specialized knowledge of a trade, for which commissions or fees are charged. All these are based on asymmetric information: the counterparties do not know each other, or the details of the transaction, but the intermediary knows. If we knew where the right apartment is becoming available, or if we knew which editor at which publishing house might like our book, or if we knew which wholesaler or distribution chain in another country might be suitable for and interested in our product, would we pay the 3%, 15% or sometimes higher agency fees? If we start up a hedge fund, we will need to raise money. Would we offer up to 50% of all the revenues to the fund 'introducer' – agents who market the fund to their contacts – as is often happening, if we knew the names and contact details of those pension funds, funds of funds or family offices that are interested in our hedge fund?
- entire industries would not exist, such as
  - the entire financial sector, including banking, fund management, investment advisers and stockbroking (if investors knew about who needed money, they could invest directly without financial intermediaries), ratings agencies as well as stock market index compilers and disseminators of such indices
  - the entire telecommunications and internet industry, which works on relaying information
  - the consulting industry
  - accounting and auditing firms (the accuracy or inaccuracy of accounts would be well-known)
  - scientists, teachers or instructors
  - lawyers, who inform about laws and how to proceed with defending one's rights
  - doctors, who use their knowledge to diagnose diseases and prescribe suitable therapy
  - tax advisers and qualified accountants, who perform the service of advising on ways to account for transactions appropriately and minimize taxes; with perfect information unqualified clerks could just perform the obvious duties of inputting data into spreadsheets
  - police officers working on solving crimes
  - economists.

The list could go on. If there was perfect information, people would not spend much time or money on gathering and relaying information. Monitoring an average day of an average employee should show that usually the majority of our time is spent on this activity: in the morning, reading the newspaper, checking the mail, attending the morning meeting, checking email, checking a few internet websites, researching in libraries, looking up company reports, looking up files, searching for files or searching for information, calling up colleagues and contacts to find out something, receiving enquiries from potential customers, colleagues, subcontractors, suppliers who ask many questions, meeting colleagues for lunch to discuss matters, visiting potential customers to explain products and services, visiting suppliers to clarify requirements and specifications or to avoid misunderstandings, having business dinners to facilitate communication, going home and seeing advertisements on the train, watching the news or commercials on TV, asking the spouse how their day was ...

It is no exaggeration to say that each one of us spends most of our time gathering, analysing, disseminating information and communicating with others. It is the very essence of our activities. It is the essence of commercial activity and hence of what happens in an economy. To assume perfect information is to assume that none of this happens.

In the real world people and companies make money *because* others do not know everything. The information that others do not have is their advantage. It is their value added. Asymmetric information is not an eccentric exception to models, as economics textbooks make it appear. Instead, it is the very essence of business and economic activity. Where information asymmetries are largest, the profits are largest. This is why in transparent and highly competitive industries profits are smaller. They are largest in the financial sector, because least is known about the actual working of financial markets and economies – partly thanks to neoclassical economics.

Information is at the very heart of the economy. Its value lies precisely in the fact that it is not perfectly and symmetrically distributed. To assume perfect information means to assume away the most crucial aspects of the reality we live in. It is tantamount to assuming that the moon is made of cheese, and then building theories on this premise.

Despite these facts, the majority of economists has for several decades happily worked on the assumption that there is perfect information. This is particularly worrying, since this and other assumptions are crucial to obtain the conclusions emphasized by the neoclassical theories. What should be of interest to anyone is the question of what happens when we acknowledge the reality of pervasive information imperfections. Neoclassical economics has made little contribution to this important question.

But there are other necessary assumptions to obtain the neoclassical conclusions, and they are equally unrealistic. Most models assume perfect competition, despite the reality of oligopolies and monopolies in most mature markets. Most models ignore the importance of increasing returns to scale (by assuming constant or diminishing returns to scale), when there is evidence that scale economies are pervasive and important for much economic activity. Another necessary assumption for neoclassical theories to work is the assumption that resources are always fully employed. This not only defies the reality of markets and economies, but also the facts of human nature: on an individual level, neoclassical economics assumes that individuals always use their talents and abilities, always work at 'maximum capacity utilization'. In reality, humans are not machines. They need to be motivated. If they are not sufficiently motivated, they may not put as much effort into their activities as might theoretically be possible. Once this reality is acknowledged, the subject of how humans can be motivated becomes of crucial importance. This is where rules and norms, social institutions and hierarchies come into play, and the question of how such incentive structures should be designed in order to elicit maximum potential. One only needs to consider how motivation can influence physical performance in the case of sports, and the role of coaches. Similarly, soldiers, as well as indeed anyone who is part of an organization or hierarchy, will be subject to motivational policies implemented in order to obtain the type of performance desired. Indeed the motivation – and also manipulation – of people is a major activity engaged in by large industries. Incentives and the type of information provided are used as tools to get people to do what is desired by others.[23]

Another area where assumptions of traditional economics are crucially flawed, thus compromising the entire model, is the theory of the consumer. Individuals are assumed to be only motivated by their own self-interest and individual utility functions are assumed to be independent. The present book is focused on macroeconomics and this issue will thus remain outside its scope. What can be said here is that this model of the individual also has little to do with reality. Individuals are born into society and mostly are interested in relating to others in society. Their status and ranking in society is an important motivation that has been ignored by mainstream economics. An inductivist approach would form a model of individual behaviour based on reality. Only then are conclusions likely to be relevant and accurate. The realistic study of incentives leads to the conclusion that institutions, hierarchies and ranking are important. Thus incentive structures that are designed to increase motivation take this into consideration. Institutional design is therefore a crucial paradigm in economics that has so far been neglected by the mainstream. As we will find, credit creation is another.

The reality of human nature, the reality of imperfect information, the reality of increasing returns to scale, the institutional reality of financial markets, the reality of large-scale businesses, all must be possible in the new economics, if not integral features of economic models.

Ingredients of the East Asian economic 'miracle'

Since economic activity is always the result of human activity, this means that the design of rules and settings, within which markets are embedded, becomes a powerful tool of government intervention to enhance economic performance successfully. It is one that is ignored by the mainstream economics paradigm. But it is one that was at the heart of the East Asian economic success, including Japan's.

With imperfect information, markets do not clear. This includes the market for money and credit. Markets that do not clear are rationed. Rationed markets are determined by quantities, not prices, according to the 'short-side principle': whichever quantity of demand or supply is smaller will determine the outcome. The limited liability of directors within corporations means that incentives are skewed such that entrepreneurs who borrow money may gain disproportionately compared to their potential downside. This has been one of the driving forces of capitalism. Concerning the market for money and credit, it means that demand is likely to outstrip supply, leaving it supply-determined. This, then, becomes the central focus of our investigation: the institutional setting of the supply of money and credit and its implication. For this purpose, inductive research into the development and operation of the banking system is necessary. It is found that banks are truly special, although their unique feature has not been recognized by mainstream economics, or by banking and finance textbooks.

In rationed markets, an allocative decision is made. Thus market rationing provides a justification for government intervention to ensure that resources are allocated such that welfare is enhanced. However, heavy-handed government intervention is unlikely to work. The East Asian economic success story in general and the Japanese in particular were based on clever government intervention, which took mainly two forms: institutional design to shape the incentive structure and direct allocative intervention largely limited to one specific area, namely the credit market. Here, a powerful credit control tool was used that remains largely unknown, despite the fact that it has been at the heart of the East Asian economic miracle, and indeed at the core of the success of a number of other economies, including Germany.

Sometimes the success of the East Asian 'miracle' economies is claimed by neoclassical economists as evidence of the success of market-based capitalism and hence of the neoclassical paradigm.[24] This, however, is an empirical question: did the Japanese and East Asian policies originate from neoclassical policy advice? Or did they originate from theories quite explicitly and fundamentally opposed to the neoclassical approach?

But just when more present-day economists are beginning to recognize some of these issues in the latest, revised theories, Germany and Japan are in the process of adopting the British and US neoclassical model through liberalization, deregulation and privatization. If this process continues, shareholder fundamentalism will reshape society and increase the share of economic activity devoted to profit-seeking by shifting ownership certificates from A to B. After all, adopting US-style capitalism means that Germany and Japan are importing its disadvantages and social problems.

If the structural reforms in Europe and Asia continue, there may soon be less talk of an alternative model to the Washington consensus policy package, as the most outstanding examples of successful development policies (as opposed to those favoured by the international institutions) will have been dismantled. Then, neoclassical economics may remain the entrenched and dominant economic ideology. This is another reason why it is high time to re-examine the neoclassical paradigm, especially in the context of the Japanese economy, and test whether an alternative approach can be found that is empirically superior.

Joseph Stiglitz has called for a new paradigm in economics. He has laid the foundations and done much to make the world aware of the problems with mainstream economics. The present book merely represents another step towards laying the groundwork for the new paradigm in the area of macro-economics. Much work remains to be done in this exciting and vast research programme on a new kind of economics.

Work on the new kind of economics must be rigorously tested, using the most difficult challenges to macroeconomics. One of the most powerful empirical challenges has been posed by Japan, which is where many of the empirical data for the present book are drawn from. The new economics should not only explain whatever the old theories could explain. It should also be able to explain the many 'anomalies' that the previous neoclassical paradigm could not account for. Finally, the new kind of economics should offer solutions – workable, actual solutions – to many of the world's problems. For, as John F. Kennedy said, man's problems are manmade. They can therefore also be solved by man.

1
Japanese Economic Performance During the 1990s

> But Japan worries me. It's not just that we are talking about a huge economy here, an economy whose woes can drag down a lot of smaller countries with it. What really disturbs me is this: If we don't really understand what has gone wrong in Japan, who's to say the same thing can't happen to us?
>
> Paul Krugman (1998b)

> Interest rates have been cut again and again. Government deficits are rising fast. In short, the authorities are doing everything the economics textbooks suggest to stave off the twin threats of deflation and recession. But what if the textbooks are wrong and the fiscal and monetary easing proves ineffective? After all, that was the experience of Japan in the 1990s. Interest rates were brought down to zero and the government deficit exploded thanks to a host of public spending projects. But a series of Japanese recoveries has spluttered and died and the Tokyo stock market is still just a quarter of its peak.
>
> Philip Coggan, Financial Times, July 2003[1]

> [T]he Bank of Japan and the Japanese government have not yet succeeded to bring the Japanese economy on a sustainable recovery track, in spite of the extreme monetary and fiscal packages. It means that the problem to be solved lies in the private sector.
>
> Kunio Matsuda, Chief Representative in Frankfurt, Bank of Japan[2]

As is readily seen from Figure 1.1 and Table 1.1, Japan's economic performance has been disappointing for much of the 1990s. Economic growth decelerated in 1992, with nominal GDP growth falling from 6.2% in 1991 to only 2.6%. Over the following year, growth fell further to only 1%. With the exception of 1996 and 1997 (when growth recorded 2.6% and 2.2%, respectively), nominal GDP growth stayed below 1.5% throughout the decade

Figure 1.1 Japanese nominal GDP growth between 1981 and 2003
Source: Cabinet Office, Government of Japan.

1992–2002. In 1998, 1999, 2001 and 2002, it even recorded a significant contraction of over 1% (culminating in the 1.5% contraction of 2002).

Retail sales fell 0.6% on average during the 1990s. Meanwhile Japan experienced disinflation in the first half of the 1990s and outright deflation in the years since 1998 – with five consecutive years of deflation, breaking the deflation records of all modern industrialized countries.

The high (by Japan's standards) unemployment rate suggests less than full employment output for much of the 1990s (Figure 1.2). Wages, as measured by the Labour Ministry's wage index, were under downward pressure during the 1990s, and declined by over 1% in the financial years 2000 and 2001.

Financial and personal distress have been evident. Since 1990, over 220,000 companies have gone bankrupt. Meanwhile, the number of suicides rose from 22,104 in 1992 to a record high of 33,048 in 1999, with continued high annual incidence of suicides since then (see Figure 1.3). This surge in suicides was not a coincidence. According to the National Police Agency, most of the additional suicides during the 1990s occurred in the 50–60 years age group and were found to have been related to Japan's weak economic performance, which resulted in unprecedented layoffs, financial distress, debts with loan sharks and bankruptcies.

Given these facts, it cannot be surprising that the 1990s has variously been described as the 'lost decade' (Harada, 1999) or the 'ten-year slump'.

This disappointing performance occurred not because of a lack of official policies, nor because of a lack of explanations and suggestions by observers. Japan adopted one of the largest fiscal stimulation programmes on record, while Japan's central bank repeatedly lowered interest rates until they reached virtually zero. Defying economics textbooks, Japan's economy appeared immune to cyclical stimulation policies. 'The usual counter-cyclical

Table 1.1 Key indicators of macroeconomic performance in Japan during the 1990s

CY (YoY %)	Nom. GDP	Real GDP	GDP deflator	Nation-wide CPI (ave)	Dom. WPI (ave)	Wage Index (ave)	Unemployment rate s.a. (ave)	Total no. of bankruptcies
1991	6.2	3.1	3.0	3.3	1.0	4.4	2.1	10,723
1992	2.6	0.9	1.7	1.6	-0.9	2.0	2.2	14,069
1993	1.0	0.4	0.6	1.3	-1.6	0.3	2.5	14,564
1994	1.1	1.0	0.1	0.7	-1.7	1.5	2.9	14,061
1995	1.2	1.6	-0.4	-0.1	-0.8	1.1	3.1	15,108
1996	2.6	3.5	-0.8	0.1	-1.6	1.1	3.4	14,834
1997	2.2	1.8	0.4	1.8	0.7	1.6	3.4	16,464
1998	-1.2	-1.1	-0.1	0.6	-1.6	-1.3	4.1	18,988
1999	-0.8	0.7	-1.4	-0.3	-1.5	-1.3	4.7	15,352
2000	0.3	2.4	-2.0	-0.7	0.1	0.5	4.7	18,769
1990s av.	1.5	1.4	0.1	0.8	-0.8	1.0	3.3	15,293
1980s av.	6.2	4.1	2.0	2.1	-0.4	3.6	2.5	14,747

Sources: Cabinet Office, Bank of Japan; Statistics Office, Ministry of Health, Labour and Welfare.

32

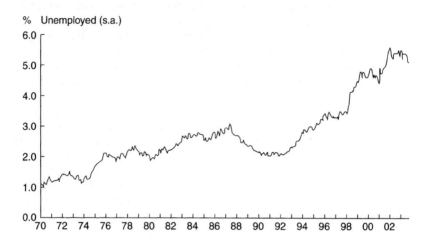

Figure 1.2 The official unemployment rate in Japan

Source: Labour Force Survey in 2003, Ministry of Public Management, Home Affairs, Posts and Telecommunications.

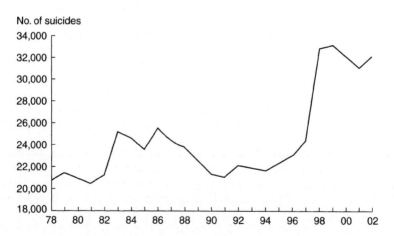

Figure 1.3 The official number of suicides in Japan

Source: Suicide Statistics in 2002, National Police Agency.

macroeconomic policies have not worked in Japan' is a typical assessment.[3] Over the past decade, the second largest economy in the world once again posed a disturbing challenge to traditional economic models.

Not surprisingly, the 'enigma' of Japanese cyclical policy ineffectiveness during the 1990s has attracted much interest among economists and policy-makers worldwide. The stakes have been high: the economic loss, in the form of lost output and national income, amounts to trillions of yen.[4] The social and human cost is not measurable in monetary terms.

Mainstream economics has responded to these challenges by ignoring them. With the exception of a small number of economists, including Joseph Stiglitz and his collaborators, hardly any attempts have been made to explain seriously what has been wrong with standard theories and why they could not explain events in Japan or produce viable policy solutions.

Given the apparent failure of anti-cyclical demand management policies, supply-side policies in the form of fundamental structural reforms were sug-gested more frequently.[5] These are usually defined to include far-reaching changes in the institutional framework of the economy, including labour markets, corporate governance, administrative systems and the regulatory environment – in other words shifting from a Japanese-style 'bank-centred and relationship-based system' to a US-style 'market-based and competitive system' or from 'welfare capitalism' to 'shareholder capitalism'.[6]

The Japanese central bank, although in charge of a key cyclical policy, has been among the most consistent proponents of such changes. The govern-ment of Prime Minister Junichiro Koizumi also adopted this view in 2001. Accordingly, fiscal stimulation was scaled back and a less interventionist view of monetary policy taken. The key policy initiatives of the govern-ment have centred on a programme of structural reform, including deregu-lation, liberalization, privatization and institutional reforms to increase the influence of shareholders and reduce that of employees and civil servants.

The general consensus in Tokyo, as well as outside Japan, has become that at least a substantial part of 'the problem', as the Bank of Japan's Matsuda put it, lies in the private sector. Many voices, foremost of which is the Bank of Japan itself, have been calling for a radical structural transformation of the Japanese economy. Given the significant ramification and long-term impact of structural changes, it appears of importance first of all to make sure that the cause of Japan's problems has been correctly identified and that all possible and suitable demand-management actions have indeed been taken.

Krugman already warned in 1998 that it is of utmost importance for all of us to understand Japan's experience (Krugman, 1998b). Indeed, recently the spectre has been raised that a Japanese-style economic problem may possibly also be a potential danger in the US or European economies.[7] While this threat has clearly receded, it is worrying that few economists can explain why this is so, and why we can be assured that it will not return. It is therefore imperative to examine these issues further, for the sake of Japan, the sake of economics as a coherent theory consistent with facts, and for the sake of preventing a potential future repetition of the Japanese experience in other countries.

Part II

Enigmas: Challenges to the Traditional Paradigm

The state of Japan is a scandal, an outrage, a reproach. It is not, at least so far, a human disaster like Indonesia or Brazil. But Japan's economic malaise is uniquely *gratuitous*. Sixty years after Keynes, a great nation – a country with a stable and effective government, a massive net creditor, subject to none of the constraints that lesser economies face – is operating far below its productive capacity, simply because its consumers and investors do not spend enough. That should not happen; in allowing it to happen, and to continue year after year, Japan's economic officials have subtracted value from their nation and the world as a whole on a truly heroic scale.

The fault does not, however, lie merely with those officials. Japan has also been badly served by the economics profession, both in Japan and outside. The great majority of economists – including those who specialize in issues of economic stabilization and growth – seem oddly uninterested in Japan's plight, as if the failure of conventional macroeconomic policy in the world's second largest economy were a subject of merely parochial interest, with no lessons for the rest of us.

Paul Krugman (1999)

2
The Enigma of the Ineffectiveness of Fiscal Policy in the 1990s

As in other countries, Japanese fiscal policy has been the exclusive domain of the government, which proposes fiscal spending measures to parliament whose funding is detailed in budgets and supplementary budgets. In principle, the government has been following a balanced budget policy in the postwar era. The Finance Law of 1947 prohibited the issuance of government bonds. As a result of the 1965 recession, it was amended and government bonds were issued for the first time.[1] Oil shock recessions and increased spending programmes produced sizeable deficits in the 1970s.[2] The elimination of fiscal deficits ('fiscal reconstruction') has been a priority since the late 1970s, with the Finance Ministry pursuing a 'zero [growth] ceiling' on budget requests since 1982. Thanks to some tax rises (including the introduction of the consumption tax in 1989), high nominal GDP growth and asset price rises in the second half of the 1980s, the target of fiscal reconstruction was achieved in 1991.

Since 1992, the government has embarked on a series of fiscal stimulation packages to increase economic growth. Government policy documents stated the view that fiscal spending needed to be increased, in order to boost domestic demand and stimulate the economy.[3] The first fiscal stimulation package was implemented in 1992. This was followed with a string of additional packages in every year, except 1996 and 2000. Table 2.1 lists the packages and supplementary budgets. As can be seen, the ten fiscal stimulation packages amounted to ¥146 trillion. Eighteen supplementary budgets were passed, amounting to ¥38.1 trillion over a decade that often also saw a significant expansion in the regular budgets.

Since the government may have had political motives to overstate fiscal stimulation packages through double-counting, a more accurate measure of the fiscal stance may be total government expenditures, as calculated by the national income accounts (aggregating government consumption and investment, as well as inventory data).[4] Government spending increased from a total of ¥705 trillion in the 1980s to ¥1136 trillion in the 1990s. As a percentage of nominal GDP, this represented an increase from 20.9% on

38

Table 2.1 Fiscal stimulation packages and supplementary budgets in the 1990s

FY		1991	1992	1993	1994	1995	1996	1997	1998	1999	2000	Total
Fiscal stimulation packages	No.	0	1	2	1	2	0	2	1	1	0	10
	Size (¥ trn.)	0	10.7	19.2	15.3	21.2	0	40.6	24.5	14.9	0	146.4
Supplementary budgets	No.	1	1	3	2	3	1	3	2	1	1	18
	Size (¥ trn.)	0.3	−0.7	5.1	0.4	7.1	1.1	10.3	7.2	4.8	2.7	38.1

Source: Cabinet Office, Ministry of Finance.

average in the 1980s to 22.7% in the 1990s. On a growth basis the more positive fiscal stance during the 1990s becomes obvious. Table 2.2 shows the breakdown by contribution to growth of each GDP component. On average, government spending contributed almost half of growth in the 1990s, while it only contributed a sixth of growth in the 1980s.

While the government contribution to growth increased, government revenues fell significantly, as the weaker economy reduced tax revenues.[5] As a result, Japan's government registered the largest budget deficits of any industrial country in the postwar era, averaging over 6% of GDP during the period 1993–2000.

Government revenue shortfall

Textbooks tell us that there are two options to fund the revenue shortfall: debt finance or money finance. In the former case, the government borrows from the private sector; in the latter, it either creates money directly, or borrows from the central bank, which pays by creating money.[6] In Japan's case the issuance of legal tender has been delegated to the Bank of Japan, which, since at least the late 1970s, has in practice acted largely independently from the government. Moreover, the Finance Law does not allow the central bank directly to underwrite government bonds.[7] This has left the government no choice but to fund the public sector borrowing requirement from the private sector, which has happened via bond and bill issuance (Table 2.3).[8]

New government borrowing increased by ¥300.4 trillion during the 1990s (58.6% of 2000 nominal GDP). This raised total outstanding debt to ¥522.1 trillion by the end of 2000, amounting to 101.8% of GDP. Adding the new borrowing of ¥60.36 trillion during 2001, the national debt figures recorded a new high of ¥582.46 trillion, about 120% of GDP, by the end of 2001. The debt continued to rise during 2002 and 2003. At the end of 2003, the government estimated that, with its budgeted new bond issuance of ¥30 trillion in fiscal year 2004, the outstanding balance of government debt would reach over ¥700 trillion by the end of March 2005.

According to mainstream textbooks, such counter-cyclical expansion of the public sector part of the economy should act as an 'automatic stabilizer' during recessions. However, the 'automatic stabilizers' failed to stabilize economic growth. The path of nominal GDP growth remained on a downward trajectory during the 1990s. Quite contrary to standard theory, fiscal policy seemed to have a negative impact on private demand (Figure 2.1). Indeed, there was even the suggestion that every yen in government spending would crowd out private demand by one yen.[9]

'Fiscal policy was effective'

The question whether fiscal policy has been effective in stimulating Japan's economy has triggered a lively debate. We first consider the theoretical

Table 2.2 Contribution to nominal GDP growth in the 1990s

CY %	Consumption + housing	Capex (+ inventories)	Net exports	Private demand	Government consumption	Government investment (+ inventories)	Total government	Nominal GDP
1991	2.6	1.6	1.3	4.9	0.8	0.4	1.2	6.2
1992	2.0	-1.6	0.8	0.8	0.8	1.2	2.0	2.6
1993	1.7	-2.1	0.1	-0.6	0.7	1.2	1.8	1.0
1994	2.1	-1.4	-0.2	0.4	0.5	0.2	0.7	1.1
1995	0.3	0.8	-0.4	0.5	0.7	0.0	0.7	1.2
1996	2.0	0.5	-0.3	1.6	0.5	0.5	1.0	2.6
1997	0.2	1.9	1.4	2.6	0.4	-0.7	-0.4	2.2
1998	-0.7	-1.1	1.2	-1.1	0.3	-0.3	0.0	-1.2
1999	0.4	-1.3	-0.2	-1.4	0.4	0.2	0.6	-0.8
2000	-0.2	1.1	-0.1	0.7	0.6	-0.8	-0.3	0.3
1990s av.	1.0	-0.1	0.4	0.8	0.6	0.2	0.7	1.5
1980s av.	3.4	1.5	0.3	5.2	0.8	0.2	1.0	6.2

Source: Cabinet Office, December 2001.

Table 2.3 Government borrowing and debt in the 1990s

CY	New borrowing (¥ trn.)	New borrowing/ nGDP (%)	Total outstanding debt (¥ trn.)	Total outstanding debt/nGDP (%)
1991	4.65	1.0	226.35	47.7
1992	14.71	3.0	241.06	49.9
1993	17.33	3.6	258.38	53.0
1994	27.15	5.5	285.53	58.0
1995	27.21	5.4	312.74	62.3
1996	30.94	6.0	343.68	66.7
1997	24.92	4.8	368.60	70.9
1998	58.38	11.4	426.98	83.2
1999	50.79	9.9	477.76	92.9
2000	44.34	8.6	522.10	101.8
Total	*300.4*	*6.0*		

Source: Bank of Japan.

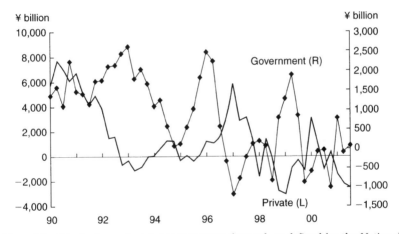

Figure 2.1 Private demand versus government demand, as defined by the National Income Accounts GDP figures (year-on-year absolute changes)

Source: Cabinet Office, Government of Japan.

arguments, starting with what probably remains the majority view in Japan: the list of economists who would call themselves Keynesian or fiscally inclined is a long one in Japan.[10] There has therefore been widespread support among economists of the government's attempts to stimulate the economy through fiscal spending. The need for and usefulness of fiscal stimulation has, among others, been argued by Nagatani (1996), Yoshitomi (1996), Koo (1996, 1998, 1999), Posen (1998) and Ito (2000).

The extreme position of a pure fiscalist stance is represented by Koo (1998, 1999) and also referred to in Ito (2000). Koo argues the general case for fiscal policy effectiveness: while money is neutral, fiscal policy – and only fiscal policy – is highly effective. At a time when short-term interest rates were several hundred basis points above zero, he argued that monetary policy would not affect the economy, based on the view that money is neutral. This view has theoretical support in the neoclassical literature, for instance in the form of the real business cycle approach. However, the models are based on highly restrictive assumptions and empirical evidence remains scarce. In particular, the fiscalist view cannot explain why the above significant fiscal stimulation failed to stimulate a significant and lasting economic recovery during the 1990s. As there is no research in support of this view, we shall not further concern ourselves with it.

The special case for fiscal policy effectiveness is made by Ito (2000). At the end of the 1990s, when short-term nominal interest rates had approached zero, he argues that the economy is in a liquidity trap, the demand for money is perfectly interest-elastic and, in a traditional IS-LM model, the LM curve, representing equilibrium in the market for real money balances, is horizontal. Since interest reductions had not stimulated investment, he argued that investment was perfectly interest-inelastic and the IS curve, representing equilibrium in the goods and services markets, vertical. In such a model, monetary policy is ineffective and fiscal policy unusually effective, without any crowding out effects.[11] This is why Ito advocates fiscal stimulation, not monetary stimulation in a zero interest environment.[12] There is a theoretical problem with this argument, as well as an empirical one. By arguing for a horizontal LM curve, describing the case of short-term nominal interest rates that have fallen to such low levels that they do not fall further, Ito restricts his argument to time periods that exclude the entire decade of the 1990s – during this decade interest rates did indeed fall steadily.

An empirical evaluation of the effectiveness of fiscal policy also depends on the size of the expected impact of fiscal expenditures. While the basic Keynesian model implies a 'multiplier', such that ¥1 trillion of fiscal expenditures would result in a rise in economic activity larger than ¥1 trillion, many proponents of fiscal policy effectiveness have adopted a far more cautious approach to fiscal policy effectiveness – indeed one that denies its existence: there has been hardly any expectation or even discussion of any second- and third-round effects, with the biggest hoped-for effect being merely the primary one-for-one impact. Thus government and private sector economists frequently argued that a public works project worth ¥1 trillion would boost nominal GDP by ¥1 trillion. A spending package amounting to 2% of GDP was commonly expected to boost GDP by 2 percentage points.[13]

Concerning the empirical evidence, Posen (1998) argues that fiscal policy has been effective in Japan during the 1990s. In his view, actual fiscal spending has been smaller than the headline figures for the packages. He argues that therefore fiscal spending has simply not been sufficiently large to stimulate the economy. A suitably sized fiscal expansion would, in his view, have been effective in ending economic stagnation and deflation. When the actual spending reached substantial size – in 1995, according to him – a recovery followed (in 1996).[14] However, actual GDP-based expenditure data as cited above, or statistics for the government borrowing requirement yield reasonably accurate measures of the fiscal stance. Yet Posen provides no empirical evidence for the effectiveness of fiscal policy. The figures above suggest that sizeable fiscal stimulation did take place and that it failed to stimulate the economy. Furthermore, there is no evidence that even the first-round effect resulted from the spending.

Ito (2000) also remains convinced of the effectiveness of fiscal policy. While he concedes that the unprecedented six fiscal stimulation packages that were implemented between 1992 and 1994 have had 'little impact' (p. 102), he argues that this does not disprove fiscal policy effectiveness. This however, depends on the definition for effectiveness chosen.

In principle, two definitions are possible. One is a *mutatis mutandis* requirement for effectiveness, defining it as the ability to create significant positive economic growth. This is the strictest definition, and the one that matters to policy-makers, investors and the population at large. The goal of fiscal spending packages is to boost GDP growth, no matter what. If that goal is not achieved, then by this definition fiscal policy has not been effective. In the first half of the 1990s, most private sector economists, forced to make *mutatis mutandis* forecasts, actually predicted significant economic recoveries, mainly based on the sizeable fiscal stimulation. However, this did not happen. Thus by the original definition of most economists who believed in the ability of fiscal policy to stimulate the economy, fiscal policy was ineffective.

There is another definition of policy effectiveness, which is the one employed by Ito (2000). It is based on the *ceteris paribus* assumption:

> Without any fiscal stimulus, the economy undoubtedly would have contracted. The underlying economy was so weak that fiscal stimulus did not bring the economy all the way to its potential growth rate but it arguably kept things from becoming worse. (p. 102)

Supporters of the efficacy of fiscal spending, including Posen (1998), feel that even more fiscal stimulation is the solution for Japan.[15] The difficulty of establishing clear-cut proof is apparent: the *ceteris paribus* condition is invoked, only to claim its violation. The argument relies on counter-factual analysis: things would have been worse without the fiscal spending. Ito thus relies on unspecified shocks, rendering economic growth exogenous to fiscal and monetary policy.[16] These undefined exogenous shocks cannot be isolated or quantified. What is worse, by invoking a violated *ceteris paribus* assumption, the fiscal policy effectiveness claim cannot be falsified – it leaves the realm of testable hypotheses.[17] In science counter-factual analysis is considered inferior to fact-based analysis. In any case, Ito's attempt at reconciling inconvenient facts with a theory through the use of *ad hoc* assumptions about exogenous shocks cannot be construed as constituting supportive empirical evidence. Hence the claim that fiscal policy has been effective remains unsubstantiated by empirical evidence.

'Fiscal policy was ineffective'

Three types of arguments have been proposed over the years why Japanese fiscal policy may be ineffective. All three point out that the positive gross effects of fiscal policy may be partially or completely negated by negative effects that result from the need of the government to procure the money in order to fund the fiscal expenditure. The first is based on a Keynesian relationship between interest rates and investment and argues that crowding out of fiscal expenditure may occur via higher interest rates. The second is based on a reduction in consumption and an increase in savings that is induced by increased fiscal spending. It is commonly referred to as 'Ricardian equivalence'. The first two views will be reviewed briefly below, while the third, based on the new paradigm, will be examined in detail in Part III of this book.

Interest rate-based crowding out

A number of studies have argued that the effect of increased government expenditure depends on how it is financed. Lerner (1943) emphasized the distinction between money-financed and bond- or tax-financed government deficits. As discussed above, the Japanese government relied almost entirely on bond finance during the 1990s. Lerner rejects tax-financed government deficits (as they would not fulfil the purpose of government deficits, namely to increase overall spending), as well as bond-financed government deficits. The latter would reduce the amount of money available to the private sector, thus increase interest rates and hence reduce private sector investment. Thus while fiscal policy has been given prominence in policy-making in most industrialized countries since the 1960s, the initial argument of the large multiplier effects was greatly diminished by a growing body of literature that pointed out the errors of such analysis: the original, large multipliers only showed the gross, first-stage impact, without considering the negative effect of funding such spending through bond issuance. Following Lerner's seminal work, Christ (1968), Blinder and Solow (1973), Hansen (1973) and others showed that the increase in interest rates triggered by debt funding of the deficits would greatly reduce the net effect of fiscal expenditure.

This proposition of fiscal policy ineffectiveness is similar to classical theory, which argued that government expenditure would result in an equal reduction in private demand, via an increase in real interest rates. The crowding out effect of increased government expenditure via higher interest rates is reflected in standard Keynesian models and the IS-LM synthesis, but also the mainstream monetarist models (such as Friedman, 1956; Brunner and Meltzer, 1976).[18] While they differ in the size of the net effect of fiscal policy, they agree that the transmission mechanism (and potential crowding out) occurs via interest rates. Indeed, the substantial literature on the possibility and size of crowding out of debt-financed fiscal expenditure has in common that it centres on interest rates as the adjustment mechanism.[19] What all these formulations (classical, Keynesian and post-Keynesian) share is that the ineffectiveness of fiscal policy is the result of increased interest rates.

In the case of Japan it was indeed argued by some economists during the first half of the 1990s that increased bond issuance to fund fiscal spending would lower bond prices and push up long-term interest rates. This rise of interest rates would negatively affect investment and economic activity, it was said. A proponent of this interest rate-based crowding out argument is, for instance, Yoshida (1996), who additionally warned that the long-term interest rate rises would tend to strengthen the yen and hurt net exports.[20]

The main problem with these interest rate-based arguments for fiscal policy ineffectiveness is that there is no empirical evidence to support them.[21] Despite brief periods of rising long-term nominal rates, nominal short-term (as measured by call rates) and long-term interest rates (as measured by ten-year Japanese government bond (JGB) yields) have trended down during the 1990s. Ten-year government bond yields fell for most of the decade. As can be seen in Figure 2.2, there are only two instances where they rose: from 4.3% on average in 1993, to 4.4% in 1994, and from 1.3% in 1998 to 1.8% in 1999. However, in both cases rates subsequently resumed their decline to new lows.[22] None of these instances constituted a reversal of the trend of falling or at least steadily low interest rates. Considering the prime lending rate, we notice that its annual average has declined every single year during the 1990s.

Calculating real interest rates as the difference between these nominal interest rates and consumer price inflation (as measured by the CPI), we find that short-term real interest rates fell from 4.2% on average in 1991 to 0.11% on average in 2000, while long-term real interest rates fell from 3.0% on average in 1991 to 0.7% in 1998, though rising again to 2.5% on average in 2000 (see Table 2.4). These real rates were lower than during the 1980s. Using the more relevant prime lending rate, we come to the same conclusion: there is no evidence for rising interest rates.

These facts are in contradiction to traditional crowding out arguments. To rescue the argument of interest rate crowding out, one would have to resort once again to invoking a violated *ceteris paribus* definition.[23] Then the theoretical argument might be conceivable that the fall in interest rates happened

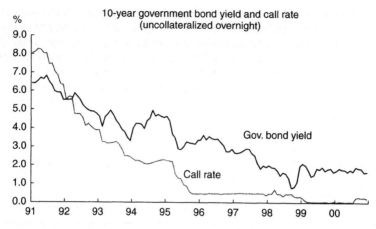

Figure 2.2   Nominal interest rates in the 1990s
Source: Bank of Japan.

Table 2.4   Interest rates in Japan during the 1990s

CY (%)	ODR	Call rate (uncoll. overnight)	Real call rate (Call-CPI)	10-year JGB yield	Real JGB yield (JGB-CPI)	Long-term prime lending rate
1991	5.66	7.53	4.2	6.33	3.0	7.5
1992	3.73	4.66	3.1	5.31	3.7	6
1993	2.38	3.06	1.8	4.31	3.0	4.8
1994	1.75	2.20	1.5	4.39	3.7	4.6
1995	1.02	1.21	1.3	3.42	3.5	3.4
1996	0.50	0.47	0.4	3.12	3.0	3.1
1997	0.50	0.48	−1.3	2.35	0.6	2.6
1998	0.50	0.37	−0.2	1.33	0.7	2.4
1999	0.50	0.06	0.4	1.76	2.1	2.3
2000	0.50	0.11	0.8	1.76	2.5	2.2

Note: All figures are annual averages.

Source: Bank of Japan (data).

despite the crowding out, and as a result of exogenous shocks, without which interest rates would have risen. Just as with the argument that fiscal policy was effective in Japan during the 1990s, as without it things would probably have been worse, proponents of this view are faced with the difficulty of having to isolate the exogenous shocks needed to justify the absence of interest rate rises.[24] Furthermore, this exercise in attempting to reconcile the contradictory empirical record with the theory through the use of auxiliary assumptions does not constitute supportive empirical evidence. Thus the fact remains that the argument of interest rate-based crowding out is not supported by the empirical record. Given the historical and dramatic declines in short, long, nominal and real interest rates, it can be safely said that few if any observers seriously entertain the interest rate crowding out argument.[25]

Ricardian equivalence

The case for a different kind of crowding out has been made by Krugman (1998c). Applying his model of intertemporally optimizing rational, perfectly informed and forward-looking representative agents to Japan, he obtains Ricardian equivalence of the type Barro (1974) proposed: Japanese consumers believe that any fiscal spending funded by the issuance of government debt (as most of it has in fact been) will require the debt to be fully paid off at some stage in the relevant future; and that the money needed to pay off the debt will come from increased taxes on individuals. Under these assumptions, for every yen the government spends in fiscal policy, rational consumers would increase savings by a yen – in order to prepare the money that will be necessary to pay back the government in the future.

One major analytical problem with this model is that it does not allow for the possibility that the debt will be paid off by other means – such as money creation, higher corporate taxes, economic growth that boosts tax revenues without raising individual taxes, or asset sales to foreign investors. It is not clear why rational consumers would not consider these possibilities plausible.[26] Another problem is that the assumptions on which it is based are restrictive. Thus if there is a simpler explanation, relying on fewer assumptions (such as the counter-factual assumption of full employment), the fundamental principles of logic suggest that it would be preferable.

Meanwhile, the empirical record of the Ricardian equivalence argument remains important to assess its relevance. The most basic test of Ricardian equivalence would be a comparison of the change of household savings and government expenditure or borrowing within a fully specified savings function. Proponents of this explanation of fiscal policy ineffectiveness have not provided such evidence, as far as the author is aware.[27] Indeed, Walker (2002) holds that 'It seems unlikely that anything as austere as full Ricardian equivalence would obtain in the real world' (p. 286).[28]

Conclusion

In conclusion, there is little, if any evidence in favour of fiscal policy effectiveness. In practice, this has become the consensus view: it seems obvious to many observers that fiscal policy has not succeeded in achieving what it was aimed at during the 1990s. However, the question of just why this was the case has not been answered by traditional approaches – neither interest rate crowding out nor Ricardian equivalence. The debate has therefore remained unresolved. Given this and the fact that fiscal policy is most directly linked to the political process that establishes constituency support for the election of Members of Parliament, it is easy to see why many politicians have continued to favour fiscal policy. However, it is remarkable that few economists have embarked on the important task of solving the mystery of just why record-sized fiscal policy has clearly failed to lift Japan's economy out of recession. Mostly, answers were simply assumed – such as the claim that it was due to structural problems – without serious evidence. We will return to the riddle and consider a proposed solution in Part III.

3
The Enigma of the Ineffectiveness of Interest Rate Policy in the 1990s

Most leading macroeconomic theories postulate that nominal interest rate reductions, as implemented by central banks in many countries over the past several years, operate towards stimulating the economy. Since about the 1980s, central banks have come to emphasize interest rates in their official publications as the dominant tool of monetary policy implementation. It has come to be described as the 'new consensus' in macroeconomics (Arestis and Sawyer, 2002). In their discussion of the Bank of England model, Arestis and Sawyer note that monetary aggregates have been relegated to a minor role, while 'interest rate policy has become demand policy' (2002, p. 12):

> Policymakers attempt to achieve a certain inflation goal by using their control over interest rates to restrain the total demand for goods and services in the economy. (Arestis and Sawyer, 2003a, p. 9)

> Monetary policy can be seen as aggregate demand policy in that the interest rate set by the central bank is seen to influence aggregate demand, which, in turn, is thought to influence the rate of inflation. (Arestis and Sawyer, 2003a, p. 17)

Taylor (2000) reflects the consensus view, when he reports his finding that even if there are alternative views of the monetary transmission mechanism, 'the same simple monetary policy rule – one in which the central bank's target short-term interest rate reacts to inflation and to real output – would perform well' (p. 60).

From 1942 until 31 March 1998, *de jure* Japanese monetary policy was, like fiscal policy, the responsibility of the democratically elected government. Unlike fiscal policy, however, it has never required parliamentary approval. Moreover, the task of monetary policy implementation has been delegated to the Bank of Japan. On 1 April 1998, the central bank obtained legal e from the government concerning its policy-making and ion.[1] Yet it is widely recognized that already before this date the was *de facto* virtually independent from the government. For ௺௺ pre-1990s period this is argued by Cargill (1989), Horiuchi (1993) and Werner (1998d, 1999a, 2001a, 2002a, 2003c). The same is argued for the 1990s by Cargill et al. (1997, 2000).[2] The independence of the Bank of Japan is highlighted by the previously unprecedented public policy dispute between the government and the central bank that erupted several times during the 1990s.[3] There is little doubt that throughout the decade the views of the central bank prevailed. It is the Bank of Japan's views, therefore, that we will refer to in an attempt to understand the 'official view' of monetary policy in Japan in the 1990s.

For most of the postwar era the primary interest rate used by the central bank to convey monetary policy signals was the official discount rate (ODR). Since the 1980s, call market operations have gradually been expanded, rendering the overnight (uncollateralized) call rate increasingly important. By the mid-1990s, the call rate had been officially declared as the 'target operational rate' of the central bank and can be considered Japan's equivalent of the US 'Federal funds rate'.

The central bank's views have been articulated in public statements or publications by central bank organs or its staff throughout the 1990s.[4] They can be summarized as follows: nominal short-term interest rates constitute the only practicable policy tool of the central bank. Their repeated reduction demonstrates that the Bank of Japan has acted vigorously to stimulate the economy; their lowering to zero is proof of the central bank's resolve. However, with such low short-term interest rates, there is no more room for further significant monetary policy stimulation. The weakness of the economy, despite 'unprecedented' monetary stimulation, is evidence that the true cause of the recession lies in non-monetary phenomena, especially problems with Japan's economic structure.[5]

During much of the 1990s, the movement of the ODR and call rate exhibited a steady decline. The Bank of Japan lowered the ODR ten times in the decade of the 1990s, beginning with the first reduction in July 1991, before which it stood at 6%. Until September 1993 it was lowered seven times, reaching a historical low of 1.75%. The ODR was further lowered to 1.0% in April 1995 and to 0.5% in September 1995. In October 1995, the uncollateralized overnight call rate was guided below the ODR for the first time (at about 0.47%). Three years later, in October 1998, the Bank of Japan guided the call rate further down to a new record low of 0.33%. In February 1999, the call rate was even further reduced to 0.1% – what at the time began to be called a 'zero interest rate policy'. After a temporary (and modest) hike in August 2000, the call rate was lowered again to 0.12% in March and 0.02% in April 2001. In September of that year, the ODR was lowered to 0.1% and the call rate to 0.003%.

As we saw in the previous chapter, long-term interest rates, as measured by bond yields also exhibited a significant decline during the 1990s. Using the long-term prime lending rate as a measure of nominal long-term interest rates, we find that the trend has been even more obviously unidirectional: the average annual prime rate fell each year short of the previous year's average. Peaking at 7.5% in 1991, by 2000 it averaged only 2.2% for all banks. We also found that while real interest rates fell less during the 1990s, they also declined significantly and reached record low levels.

To assess the performance of interest rate policy, it is necessary to compare the planned or desired outcome of the policy action with the actual result. Both government and central bank argued that lowering interest rates would operate towards strengthening economic growth and stimulate a lasting economic recovery. As we saw in Chapter 1, this is not what happened.

The fact that significant declines in nominal and real, long- and short-term interest rates have failed to trigger a significant economic recovery has attracted some attention by economists during the past decade. In this section, we consider how the literature has attempted to deal with this reality.

We shall divide the debates that were sparked by the events in Japan into those centring on the unusual circumstances surrounding the near-zero interest rate policy (starting in about late 1998), and the earlier, more general debates (starting about 1992). As it turns out, much of the critique specific to the zero-interest rate era can be identified as a special case of the more general critique of the central bank's policies in the earlier period.

The special case: the debate since late 1998

The lowering of the overnight call rate to about 0.3% in September 1998 coincided with a dramatic fall in ten-year government bond yields to 0.7%.[6] Both events triggered much talk about near-zero nominal interest rates in Japan. Since then, despite temporary rises, interest rates have declined further and an increasing number of observers abroad and in Japan have made the case that interest rate policies were reaching their limit, yet with unimpressive results.

The liquidity trap argument

Probably the most influential argument addressing this issue was proposed by Krugman (1998a, 1998b, 1998c). Subsequent variations on the same theme have been proposed by Bank of Japan staff, as well as Ito (2000), which will be discussed below.

Choosing the definition that an 'economy is in a liquidity trap if aggregate demand consistently falls short of productive capacity despite essentially zero short-term nominal interest rates', Krugman (1998a) finds Japan to be an example.[7] Krugman is careful not to imply that he is referring to Keynes' original definition of a liquidity trap or Hicks' interpretation (Keynes primarily referred to long-term interest rates, and his argument was not tied to any absolute nominal interest rate level, but to the expectation of capital losses incurred by investors from rising interest rates; Hicks referred to a perfectly interest-elastic money demand function and LM schedule).[8]

Krugman's model assumes, among others, identical, eternally living individuals with identical time preference. There is no banking system, and hence no credit. Cash is created by open market operations by the government – there is no independent central bank.[9] There is perfect information and hence no market rationing. However, prices are sticky. Based on his definition of a liquidity trap and the above assumptions, Krugman explains why interest rate reductions have failed to stimulate the economy as follows. There are exogenous expectations that future productive capacity will be lower than current productive capacity (for instance due to exogenous demographic problems). This results in deflationary expectations, such that even with nominal interest rates close to zero, real interest rates are above their full-employment equilibrium level, which is negative.[10] Since Krugman assumes that the central bank cannot lower nominal rates below zero, and since in this model monetary policy affects the economy only via its influence on real interest rates, there is a problem – a 'liquidity trap'. As empirical evidence in support of his argument, Krugman musters the fact that short-term interest rates approached zero, and that the broad deposit aggregate M2 + CD was not growing sufficiently, despite significant increases in high powered money by the central bank.[11]

Ito (2000), as well as the IMF's Kumar et al. (2003) follow Krugman's analysis, although they define the liquidity trap somewhat differently. Ito and the IMF researchers use a Hicksian description of the liquidity trap, based on a horizontal LM curve. Ito (2000) also makes the somewhat doubtful assertion that the existence of a liquidity trap 'in Keynesian economics' is defined by the relative growth rate of different monetary aggregates: an 'expansion in the monetary base (it is increasing at around 9%) has not resulted in much increase in M2 (it is increasing at around 3%). A situation like this is termed a liquidity trap in Keynesian economics' (p. 101).

Inflation targeting

Krugman dismisses fiscal stimulation for Ricardian equivalence reasons (which would follow from his model). He also dismisses the effectiveness of structural reforms, because they constitute a supply-side policy that does not increase demand.[12] Instead, Krugman recommends raising inflationary expectations sufficiently to render real interest rates negative.[13] This can be achieved by the central bank, he argues, if it can make a credible commitment that it will pursue 'irresponsible monetary policy', instead of price stability or deflation. Since Krugman argues that agents had so far considered interest rate reductions as temporary – to be reversed the moment prices start to rise – they were not effective. However, a credible commitment to a permanent increase in prices, even when inflation appears, would reverse expectations. Krugman (1998c) deduces from this the need for an inflation target. He therefore suggests legal changes to impose an inflation target on the Bank of Japan (his suggestion is 4% for 15 years), with the aim of creating 'managed inflation' (referred to in the Japanese literature as *chousei infure*).

Cargill et al. (2000) agree with Krugman's inflation targeting proposal, and merely differ in the size of the recommended inflation target, suggesting a '1 to 3 percent target' as being sufficient for the late 1990s.[14]

Problems with Krugman's argument

Firstly, Krugman's model operates on the basis of a number of premises that may unnecessarily restrict it. It is not obvious that a central bank cannot impose negative penalty-type interest rates, for instance, on excess reserves.[15]

Secondly, Krugman's transmission mechanism is based on interest rates and does not allow for any form of quantity effects. For instance, he argues that 'no matter how much money the Bank of Japan prints *now*, it doesn't matter...' (1998b, p. 4). This is a problem for the policy recommendations suggested by Krugman: as Bank of Japan spokesmen (among others, Okina, 1999) subsequently relished in pointing out, if there is a liquidity trap and nothing more can be done by monetary policy, how can the central bank possibly make a *credible* commitment to create inflation? Since the model describes no physical mechanism by which demand is stirred, it all depends on the credible commitment affecting expectations. But credibility is hindered by the knowledge that the central bank is merely trying to conjure up inflation expectations, while it cannot affect the economy in any physical sense. Realising that the central bank is only trying to 'fool' agents without being able to follow up with effective deeds, the commitment will not be credible and inflation expectations cannot be stirred.

Pressed on the question what would happen, if the announcement of an inflation target failed to work, Krugman (1998c) makes a surprising retreat: then, he concedes, there is nothing that can be done by monetary policy. 'In this case the temporary fiscal jolt once again comes into its own' (Appendix C, p. 59). Moreover, Krugman has since argued that this worst-case scenario applies to Japan and that, therefore, monetary policy remains ineffective. In a liquidity trap, he now believes, 'Additional cash pumped into the economy – added liquidity – sits idle, because there's no point in lending money out if you don't receive any reward. And monetary policy loses its effectiveness' (Krugman, 2003).[16]

Variations on Krugman

A number of other authors have come to agree with much of Krugman's analysis.[17] Some came to somewhat different policy recommendations, based on their critique of Krugman's work of 1997 and 1998. This includes the Bank of Japan, which has utilized Krugman's liquidity trap argument to support its case that the central bank had already done all that was possible to stimulate the economy. Its Ueda (2001b) argues that because of the liquidity trap, monetary policies, including an inflation target, would not work due to the lack of credibility. Ueda (2001a) argues that the central bank is already operating a 'weak form' of an inflation target, with little success.[18] Any stronger version, such as naming a clear timeframe, would not help, because the central bank would probably not be able to meet a more specific target, and hence would lose credibility, which would be counterproductive.[19] In its frequent publications, the Bank of Japan has concluded from such analysis that monetary policy is ineffective, and hence other policies outside its mandate (such as fiscal stimulation or structural reform) should be pursued.

McKinnon (1999) takes the same stance by arguing that, due to the liquidity trap, inflationary expectations cannot be raised.[20] Instead of the attempt to create expectations of inflation, he suggests stirring expectations of yen depreciation 'through joint action by the Japanese and US governments' (p. 187). It is not clear, however, through what, presumably different, transmission mechanism this depreciation should be achieved within McKinnon's model, and why such a policy would, within his model, be any more credible than the policy to establish an inflation target.

Ito (2000), though in agreement with Krugman's liquidity analysis, also does not follow Krugman's initial conclusion that monetary policy remains relevant, and, like the Bank of Japan and MacKinnon, argues that fiscal policy can stimulate the economy. Ito also disagrees with McKinnon's proposal to set an exchange rate target – not because the policy would be ineffective, but because of its effectiveness, as a result of which Japan's trade partners would be negatively affected, and hence Japan itself.[21] It is not obvious, however, that Ito's definition of a liquidity trap, based on a described dichotomy of high narrow money and low broad money growth, is meaningful. The Keynesian liquidity trap argument requires an increase in monetary aggregates that is not translated into an increase in bond holdings, and hence no fall in long-term interest rates. What the suitable actual measures are to represent money in IS-LM models remains subject to dispute. Moreover, the use of an IS-LM-based definition of the liquidity trap means that zero short-term interest rates *per se* cannot be used as evidence of a liquidity trap, though many observers, including Ito, appear to have done so. Instead, Ito's Hicksian definition of a liquidity trap requires a horizontal LM curve (at any interest rate), below which rates could not be lowered.

There are three fundamental problems with the liquidity trap argument as presented so far. Firstly, by the definition of its various proponents, there actually was *no* liquidity trap throughout much of the 1990s in Japan. Secondly, the liquidity trap argument fails to answer the paramount question that should concern us: why have interest rate *reductions* failed to stimulate the economy. Thirdly, despite the widespread support for the liquidity trap argument by economists, the central bank and commentators in the media, there has been little empirical support for it. Attempts at defining Japan's situation before September 1998 as a liquidity trap exist, but they failed. Weberpals (1997) tested for the existence of a liquidity trap and found no empirical support. Instead, she concludes that Japan's experience has been 'unique', leaving the enigma of interest rate policy ineffectiveness unsolved.

More fundamentally, if the liquidity trap is defined as either a situation where short-term nominal interest rates are at their zero (or close to zero) lower bound (as Krugman and others do), or in the Keynesian and Hicksian (IS-LM) sense as a situation where short-term interest rates cannot be lowered any further, then by definition no liquidity trap existed during the 1990s. Strictly speaking, there could not have been a liquidity trap before 20 March 2001, since short-term nominal interest rates in earlier periods were subsequently followed by even lower rates. Even if we are willing to ignore the reductions of call rates subsequent to the September 1998 reduction to 0.1% (namely by a factor of 100 to as low as 0.001%), then also by this definition there could not have been a liquidity trap until September 1998.

Those who adopt the Hicksian IS-LM version of the liquidity trap argument are additionally handicapped by its static nature. For instance, if the demand for money was perfectly elastic with respect to interest rates, not only would subsequent falls in nominal interest rates be impossible, but also rises. However, both short-term and long-term interest rates not only fell, but also rose during the observation period (in late 1998, interest rates on ten-year government bonds rose from 0.7% to about 2%; short-term interest rates rose in the summer of 2000, duly reflecting Bank of Japan policy).

The liquidity trap model is concerned with the comparative statics of a liquidity trap (when interest rates reached the point where they would not fall further), but not the question of how it developed. It cannot explain why *pre*-trap interest rate *reductions* throughout the 1990s have failed to stimulate the economy. That, however, is the interesting question that we set out to solve. The liquidity trap model of Krugman and its variations proposed by others do not attempt to address, let alone answer this question. Similarly, the Hicksian liquidity trap model does not ask the question why the demand for money *became* perfectly elastic with respect to interest rates.

As Krugman admits, there are few solid reasons why there should be negative growth and inflation expectations. He suggests capital and credit market imperfections as a possibility, but argues that 'demography seems to be the leading candidate' (1998a, p. 9). In Krugman's version, the ultimate cause is exogenous expectation of declining growth in the future. The questions of where this suddenly came from and why it seems to have hit Japan so badly appear to be at the core of understanding the problem and suggesting solutions. However, these are issues that remain outside the model. If this is so, then why are other countries that have similar or worse demography, such as Italy, not suffering from a liquidity trap? The debate about the liquidity trap (and the many subsidiary papers it has spawned) is by definition incapable of addressing, let alone solving the question that we asked at the outset of this chapter, namely why interest rate reductions have not produced an economic recovery.

The liquidity trap argument is thus fundamentally flawed. It elevates what is merely a faulty description of symptoms to a proper diagnosis of the disease and its causes. Hence the proscribed therapy remains doubtful. Upon closer inspection, it implodes to a tautology, namely that short-term nominal interest rates cannot fall further, because they have fallen by as much as they can fall. We therefore turn to the literature formulating the general case for ineffectiveness of interest rate policy.

Quantitative easing

Since economists eventually recognized that nominal short-term interest rates close to zero implied the end of interest rate policy, several began to argue that the central bank might wish to consider tools other than interest rates. After all, as Bernanke (2000) reminds us, even zero interest rates are not a sign that monetary policy is stimulatory, since 'low interest rates may just as well be a sign of expected deflation and monetary tightness as of monetary ease' (p. 155). Thus the unusual circumstances of near-zero interest rates have prompted economists that normally argue in favour of interest rates as the key monetary policy tool to abandon the price of money, and instead use the quantity of money as operating target. Hence those monetarist economists that had been calling for quantitative expansion earlier (and will be discussed below on the general case) were joined by the likes of Krugman (his work of 1998 and 1999), Hayashi (1998) and others, who argued that the central bank should increase the quantity of money it supplies to the economy. In Hayashi's model, as well as Krugman's subsequent models (such as 1998c), the transmission mechanism from such quantitative policy to the economy operates via expectations: the announcement of 'quantitative easing' would prompt inflationary expectations, which would lower real interest rates and these would, in turn, act to stimulate investment and economic growth.

Structural reform argument

There is an alternative argument why neither monetary nor fiscal policies during the 1990s were effective and why none of the above policies would stimulate growth. According to this view, represented for instance by Katz (2001), Wilson (2000), Ikeo (2001) and others, Japan's recession has been caused by supply-side problems, mainly low productivity and efficiency resulting from the Japanese economic structure. The policy advice is therefore to reform Japan's economic structure fundamentally.

The problem with the structural argument is that it is concerned with potential growth (which is a function of the quantity of factor inputs and total factor productivity). It thus fails to address the main question, namely why Japan's actual growth rate has remained below potential (as evidenced by consistently low capacity utilization in the factor markets). The only way to explain weak demand with this supply-side argument is via the problems in the banking sector. It is in this context that we will return to this argument below.

The general case

A number of economists have argued for at least a decade, beginning at a time when Japanese interest rates were far from zero, that mere rate reductions would be insufficient to stimulate the Japanese economy. Their arguments are based on one of the following four schools of thought, all of which have existed longer than the Japanese macroeconomic problems.

Neutrality of money

Some economists argue that monetary policy is generally incapable of affecting the economy, since money is neutral. This view is in line with new classical models of the macro economy (such as Lucas, 1972) which usually rely on a restrictive set of assumptions. Within the context of the debate about Japan's economy, Koo (1998, 1999) has been a proponent of the first school of thought.

However, there is little empirical evidence that money is indeed neutral.[22] On the contrary, economists have for years had to grapple with the reality that money does affect the economy.[23] Specifically, using a different concept of causality, namely superexogeneity or 'control causality' (the ability to predictably affect B through one's control of A, as proposed by Engle et al., 1983, and Hoover, 1988, respectively) Perez (2002) found that monetary policy does matter in the US. We will therefore not consider this case in greater detail. For all practical purposes the general case against interest rate policy ineffectiveness has been debated by adherents of the remaining three schools.

Endogeneity of money

The second school of thought argues that causation does not run from money to economic activity, but in reverse order, and hence traditional monetary policy is powerless. This view is shared by Kaldor (1970) and many post-Keynesian economists who argue that the money supply is endogenous.[24] Many proponents of this view also argue that the credit supply is endogenous (Moore, 1988). Concerning the role of interest rates, this school of thought argues that the 'ability of the monetary authorities to control the rate of expansion of bank credit and hence the money stock in the absence of credit controls lies primarily in their ability to determine short-term interest rates, and so the level of administered bank lending rates' (Moore, 1988, p. 232, see also Arestis and Howells, 1996). Noting that there has been little statistically significant evidence that nominal rates are indeed negatively correlated with the quantity of money or credit, Moore argues that 'the authorities' power to control the total volume of credit expansion by this means is very slight' (p. 232). Essentially, the endogenous money school argues that the credit market is not in equilibrium, but rationed and determined by loan demand. The loan demand is, in turn, determined by various factors inherent to the corporate sector (such as costs, taxes, inventories or other aspects of the corporate balance sheet).

Since this approach in effect absolves central banks from much responsibility (they are passive bystanders without much ability to affect the economy), it has proven to be popular among central banks. In Japan, the Bank of Japan has consistently adhered to this approach during the 1990s.[25] Among economists who are not full-time staff of the Bank of Japan, Yoshikawa (1993) has been a proponent of this view.

The Bank of Japan's Okina (1991, 1993a, 1993b) provides the most detailed description of this model, closely following Moore (1988) and others. His starting point is the observation that the central bank fulfils the double function of conducting monetary policy and acting as the lender of last resort that has to protect the stability of the financial system. Currency in circulation, at the end of 1992 accounting for 93% of high powered money, is not supplied by the central bank at its discretion, but only on demand from the public (for instance, when bank deposits are withdrawn and turned into cash for spending; banks are passive and cannot initiate this, and neither can the central bank). This demand is largely transaction-based and hence closely related to nominal consumption. Therefore, 'in the short run, the central bank cannot control currency in circulation unless it drives up short-term interest rates dramatically so as to affect nominal consumption' (Okina, 1993a, at a time when methods to slow the economy were discussed). However, in its function as lender of last resort, the central bank cannot allow dramatic interest rate fluctuations, as they might endanger the stability of the financial system. Furthermore, bank reserves, the other component of high powered money, also cannot be controlled for a similar reason: As the deadline for banks to meet their reserve requirements approaches on the 15th of the month, the central bank may be forced to inject more money into the call market (or absorb money from it), in order to prevent 'dramatic' volatility in short-term interest rates. Hence high powered money is not under the control of the central bank and not an exogenous policy variable. It is 'not the cause, but the result' (Okina, 1993b, p. 104). Having no control over the money supply, the central bank's activity is reduced to smoothing the call rate, which becomes the only viable operational target. However, the Bank of Japan is also aware of the severe limitations of this tool: even the call rate 'cannot exert substantial influence on corporate or household expenditures' (p. 87), since it has to work through other, longer term interest rates, which in the long run might have some influence over the money supply and domestic demand.

Yoshikawa (1993) agrees with the Bank of Japan's view that the money supply is largely endogenous to 'real shocks' in the short run, because 'central banks smooth the nominal interest rate' (p. 122), especially in the face of seasonal variations. At the same time, he points out that, like in other countries, in Japan Granger 'causality' also tends to run from money to output. His own empirical work finds that 'monetary policy, represented by changes in the call rate, exerts substantial effects on real output in Japan mainly through its effect on fixed investment and imports' (p. 156). This is because 'When the BoJ changes its policy stance ... it affects real output.'

The Bank of Japan's and Yoshikawa's endogeneity appears restricted to the very short-term, seasonal movement of the economy, within a medium- to long-term setting of exogenous monetary policy. Beyond seasonality, Yoshikawa concedes that the Bank of Japan 'at times ... even actively changes the interest rate during the business cycle' (p. 157). As there is no reason why the base money targets could not be seasonally adjusted, the argument of short-run money endogeneity depends on a narrow definition of what constitutes the short run.

The Japanese experience of low income elasticity of interest rates would appear to fit the endogenous money school, since in a demand-rationed credit market interest rates are not necessarily inversely correlated with economic activity. However, the overall empirical evidence in favour of this approach remains mixed, as other parts of the argument have not found convincing support.

Much of the endogenous money school has focused on the problems by central banks in moving towards tighter monetary policy. As the above quote from Moore clarifies, the endogenous money school of thought assumes the absence of credit control in periods where the central bank wishes to slow the economy. However, it needs to be established that this assumption does apply to Japan's case of the 1980s and early 1990s. During the remainder of the 1990s, the problem was weak credit growth. Here, however, the assumption of the endogenous money school that the central bank can only rely on interest rates to implement monetary policy is also inapplicable. Surely the central bank remains able to *increase* the supply of money and credit to the economy, for instance by autonomously deciding to step up its purchases of private sector assets (such as bills, commercial paper, bonds, equity, real estate, and so on).

Secondly, Moore (1988) and others provide empirical evidence that credit Granger-'causes' (that is, is consistently useful in predicting) money supply. There is also some evidence that certain parts of total credit, namely bank lending to industry and commerce, especially by larger firms, may be endogenous to other factors (such as costs, inventories, taxes, or other aspects of corporate balance sheets), as Moore and Threadgold (1980, 1985) have found in the UK. However, even if these findings can be generalized, they do not imply that total credit is endogenous to such factors and that the central bank cannot autonomously increase the supply of credit.

Thirdly, there has been little empirical evidence that money or credit supply are endogenous to economic activity. To the contrary, empirical research on the relationship between money or credit aggregates and economic activity (such as nominal GDP) has more often than not yielded evidence that the monetary variable 'Granger-causes' economic activity (see, among others, Sims, 1972; Stock and Watson, 1989; Blanchard, 1990; Romer and Romer, 1994; Cheung and Fujii, 1999). As will be seen below, this also holds in the case of Japan in the 1990s. While such findings do not constitute 'proof' that causation runs from monetary variables to economic activity, it can be said that they fail to support the hypothesis of endogenous money.[26]

Fourthly, upon closer inspection, it emerges that the Bank of Japan's version of the endogeneity argument, despite close affinity to Moore (1988) and other post-Keynesians, does not explain why interest rate reductions failed to stimulate the economy: although the main proponent of endogeneity, the central bank's Okina, argues for endogeneity of the money supply to economic activity, he simultaneously argues that interest rates remain relevant. According to his theory, 'over a long time period, a reduction in interest rates, through stimulation of economic activity, increases income and raises asset prices, which can be expected to increase the appetite to hold money. Through this route, the central bank can control the money supply' (Okina, 1993b, p. 174).[27] Since a decade should be sufficiently long for Okina's theory to be applicable, it has failed to find empirical support. Furthermore, since according to the 'BoJ Theory' (as it was dubbed by Iwata, see below), it is interest rates which, after all, determine economic activity and GDP growth, the Bank of Japan's theory of money endogeneity is disqualified as a potential explanation of the question that concerns us in this chapter, namely just why interest rate reductions have failed to do what the Bank of Japan claims they should have achieved. It is likely that this fatal claim of the 'BoJ Theory' led to its demise in 2001, as we find below.

Fifthly, the endogenous money school, like other macroeconomic theories, assumes the conventional equation of exchange to hold, where the velocity V is assumed constant. Moore (1988), for instance, refers to what he calls the 'quantity identity':

(1) $Y \equiv MV$

with Y representing nominal GDP, M the money supply and V the velocity. The endogenous money approach (like the monetarist, exogenous money approach) assumes that, at least for longer time periods, the velocity is constant (Moore, 1988, p. 305). However, the Bank of Japan's Ueda (2001b), referring to the traditional quantity theory relationship

(2) $MV = PY$

and defining M as high-powered money, Y as real output, P as the GDP deflator, points out that the velocity V has fallen, instead of remaining constant. In his view this is due to the liquidity trap, which, in line with Krugman, he defines as a situation of near-zero short-term interest rates. Since increases in M coincide with further declines in V, there is no impact on nominal GDP (PY). Thus Ueda argues that increases in the monetary base become practically 'meaningless'. As evidence he points to the frequent incidents of money market bids falling short of the total offer, reflecting a 'lack of demand' for the money the central bank is trying to supply. But he fails to provide a reason of just why velocity has been falling or why the liquidity trap came about in the first place.

In conclusion, the money endogeneity argument does not fit well with the Japanese experience of the 1990s. Moreover, it turns out that the main Japanese proponents do not actually use it to explain why interest rate reductions have failed to stimulate the economy. Instead, the Bank of Japan appears to have abandoned its long-standing endogenous money view in favour of a version of Krugman's liquidity trap argument – which in turn fails to address our main question of interest.

The monetarist view

The third school of thought holds the opposite view to the second: its adherents see monetary policy as being exogenously determined by the central bank and capable of affecting output.[28] Milton Friedman (1968, 1984), Poole (1982), Brunner and Meltzer (1983), McCallum (1985) and others argue that it is possible for the central bank to control high powered money exogenously in order to implement monetary policy and manipulate the economy. McCallum (1993) points out that the Bank of Japan admits that it *can* control high powered money, if it allowed greater interest rate fluctuations (while Okina failed to clarify what would constitute a 'dramatic' interest rate movement). McCallum also points out that Okina's (1993a) justification of money endogeneity through lagged reserve requirements fails to allow for the desirable institutional change to contemporaneous reserve requirements.

In line with this view, Iwata (1992b, 1992c, 1994) argues that the Bank of Japan's explanation and conduct of monetary policy – what he termed the 'BoJ Theory' – is fundamentally flawed. He argues that the central bank can exogenously manipulate the quantity of high powered money, that there is a stable relationship between high powered money and deposit aggregates (such as M2 + CD), and in turn a stable relationship between deposit aggregates and GDP. Therefore, the central bank can manipulate economic growth by controlling high powered money. The latter is, in his view, a more appropriate measure of the stance of monetary policy than interest rates. Using this analysis, Iwata points out that the central bank tightened monetary policy too late (high powered money growth continued to rise for one and a half years after the central bank had raised interest rates for the first time in May 1989), and then failed to stimulate the economy for too long (while interest rates had been falling since 1991, the supply of high powered money contracted during much of 1992).[29] He therefore urged in 1992 that the central bank abandon its 'BoJ Theory' and shift its operating target from interest rates to high powered money (Iwata, 1992c).[30]

However, the monetarist case also suffers from some of the theoretical shortcomings of the liquidity trap argument, because the transmission mechanism of the monetary stimulus is often said to operate via expectations, just as in Krugman's (1998c) model. Allan Meltzer, a leading monetarist, for instance, argued as follows: 'An announcement by the Bank of Japan and the government that the aim of policy is to prevent deflation and restore growth by providing enough money to raise asset prices would change beliefs and anticipations' (Meltzer, 1998). Thus a credible announcement by the Bank of Japan that it would provide more money would change expectations, which in turn would stimulate the economy. If, however, increases in monetary aggregates fail to trigger such expectations (because they are seen to lack credibility), then the economy would not be stimulated.[31]

Subsequent to Iwata's arguments of 1992, high powered money, M1 and M2 + CD growth increased sharply. However, these increases in the money supply failed to be associated with commensurate increases in economic activity. Contrary to the monetarist framework, the monetary indicators were not in a stable relationship with nominal GDP growth. This silenced many proponents of this view for many years. Many economists who noticed that M1 growth rose significantly in 1992 and 1993 predicted no further problems with Japan's economy and argued that there was no reason to fear a credit crunch or other monetary obstacles to growth (see, for instance, Morgan, 1994a, 1994b).

Just like the endogenous money view, the monetarist case also rests on the assumption of a stable velocity in equations (1) or (2) (even though causation is said to run the opposite way). It had already been observed in many other countries that the stable relationship between money and GDP 'increasingly came apart at the seams during the course of the 1980s' (Goodhart, 1989a). A large body of literature has tried to grapple with this 'anomaly', but the problem remained: 'recurring bouts of instability in money demand' (Goldfeld and Sichel, 1990, p. 349). Indeed, central banks in the UK and US were forced to abandon targeting monetary aggregates, since they were in no stable relationship with economic activity.[32] 'Once viewed as a pillar of macro-economic models, it is now widely regarded as one of the weakest stones in the foundation' (Boughton, 1991).

The Japanese experience of both the 1980s and 1990s was no exception. Many publications by the Bank of Japan therefore pointed out the problem of an unstable velocity (such as Okina, 1993b). Ueda (2001b), citing equation (2), notes that V declined throughout the 1990s. Other, broader monetary indicators did not fare better. Apparently there was no clear-cut link between money and the economy.

The monetary transmission mechanism proposed in monetarist models such as Brunner and Meltzer's (1968) or Meltzer's (1995) operate through a rebalancing in other asset markets. However, the significant monetary stimulation via lower interest rates and expanded monetary aggregates failed to boost asset prices significantly during the 1990s. Meltzer (2001) is thus forced to argue that the monetary stimulus was simply not strong enough.[33] Thus, despite the record expansion in money aggregates and record low interest rates, monetary policy in fact remained 'deflationary'. However, the issue of why a decade of interest rate reductions failed to show the otherwise familiar effect is skirted.

Despite the lack of empirical support for the monetarist case (but presumably prompted also by the lack of support for its own prior money endogeneity theory), the Bank of Japan on 19 March 2001 abandoned its long-standing interest rate targeting regime and adopted a reserve target, just as the monetarists had advised almost a decade earlier. Thus the Bank of Japan became the first central bank to reintroduce explicit monetary targeting in over a decade, despite the ineffectiveness of this practice in the past. Bank reserves with the central bank were aggressively increased, rising 114% year on year in the second half of 2001. Just as the monetarists predicted, and the endogeneity theory denied, the central bank succeeded in meeting its reserve targets (and raised growth of high powered money), without visible volatility in short-term interest rates. However, the expected recovery in the economy had failed to materialize, as of August 2003. The 'anomaly' of an unstable velocity persisted and undermined the monetarist argument.

When interest rates had fallen close to zero, the Bank of Japan used this as further evidence of the inability of monetarist policies: Ueda (2001a) argued that with zero interest rates an injection of any quantity of money will not affect the economy, as it would merely increase the banks' idle excess reserves.

While the monetarist argument does not explicitly address the question why falling interest rates have failed to stimulate the economy, the monetarist model postulates an equilibrium in the market for money and hence a unique relationship between quantity of money variables and interest rates. Interest rates are considered endogenous to the exogenously controlled quantity of money variable(s). For monetarists, the question why interest rates have not stimulated the economy is thus equivalent to asking the question why rises in the various monetary aggregates have failed to stimulate the economy. This, however, remains a puzzle that the monetarist theory has failed to explain.

The credit view

The main alternative explanation for the ineffectiveness of interest rate reductions to stimulate the economy is provided by the 'credit view'. There are three versions of it, often interrelated: The 'bank lending channel' or 'lending view', the credit rationing argument, and the 'balance sheet channel'.

The lending view

The pure 'lending view' argues that monetary policy actions not only affect the economy through private sector assets (the money supply), but also through private sector liabilities (borrowing and credit).[34] When the central bank tightens monetary policy by reducing high powered money or bank reserves, deposits decline, but banks' access to loanable funds is also reduced and hence the supply of bank loans falls (Bernanke and Blinder, 1988; Bernanke, 1993; Gertler and Gilchrist, 1993). This lending channel is said to work over and above the traditional money supply and interest rate effects, such as represented in IS-LM analysis. As a result, proponents of this view believe that the effect of monetary policy is larger than that attributed to interest rates and the asset channel alone. Unlike the money view, the bank lending view usually distinguishes between large and small borrowers (the latter assumed to be mainly dependent on bank lending). The Japanese situation in the 1990s provides an interesting application of this theory, because it proclaims that 'even under extreme conditions where either interest rates do not respond to monetary policy actions or where spending is unresponsive to changes in interest rates, monetary policy actions affect the economy because of their direct effect on bank loans' (Thornton, 1994, p. 32).

As Bernanke (1993), Gertler and Gilchrist (1993) and Kashyap and Stein (1997) argue, two necessary conditions must be satisfied for a lending channel of monetary policy to exist. Firstly, the central bank can affect the supply of bank loans, and lending is imperfectly substitutable for borrowing in the capital markets (or other forms of raising funds). For this condition to hold, bank loans and securities must be imperfectly substitutable in banks' portfolios (otherwise banks could offset a decline in reserves due to monetary policy by increasing CDs to maintain an unchanged amount of loans in their portfolios).[35] The second condition for the lending view is that other intermediaries or the capital markets fail to satisfy an excess demand for loans. Thus a convincing explanation why banks (or 'lenders') are special must be presented, and be consistent with the empirical record.

In a Modigliani-Miller world, borrowers whose banks do not lend to them could obtain funding from other sources. When asymmetric or imperfect information is the basis of the special role of banks, it is argued, as in Diamond (1984), that banks carry out delegated monitoring of borrowers on behalf of depositors or, as in Fama (1985), that banks have a special role as accumulators of specific information about borrowers. However, it is not readily visible why other financial intermediaries, such as non-bank financial institutions, should not be able to act as delegated monitors or accumulators of information. Thornton (1994) argues that the bank lending view comes to appreciate bank lending as a special factor just at a time when financial innovation and disintermediation renders bank lending less 'special' than it may have been in the past.

Since bank loans are private sector liabilities, empirical researchers have responded to this difficulty on occasion by adding other types of private sector liabilities to their definition of 'lending'. Some therefore assume that funding from banks and other, non-bank financial institutions is perfectly substitutable, while it is imperfectly substitutable with funding from capital markets ('direct financing' via the issuance of debt or equity). Others argue that all debt financing is perfectly substitutable (grouping bank, non-bank financial institutions and debt origination in capital markets together), while arguing that it is different from (and imperfectly substitutable with) equity financing (Bayoumi, 2000; Nishimura and Kawamoto, 2003).

The contradictory claims of substitutability between different funding channels does little to enhance the intellectual appeal of the credit approach. The broader the definition of 'lender' becomes, the less convincing the argument that 'lending' is imperfectly substitutable for other forms of fundraising and the less distinguishable the lending view becomes from the familiar representation of banks in finance textbooks as mere financial intermediaries between savers and investors (see, for instance, Miller and VanHoose, 1993). This analytical and empirical weakness of the lending view is reminiscent – indeed a 'credit counterpart' – of the travails experienced by the monetarist approach. Here, private sector assets are used to define 'money'. However, when the initially favoured narrow monetary aggregates exhibited 'instability', ever broader definitions of private sector assets were employed (and this practice justified theoretically). The analytical problem was, as Milton Friedman recognized, that 'there is no hard-and-fast line between "money" and other assets' (Friedman, 1956, p. 158). Though focusing on private sector liabilities, the credit view faces a similar problem. There is a continuum of private sector liabilities, yet so far no robust justification of any specific definition.

To establish the lending view empirically, it would have to be demonstrated that (1) central bank actions affect bank lending, even when demand does not respond to interest rate actions, because of the direct effect on lending;[36] (2) the effect of monetary policy action is larger than the effect of the traditional monetary channel alone; (3) lending must be special and non-substitutable for other forms of fundraising.

The evidence has not been compelling on either count. While Kashyap and Stein (1997) report significant evidence of a bank lending channel from panel data on commercial banks, especially small banks, and Bernanke and Blinder (1992) showed in a VAR model that credit aggregates fall after a rise in short-term interest rates, the results were not easily duplicated for other countries.[37] Although Kashyap and Stein (1997) concluded on the basis of qualitative indicators that the lending channel is more likely to be relevant in Germany than in most other countries of the European Union, VAR studies by Barran et al. (1995), Guender and Moersch (1997) and Kakes et al. (2001), concluded that a bank lending channel is not an important transmission mechanism of monetary policy in Germany.[38] Furthermore, a number of studies, including Bernanke and Lown (1991), Driscoll (1994) and Haubrich (1990), fail to find support for the lending view. Only very limited support is cited by King (1986), Ramey (1993) and Hubbard (1995). Romer and Romer (1990) have shown that since about 1980, banks' ability to raise funds through CDs, securitized loans or equity issues has improved. There has been little empirical support of the monitoring rationale advanced by Diamond (1984) and Fama (1985).[39] Thornton (1994) shows that financial innovation and deregulation have increased banks' access to financial markets and reduced their dependence on funds subject to the central bank's reserve requirements. While Thornton finds a statistically significant relationship between Federal Reserve actions and both bank lending and bank deposits prior to the early 1980s, the effect was small, and became negligible afterwards. He concludes that there was little empirical support for the lending view.

In the end, proponents of the lending view conceded: 'Clearly, the Bernanke and Blinder (1988) model is a poorer description of reality than it used to be, at least in the United States' (Bernanke and Gertler, 1995, p. 41).[40] 'In summary, because of financial deregulation and innovation, the importance of the traditional bank lending channel has most likely diminished over time' (p. 42).

In Japan's case, the bank lending view is quickly dismissed, since the first condition cannot be met: bank lending failed to respond to significant rises in reserves and high powered money or reductions in interest rates throughout the 1990s.[41] Several authors who have argued that they have found evidence for a lending channel in Japan turn out to have found evidence that the credit market has been rationed. That, however, is a different argument that should not be confused with the lending view.

The credit rationing argument

In order to justify why certain types of loans are special, the argument is often made that small firms are dependent on borrowing and have limited access to capital markets. Credit rationed small firms might fail to increase plant and equipment investment by as much as they otherwise would. As Bernanke (1993), Bernanke and Blinder (1988), Gertler and Gilchrist (1993), Kashyap and Stein (1993) and Friedman and Kuttner (1993) recognize, credit rationing is neither a necessary nor a sufficient condition for the operation of a lending or credit channel of monetary policy transmission. This does not mean that credit rationing is not an important phenomenon in its own right that might explain events in Japan in the 1990s. In the words of Blanchard and Fischer (1989),

> a recurrent theme in the literature and among market participants is that the interest rate alone does not adequately reflect the links between financial markets and the rest of the economy. Rather, it is argued, the availability of credit and the quality of balance sheets are important determinants of the rate of investment.

Jaffee and Russell (1976) and Stiglitz and Weiss (1981) showed that credit markets would be rationed even when agents are maximizing, as long as information between borrowers and lenders is asymmetric. Due to the risk of default, the lender maximizes returns by setting interest rates below the market-clearing level. This is said to provide 'a firm theoretical basis' (Dimsdale, 1994, p. 35) for Keynes' (1930) argument that there is a 'fringe of unsatisfied borrowers'. Based on the case for credit rationing, Jaffee and Stiglitz (1990) conclude that the availability of credit is more important than the price of credit. Stiglitz and Weiss (1992) argue that with credit contracts that include both an interest rate and a collateral requirement, all types of borrowers may be rationed. As a result, interest rates charged borrowers may move either pro- or counter-cyclically.

While many post-Keynesian economists argue in favour of endogenous money and endogenous credit, the view that the supply of credit is of importance, and may be rationed, has also been gaining ground among them. A notable example is Arestis and Sawyer and their discussion of monetary policy channels, in which they argue that

> credit channels are only indirectly affected by monetary policy in that when interest rates rise there may be some impact on the willingness of banks to grant credit; in other words the extent of credit rationing changes. This may be seen to enhance the impact of monetary policy in that changing interest rates not only have a 'price effect' on investment and other forms of expenditure, but there is also a credit rationing effect. However, the size of this credit rationing impact depends on the liquidity preference of banks and their willingness to grant credit. (Arestis and Sawyer, 2003b, p. 12)

Evidence in support of credit rationing has been provided by Bernanke (1983), as well as Gertler and Gilchrist (1993, 1994), who considered the impact of a liquidity shortage on different types of firms (small versus large) and found significant differences in their behaviour. Unlike large firms, small firms are more likely to cut working hours and production, as they apparently have limited access to short-term credit markets. DeYoung et al. (1999) report that younger banks lend more to small firms than older banks.

However, many studies on credit rationing are susceptible to the argument that reduced loan demand may explain the reduction in lending. Ludvigson (1999) devised a test that is immune to the demand argument by focusing on car loans and observing whether lending patterns by banks would differ from that of financing companies. She finds tighter monetary policy reduces lending by banks, but not of financing companies. There is also empirical evidence for severe credit rationing (a 'credit crunch') from Korea and Thailand (Ferri and Kang, 1998; Agenor et al., 2000). On the other hand, a study of several thousand US loan contracts by Berger and Udell (1994) did not provide evidence of significant credit rationing.

In Japan's case, most studies found that there was no evidence for a 'credit crunch' before 1997, but there has been since (Baba, 1996; Motonishi and Yoshikawa, 1998; Woo, 1999; Bayoumi, 2000; Morsink and Bayoumi, 2000).[42] Yet, even the studies that find evidence for a credit crunch during or after 1997 suffer from several defects. For instance, there are several limitations to Bayoumi's (2000) analysis: declining lending is explained by asset price movements, which remain an exogenous variable. The definition of bank lending – crucial for the argument – consists of the 'sum of liabilities of the corporate sector and borrowing by the private sector' (p. 43). However, liabilities of the corporate sector include borrowing directly from the capital markets through the issuance of commercial paper, corporate bonds, and so on.[43] Furthermore, Bayoumi (2000) warns of the limitations of VAR analysis (which applies to many of the other empirical studies), especially the assumption that the underlying responses are linear and unchanging over time. In reality, individuals

> could react differently to events depending on the state of the macro-economy, with behaviour at the tip of a cyclical upturn being rather different from that at the bottom of a downturn. Similarly, the impact of financial sector deregulation since 1980 may have altered the relationship between the corporate sector and the banking system. (p. 42)

Meltzer (2001) rejects the rationing argument outright in the case of Japan:[44]

> I find the argument about banks' unwillingness to lend puzzling for two reasons. First, it does not fit well with another common argument about Japanese banking – that banks went heavily into real estate lending in the 1980s because, after deregulation, corporate borrowers greatly reduced their reliance on banks. Second, evidence from many countries suggests that loans, including very risky loans, increase in weakened financial systems with many insolvent banks. This is the familiar moral hazard

argument. Both of these arguments suggest that much of the decline in lending reflected reduced demand for loans.

Krugman (1998c) also dismisses the credit crunch argument on the basis of the moral hazard argument.[45] Indeed, from 1991 to 1994 bank lending to the real estate sector increased faster than loan growth to other sectors (Werner, 1996d).

Kashyap (2002), formerly a proponent of the credit view and credit rationing, appears to have accepted such arguments, as he is now criticizing Japanese banks for lending *excessively*, thereby keeping 'deadbeat borrowers' in business by 'routinely rolling over loans rather than pulling the plug on bankrupt firms' (p. 54). Too much lending has been detrimental, because 'suppressing the normal process of creative destruction leaves all banks with fewer good borrowers to lend to. Without good borrowers, the banks have an even greater inventive to roll over loans to deadbeat borrowers', which in turn has been a 'covert unemployment compensation programme' (p. 54). In other words, far from restricting demand by lending too little, banks are said to have engaged in policies that governments normally adopt to prop up demand – and they are said to have done too much of it.

Kashyap (2002), Fukao (2003) and the BIS (2002) also criticize the 'strong competition from government sponsored financial institutions' (BIS, 2002, p. 133), which they argue has held bank loans back. Kashyap thus recommends shutting down the public banks (p. 54). The IMF (2002) even recommends that Japan reduce the number of commercial banks and public financial institutions through 'exit'. If their reasoning is accurate, then banks have been willing to lend, but borrowers had a choice of other funding sources, and opted against the banks. Thus a large number of economists does not believe that lack of fund supply has been a key problem.

The rapid growth of non-bank financial intermediaries and sub-prime lenders ('loan sharks') during the 1990s, as well as the historically unprecedented rise in incidents of illegal usury and the number of victims of loan sharks suggests that certain types of borrowers did face credit rationing.[46] However, while bank lending to some borrowers may be rationed, the main difficulty of the credit rationing argument is that such a finding in itself would be insufficient to explain why the economy failed to recover: the very increase in funding from non-bank sources is evidence that there are substitutes for bank lending. While the credit view attempts to make the macroeconomic case that monetary policy also functions through a bank lending channel (which fails in the case of Japan), the credit rationing argument is essentially a microeconomic argument. Evidence for the existence of credit rationing does not demonstrate that economic growth must be negatively affected by it. For that, it is necessary to show that fund raising and spending by others (such as large firms or the government) and through other means (such as from insurers, public banks, capital markets, borrowing from abroad, trade credit, and so on) could not compensate for the decline in fund raising by small firms (which account for only about a third of total business investment). It is not clear why the rationing of small firms has an especially large effect on the economy, quite disproportional to their size. Even in Japan, where small firms are an important part of the economy, their business investment (capital expenditure) amounts to only 24% of all capital expenditure.[47] Indirect financing continued to grow significantly in Japan during the 1990s. Most of all, fundraising by the Japanese government has been at record-breaking levels.

As Meltzer (1995) argues, for credit rationing to explain downturns, lending must drop by more than other fund raising in capital markets. To apply the credit rationing argument to Japan means that it must be shown that other forms of fundraising were also not available.[48] Meltzer (2001) argues that as an open economy with deregulated capital flows, Japanese borrowers have not only domestic financial markets open to them, but the world's financial resources:

> Large Japanese corporations can borrow abroad, and they do. Borrowing abroad declined in the 1990s, suggesting that the decline in lending reflected reduced demand to borrow. Consumption lending by banks has been relatively small, or non-existent, during most of the postwar. Further, Japanese households have maintained a high saving rate throughout the decade. Lending gives less support to consumption spending in Japan than in the United States.

There is international evidence that bank lending is substituted by other forms of lending. Calomiris et al. (1995) found that a reduction in bank lending is met by an increase in the extension trade credit and other forms of direct financing. Mateut et al. (2003) show that bank lending is substitutable with trade credit in the UK.[49] Kashyap (2002) also concludes that in the Japanese case the loan supply from banks, due to balance sheet problems of banks, cannot be the main problem:

> There have always been international banks (and insurance companies) operating in Japan, and the number rose substantially as a result of the so-called 'Big Bang' deregulation ... These foreign firms are solvent but are choosing not to lend much in Japan. So the problem is not just that the domestic financial institutions are undercapitalized. (p. 43)

These findings on Japan mean that for the majority of the 1990s, even the credit crunch argument cannot answer the question why significant declines in interest rates failed to stimulate economic activity. No empirical paper on Japan has so far attempted to explain why the borrowing from other sources and spending by others that *did* take place to a significant extent could not make up for the decline in small firm borrowing. Thus today many observers have concluded that credit rationing by banks cannot explain Japan's predicament.

Eye inspection of the annual flow of funds data provided by the Bank of Japan can be used to check the 'stylized' facts on fundraising in Japan during the 1990s.[50] Table 3.1 breaks down fundraising by the non-financial sector via domestic markets into the type of financial institution and the type of non-financial intermediary that provided the funds. It transpires that during the 1990s, deposit-taking financial institutions did reduce their lending significantly in FY1994, FY1996, FY1998 and FY2001. However, from FY1994 to FY1997, nominal GDP growth was above average. As can be readily seen, in FY1994 and FY1996, loans by insurers and pension funds rose to the decade's average or above-average level, partially making up for the decline in bank loans. In those years, as well as in FY1998, lending by other non-bank financial intermediaries was also close to the decade's average. As a result, we find that fundraising from all financial institutions remained fairly stable throughout the 1990s, with the first significant drop only occurring in FY2001 (followed by the first net repayment of funds in FY2002). Thus apparently borrowing from banks was substitutable with borrowing from other financial institutions, at least in aggregate. The right half of the table indicates that in crucial years, such as in FY2000 and FY2001, when funding from financial institutions was relatively scarce, direct finance stepped in. Thus funding from financial institutions was, at least in aggregate, to some extent substitutable.

From the flow of funds table it also transpires that one of the most frequently repeated claims by the central bank, namely that it has been providing the economy with 'ample liquidity' (for example, Hayami, 1999), is not supported by the empirical record: the central bank withdrew funds from the non-financial sector in FY1998, FY1999 and FY2000. This finding seems puzzling at first, but it is in line with an alternative measure of central bank liquidity provision proposed in Part III, in the context of a modified credit view perspective.

When adding the borrowing in the form of trade credit, we obtain the figures for all fundraising in the domestic markets (Table 3.2). We obtain total fundraising by Japanese entities, if we also add fund raising undertaken from overseas markets. This table also breaks down the borrowing via financial institutions in a different way, namely whether funding was in the form of loans, or in the form of purchases of securities by financial institutions or credit from public institutions.

From Table 3.2 it can be seen that fundraising via domestic markets only dropped sharply in one year, namely in FY1998, to ¥3.5 trillion. During that year, the sharp withdrawal of trade credit was a more important factor than a reduction in loans. Fundraising immediately recovered in FY1999, reaching a higher volume than even in prosperous 1991. In the possible 'crunch'

72

Table 3.1 Fundraising via domestic markets, broken down by source

FY ¥ trillion	Via financial institutions	BoJ	Depos. instit.	Insur., pension funds	Other financial intermed.	Via non-financial sector	Securities other than shares	Shares & other equities	Of which		
									Non-financial corporations	Government	Households
1990	74.9	-1.1	45.1	18.0	10.7	10.4	2.6	7.7	1.8	6.1	1.5
1991	50.2	-8.0	20.4	14.8	18.8	0.9	-2.4	3.3	-1.6	4.0	0.2
1992	52.0	1.4	10.2	16.7	20.7	4.7	0.9	3.8	-2.9	6.4	1.6
1993	65.0	8.0	11.4	12.7	29.2	2.2	-2.4	4.6	-1.3	2.7	-0.8
1994	44.6	0.6	8.4	20.9	17.5	14.3	9.8	4.5	0.1	11.5	2.0
1995	52.7	10.3	24.6	19.4	16.7	6.1	2.0	4.1	-0.6	4.2	1.1
1996	37.6	5.8	0.1	14.2	21.4	7.8	5.3	2.5	1.8	4.4	0.2
1997	47.0	8.3	16.8	7.3	19.0	6.7	4.5	2.2	-1.6	3.1	0.6
1998	35.0	-0.7	2.2	6.9	16.9	2.6	0.0	2.5	-1.0	5.1	0.1
1999	59.5	-9.5	10.6	17.1	33.4	2.6	1.0	1.6	1.9	0.4	-1.5
2000	29.4	-3.9	18.0	10.9	6.7	11.0	4.5	6.5	5.7	4.6	3.4
2001	13.1	36.8	2.5	8.6	-18.9	20.9	13.1	7.8	2.9	11.9	3.0
2002	-6.6	3.1	5.0	5.4	-14.8	8.8	3.3	5.5	2.1	6.2	-0.1

Source: Flow of Funds, Bank of Japan, 2003.

Table 3.2 Fundraising by the domestic non-financial sector, broken down by source

FY ¥ trillion	Fundraising by domestic non-financial sector	Via overseas market	Via domestic market	Via financial institutions				Via non-financial sector			Trade credits
					Loans	Securities other than shares	Shares & other equities	Public institutions		Securities other than shares	Shares & other equities	
1990	117.9	1.0	116.8	74.9	73.9	3.0	-2.0	15.7	10.4	2.6	7.7	31.6
1991	58.5	7.1	51.4	50.2	43.2	7.4	-0.4	19.5	0.9	-2.4	3.3	0.3
1992	21.3	-5.0	26.2	52.0	28.7	22.5	0.9	26.2	4.7	0.9	3.8	-30.4
1993	57.9	-1.1	59.0	65.0	35.7	30.5	-1.2	38.4	2.2	-2.4	4.6	-8.2
1994	62.4	0.0	62.4	44.6	23.9	19.3	1.4	30.8	14.3	9.8	4.5	3.5
1995	88.2	6.6	81.6	52.7	24.3	29.0	-0.7	37.0	6.1	2.0	4.1	22.8
1996	63.9	5.6	58.2	37.6	12.7	21.3	3.6	35.3	7.8	5.3	2.5	12.9
1997	15.0	-12.8	27.8	47.0	21.3	24.0	1.7	36.0	6.7	4.5	2.2	-25.9
1998	5.2	1.7	3.5	35.0	8.8	25.9	0.3	27.7	2.6	0.0	2.5	-34.1
1999	80.1	4.7	75.4	59.5	1.1	60.0	-1.6	20.0	2.6	1.0	1.6	13.3
2000	42.2	-5.5	47.7	29.4	-5.1	30.5	4.0	-2.0	11.0	4.5	6.5	7.3
2001	8.0	-7.0	15.0	13.1	-2.3	17.9	-2.5	47.3	20.9	13.1	7.8	-18.9
2002	21.1	5.6	15.6	-6.6	-31.1	26.1	-1.5	0.7	8.8	3.3	5.5	13.4

Source: Flow of Funds, Bank of Japan, 2003.

year of FY1997 sharp falls in trade credit and loans from overseas (possibly triggered by the collapse of Yamaichi Securities), were largely compensated by more abundant funding from domestic financial institutions. Although loans by financial institutions have turned negative since FY2000, this could be largely compensated by other funding sources. Thus we are left with two years during the 1990s, when fundraising by the non-financial sector was reduced to only ¥5.2 trillion and ¥8.0 trillion (FY1998 and FY2001, respectively). In both cases, the single biggest negative factor appears to have been a withdrawal of domestic trade credit (and also overseas funding in the case of FY2001).

We conclude that there is little evidence that other sources of funding have not been able to make up for any potential decline in either bank lending or lending from financial institutions. The evidence in support of the lending view, or in support of the argument that credit rationing hampered growth must therefore be considered insufficient and not in line with the theoretical requirements of the respective theories.

There is another way to break down the data for fundraising by the non-financial sector in the domestic financial markets, namely by type of borrower (Table 3.3). As can be seen, corporations repaid funds in four years during the 1990s, namely in FY1997, FY1998, FY2000 and FY2001. However, it is apparent that falling borrowing by firms (and recently also households) was more than compensated by increased borrowing by the government.

Table 3.3   Fundraising by the domestic non-financial sector

FY ¥ trillion	Domestic non-financial sector	Corporations	Government	Households	NPOs
1990	117.9	74.7	8.6	33.8	0.8
1991	58.5	31.2	11.5	15.8	−0.1
1992	21.3	3.5	12.1	4.6	1.0
1993	57.9	20.5	26.3	10.9	0.1
1994	62.4	19.8	32.1	10.3	0.2
1995	88.2	24.4	47.6	15.8	0.3
1996	63.9	20.2	31.8	10.9	0.9
1997	15.0	−28.9	36.3	7.5	0.1
1998	5.2	−47.4	55.7	−2.8	−0.2
1999	80.1	8.2	68.5	3.5	−0.2
2000	42.2	−8.6	52.1	−1.8	0.5
2001	8.0	−34.1	43.7	−1.1	−0.4
2002	21.1	−8.0	39.1	−9.4	−0.6

Source: Flow of funds, Bank of Japan, 2003.

A satisfactory theory of Japan's recession should also be able to explain why the government, as a zero default-risk borrower, succeeded in raising significant amounts of money, but when it spent it, the impact on the economy was apparently small. Thus a further test of the various models is their views about the effectiveness of fiscal policy. The following chapter is devoted to this question.

The balance sheet channel

The 'balance sheet channel', proposed by Gertler and Gilchrist (1993), argues that monetary policy actions induce changes in interest rates and prices that are propagated through their effect on borrowers' balance sheets, which in turn affect their external finance premium. The finance premium determines overall terms of credit and hence access to funding. The balance sheet channel thus recognizes the possibility of financing constraints, especially for small firms – effectively incorporating the credit rationing argument, discussed above. At the same time, it also argues that fund demand is important, as the financial position also determines the demand for funding (see Bernanke and Gertler, 1995; Bernanke et al., 1996).

Figure 3.1 shows the chain of causation postulated by the balance sheet channel of monetary policy transmission. Monetary policy, through its effect on interest rates and prices, affects the firms' financial position, as reflected by the state of corporate balance sheets. This, in turn, affects both supply of funds to the firm (via the external finance premium) and the firm's demand for loans.

According to the theory, the financial position depends on net worth, which may also be important as collateral. Unlike the lending channel, this channel is operative 'even if the central bank has no direct leverage over the flow of bank credit' (Gertler and Gilchrist, 1993, p. 7). However, it requires monetary policy to affect corporate balance sheets, such that higher interest rates will worsen the balance sheet position of potential borrowers (Bernanke and Gertler, 1995).

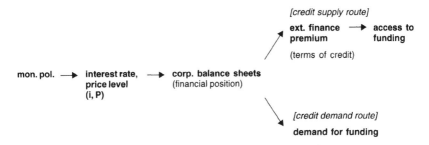

Figure 3.1 Causation in the balance sheet channel

There are two problems. The balance sheet channel needs to demonstrate that stimulative monetary policy (such as lower interest rates) actually affects corporate balance sheets positively. Secondly, just like the credit rationing argument, it must demonstrate that any negative impact of the balance sheet situation of certain borrowers (in practice, small firms) on their fundraising cannot be compensated for through fundraising by other borrowers. Since small firms account for only a small part of total investment, there is the need for some kind of multiplicator of the effect (what Bernanke and Gertler, 1995, call an 'accelerator'). Kiyotaki and Moore (1997) offer a theoretical model of the 'balance sheet channel' with an accelerator. They show that in a world in which lenders require collateral for loans, demand shocks may have prolonged real effects amplified by the effects of asset price fluctuations. The value of real assets as collateral constrains the supply of loans (the credit market is rationed). If a shock increases the supply of loans, this stimulates the firms' investments and raises the value of real assets owned by the firm. Thus when debt has to be secured by collateral, such as land, and the collateral is also an input in the production function, a small negative shock reducing the net worth of credit-constrained firms leads them to reduce their investment in land. Land prices and output fall. This further reduces the capacity of firms to obtain loans, which will additionally reduce land prices and output. With their model, Kiyotaki and Moore have demonstrated that the conditions under which a disproportionate effect of small firm balance sheets can be shown are non-trivial and not immediately recognizable as realistic. The model relies on a number of behavioural relationships and assumptions, including exogenous productivity shocks, sticky prices, direct control of credit by the central bank and imperfect substitutability of loans and bonds for both banks and borrowers.

The primary argument of the balance sheet channel, that higher interest rates slow the economy via this channel, and that lower interest rates stimulate it, is not consistent with the Japanese experience of the 1990s. Despite significant reductions in interest rates, balance sheets apparently failed to improve sufficiently to stimulate a lasting recovery. Secondly, the credit rationing argument has not been adequate in explaining the Japanese economic performance, as discussed above. Third, there is no evidence that the fall in land prices in Japan during the 1990s was triggered by firms selling their land assets, as Kiyotaki and Moore postulate.[51] It appears that land prices declined before any substantial selling of land by firms occurred.

More direct empirical tests of the balance sheet channel have been inconclusive. In this context, Ogawa's (2000) VAR estimates are notable, as he reports empirical support for the balance sheet channel, working through land used as collateral by firms.[52] However, land prices themselves are postulated to depend on monetary policy: 'Monetary policy affects the interest rate, which in turn influences the asset price' (p. 388). Yet lower interest rates during the 1990s did not raise asset prices. That land data correlate well with bank borrowing was already well-documented, and does not in itself constitute unambiguous evidence of a balance sheet channel (see Werner, 1992, 1997d). Thus Ogawa has merely replaced one puzzle (why interest rates have failed to boost the economy) with another (why interest rates have failed to boost land prices). As a result, the main question of concern, why interest rate reductions have failed to stimulate a lasting recovery in Japan in the 1990s, remains unanswered.[53] There are other problems.[54]

In summary, the empirical record of the bank lending, credit rationing or balance sheet channel theories, what we have termed as the 'credit view', has remained patchy at best. Most of all, it does not fit the Japanese experience well. As a result, we saw that leading experts, including the IMF, now assume that bank financing is perfectly substitutable with other funding sources. This is why Hoshi and Kashyap (2000) argue that, while the bank credit channel is impaired, accelerated structural reforms in the financial sector should facilitate fundraising. Thus they advise Japan to 'fully open the markets now, most importantly to foreign financial institutions'. The IMF and others argue that both public and private banks should be closed down in Japan. However, until a satisfactory explanation is found, caution towards policy advocacy based on theories not backed by the empirical record seems advisable.

Conclusion

We must conclude that none of the various theories to explain the Japanese economic performance has been supported by the empirical evidence. The enigma why interest rate policy has been ineffective during the 1990s has not been solved by traditional approaches, and even the more innovative recent 'credit school' approaches have failed to provide an answer.

While the precise theories advanced so far have not been satisfactory, there may be a reason why credit rationing and the notion that there is something about banks that makes them 'special' are 'recurrent themes' (Blanchard and Fischer, 1989). In many ways, the bank lending or credit rationing views that small firms are credit rationed remain empirical concepts in search for a simple and compelling explanation why this should have such a large impact on the economy. An attempt at providing one, reconciling aspects of the various alternative approaches and the empirical record, is made in Part III.

4
The Enigma of Japan's Long Recession

The neoclassical view

Adherents of the real business cycle approach or similar neoclassical and new classical theories follow the deductivist approach of constructing theoretical models from first principles, based on a number of axiomatic assumptions, including perfectly competitive and complete markets, flexible prices and no transaction and information costs. It is then shown that, under such assumptions, unique equilibrium solutions exist. For instance, under such assumptions the markets for factor inputs, such as labour, are in equilibrium and aggregate demand equals aggregate supply. Output therefore always operates at its full employment level in such an imaginary environment. Since this hypothetical situation is already assumed to be optimal, any disturbance or departure from it must by definition be suboptimal. Existence theorems and equilibrium models of this type focus on allocative efficiency within perfectly competitive markets, and are constructed such that any intervention by the government must disturb that efficiency. Since the economy is *assumed* to always perform optimally, the adherents of such models also assume that there is nothing the government can do in terms of cyclical policy. By definition, in the more extreme versions of these models (which have a tendency to appear in textbooks and IMF reports) any attempt to stimulate demand through policy intervention cannot boost output – it is already at the full employment level. Hence it must instead trigger inflation or create other harmful distortions.

Due to the rise of Keynesian economics, a synthesis had developed in the postwar era that argued that limited demand-management via fiscal stimulation or interest rate policies can be effective. However, pure neoclassical economists had always been suspicious of the type of demand-management policies we have examined in the previous two chapters. Thus their lack of results in the Japanese case revived the purely neoclassical argument, according to which demand-side policies cannot help, indeed would just lead to further distortions. In this chapter we will therefore examine how the mainstream neoclassical theory has dealt with Japan's experience of the 1990s.

Can neoclassical economics explain the performance of the 1990s?

The neoclassical view has been favoured for many years by US trade negotiators, who have since the 1970s argued the case that Japan's economic structure was not only responsible for lost market shares of US companies, but also of great disadvantage to Japanese consumers in particular and Japan's economic performance in general.[1] Naturally, for the first 45 years since World War II, it has been difficult to convince Japanese policy-makers that the very system that outperformed its European and North-American competitors in terms of growth, unemployment and inequality measures was an obstacle to even better performance and needed to be changed. Inside Japan, the neoclassical view did not immediately find many supporters.

However, the experience of the 1990s changed the picture. As we saw above, Japan's economy has apparently and mysteriously failed to respond to seemingly vigorous attempts of traditional cyclical demand-management. This, however, is no puzzle or mystery for adherents of neoclassical economic models. To the contrary, according to their models, Japan's economic performance could not be but dismal. The long recession of the 1990s has therefore been seized upon by new classical economists as evidence in favour of their models. Finally, Japan seemed to conform to their models.

But is this actually true? Did Japanese economic reality of the 1990s really conform to neoclassical, new classical or supply side economic theories? This is an issue that must be established by objective empirical research.

To do this, it is first necessary to identify the precise theoretical foundations of the structural reform argument, in order to formulate testable hypotheses. In general – and not specific to neoclassical theory – actual economic growth is due to two sets of variables: firstly, the quantity of factor inputs (QFI) which are employed, such as land, labour, capital and technology; secondly, total factor productivity (TFP) of those factor inputs that are employed (equation (1)).

(1)   actual growth = f(QFI; TFP)

Moving on to neoclassical growth theory, we observe that it is built on a number of assumptions. Depending on the model, these may vary, but they usually include the assumptions of perfect information, complete markets, no transaction costs and perfectly flexible prices. In a theoretical world with such characteristics, markets are always at their full employment equilibrium. As all resources are fully employed, actual growth is equal to potential growth. Thus in addition to equation (1), which is generally true, neoclassical growth theory assumes equation (2) to hold true as well:

(2)   actual growth = potential growth

Since equation (2) is considered true by assumption, it is not questioned. As a result, mainstream neoclassical growth theory allows only two possible arguments to explain the Japanese economic underperformance of the 1990s: firstly, the quantity of total factor inputs available (QFI) has declined. This argument is supported by Krugman (1998a), who maintains that Japan's demography has deteriorated and thus negatively affected Japan's potential growth rate. Others argue that Japan's capital stock has become outdated or that its technology is lagging behind. Secondly, the total productivity of the employed factors of production (TFP) has declined. This case is made by Ikeo (2001), Hayashi and Prescott (2002) and others.

It is already apparent that neoclassical theory cannot explain Japanese economic performance before 1990. To test whether it can actually explain Japanese performance since then, we can simply determine whether

1. productivity of the employed factors of production has fallen sufficiently to explain Japanese weak economic performance of the 1990s;
2. the supply of available factor inputs has fallen significantly;
3. there are factors of production that have not in fact been utilized, and hence actual growth may have fallen short of potential growth (in which case the neoclassical growth theory has been proven to be inapplicable to the Japanese case).

These three hypotheses will be tested below.

Evidence on the productivity decline in Japan

The measurement and accurate comparison of productivity is not a straightforward matter. In the words of *The Economist*, the 'productivity debate is surrounded by a thick statistical fog'.[2] Since output is measured in local currency, international comparisons must deal with the issue of how to convert this to comparable values. Given their high volatility, market exchange rates are usually not considered useful. Alternatives, however, have to be calculated first and depend on assumptions, such as purchasing power parity exchange rates, which crucially depend on the choice of basket.[3] There are even graver statistical issues.

During the 1990s, many studies have referred to evidence that Europe and Japan have lagged behind the US in productivity or productivity growth. Since the beginning of 2000, European productivity has risen by only 0.9% according to the ECB, while it has risen by 7.9% in the US, according to the Bureau of Labor Statistics.[4] However, productivity should be defined as the productivity of employed factors of production. Thus labour productivity must only measure the productivity of the actually employed workforce. The fact that unemployed workers are not productive *per se* cannot be counted as productivity declines. Likewise, output increases that are due to increased factory capacity utilization also cannot be counted as productivity increases. The statistics by the US Bureau of Labor Statistics, however, are calculated by simply dividing the volume of produced goods by the number of working hours. Thus economists have pointed out that US 'productivity increases' may in actual fact merely reflect a greater utilization of factor inputs. Burnside et al. (1995) and Basu (1996) have argued that there is a risk to over-estimate (underestimate) TFP growth, if we do not take account of an increase (a decline) in the capacity utilization rate.

Furthermore, if employees work longer hours in the US than in Europe and Japan, this also cannot be allowed to increase productivity figures. To be comparable, productivity statistics must refer to equivalent time periods. Often productivity is, however, defined as GDP per person employed, without reference to the time required. By this measure, US productivity stood at $59,081 in 2001, according to the ILO (2003).[5] However, US workers were employed for 1825 hours in 2002, far longer than in many leading European economies, though about the same time as in Japan (ILO, 2003).[6] If output per worker has increased due to longer hours per worker, it is not an efficiency gain, but an increase in factor inputs. Indeed, when productivity is calculated as GDP per hour worked, the US, at $31.45 per hour worked, ranks behind France and several other European and Asian economies. In the words of Lou Dobbs, 'there is no denying that the people who are lucky enough to have jobs are simply working more'.[7] Not only do US employees work more hours than those in most other industrialized countries, but they also have no mandatory holiday periods.[8]

'There are many ways to measure productivity. America has chosen the most flattering one, the euro area the least flattering', concludes *The Economist*.[9] 'The figures certainly show that when they are actually at their desks (or lathes) the Germans, French and Dutch (though not the British) are more productive than Americans.'[10] Gordon (1999) has shown that 'after adjusting for the effects of the economic cycle, all of the increase in labour productivity was concentrated in the manufacturing of computers, with no net gain in the rest of the economy'. Further distortions include the way the US has chosen to measure corporate spending on software and information technology. In the US it is counted as investment, thus contributing to final GDP (and hence the output used to calculate productivity). Price increases in the software sector were often counted as increases in the quality of software (and hence as productivity gains).

Let us now turn to the evidence that a decline in Japanese productivity can explain Japan's weak economic performance of the 1990s. Pilat (1993) studied the long-term pattern of Japanese manufacturing productivity and compared it with the US. He concluded that by the early 1990s Japan's had reached US levels. US government statisticians concluded as recently as 1997 that, on the basis of a 1995 comparison of eleven industrialized countries, only three countries exceeded US productivity growth, namely Japan, Italy and Sweden (Sparks and Greiner, 1997). One of the countries with worse productivity growth than the US was the UK (recording negative productivity growth). Furthermore, they find that over the longer time period from 1975 to 1995, the US fared even worse, recording lower productivity growth than all but three of these eleven industrialized countries. Their measure of productivity was based on output per hour.

However, more recently Hayashi and Prescott (2002) have argued that Japan's weak growth since the early 1990s has been due to an exogenous productivity shock and not demand-side factors. Assuming that all factors of production were fully employed, they find that the productivity of the workforce declined during the 1990s and thus total factor productivity growth slowed significantly, from 2.4% during the period from 1983 to 1991, to only 0.2% in the period from 1991 to 2000.

Fukao et al. (2003) demonstrated that Hayashi and Prescott (2002) incorrectly counted as productivity decline what was actually a decline in factor utilization. By adjusting the calculations of factor productivity for the decline in factor utilization, Fukao et al. (2003) find that in actual fact Japanese productivity did not decline much during the 1990s. While Hayashi and Prescott (2002) claimed that the decline in total factor productivity from the 1983–91 period to the 1991–98 period was as large as 2.2 percentage points, Fukao et al. (2003) found only a decline of 0.20 percentage points. 'Hayashi and Prescott (2002) seem to have overestimated the size of the TFP growth decline' (p. 20), they conclude. Needless to say, the figures of Fukao et al. do not lend any support to the argument that Japan's recession of the 1990s was due to a decline in productivity.

Another study, by Jorgenson and Motohashi (2003), came to different conclusions still. Their study, unlike others, treated land as a factor input and, similar to US practice, included consumer durables and computer software as capital input. They also constructed their own IT product deflator, in order to distinguish price changes from quality changes in the IT sector, by using a method similar to the US. They found that Japan's TFP growth rate declined from 0.96% in the period 1975–90 to 0.61% during the period 1990–95, but actually accelerated to 1.04% during the period 1995–2000. We conclude that according to the more careful studies of Fukao et al. (2003) and Jorgenson and Motohashi (2003), there is no evidence that Japan's productivity declined significantly or sufficiently to account for Japan's weak economic performance of the 1990s.

According to neoclassical trade theory an alternative measure of Japanese productivity can be found in Japan's trade performance. Indeed, during the 1980s, many US economists and management experts spent much time

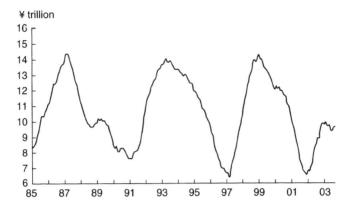

Figure 4.1 Japan's trade surplus (annual moving sum)
Source: Ministry of Finance.

examining the Japanese productivity advantage over the US. Formal Congressional hearings were held under the title 'Japanese Productivity – Lessons for America'. They derived their assessment of the higher Japanese productivity from the more successful trade performance of Japan. What is the evidence on Japanese productivity during the 1990s by this measure? As Figure 4.1 shows, Japan continued to record sizeable trade surpluses with the world during the 1990s, even rivalling the record surpluses of the 1980s. It is noteworthy that these surpluses came about despite a stronger average yen exchange rate than during the 1980s. Low rankings awarded to Japan in (largely arbitrarily assessed) international 'competitiveness' comparisons notwithstanding, the facts of international trade indicate that Japanese goods and services have remained highly competitive throughout the 1990s. We conclude that there is no empirical support for the structural reform argument deriving from the claim that Japanese productivity declined during the 1990s.

Evidence on the decline in available factor inputs

The Japanese population continued to grow during the 1990s, but its growth rate slowed during the 1990s, from 0.4% in 1992 to 0.3% in 2001 (Figure 4.2). However, larger drops in population growth during the 1970s and 1980s do not appear to have been linked to decade-long stagnation. Considering the workforce, we initially seem to find some evidence in support of the structural reform argument (Figure 4.3): growth of the workforce slowed during the 1990s and by 2001 the workforce even contracted. Is this the exogenous demographic shock referred to by some economists? Once again, there is a danger that cyclical factors are misinterpreted as structural.

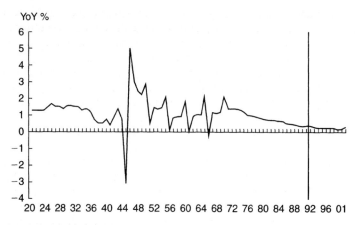

Figure 4.2 Population growth in Japan

Source: Population Estimates of Japan, 2002, Ministry of Public Management, Home Affairs, Posts and Telecommunications.

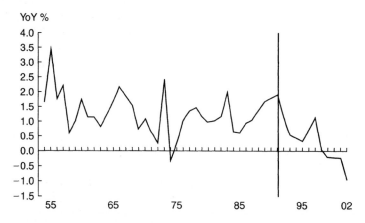

Figure 4.3 Growth of the official workforce

Source: Labour Force Survey, 2002, Ministry of Public Management, Home Affairs, Posts and Telecommunications.

The growth rate of the workforce has cyclical characteristics, since in Japan a significant part of the workforce tends to withdraw during periods of economic stagnation (such as non-permanent staff, especially female staff), only to re-emerge among the official workforce when the economy recovers. This effect has indeed contributed to keeping the official unemployment rate at low levels (understating actual unemployment, according to many observers). As with productivity, if we misread a decline in the utilization of labour as a decline in its availability, we will underestimate Japan's potential growth rate. Another indication that the supply of labour may not have declined is provided by the statistics on wage trends. Wages, as measured by the Labour Ministry's wage index, have been under downward pressure during the 1990s and declined by over 1% in FY2001 and FY2000. This is difficult to reconcile with the argument that the supply of labour declined and restricted economic growth – which one would expect to place upward pressure on wages.

Another measure of the growth of the potential workforce is the number of new university graduates (Figure 4.4). As can be seen, not only did it continue to grow during the 1990s, but it has accelerated since the recession started in 1992. These figures are hard to reconcile with the claim that Japan has moved into recession because the supply of labour declined exogenously. The figures may also shed light on the above observed decline in the workforce: students unable to find jobs may have left the workforce temporarily to pursue higher degrees. The greater increase in graduates from postgraduate courses seems to support this argument.

We conclude that the evidence concerning the supply of labour is mixed, though without clear-cut support for the structural reform argument. While further research is needed on this issue, the question whether the weak growth in the workforce was due to supply factors (a lack of people in the workforce) or demand factors (a lack of employment opportunities, forcing retirement from the workforce) will become clearer below, when the

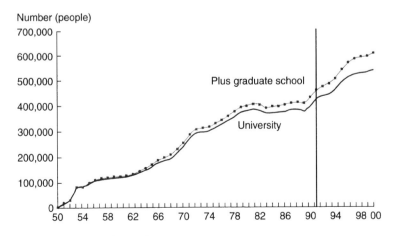

Figure 4.4 New university graduates

Source: Education Statistics, Ministry of Education, Culture, Sports, Science and Technology.

hypothesis is directly tested that potential growth equals actual growth, and hence that all factors of production are always fully employed.

Next, consider the evidence on the supply of capital. One way to measure this is via savings. Those have indeed increased throughout the 1990s: the personal savings rate has risen steadily during the 1990s while its inverse, the propensity to consume, has fallen. Thus there has been no reduction in the supply of savings capital.

Another way is to measure the physical stock of capital. As can be seen in Figures 4.5 and 4.6, the capital stock continued to grow during the 1990s. However, its growth rate fell during the 1990s. Similar to the workforce decline, the possibility cannot be dismissed that weak capital expenditure was due to weak demand, not a lack of supply of physical capital. Since economic growth requires investment, the close correlation between capital expenditure and final growth is not surprising. However, few would support the case that Japan's weak plant and equipment investment was the result of supply bottlenecks. Again, our examination of the evidence on whether resources were in fact fully employed, as conducted below, will shed light on this issue.

Next, consider the evidence on the supply of technology inputs – a factor of production that may be less affected by cyclical distortions. Figure 4.7 shows our proxy, the net new patents and trademarks registered. Their number did not decline during the 1990s, but accelerated significantly. Finally, the evidence concerning the supply of land as a factor of production is straightforward: there is no evidence that Japan's landmass has significantly changed during the 1990s.

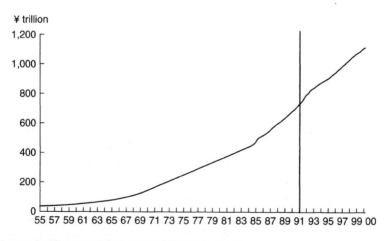

Figure 4.5   The outstanding stock of capital in Japan

Source: Quarterly GDP Estimates, Cabinet Office, Government of Japan.

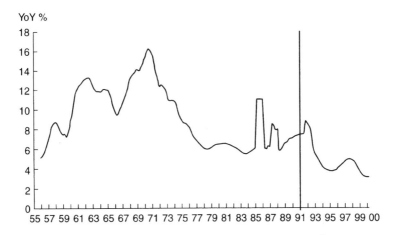

Figure 4.6   Growth of the stock of capital

Source: Quarterly GDP Estimates, Cabinet Office, Government of Japan.

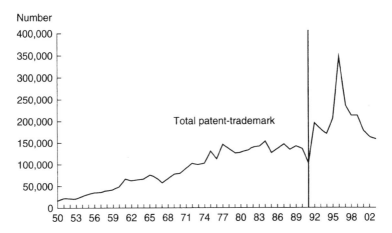

Figure 4.7   The number of new patent and trademark registrations in Japan

Source: Number of Applications and Registrations in 2002, Japan Patent Office.

Evidence on whether all factors have been fully utilized

The ultimate test of the applicability of the neoclassical growth theory is to
confirm whether there have been factors of production that have not been
fully utilized. As outlined above, this version of the structural reform argument relies on the assumption that all resources are always fully employed

and hence actual growth is always equal to potential. If that was the case, a decline in growth would have to be due to a decline in the supply of the factors of production. However, if it can be shown that potential growth is not always equal to actual growth, as some resources remained unemployed, this neoclassical foundation of the structural reform argument must be dismissed entirely.

We proceed by considering measures of factor input utilization. Figure 1.2 in Chapter 1 showed the unemployment rate. As discussed, there is some indication that this measure understates actual unemployment. Nevertheless, the unemployment rate has risen significantly since about 1992, when it stood at just above 2%, to reach a postwar record high of 5.4% in October 2001. This statistical series provides evidence that actually utilized labour input is not equal to maximum available labour supply. This finding is supported by the statistics on wage growth, which has shown a steady decline during most of the 1990s.

There is alternative evidence on the lack of utilization of human resources. We also noted in Chapter 1 that Japan's suicide rate rose from 22,104 in 1992 to a record high of 33,048 in 1999 (Figure 1.3 in Chapter 1). Needless to mention, the destruction of human resources – voluntary exits from the market opportunities of this world? – is an indication that factor inputs are not fully utilized (and also that the neoclassical conception of market clearing and individual behaviour may be inadequate).

To consider the utilization of capital in the manufacturing sector, we turn to the seasonally adjusted operating rate. Figure 4.8 shows that the operating rate peaked in 1990/91 at an index reading of 117.1 and then declined significantly, hitting a low of 87.7 in December 2001. Despite temporary upswings, it stayed on a downward trajectory during the past decade. From this it would appear that a significant stock of capital remains underutilized in Japan. This contradicts the fundamental assumption of the neoclassical model and the structural reform argument based on it that all resources are always fully employed.

There is another indicator that physical capital may not have been fully utilized during the 1990s. This is the number of bankruptcies. From January 1990 to November 2003 alone, 212,660 companies had gone bankrupt. Bankruptcies often involve write-downs of assets, lost capital and discontinuity in the use of facilities. Furthermore, bankruptcies are more frequently observed in times of weak demand than in times of excess demand and lack of supply.

Price data also appear at odds with the neoclassical assumption that actual output is equal to potential. Figure 4.9 shows Japanese consumer price inflation, as measured by the year-on-year growth rate of the domestic consumer price index (CPI).

Inflation declined during the decade of the 1990s, and since 1999 has given way to deflation. The only exception is the twelve-month period between April

Figure 4.8 Capacity utilization as measured by the operating rate

Source: Report on Indices of Industrial Production, August 2003, Ministry of Economy, Trade and Industry.

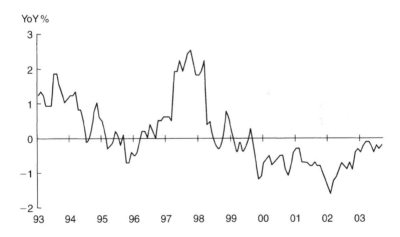

Figure 4.9 Consumer price inflation, as measured by the CPI

Source: Ministry of Public Management, Home Affairs, Posts and Telecommunications.

1997 and March 1998, when the increase of the consumption tax from 3% to 5% gave the impression of higher inflation. Japan's experience of four consecutive years of deflation since 1999 is unique among G7 nations. These findings are hard to reconcile with the argument that Japan's recession has been due to supply bottlenecks, which tend to place upward pressure on prices.

Conclusion

Although the neoclassical approach claimed Japan's experience of the 1990s as corroboration of its theory, this argument is not convincing. Firstly, the experience of the 1990s remains a briefer period than the 40 years from 1950 to 1990. If the neoclassical approach was relevant, why, then, did Japan's cartelized and controlled economy perform so well during this longer period? Secondly, the argument fails to explain precisely what changed between the longer, first period, and the shorter 1990s. Thirdly, if one was to examine the differences between the 1990s and the earlier time period, one would notice that the economic structure did change. However, as we will examine in greater detail below, this change did not occur in the direction suggested by new classical analysis. Fourthly, and most damning, it turns out that neoclassical growth theory is not even supported by the empirical record of the 1990s, when Japan's growth rate was very low. Specifically, the evidence for a decline in the productivity of employed factor inputs and for a decline in the supply of the available factor inputs remains insufficient to explain weak Japanese economic performance during the 1990s. The hypothesis that the Japanese recession is due to an under-utilization of available factor inputs is logically and empirically more compelling. In this case, actual economic growth will fall short of potential growth and neoclassical growth theory cannot be employed to support the structural reform argument. Thus it must be concluded that neoclassical growth theory cannot explain the Japanese long-term growth performance of the postwar era.

The argument that high unemployment was caused by an economic structure that is holding back the potential growth rate is not supported by the facts: there is evidence that actual growth has remained far below potential, so that the potential growth rate has not been the problem. Therefore, neoclassical growth theory cannot explain the enigma of Japan's long recession of the 1990s. The neoclassical growth theory thus also provides no support for the policy advice that Japan give up demand-side policies and focus on supply-side structural reforms.

This finding has implications. Let us for sake of argument assume that structural reform does indeed lead to higher potential output, as its supporters claim (whether or not this claim is empirically tenable will be tested in the following chapter). Since actual output and actual growth remain below potential, raising potential growth would merely cause the gap between actual and potential output to widen. Since deflation tends to be caused by excess supply, that is, actual demand being smaller than the supply potentially produced by the economy, we must conclude that structural reform would not produce positive results. To the contrary, it would have negative effects, such as to exacerbate deflation.

5
The Enigma of the Ineffectiveness of Structural Policy

> Of those who do make pronouncements on Japan, many if not most have taken the easy way out: blaming the victim, absolving themselves of responsibility for proposing solutions by asserting that Japan's problems are deep, structural, beyond the reach of technical fixes. Well, maybe; but maybe not. Sometimes big problems have small causes; sometimes a simple technical fix can work miracles.
>
> (Krugman, 1999a)

The lack of apparent success of fiscal and monetary policies was taken by many economists as evidence that demand-side policies did not work. So they advanced supply-side policies that focus on structural change. Japan, we were told had to implement 'badly needed' structural reforms.

The call for structural reform by macroeconomists was also supported by finance experts who were analysing the problems of the Japanese financial system. By the mid-1990s, many such experts, including adherents of the 'credit view', had come to agree with the analysis that the main cause of the Japanese recession had been the bad debt problem.[1] Since this literature considers banks as financial intermediaries fulfilling the same function as other intermediaries (such as non-bank financial institutions) or the capital markets, it was thought that any sign of a credit crunch or imperfect substitutability of bank funding with other forms of financing were indicators that the capital market structure was not efficient enough.[2] Therefore, it was concluded, Japan needed structural reforms of its financial markets as well. Hoshi and Kashyap (2000), for instance, advise Japan to stimulate its economy through policies to 'fully open the markets now, most importantly to foreign financial institutions'. Structural reforms, it was argued, would improve the efficiency of the financial sector.

Since the second half of the 1990s, therefore, the chorus of voices had become overwhelming arguing that the disappointing economic performance of the 1990s was due to Japan's economic structure and hence demanding far-reaching reforms. With the arrival of the Koizumi administration this view was elevated to official government policy, as illustrated in the widely-quoted slogan 'no economic recovery without structural reform'.

Given its dominance in the media, among experts and decision-makers, one may be excused for assuming that this argument had been thoroughly tested and found supported by the empirical evidence. This is not the case.

It is thus necessary to review the evidence. To do this, we need to consider the precise theories that have been advanced to support the structural reform argument. There are two arguments within neoclassical theory that support the structural reform case. The first was examined in the previous chapter, namely neoclassical growth theory, which simply assumes that growth is always at its maximum potential, and thus any weak economic performance must be due to low productivity or a decline in the supply of factor inputs. Since these are supply-side factors, it was argued that structural changes would be necessary to stimulate the economy. We have already examined the empirical evidence for this argument and found it lacking on all three fronts: there is no evidence that the quantity of factor inputs supplied, nor the productivity of employed factors of production declined sufficiently to explain the weak economic performance of the 1990s. Furthermore, and most damning, it was found that actual output and actual growth were below potential, thus discrediting this entire argument. Neoclassical growth theory is simply not relevant to the type of world we know.

However, there is a second line of reasoning to justify the structural reform argument, which derives from neoclassical welfare economics. Surely it is supported at least on this front? It is the fundamental theorem of neoclassical welfare economics, which identifies the particular set of assumptions under which the competitive economy is Pareto efficient. These assumptions, which include perfect information, complete markets, no transaction costs, and so forth, define an economy where interventions, such as by the government, cannot but reduce allocative efficiency. Of course, Japan's economy has at no time during the postwar era resembled such an economy. To the contrary, until the end of the 1980s, the postwar Japanese economic structure was characterized by restricted and incomplete capital markets, reliance of corporate finance on bank funding, weak shareholder influence, a large number of government regulations, direct government interference in the form of 'guidance', a large number of formal and informal cartels, inflexible labour markets characterized by a division into full-time staff at large enterprises enjoying job security, promotion based on the seniority in terms of years spent with the firm and in-house company unions, on the one hand, and other staff more exposed to competitive pressures in the labour markets, on the other.[3] Therefore, according to neoclassical welfare economics, its economy must be inefficient, and the solution to Japan's problems is to change the economic structure in order to move more in line with the theoretical model of free and unimpeded markets. Deregulation, liberalization and privatization will do the job.

Before Japan proceeds to implement these historic changes, objective scientists would wish to put this argument for structural change to the test. Indeed, we can formulate two testable hypotheses derived from the predictions of neoclassical welfare economics. The first concerns the link between the economic structure and economic growth. The second concerns the question of how structural reform, that is, a change in the economic structure, would affect economic growth. They are examined in turn below.

The link between type of economic structure and economic performance

Japan's postwar macroeconomic performance was the first major challenge to standard economic models. In the 1960s, its economy recorded extraordinarily high growth, dubbed an 'economic miracle' by financial commentators (Table 5.1).

What was remarkable was not just the high growth rates themselves, but rather the fact that such unusually high growth was recorded despite an economic structure that differed vastly from the new classical theories. There was no doubt that regulation and intervention were substantial. Moreover, the incentive structure and corporate governance of corporations was markedly at odds with the theories proposed by new classical or neoclassical economists. Shareholder influence, for instance, was small, and companies were often operated for the joint benefit of other stakeholders, such as employees. Japan's economic model seemed like a third way between the textbook neoclassical system and the socialist planned economy structures in place in communist countries during the Cold War.

According to neoclassical theories, such an economy could not hope to produce efficient results, since it was operating on principles virtually diametrically opposed to the assumptions of new classical models as it appeared cartelized, controlled and closed. Yet the success of Japanese exporters was so significant that many European and North American industries were negatively affected. The persistent balance of trade surpluses resulting from

Table 5.1   Postwar Japanese real GDP growth

Period	Real GDP growth (%)
1950–59	9.4
1960–69	10.1
1970–79	6.6
1980–89	4.0
1990–99	1.7

Source: Bank of Japan.

Japan's economic success were of such proportion that they triggered serious and repeated government intervention by the US. This was reflected in a string of protracted trade negotiations, during which US trade representatives listed the ways in which Japan's economy differed from the theoretical new classical models and demanded that it change. The most comprehensive such list of structural change demands was compiled as part of the Structural Impediments Initiative.

While it is sometimes argued that nothing about Japan's growth was 'miraculous', since by definition growth is the result of high investment and Japan simply invested a lot, the neoclassical theory fails to explain just why Japan was able to invest so much, while other countries that attempted to do so failed.

However, when discussing just one country and its apparent contradiction of mainstream theory, it is always possible to make the objection of special reasons or unusual circumstances. This does imply the use of *ad hoc* auxiliary assumptions, and hence weakens the argument. It would be more convincing if it could be established that there is a consistent pattern, and Japan's case is not just a fluke. Thus, when examining the link between Japan's economic structure and its economic performance, a comparison with other countries is useful to increase our data set. There are indeed several major economies that have had similar economic structures to Japan's (similarly far removed from the free market ideal of the neoclassical theory) and there are also several economies more closely resembling the market-oriented model envisaged by neoclassical welfare economics: over most of the postwar era, the Japanese and Korean economic systems have shared key features with the German economic system, including incomplete capital markets, reliance on bank funding, cross-shareholdings, few outside board directors, an absence of a flexible labour market (that is, greater long-term job security), a low penetration of high-value-added imports (predominance of raw material imports), policy coordination between industry associations and government authorities, and the presence of cartels and government regulations or government intervention (see Aoki et al., 1997; Dore, 2000; or Werner, 1993, 2002c, 2003d).

On the other hand, leading decision-makers of the UK and US economies have been vocal supporters of free markets, and have strongly supported deregulation, liberalization and privatization, while their financial systems rely more on stock markets, shareholder influence is larger, there is less job security, and less government intervention.

Hoshi and Patrick (2000) and others have pointed out that the type of structural reforms envisaged in Japan basically amount to the introduction of a US- or UK-style economic system. The neoclassical argument is that Japan's downturn has not been due to cyclical demand-side factors, but the economic structure, and that therefore the introduction of a US- or UK-style economic system are necessary and sufficient conditions for Japan's economy to recover.

Given these facts, neoclassical welfare economics generates three easily testable hypotheses. Firstly, if the introduction of a US-style economic system in Japan is the solution to Japan's recession and will lead to a recovery (as is claimed by the structural reform view), then the US and the UK economies – already in full possession of a US- and UK-style economic structure – could not possibly suffer from significant economic downturns. What is the evidence on this count? According to the US National Income Accounts, US real GDP declined by 1.3% in 1991. Furthermore, growth slowed significantly in 2000 and 2001. The fact is that the US and the UK, the alleged role models for a deregulated and liberalized economy, both experienced recessions in the past decades. Indeed, it is fair to say that economic downturns have occurred in virtually any economic structure and any type of system (from the Soviet Union to the US). Such findings are in contradiction to the predictions of the structural reform view. However, they might be considered as statistical flukes. Thus more long-term empirical evidence is desirable.

A second testable hypothesis derived from neoclassical welfare economics is that the type of economic structure existing in Japan, Germany and Korea should perform less well than the economies of the US and the UK, as the latter are more in line with the necessary preconditions for economic efficiency. This hypothesis is also readily tested, by reference to actual economic growth of these countries over a suitably long timespan to abstract from cyclical factors: Figure 5.1 shows the economic growth performance of the US, the UK, Germany, Japan and Korea over the time period from 1950 to

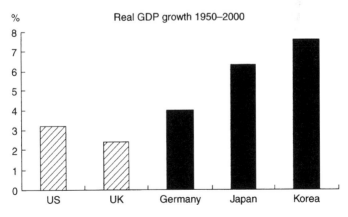

Figure 5.1   Real GDP growth over the half-century from 1950 to 2000
Source: Bank of Japan.

Table 5.2 Comparison of key economic performance
indicators since 1950

Period 1950–2000 average	Real GDP growth	Gini coefficient
US	3.2	40.8 (1997)
UK	2.4	36.1 (1991)
Germany	4.0	30.0 (1994)
Japan	6.3	24.9 (1993)
Korea	7.6	31.6 (1993)

Source: Bank of Japan, World Bank (World Development
Report, 2000/01).

2000, as represented by the average real GDP growth rate. The actual average real GDP growth rates over this time period are also listed in Table 5.2, which also considers another important measure of economic success, namely how the wealth generated by growth is distributed. This is done with the Gini coefficient, whereby a high figure indicates more inequality and a low figure more equality (a figure of 100 would represent complete inequality).

As can be seen, during the second half of the twentieth century, the US and the UK delivered a respectable performance of 3.2% and 2.4% growth, respectively. According to neoclassical economics and the structural reform view supported by it, the economies of Germany, Korea and Japan, where there has been greater cartelization, regulation and weaker shareholders, economic performance should have been weaker. However, average real GDP growth over this half-century has been significantly larger in all three economies. Japan, the main focus of this book, recorded an average real GDP growth rate of 6.3%, almost twice as high as the growth rate of the US and not far short of three times as high as the UK average growth rate. This feat was achieved despite the fact that for one-fifth of the observation period Japan's economy was held back by a severe recession that increased unemployment and prevented the full utilization of Japan's resources.

In developing countries, it is often found that even high overall economic growth rates hide the extent of poverty and destitution of the majority of the population, since aggregate indicators such as GDP growth do not say anything at all about how the newly generated income is distributed. This can be seen from the Gini coefficient. Here we find that in Korea, Germany and especially Japan income is significantly more equally distributed. This means that even if real GDP growth rates were the same as in the UK and US, the majority of the population will have benefited more from this growth. The combination of much lower Gini coefficient and much higher real GDP growth leads us to the conclusion that the economic performance of Korea, Germany and Japan has been far superior to that of the UK and the US over this half-century.

If further indicators of the level of development were included in the analysis, such as the crime rate, the percentage of the population held in prisons, life expectancy and other quality of life statistics, there can be little doubt that the conclusion would be strengthened. These findings contradict the claims of neoclassical welfare economics. In other words, whether measured by standard measures of economic growth or by social welfare indicators, the 'corporatist' model performs well. There certainly is no long-term evidence that the economic structure of the 'shareholder capitalist' model of the US and UK is superior in terms of economic performance.

Evidence on the link between structural change and economic performance

So far we have engaged in comparative statics by comparing two different types of economic systems with each other and noting their respective economic performance. The purpose of this section is to examine the dynamic issue of how structural change, that is, a reform in the economic structure away from the Japanese-style system and towards a more market-oriented system, affects economic performance.

The testable hypothesis derived from neoclassical welfare economics is that a shift away from the Japanese-style economic structure, towards a US/UK-style more deregulated, liberalized and privatized economy will increase economic growth. This is also quite directly the claim made by the structural reform camp. Economists do not often have ready access to controlled experiments. However, economic history provides many case studies that can be drawn upon, which come close to experiments. Here we will restrict ourselves to one specific instance, which is also the main focus of this chapter, namely Japan's postwar experience.

The Koizumi administration's call for a fundamental structural reform of the Japanese economy towards a deregulated, liberalized and privatized system is not original. During the 1990s, the Hashimoto, as well as the earlier Hosokawa cabinets had produced similar reform agendas. For instance, beginning in 1997, the Hashimoto government tightened fiscal policy and significantly reduced political pressure on the central bank by preparing and, in 1997, passing the new Bank of Japan Law. This law became effective on 1 April 1998. It granted the central bank complete independence from the government. Among the significant structural changes introduced by the Hashimoto administration was a far-reaching programme of administrative reform that effectively dismantled the *Ōkurashō* (Ministry of Finance) and created an independent Financial Supervisory Agency.[4] Furthermore, the role and powers of the prime minister and the Cabinet Office were strengthened. Key government agencies, such as the former Economic Planning

Agency, were directly incorporated into the Cabinet Office and direct reporting to the prime minister was expanded. The Hashimoto administration's structural reforms also included a sweeping deregulation programme that centred on the 'Big Bang' reforms of the financial sector, beginning in 1998, which liberalized foreign exchange transactions, deregulated the sale of investment trust funds, liberalized licensing and commissions of securities companies, and so on.

What has been the empirically observed, actual result of the Hashimoto administration's structural reforms of 1997/98? They were not followed by improved economic performance. In 1996, before the implementation of Hashimoto's structural reforms, real GDP growth of 4% was recorded. By contrast, the reforms were accompanied and followed by what was then the largest shrinkage of nominal GDP and consumer prices in the postwar era in Japan.

A counter-argument against the above evidence would be that the question of how structural reforms and, indeed, different economic structures affect economic growth can only be addressed over the long run, and not over such relatively short time periods as a decade or so. In other words, the lack of success of the structural reforms of the late 1990s may simply be due to the fact that the observation period has been too short and we have not yet been able to get a better picture of the long-term impact of such reforms.

Indeed, since the 1960s, when Japan joined the OECD, the Japanese government has implemented a large number of structural reforms. As noted above, the Bank of Japan's leadership has demanded deep structural reforms since the 1970s, which closely resembled the demands US trade negotiators had made since the late 1960s. Under severe political pressure from the US, the system started to change significantly from the 1970s onwards. As a result, deregulation, though gradual, was introduced well before Prime Minister Koizumi.[5] While reform was initially slow, and certainly continuously failed to satisfy US trade negotiators or reform supporters in Japan, such as the Bank of Japan, it remains a fact that Japan has gradually implemented structural changes since the early 1970s. Thus for about 30 years out of the 50-odd postwar years, structural reform has been undertaken in Japan and Japan's economy has been gradually moved away from the original 'corporatist' model described above to become more and more similar to the US-style 'shareholder capitalism'.

The progress of these structural reforms can be numerically represented by data on some of the key indicators identified above. On most counts it is clear that during much of the postwar era Japan moved measurably towards the US/UK prototype of deregulated, liberalized and privatized capitalism with an independent central bank and corporations working for the benefit of shareholders, not other stakeholders in society.

The percentage of imports accounted for by manufactured goods has risen steadily, and almost tripled between 1982 and 2000. Corporate financing via bank loans started to decline during the 1980s and virtually came to standstill in the 1990s. Previously government-owned companies were increasingly privatized from the 1980s onwards. The number of government regulations gradually fell, especially from the late 1980s onwards. Job mobility increased steadily, especially since the 1980s. There can be no doubt that in the 1950s and 1960s Japan's economic system, however one might want to describe or label it, was still closer to the 'typical Japanese' ideal and by the end of the 1990s it had moved significantly closer to the US model.

The many reform packages and structural changes were initially sector-specific and they are not easily measured or aggregated. However, there is one readily available measure of the degree of change in Japan: one of the main targets of US criticism has been the fact that the traditional postwar Japanese economic system relied on a large number of explicit cartels (official exemptions from the Anti-Monopoly Law granted by the Fair Trade Commission). In line with a gradual increase in the role of markets since the early 1970s, the number of cartels has declined steadily. It can thus be used as a useful proxy of structural change in Japan during the postwar era. As Japan steadily, if slowly, moved away from its original 'typical' economic model that existed in the 1960s, the number of cartels declined steadily.

We can therefore directly test the claim by neoclassical welfare economics and the structural reform camp concerning the effect of structural reform towards a free market economic system on economic growth by considering whether a correlation exists between the number of cartels in postwar Japan and Japanese economic performance. According to neoclassical welfare economics and the structural reform view, as the number of cartels declines and market forces become more widespread, economic performance should improve. As the number of cartels increases (as happened in the 1950s), economic performance should deteriorate. In other words, the number of cartels and GDP growth should be negatively correlated. Figure 5.2 shows the empirical record. As can be seen, the number of cartels initially rose from 401 in 1958 to a postwar high of 1079 in 1966. This was the build-up to the system of a controlled and cartelized economy, with fairly direct resource allocation and pervasive official intervention (see Werner, 2003c). As can be seen, the post-oil shock period was characterized by a sharp decline in the number of cartels. This phase saw much soul-searching, not unlike the late 1990s, about the need for more deregulation, liberalization and privatization. As such reforms were gradually implemented under political pressure from the US, the number of cartels declined steadily throughout the 1980s. Then in the late 1990s, as structural change had become 'remarkable' (Hoshi and Patrick, 2000), the number of cartels finally dropped to zero.

According to neoclassical economics and the supporters of structural reform, the decade during which the number of cartels increased (the 1950s) should have been characterized by a decline in economic performance, and the entire period of gradual structural change towards greater market orientation

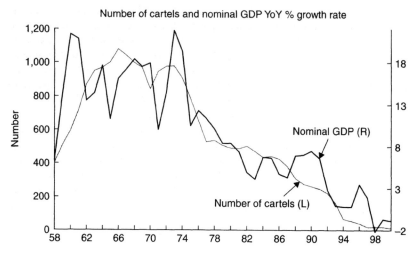

Figure 5.2 The number of official cartels in Japan (official exemptions from the Anti-Monopoly Law granted by the Fair Trade Commission)

Source: Fair Trade Commission of Japan.

since the early 1970s should have been characterized by improving economic performance. Growth should have been most dismal during the 1960s, when the number of cartels peaked. However, as can be seen from Figure 5.2, there is no empirical evidence in support of this claim. Quite to the contrary, there seems to be a positive correlation between the number of cartels and nominal GDP growth. As more cartels were introduced by policy-makers during the 1950s, economic growth accelerated sharply. The highly cartelized economic system of the 1960s, when there were over 1000 cartels and the command economy system originating from the wartime era was in its purest form, is associated with double-digit GDP growth. As the number of cartels declined and Japan became more market-oriented, economic performance deteriorated, culminating in the structural reform era of the late 1990s. By the end of the 1990s the scale of structural reforms had reached such proportions that even structural reform proponents were in awe.[6] Thanks to 'a sense of impending crises' a 'major transformation' of the Japanese financial system was achieved, shifting it 'from a bank-centered and relationship-based system to a market-based and competitive system' and triggering 'the most surprising and fascinating events of the tumultuous 1990s', namely the 'sharp decrease in the power and position of the hitherto seemingly omnipotent Ministry of Finance, the most powerful and elite central government bureaucracy in a country where bureaucrats rule and politicians simply reigned' (Hoshi and Patrick, 2000, pp. xi, 22).

But when such historic structural change towards deregulation, liberalization and privatization had taken place and the number of cartels had reached zero, economic growth had completely come to a halt and even turned negative. As US-style hiring and firing was gradually adopted, unemployment rose significantly – low unemployment being another mark of the original 'corporatist capitalism' of the 1960s. As US-style shareholder capitalism spread, income and wealth disparities rose. Not only suicides rose, but also incidents of violent crime. Measured in social welfare terms, there can be little doubt that the decline in performance of Japan's economy has been far larger than merely the reported fall in GDP growth rate.

If anything, the empirical record yields evidence in support of the hypothesis that the more Japan moved away from its 'traditional' postwar structure, the weaker its economic performance became. The hypothesis that Japan's traditional postwar economic system is good for growth is not contradicted by the evidence.

Conclusion on empirical examination of neoclassical welfare economics

The alternative theoretical support of the structural reform view is based on neoclassical welfare economics theory, which says that only deregulated, liberalized and market-oriented structures without direct intervention or cartels are economically efficient. From this, the testable hypotheses can be derived that deregulated and market-oriented structures should record superior economic performance to regulated structures. However, there is no evidence to support this hypothesis. To the contrary, Japanese growth has outperformed that of the US and the UK over the past 50 years. Furthermore, the other hypothesis derived from neoclassical welfare economics, namely the frequently cited claim that an increase in the market-orientation of an economy via deregulation, liberalization and abolition of cartels will result in improved economic performance is also not supported by the empirical record. To the contrary, there is evidence that the gradual structural reform during the postwar era is associated with steadily declining economic performance. It must be concluded that neoclassical welfare economics also provides no support for the structural reform theory. Since we found in the last chapter that the argument for structural reform derived from neoclassical growth theory was also rejected by the empirical evidence, we must conclude that the entire structural reform argument remains without merit.

The financial press and learned commentators assert almost on a daily basis that Japanese economic performance will improve if US-style capitalism is adopted. However, the truth is that there is no empirical foundation for such a claim. The structural reform argument must be considered an unfounded theory. If one did consult the empirical record, then one can only conclude that Japan's structural reforms towards deregulation and liberalization have been accompanied by a steady reduction in economic growth, both in the short term and in the long run. Reforms may be 'badly wanted' by certain parts of society. However, it is far from clear that they are 'badly needed'.

Especially in the 1990s the proponents of structural reform in Japan have dealt with this uncomfortable fact by simply moving the goalposts on the definition of structural reform. As the recession of the 1990s continued despite accelerating structural reform, it is simply claimed by the reformers that the continued weak economic performance is due to the insufficiency of reform: if even further-reaching reforms had been implemented, economic performance would surely improve. Obviously, this merely expands the range of unsubstantiated assertions, but does not constitute factual evidence.

The question of why Japan's old corporatist economic system, indeed the German and Korean systems as well, should have been superior in their performance to the US/UK-style shareholder capitalism is a mystery to neoclassical economists. How could the less market-oriented capitalist economies have clearly outperformed the more market-oriented capitalist economies? Worse, there is empirical evidence that Japan's economic performance deteriorated, the more it moved away from its system and towards the freer market economy system of the US and the UK. For neoclassical economics, both empirical facts remain enigmas that the approach fails to address, let alone offers solutions to.

This result will not come as a surprise to those not slavishly following neoclassical economics. The axiomatic, deductivist models of neoclassical economics have no bearing on economic reality, and thus it would have been far more surprising, if there actually had been any empirical support for their arguments or predictions. Instead, economic theories built on inductivist reasoning and empirical evidence are more likely to be relevant. It was such theories that were indeed used to develop the German and Japanese-style corporatist capitalism. Its superior performance is thus also a reflection of the soundness of the methodology used for their theories.[7]

It remains to be concluded here that the mystery of why Japan's economy remained in a prolonged slump during the 1990s can also not be solved with the structural reform explanation.

6
The Enigma of
Economic Growth

In May 2002, Bank of Japan Governor Masaru Hayami proclaimed that Japan was entering its third recovery since the bursting of the bubble economy.[1] Although the 1990s were marked by economic stagnation, there were two periods of brief but remarkable economic growth, namely 1996, when close to 4% real GDP growth was recorded, and 2000, when over 2% growth was achieved. In both cases, very few, if any, economists had forecast such sudden recoveries. Similarly, many economists were surprised by the sharp upturn recorded in most economic indicators in early 2002.[2]

The enigma of the upturns, especially the one in 2002, was a problem for the supply-side economists. They had argued only in 2001 that new and more sweeping structural reforms would be necessary to create an economic recovery. Well aware of the experience of the Hashimoto-era structural reforms, Prime Minister Koizumi repeatedly asserted in 2001 that (a) no recovery would happen without structural reform and (b) in the short-term, for at least the first two years, his planned structural reforms would worsen the economic situation, reduce growth and increase deflationary pressure.

In his June 2002 speech in Sydney, Koizumi said: 'It is an economic certainty that Japan will have "no growth without reform".'[3] The message 'no recovery without structural change' had been broadcast almost on a daily basis during 2001. To leave no doubt, Koizumi reiterated precisely what his reform plans were:

Our structural reform includes the disposal of non-performing loans over the course of the next two or three years, the reform of government-affiliated corporations, the participation of private capital in postal businesses, the abolition of regulations preventing free economic activities in the private sector and changes in rigid fiscal and social systems.

Unfortunately, during the first year of his government Koizumi failed to implement any of the major reforms he had envisaged. Given the far-reaching nature of these reforms, it is natural that the prime minister felt obliged to admit that they would take years to implement:

> I often hear the questions, 'Why isn't structural reform occurring faster? Why don't we see more results?' I would point out that Great Britain experienced negative growth for the first two years after Prime Minister Thatcher's reforms were inaugurated. Likewise, the United States under President Reagan suffered negative growth before enjoying the fruits of his reforms several years later.[4]

The implication for the economy was that, according to Koizumi and supply-side economists, there could not possibly be an economic recovery, since none of the planned structural reforms had been implemented. However, with Hayami's declaration of a recovery in May 2002, Koizumi's claims had been proven wrong. Once again, Japan's economy puzzled observers: although far-reaching structural reforms had been widely considered a necessary condition for a recovery, the economy recovered without any of Prime Minister Koizumi's reforms having been implemented.[5]

This is further evidence against the new classical and supply-side theories that blamed Japan's low GDP growth rate during much of the 1990s on Japan's economic structure. Clearly, there are other factors at work in explaining GDP growth, besides Japan's economic structure. However, the supply-side economists were not the only ones puzzled by Japan's economic performance. The still more widespread demand-side economic models also failed to predict the short-lived upturns of the 1990s. As we saw, the demand-based models could not explain why neither fiscal stimulation nor interest rate reductions seemed to make much impact on the economy.

What, indeed, are the standard explanatory variables of economic growth? According to analysts of the major financial houses, as well as most standard macroeconomic models, the single most important variable explaining economic growth is the rate of interest. This is what we are told on a daily basis in the financial press. Lower interest rates will stimulate private investment, which in turn will boost overall economic growth. Conversely, higher interest rates will slow economic growth.

What is the empirical evidence for this theory, in the case of the largest and second-largest economies? Figure 6.1 shows a time series graph of the overnight call rate and nominal GDP growth.[6] Eye inspection seems to reveal little evidence that lower call rates have been followed by higher growth. If anything, it appears that higher growth is followed by rising call rates, and lower growth by lower call rates. Indeed, a scatter plot of the same data appears to yield a positive relationship between the two variables (Figure 6.2).

It is true that central banks virtually determine the overnight short-term interest rate (the call rate, in Japan; in the US this is called the Federal funds

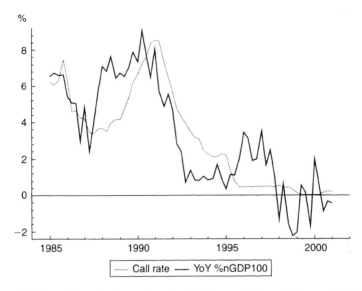

Figure 6.1 Overnight call rates and nominal GDP growth (overnight uncollateralized call rate; nominal GDP growth)

Sources: Bank of Japan; Cabinet office, Government of Japan.

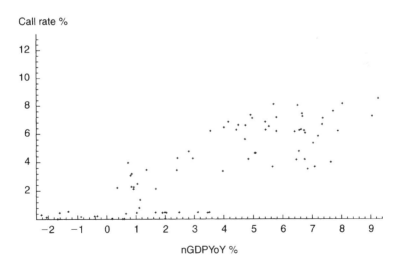

Figure 6.2 Short-term nominal interest rates and nominal GDP growth (overnight call rate, uncollateralized)

Sources: Bank of Japan; Cabinet office, Government of Japan.

rate). The empirical record suggests that central banks lower interest rates, when growth has slowed, and they raise them, when growth has risen. In other words, they adjust the short-term interest rates simply by following economic growth. This means, in terms of causation, that short-term interest rates are the result of economic growth.

There is ample evidence for this finding. The British central bank raised interest rates in 2004 in *response* to strong economic growth, and so did the Swiss central bank. The US Federal Reserve raised interest rates *after* it had become clear that economic growth had been strong. Earlier in the cycle, all these central banks had lowered interest rates, clearly *in response* to weak economic growth.

To most observers this finding is perfectly obvious. But it has important implications: if we agree that short-term rates are the *result* of economic growth, then this means that they cannot at the same time be the *cause*. In other words, lowering rates cannot possibly stimulate the economy, since interest rates do not cause growth, but rather growth causes interest rates to move. This means that we need to look for another explanatory variable of economic growth. It is clear that it cannot be short-term interest rates.

Perhaps the answer is long-term interest rates. The interest rate theory of growth should at least work here. Figure 6.3 shows a scatter plot of Japanese nominal ten-year (benchmark) bond yields and nominal GDP growth.[7]

A very strong positive correlation can be identified. There seems to be empirical evidence that not low rates and high growth occur together, but

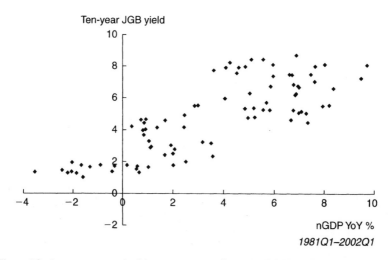

Figure 6.3   Long-term nominal interest rates and nominal GDP growth (ten-year JGB yield; nominal GDP growth)

Sources: Cabinet Office, Government of Japan; Statistics Bureau, Bank of Japan.

instead high rates and high growth. Next it will be interesting to consider which variable moves first. According to the standard mainstream theory, interest rates move first, and growth follows. Figure 6.4 shows the same data as above, but in a time series graph.

Eye inspection yields no evidence that low long-term interest rates produce high economic growth. There is also no evidence that growth follows interest rates. For instance, in 1987, growth accelerated sharply, and interest rates followed several years later. Growth also seemed to peak first, before interest rates peaked. Nominal GDP growth bottomed in the first quarter of 2002 and then picked up sharply. Long-term interest rates, however, only bottomed over a year later, in the second quarter of 2003, at a new world record low rate, before rising gently. The data also appear supportive of the hypothesis that interest rates *follow* growth. If that is the case, then we are left with the enigma of what determines economic growth. Whatever it is, it is indirectly also responsible for the movement of interest rates, because these follow growth.

Many economists are quick to argue that the solution must lie with calculating real interest rates. To them, the use of nominal variables is suspect. They argue that only real variables are of relevance. Things are not quite so easy, however. Firstly, central banks do set nominal short-term interest rates, and hence it is perfectly valid to analyse their relationship with the economy – which should be consistent, of course, and hence must focus on nominal growth. There is no convincing empirical evidence that central

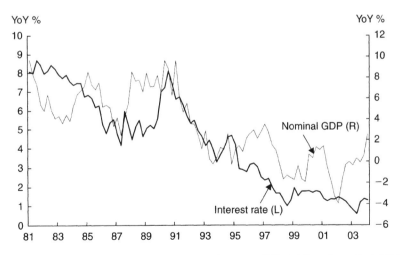

Figure 6.4 Long-term nominal interest rates (ten-year JGB yield) and nominal GDP growth (time series)

Sources: Bank of Japan; Cabinet Office, Government of Japan.

banks use real interest rates either as a target or as an operational tool of their monetary policy. Secondly, empirical observation of reality reveals that most key variables that influence the behaviour of decision-makers are in nominal terms: stock prices, wages, exchange rates. There is also little empirical evidence that in periods without high inflation agents engage in calculations of 'real' variables. Indeed, the argument that only real variables matter follows by assumption from neoclassical models. It is not an empirical finding. Thirdly, there may be a good reason for the latter finding: it is not easy to calculate 'real' prices, and thus also 'real' interest rates. To do so, the prices of all goods, services and assets that are transacted would have to be 'deflated' appropriately. There is no such price index, and agents appear not to have the perfect information that is necessary to properly calculate such 'real' variables.

Nevertheless, 'real' variables can be approximated by making a number of the usual assumptions. The 'real' call rate is then calculated as the nominal call rate minus the annual growth rate of the consumer price index (CPI) (which is merely indicative of prices of a specific basket of consumer goods). Figure 6.5 plots the resulting short-term real interest rates against real GDP growth (which is calculated by subtracting the GDP deflator, itself calculated by the authorities on the basis of a number of assumptions, from nominal GDP).

We find that, once again, there is little evidence that short-term interest rates and growth are negatively correlated. For both nominal and real, short and long interest rates, one may wish to try different leads or lags in order

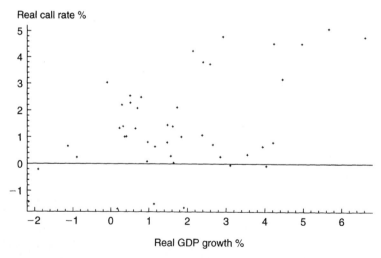

Figure 6.5   Short-term real interest rates and real GDP growth

Sources: Bank of Japan; Cabinet Office, Government of Japan.

to determine the empirically most significant relationship. Perhaps on this basis a negative correlation can be found? But this is also not the case. The correlation that is statistically strongest is the positive correlation, as eye inspection suggests.

Perhaps these findings are just another aspect of the major enigma that seems to surround the Japanese economy? In other words, perhaps Japan is a special case? Indeed, during the 1990s interest rates had fallen so low that they simply could not have an effect any more – as the liquidity trap argument proposes. There are several problems with this argument. Firstly, as we saw in Chapters 2 and 3, the liquidity trap argument applies only to the time period when interest rates had fallen to the lowest level. That, however, happened only in 2002/03 and thus fails to address the question why during the entire decade of the 1990s interest rate *reductions* remained without effect. Secondly, the above findings about the positive correlation between interest rates and growth, and the timing of rates following growth also apply to the 1980s. Simply dropping the 1990s will give us the same result.

Thirdly, the findings seem very robust across other major economies. It may be tempting to believe that when using US data we will surely find that interest rates and economic growth are in a negative correlation, and that growth follows interest rates. But is this so?

Figure 6.6 is a scatter plot of US ten-year government bond yields against nominal GDP growth.

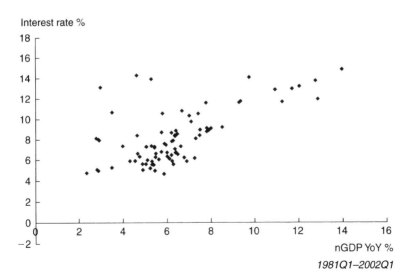

Figure 6.6 US long-term nominal interest rates and nominal GDP growth
Source: Board of Governors of the Federal Reserve System.

A time series chart (Figure 6.7) shows the close correlation between the two. Again, there is no evidence that low interest rates cause high growth. We simply observe that high growth and high rates occur together.

In terms of timing, it appears that growth bottoms and peaks before interest rates. In other words, once again interest rates appear to follow growth.

Perhaps the answer is to calculate the somewhat imprecise 'real' rates and compare them with real growth? The scatter plot is shown in Figure 6.8.

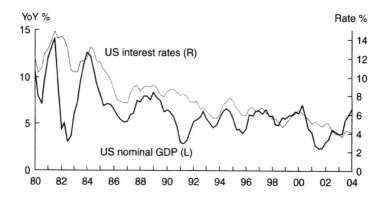

Figure 6.7   US long-term nominal interest rates and nominal GDP growth (time series)

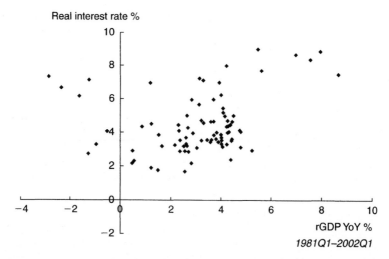

Figure 6.8   US long-term real interest rates and real GDP growth
Source: Board of Governors of the Federal Reserve System.

As can be seen, the positive correlation is somewhat weaker. But there is still no evidence of a negative correlation. Relationships that are clearly visible by eye inspection tend to be reliable also in statistical tests. Table 6.1 presents simple ordinary least square regressions of interest rates and economic growth for Japan and the US, for real variables. The same is shown for nominal variables in Table 6.2. We find that there is no evidence of a negative correlation in all four cases, as coefficients for interest rates are positive and significant.

Table 6.1 The correlation of real interest rates and real GDP

(a) Modelling US real GDP by OLS
The estimation sample is: 1981 (1) to 2002 (1)

	Coefficient	Std. Error	t-value	t-prob.	Part. R^2
Constant	1.72756	0.5967	2.90	0.005	0.0917
US real interest rate	0.311376	0.1247	2.50	0.014	0.0699

$R^2 = 0.0698846$ F(1,83) = 6.236 [0.014]*   Sigma = 1.98153   RSS = 325.897124
log-likelihood = -177.727 DW = 0.291   no. of obs. = 85   var(US real GDP) = 4.12216

(b) Modelling Japan real GDP by OLS
The estimation sample is: 1981 (1) to 2002 (1)

	Coefficient	Std. Error	t-value	t-prob.	Part. R^2
Constant	0.0763328	0.4960	0.154	0.878	0.0003
Japan real interest	0.731660	0.1331	5.50	0.000	0.2668

$R^2 = 0.266775$ F(1,83) = 30.2 [0.000]**   sigma = 1.85778   RSS = 286.462053
log-likelihood = -172.245 DW = 0.434   no. of obs. = 85   var(Japan rGDP) = 4.59633

Table 6.2 The correlation of nominal interest rates and nominal GDP

(a) Modelling US nominal GDP by OLS
The estimation sample is: 1982 (1) to 2002 (1)

	Coefficient	Std. Error	t-value	t-prob.	Part. R^2
Constant	2.73860	0.6684	4.10	0.000	0.1753
US nominal interest	0.422422	0.08135	5.19	0.000	0.2545

$R^2 = 0.254468$ F(1,79) = 26.96 [0.000]**   Sigma = 1.70643   RSS = 230.041399
log-likelihood = -157.208 DW = 0.246   no. of obs. = 81   var(US nom GDP) = 3.80938

(b) Modelling Japanese nominal GDP by OLS
The estimation sample is: 1982 (2) to 2002 (1)

	Coefficient	Std. Error	t-value	t-prob.	Part. R^2
Constant	-1.94981	0.4954	-3.94	0.000	0.1657
Japan nominal interest	1.16778	0.09885	11.8	0.000	0.6415

$R^2 = 0.641485$ F(1,78) = 139.6 [0.000]**   Sigma = 1.94283   RSS = 294.416614
log-likelihood = -165.634 DW = 0.533   no. of obs. = 80   var(Japan nGDP) = 10.2652

Needless to say, this finding contradicts most mainstream economic models. The movement of interest rates and economic growth therefore remain an enigma, if we use traditional approaches.

Given how central the inverse and leading relationship between interest rates and economic growth is to modern economics, and given how frequently we hear assertions in the leading financial press and by central banks that lower interest rates will stimulate growth and higher interest rates will slow growth, it must come as a surprise to many, especially theoretical economists, that there is no empirical evidence for this relationship.

There is another, related enigma. And again, it is not unique to Japan: mainstream theory also holds that interest rates should be in a negative correlation with money supply aggregates (low interest rates and high money growth going together on the one hand, and high interest rates and low money growth on the other). Concerning timing, interest rates are considered the driving force of broad money aggregates. This negative and leading relationship between interest rates and money growth is referred to as the 'liquidity effect'. In a detailed empirical study, Leeper and Gordon (1992) have sought to establish this liquidity effect empirically, as it had hitherto only been 'demonstrated' in theoretical models. What they found was that both causation and correlation appeared the exact opposite of what standard theory proclaims.

Despite these devastating findings, none of the above facts are pointed out to students of economics, nor to journalists or the general public. Apparently oblivious to the facts of this world, central bankers and theoretical economists keep repeating the mantra of the importance of interest rates, derived from their theoretical models, like monks spinning a prayer mill. Those who do not have the time to check the facts are easily misled by the so-called experts who are supposed to know better.

The enigma of the interest rate also means that when the next central banker asserts that he is raising rates to slow growth, or that he is lowering rates to stimulate growth, we know that he is talking nonsense. Since rates, especially those set by central bankers, are the result of economic growth, they cannot at the same time be the cause.

The other implication is that standard theories therefore do not explain what actually determines growth. The latest neoclassical theories virtually acknowledge this. Since the structural reform argument also has to be ruled out (as we saw in the last two chapters), neoclassical economists are left with the argument that all economic growth is simply the result of unpredictable 'random' shocks, and economic growth is a 'random walk' – an enigma that cannot be solved by economists, we are told.

That, however, is once again an assertion that needs to be put to the empirical test. We find in this book that much can actually be said, as long as we are willing to analyse empirical facts objectively and formulate theories based on reality (instead of being puzzled why reality refuses to conform to preconceived theory). As we saw, the assumption that the economy is always operating at the full employment level of all inputs does not hold. This means that the economy often operates below full capacity, so that instead of supply-side arguments we must return to the demand side to find an answer.

7
The Enigma of the Velocity Decline

We now turn to what may be the single most disturbing enigma. Once again it not only concerns Japan, but has arisen in many countries and many time periods around the world. It is disturbing for economics as a theory and for economists as applied social scientists.

Since the answer to the enigma of Japan's long recession is not to be found among supply-side theories, it is time to review the foundations of the major demand-side theories. Although these macroeconomic theories are presented as very different, and their proponents are often engaged in fierce arguments with each other, they turn out to have much in common: they share the same, single foundation. Since they also have in common that they cannot explain important aspects of reality, such as Japan's macroeconomic performance, it stands to reason that we should examine their common foundation to see whether it might be the problem.

If we are looking for a fundamental flaw, we need to examine the fundamentals. We thus need to review the basic demand-side theories that continue to form the foundation of macroeconomic analysis, namely the classical (and neoclassical), Keynesian, monetarist and fiscalist theories, in order to identify their common foundation.

The classical school of thought

As the name suggests, the classical theory is the oldest one. It was formulated more than a century ago in Britain, when it was the leading manufacturing power and keen to increase its exports. Classical economics provided a useful theory to persuade other countries to open their borders to British exports instead of attempting to establish competing indigenous industries. Some countries, such as the US, Germany and Japan, did not accept the classical arguments and refused to follow classical policy advice (needless to say, they did well from ignoring this advice). Nevertheless, classical theory survived in its neoclassical and new classical variants right into the twenty-first century.

Among a larger number of assumptions made by classical theory, we can emphasize the following three:

1. people are rational and aim at maximizing their utility;
2. prices are perfectly flexible;
3. everybody has perfect information about everything.

In such a theoretical world the economy will, by definition, always be at or close to its full-employment equilibrium. If there is excess demand in any market, prices in that market would rise, thus reducing demand and increasing supply, until both demand and supply are in equilibrium. In such a world there cannot really be involuntary unemployment, because wages would fall until everybody is fully employed. With the economy always at full employment, there is no positive role for government policy to increase or reduce demand. The policy advice is pure *laissez-faire*.

Fiscal policy

As is already clear from the above, government policy can't have any lasting impact. Increased fiscal spending would push up interest rates, as it draws on the savings from the private sector. This in turn reduces private sector spending, especially investment. So any rise in government demand would be counter-balanced by a fall in private demand – classical crowding out. Hence the ideal fiscal policy is to keep a balanced budget, that is, no fiscal policy at all.

Monetary policy

Classical economists employ what can be called the 'quantity equation' to describe the link between money and the economy. It is formalized as follows:

$$(1) \quad PY = MV$$

P stands for the price level, Y for output (or income) measured in volume terms, that is, real GDP. So P times Y is nominal GDP. M stands for the amount of money in the economy, the 'money supply'. V stands for 'velocity of money', which is the number of times the money supply is 'turned over' in the time period of observation, or the number of times money M is used for transactions. So M times V is the total effective money supply. Equation (1) therefore simply says that nominal national income or output equals the nominal amount of money that is actually used in the economy. In other words, the money going round in a year must buy a year's national income.

From this, a theory of the 'demand for money' is derived: It was observed that the ratio of nominal GDP to the money supply is usually fairly stable.

Since GDP is also national income, economists called the observed *ex post* relationship between national income and the money supply (that is, the ratio of M to PY) the 'money demand function', arguing that for any given level of nominal income, there is a certain 'demand for money', which has produced the observed money supply figures. This demand for money was originally thought to be due to the desire to undertake economic transactions (the 'transactions demand for money'). This is known as the 'Cambridge equation' and is written as follows:

(2) $M^d = kPY$

It simply says that the demand for money (M^d) is proportional (by factor k) to nominal income or nominal GDP, which can be broken into the price level P and real income (or output) Y. Both k in equation (2) and its inverse, V in equation (1), are assumed to be constant, so that the stock of money is directly linked to nominal GDP (PY): The central bank controls the supply of money (M^s) and since markets are assumed to be in equilibrium, the money supply equals the demand for money. If the central bank injects more money, but only a certain proportion of national income is desired to be held in money, then more money will be invested in the economy and demand will rise. So the increase in the money supply boosts GDP until money demand equals money supply and the constant share of national income PY that is desired to be held as money (k) is restored. Thus a rise in M pushes up PY proportionately.

The question is how much of that rise in PY will result in a rise in output Y and how much will result in a rise in prices P. Under the classical assumptions employment is already at the full employment level and output is already as large as it can be (at the full employment level Y_f), irrespective of the price level. This means that output is always fixed at the full-employment level. Thus equation (1) can be rewritten:

(3) $P\bar{Y} = M\bar{V}$

In other words, the aggregate supply curve is vertical (see Figure 7.1). As a result, any policy that boosts aggregate demand, whether monetary or fiscal, can only push up prices. Therefore, according to classical theory, monetary policy merely produces inflation, as with fixed V and fixed Y, any rise in M must raise P equally. Meanwhile, fiscal policy is ineffective (as the government claims savings to fund fiscal spending, thus pushing up real interest rates and hence reducing private demand by the same amount – interest-rate-based crowding out).

Modern versions

The classical theory was revived as 'neoclassical' theory earlier in the twentieth century and even more recently as 'new classical economics'. Their

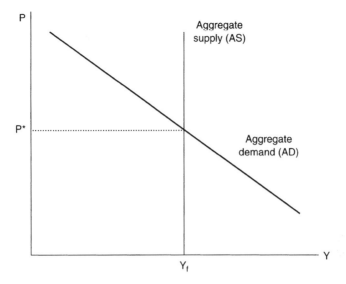

Figure 7.1 The classical (and neoclassical) vertical aggregate supply curve

research programme has involved the creation of microeconomic principles ('assume there is one firm, one good, one consumer', and so on), which will produce the desired macroeconomic models. With the same assumptions of perfect information and flexible prices, neoclassical economists come to the same conclusion as classical economics, but much faster: if individuals have all information about everything, then there is no need for money at all. Money was invented to bridge the problems of barter, where a double co-incidence of wants was necessary. That gets very complicated when many people are involved and all their wants are not known. However, with the convenient assumption of perfect information, such barter would be possible and money would not exist. Since therefore there is no money in their models, money also cannot have any effect. Neither can fiscal policy nor any other form of government intervention. Since any applied model must include the reality of money, the modern versions have also fallen back to the classical 'quantity equation'.

Similar to the neoclassical school of thought, proponents of the so-called 'real business cycle' theory argue that economic policies are not meaningful. As the economy is always at its full employment equilibrium, what you get is also always the best you can get, for any given economic structure. Any importance of money is also denied, as money is seen as a nominal variable, that cannot have real effects. Causation is seen as always emanating from the 'real economy' to monetary and financial variables. Thus 'exogenous' shocks to the real economy, such as the oil shock or structural problems with the economy, produce the 'real business cycle'.

Policy advice for Japan

The classical, neoclassical or real business cycle theories are usually billed as demand side economic theories. However, they effectively abrogate any role for demand management, by arguing that economic demand is always as good as it can be. If one wants to improve growth, then only structural policies can be successful, as they tackle the supply side. The policy advice for Japan is therefore to forget about monetary or fiscal policy. Aggregate demand policies are not interesting, because demand is not the problem. Instead, Japan should improve its economic structure, which is hampering a more efficient use of resources. We have, however, already seen that the structural change argument is not backed by the empirical evidence. Furthermore, although new classical theories argue that money supply increases will merely create inflation, significant rises in the money supply have not produced inflation – to the contrary, Japan experienced five consecutive years of deflation. New classical theories also deny any impact of fiscal policy, since under its assumptions of perfect information and rational expectations tax payers will simply save more if the government loosens fiscal policy and thus negate any effect (Ricardian equivalence). However, we found that there is no empirical evidence that personal savings rose as much as fiscal expenditure.

The Keynesian school of thought

When unemployment reached more than 20% in the early 1930s in the US, Germany and other countries, the British economist John Maynard Keynes, a hitherto leading representative of classical economics, suggested that perhaps something was not entirely correct with the mainstream theory which maintained that economies were always at their full employment equilibrium. While he agreed with the classical assumptions of rationality, utility maximization, perfect information and clearing of most markets, he observed that the labour market is not as flexible as the classics thought – he described wages as 'sticky', difficult to reduce even in the face of unemployment. He thus made what was a radical suggestion for English-language economics at the time: that not all markets might always be in equilibrium, namely that there was one exception, the labour market.

The main assumptions of Keynesian macroeconomic theory are therefore:

1. people are rational and aim at maximizing their utility;
2. prices are not perfectly flexible: wages are 'sticky';
3. everybody has perfect information about everything.

However, with inflexible prices (due to labour market 'imperfections', such as unions, long-term wage contracts, and so on), it is possible that involuntary unemployment exists. As a result, the economy can be below the full employment level for a protracted period of time. When classical economists responded to Keynes that 'in the long run' wages would adjust and the economy would eventually move to full employment, Keynes pointed out that the long run may be too long to be relevant.

Fiscal policy

The well-known policy conclusion of Keynes' analysis of the 1930s Depression was that in recessions, when private demand is weak, government demand needed to step in and boost aggregate demand until the economy was back at full employment. According to the national income accounts, GDP can be broken up into consumption C, private investment I, government spending G and net exports NX:

(4) $Y = C + I + G + NX$

so if C, I and NX slump, then Y can be expanded by increasing G, says the Keynesian analysis. In other words, unlike the classical theory, Keynesians do not believe in total crowding out of fiscal spending (they agree that partial crowding out is possible, but the net result of fiscal policy under Keynesian assumptions is always an increase in Y).

Monetary policy

Keynesian economists agree with the 'quantity equation' (1), including its assumption of a constant velocity. However, they provide for a more sophisticated transmission from money to the economy: they argue that in addition to the transactions demand for money that classical models assume, there is also significant 'portfolio demand' for money. To simplify, it is usually assumed that the portfolio of total wealth W in the economy consists of money M and bonds B ($W = M + B$). Investors try to maximize returns while minimizing risk by diversification. As a result, an increase in M arranged by the central bank means that portfolio-diversifying investors that do not wish to hold too much money M will increase their demand for bonds. This pushes up bond prices and reduces interest rates. Lower interest rates then increase investment demand, which boosts GDP. As a result, an increase in the money supply increases GDP, as the 'quantity equation' suggests. The chain of causation assumed in this Keynesian transmission from M to Y is as follows:

(5) $M \to P_B \to i \to I \to Y$

However, when this mechanism seemed to break down in the 1930s (large declines in interest rates failed to stimulate the economy), Keynes developed an auxiliary theory to explain this anomaly – his 'liquidity trap' theory. It says that when interest rates are already extremely low, monetary policy ceases to work and all a government can do is increase fiscal spending. We have already encountered this argument in our discussion of the liquidity trap in the context of Japan in the 1990s.

Keynesians also disagree with classicals about the degree to which an increase in demand (either due to monetary or fiscal policy) will result in inflation. Since with inflexible prices the economy can be below the full employment level, the aggregate supply curve is not vertically fixed at Y_f, but upward-sloping (Figure 7.2). Therefore, a boost of aggregate demand will only partially result in a rise in prices P, while (depending on the exact shape of the aggregate supply curve) output Y is also increased. The extent to which increased demand results in higher real growth and to which it results in inflation depends on how much the economy is away from its full employment level. (This idea was formalized and empirically supported by the Phillips curve relationship, which found a negative correlation between unemployment and inflation.) If demand is far below full employment output level Y_f, then inflationary pressure will be low and increases in demand will mainly boost real output.

This means that the 'quantity equation' (1) holds for Keynesians, but not equation (3), since they differ about the assumptions surrounding Y: while classical economists consider it constant, Keynesians don't, so that monetary policy may boost demand when the economy is below the full

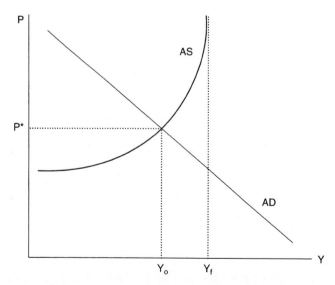

Figure 7.2 The upward-sloping Keynesian aggregate demand curve

employment level Y_f. Thus:

(6) $PY = M\bar{V}$

New Keynesian models come to the same conclusions, but are also mainly based on microeconomic models that provide for more sophisticated reasons why wages may be sticky or the economy might remain below the full employment level.

Policy advice for Japan

The policy advice for Japan according to this approach is to lower interest rates and increase government spending. We have, however, already found that lower interest rates are not negatively correlated with investment and economic growth, as they should be according to this theory. Thus the theoretically postulated chain of causation shown in equation (4) seems unsupported by empirical reality. Moreover, the liquidity trap argument fails to explain the ineffectiveness of fiscal policy during the 1990s, before the liquidity trap situation occurred. It also does not explain just why a liquidity trap came about in the first place. Finally, fiscal spending has failed to boost economic growth, although according to the Keynesian model it is supposed to be the only policy that is effective. The Keynesian model therefore, just like the classical/new classical theory, does not seem to work empirically.

The monetarist school of thought

The empirical track record of Keynesian theory seemed reasonably strong during the earlier postwar era, which is why it became a popular approach with economists trained in the 1950s and 1960s. However, in the 1970s, when economies suffered high unemployment and inflation ('stagflation'), the Keynesian model was severely criticized. Classical economists felt vindicated, as fiscal policies merely seemed to fuel inflation and higher interest rates, while unemployment persisted (that is, the Phillips curve relationship broke down). In this situation, a group of economists wanted to preserve the advances made by Keynesian theory, but combine them with some of the plausible parts of classical theories. These were the 'monetarists'. They followed the classical assumptions of rationality, utility maximisation and even the assumption of perfect price flexibility. However, they argued that the assumption of perfect information was at fault: clearly, nobody enjoys perfect information. Instead, people have to make imperfect assessments, which they revise based on how far their past forecasts went wrong ('adaptive expectations').

The main assumptions of monetarist macroeconomic theory are therefore:

1. people are rational and aim at maximizing their utility;
2. prices are perfectly flexible;
3. information is imperfect.

Monetarists distinguish between the short run and the long run, and this is essentially how aspects of both the Keynesian and classical models were preserved: In the short run, demand management policies can be effective, as an increase in demand pushes up prices (like in the classical model), but people don't realize this initially, due to a lack of perfect information. Therefore their real wages are declining (without people noticing). Firms notice, however, and thus employ more people. Employment is boosted beyond the full employment level Y_f (which in practice leaves a certain degree of 'natural' unemployment). However, in the long run people realize that they suffered from money illusion (that is, they thought nominal wage rises also meant real wage rises). As soon as they find out, they withdraw their extra labour beyond the call of duty (beyond 'natural' employment). Consequently, in the long run the economy moves back to the full employment (or 'natural' employment) output level, and only prices rise. Thus, as with classical theory, in the long run neither monetary nor fiscal policy is effective. However, in the short run, monetary and fiscal policy can boost demand, as the Keynesians have argued.

Monetary policy

Monetarists, as the name suggests, agree with the 'quantity equation' as presented by classical theories (equation (1)). More than classical economists they feel that monetary policy is the most efficient way to manipulate the economy, but can only do so in the short run. In Figure 7.3, a boost of the money

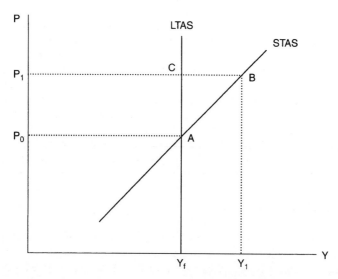

Figure 7.3 Monetarist short-term and long-term aggregate supply curves

supply that is not initially known pushes supply above its full employment level (and unemployment below its natural level). So in the short run, the economy moves from A to B and output rises from Y_f to Y_1. Prices have risen already from P_0 to P_1, but people do not know this in the short run. However, after a while, inflation becomes obvious. People supply less labour and in the long run the economy moves back to the old full employment level at C, with higher prices. Thus, in the short run the Keynesian version of the 'quantity equation' holds:

(7) $PY = M\bar{V}$

while in the long run the classical version is correct:

(8) $P\bar{Y} = M\bar{V}$

Fiscal policy

Concerning fiscal policy, monetarists are close to the classical view: they believe that it is largely ineffective, because investment is very sensitive to interest changes. Hence when the government funds its fiscal spending by issuing bonds, this is thought to drive up interest rates, which in turn will slow private investment by as much as public demand is rising. In other words, monetarists argue for almost complete crowding out via interest rate rises.

Policy advice for Japan

The policy advice of the monetarists has been for the central bank to increase the money supply, as measured by such monetary aggregates as M1, M2 or M3, and push interest rates down as much as possible. Fiscal policy is not needed. While money aggregates rose during the 1990s and interest rates were successfully reduced, we saw that this did not have the expected stimulatory effect on the economy – especially not in the short run that monetarists thought to be applicable (but also not in the long run). Moreover, we found that there is no evidence for the type of interest-rate-based crowding out of fiscal policy postulated by monetarist theory: interest rates did not rise. Therefore the monetarist approach also has considerable problems accounting for the observed reality of the 1990s in Japan.

The fiscalist school of thought

The monetarist approach became very popular from the late 1970s onwards. To a large extent driven by the forceful personality of Milton Friedman, it revived interest in the 'quantity equation' or 'quantity theory of money' and targeting of monetary aggregates in order to manipulate the economy.

However, monetarism also failed to explain important macroeconomic events – and Japan's case is only the most gregarious example of this failure. As a result of this embarrassing showing of monetarism, central banks de-emphasized the role of the money supply altogether. Indeed, they have now more or less officially adopted an entirely different school of thought – the fiscalist school.

The main assumptions of fiscalism are the same as in the Keynesian theories, namely:

1. people are rational and aim at maximizing their utility;
2. prices are not perfectly flexible: wages are 'sticky';
3. everybody has perfect information about everything.

While they also accept the quantity equation linking money and the economy, they disagree with monetarists about the direction of causation: not from money to the economy, but from the economy to money. In other words, the supply of money is thought to follow closely the demand for money (noted here by having money M, the endogenous variable, on the left-hand side of the equation):

(9) $\quad M\bar{V} = PY$

While the money supply is endogenous to demand, the demand for money, in turn, is thought to reflect autonomous processes in the economy that are not directly controllable (such as 'animal instincts', entrepreneurial 'spirits', perception of 'investment opportunities', and so on). If people feel confident and want to spend and invest more, they will have a greater demand for money. Given Keynes' use of the concept of 'animal spirits', and since this school of thought subscribes to the Keynesian analysis in virtually all aspects, except the monetary mechanism, many of its proponents would describe themselves as 'post-Keynesians'. Ironically, this school of thought has much in common with the supply-side neoclassical economists, who also argue that the economy simply moves as a result of exogenous shocks that cannot be easily controlled. Their main difference lies in the ability of fiscal policy to affect growth. Here, the policy implications are the reverse of the monetarists': while the latter claim that monetary policy is key and fiscal policy is largely powerless, the fiscalists think that monetary policy is powerless, while fiscal policy can stimulate demand. According to the national income accounting identity, if private demand is weak, an increase in public demand can compensate. That, in turn, will then increase the demand for money, which will also boost the supply for money. In other words, the only way out of recessions is fiscal policy.

Among proponents of this school of thought we find many central banks. The theory of bureaucracy argues that any bureaucracy will tend to downplay its powers in public so that responsibility can be avoided.[1] In this vein there seems to be a tendency for central banks to favour fiscalism, enabling them to argue that responsibility for demand management lies with the fiscal authorities, while the latter tend to be stronger believers in the powers of central banking and sceptical of the capabilities of fiscal policy. Supported by the statistics and research departments of central banks and their staff economists, this school of thought has slowly begun to make inroads into the economics community. Thus it often happens that straight-faced central bankers tell fund managers, economists and journalists that, sorry, they simply can't control the money supply, let alone the economy. With innocent looks they claim that they merely target interest rates and then have to supply whatever quantity of money is demanded by the markets. So as long as interest rates are low, you cannot blame the central banks for weak economic growth: they are virtually powerless institutions, facing a powerful economy that cannot be tamed. Readers will have recognized that the 'BoJ Theory' proposed by its Okina is in fact pure fiscalism. But as Forder (2002) has asked, if central banks have so little power, why were they vocal (and ultimately successful) proponents of the idea that they need to be given full legal independence?

Policy advice for Japan

The fiscalist approach has been popular in Japan for much of the 1990s, as most economists continued to argue that no economic recovery could take place without government spending. The repeated lack of success of the sizeable fiscal spending eventually silenced the fiscalists, and, probably for lack of other arguments, many have made the methodologically highly surprising switch into the camp of the neoclassical economists by agreeing that structural changes are necessary for Japan to recover. This switch has not only occurred without any empirical foundation, but it is also logically inconsistent, since fiscalist models emphasise the demand side, not the supply side. Moreover, when confronted with supply-side arguments a few years ago, most fiscalists would have had no trouble dismissing the structural change argument as irrelevant by pointing out – correctly – that Japan's recession is caused by lack of demand. Supply-side policies merely increase the potential growth rate, but do nothing to boost demand. It must thus be concluded that the fiscalist school of thought has also been unsuccessful in finding empirical support.

Testing mainstream macroeconomics

We have surveyed the fundamental propositions of the main schools of thought in macroeconomics. Each theory seems to have some appealing aspects, but also some parts that seem unrealistic or contrary to evidence. We can also identify several aspects that they have in common: firstly, they are all based on the deductive methodology, which starts by making assumptions about reality, and then proceeds to build models; secondly, they generally are based on the faith that most markets will be in equilibrium (even if the labour market may not be, as in the case of the Keynesian and fiscalist theories); thirdly, they all agree about the link between money and the economy, namely the 'quantity equation' MV = PY (even though they disagree about details), which forms the fundamental pillar on which they are built; and fourthly, they all do not work – since they are unable to explain events in the 'real world', for instance the second largest economy.

Since they have in common that they do not seem to work, it stands to reason that their other common features may be part of the problem. We can easily test this, and thereby simultaneously put all mainstream macroeconomic theories on trial, if we test their common foundation, namely their postulated link between money and the economy. The general formulation was shown in equation (1) and is reiterated here:

(1) $PY = MV$
    with $V = PY/M = \text{constant}$

For any of the above theories to work, this relationship must hold and, specifically, velocity V must be constant, which also means that the 'money demand function' is stable. If equation (1) and its assumption of stable velocity does not hold, then nothing certain can be said about the relationship between money and the tangible economy (including about the impact of monetary policy).

In the 1950s and 1960s, there were no worries about the stability of velocity. Friedman and Schwartz (1963), among others, provided empirical support from several decades of US data for a stable relationship between money and nominal GDP or between money and prices. By the late 1970s, the view that targeting of the money supply would enable control of nominal GDP growth became widespread. Even until recently, it formed the foundation of the policy decisions of key central banks (see Deutsche Bundesbank, 1992). Monetary economists were convinced to have found an immovable paradigm, as Friedman's (1956) statement illustrates:

> One of the chief reproaches directed at economics as an allegedly empirical science is that it can offer so few numerical 'constants', that is has isolated so few fundamental regularities. The field of money is the chief example one can offer in rebuttal: there is perhaps no other empirical relation in economics that has been observed to recur so uniformly under so wide a variety of circumstances as the relation between substantial changes over short periods in the stock of money and in prices; the one is

invariably linked with the other and is in the same direction; this uniformity is, I suspect, of the same order as many of the uniformities that form the basis of the physical sciences. And the uniformity is in more than direction. There is an extraordinary empirical stability and regularity to such magnitudes as income velocity that cannot but impress anyone who works extensively with monetary data. (Friedman, 1956)

In order to move to testing the relationship between money and the economy, we need to put data into equation (1), namely for money M and for nominal GDP. The latter is easily available from the national income accounts. We hit the first snag, however, when trying to obtain data for M. While economics has discussed money for several centuries, there seems no ready answer to the simple question: What is money?

Most leading university-level textbooks on monetary economics offer no proper answer. One warns: 'Theoretical models of monetary economies often provide little guidance to how the quantity of money appearing in the theory should be related to empirical measures of the money supply' (Walsh, 2003, p. 449). Another offers a variety of definitions with the comment: 'An empirical answer to the definition of the money stock is much more eclectic than its theoretical counterpart' (Handa, 2000, p. 4). Another textbook merely laments that 'money is difficult to define and measure' and that 'divergences in views about what constitutes money are likely to widen with time' (Miller and VanHoose, 1993, p. 59). The definition of money is said to be a 'major difficulty' in another, which then proceeds to recommend a 'narrow' measure of money, namely cash and notes in circulation, perhaps throwing in bank reserves with the central bank (Miles and Wilcox, 1991, p. 229). This aggregate is called the 'monetary base', 'base money' or 'high powered money'.

Historically, most researchers initially used narrow measures of money for M in the quantity equation, such as cash or the monetary base. And if we assume that all transactions must be paid in cash, then this makes sense: equation (1) shows the amount of cash used to buy all transactions that make up national income. But cash or high powered money is usually no more than 5% of all money in most economies. Cash-based transactions also only account for about 5% of all transaction values. What form does the rest of the money used in the economy take? And thus what measure of money should be used to represent M in the 'quantity equation'?

Many economists argued that money held in banks as deposits (D) were also money that had to be counted as part of the 'money supply', together with cash. Thus the sum of cash (C) and deposits (D) is usually also abbreviated with the letter M, but not necessarily identical to the M of equation (1); we thus refer to it as M' here. Such deposit money (D) is sometimes called 'inside money', while high powered money (H), which is the sum of cash (C) and reserves (R), is called 'outside money'. Since in this case M' is much larger than H, we can calculate the ratio of the two (M'/H), and give it a new name, namely the 'money multiplier' (m):

(10) $m = M'/H$

This somewhat attractive name is justified by pointing out that multiplying the smaller H with this scale factor m will give us the larger M':

(11) $M' = mH$

This is not a major feat, since that is how we *defined* m in the first place. Thus there is no informational value in either equations (10) or (11), and certainly no insights can be gained into how banking systems work or how money affects the economy. Nevertheless, we can create the impression of more complexity (and hence greater information value?) if we substitute further definitions into equation (10), namely the way we have *defined* H and M' (remember, $H = C + R$ and $M' = C + D$), so that we obtain:

(12) $m = (C + R)/(C + D)$

Next, we can divide both numerator and denominator by deposits D, with the rationale that we would like to look at deposit ratios (why not?). Thus we obtain equation (13), which is how since Phillips (1920) textbooks and leading economists have represented the 'money multiplier':

(13) $m = (C/D + 1)/(C/D + R/D)$

This so-called 'money multiplier' (m) is an illustration of how formalism in economics can serve to obfuscate. Of course, equation (13) says no more than equations (10) or (11), but has a satisfyingly scientific appeal about it. As the reader will readily discern, there are limitless ways in which this expression can be rendered more complex, without adding any information value, and this is what has actually been done.[2] This rather convoluted way of looking at the ratio between a broader money supply measure (M') and a more narrow one (H) has also encouraged researchers to postulate (without empirical evidence) that broad measures of money are in some stable relationship to narrow ones, and that bank deposits are merely an extension of narrow money measures. Consequently, for decades little need was felt to study the origin and role of deposits further, the actual functioning and economic role of banks or other institutional realities that could yield important insights into how the economy works. The deductivists could stay within their axiomatic models and did not have to venture into the vagaries of reality.

Still, it remains unclear what statistical data series should be used to measure money M when attempting to calculate the quantity equation (1) to test whether velocity V is constant. Should it be cash, reserves, high powered money, deposits or any combination or aggregation of them? The brief answer is that researchers have tried all of them. But even if we use a broad definition of money, such as the definition of M' above (the sum of cash and deposits), we will find that there is still a whole menu of such aggregates to choose from, depending on which type of deposits or other private sector assets are included. In practice, researchers seem to have experimented, often choosing whatever definition seemed to meet the goal of such empirical 'tests', namely to provide a stable velocity and thus a stable relationship between money and nominal GDP.

In Japan's case, the Bank of Japan publishes a number of measures of what it calls the 'money supply', among them: 'high powered money' (H in the equation above, is often called M0 in empirical applications), M1, M2 + CD, M3 + CD and 'Broad Liquidity'. The definitions are (together with recent figures, for May 2004):

M0 (¥100.7 trillion) = cash currency in circulation (¥63.7 trillion in notes
   + ¥4.4 trillion in coins)
   + banks' reserve deposits with the central bank (¥32.6 trillion)
M1 (¥362.8 trillion) = cash currency in circulation (¥68.0 trillion)
   + demand deposits (current, ordinary, savings, notice, special tax
   deposits) with financial institutions (¥294.8 trillion)
M2 + CD (¥693.8 trillion) = M1 + quasi-money (all other deposits, such as
   time deposits, with financial institutions; ¥311.1 trillion)
   + certificates of deposit (CDs; ¥19.9 trillion)
M3 + CD (¥1130.1 trillion) = M2 + CD + post office deposits (¥231.0 trillion)
   + deposits with credit cooperatives (¥109.8 trillion)
   + money in investment trusts of banks (¥95.7 trillion)
'Broad Liquidity' (¥1361.0 trillion) = M3 + CD + investment trusts
   (¥33.8 trillion)
   + other trusts (¥8.2 trillion)
   + bank debentures, government bonds and bills (¥188.4 trillion)
   + CPs issued by financial institutions (¥0.5 trillion)

The principle is clear: the more subsets of private sector savings are aggregated in ever broader measures of the 'money supply', the higher the M number. Textbooks and researchers have been unwilling to tie themselves down to any one measure of the money supply, partly because there is such a large variety to pick and choose from. This in itself, however, should make us suspicious: how could confidence in economics and its link to reality be high, if what surely must be one of the most important variables in economics – the amount of money circulating in the economy – cannot be measured or defined accurately?

We give the traditional approaches the benefit of the doubt by simply adopting the most generous approach and testing the stability of the velocity (that is, the ratio of nominal GDP to the money supply) with all of the above measures. The results for M0 and M1 are shown in Figure 7.4, that for M2 + CD is shown in Figure 7.5. We find that the velocity is highly variable over time. This has been recognized in the literature, as well as by

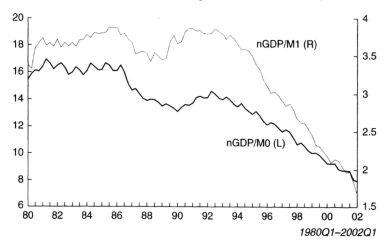

Figure 7.4   Income velocity decline in the case of M0 and M1
Sources: Bank of Japan; Cabinet Office, Government of Japan.

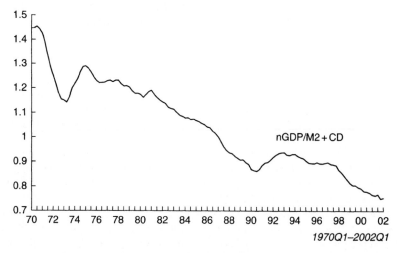

Figure 7.5   Income velocity decline in the case of M2 + CD
Sources: Bank of Japan; Cabinet Office, Government of Japan.

central bankers (Ueda, 2001b), who have lamented the extreme variability of velocity.[3]

Could it be that special factors were at work in Japan? Unfortunately, the Japanese experience is no exception. For the US, a significant instability in the velocity of money was also found by many studies (such as Belongia and Chalfant, 1990). Although for most countries the stable relationship between M and P or M and PY proposed by equation (1) appeared to hold until the early 1970s, economists documented that it 'increasingly came apart at the seams during the course of the 1980s' (Goodhart, 1989a). This was especially noticeable in the US, the UK and Scandinavian countries, as well as in Japan and several other Asian countries.

In most cases, significant declines in velocity were observed in the 1980s. Given the tremendous importance of the stability of velocity or the 'money demand function', this finding naturally attracted much attention. A decline in the velocity meant that the money supply grew faster than nominal GDP. But where did the money go?

Dozens of academic papers tried to grapple with this 'anomaly', variously termed the 'velocity decline', the 'velocity problem' (Belongia and Chalfant, 1990), the 'breakdown of the money demand function' or the 'mystery of the missing money' (see the surveys by Goodhart, 1989; and Goldfeld and Sichel, 1990). Many researchers attempted to explain the velocity decline as being due to special factors, often difficult to quantify, such as institutional changes like financial liberalization and tax changes.[4] It was also argued that it may have been due to the wealth effect, although empirical evidence was not very supportive of this thesis (Santoni, 1987). In response, increasingly broader measures of the 'money supply' were used by researchers and central banks in an attempt to revive the stable relationship between money and GDP.

While M0 had previously been a preferred measure in the UK, the government and central bank quickly moved through a succession of favourite indicators, including M2, sterling M2, M3, even M4 and, finally, the so-called 'divisia money supply' index, which is a liquidity-weighted average of an even larger aggregate of private sector assets (see, for instance, Bank of England, 1996). There are rumours that even M25 is used around London...

Several central banks suggested that the measurement of the price level could also be broadened to include asset prices (see the Bank of Japan's Shibuya, 1991), or, along somewhat different lines, the so-called P* models applied by the Bundesbank (1992).

But all this switching between various M measures of the money supply was to no avail. The problem could not be eliminated. In the UK, the sterling M3 money demand function 'comprehensively collapsed' (Goodhart, 1989a), as this monetary aggregate expanded at a brisk 20% per annum in 1987/88, while nominal incomes rose only by about half as much.

Researchers found that in the US and the UK, money aggregates and income were not cointegrated and velocity was non-stationary.[5] The movement of monetary aggregates remained 'puzzling', in the words of Federal Reserve researchers (Burger, 1988). Henceforth economists and central bankers had to deal with the persistent problem of 'recurring bouts of instability in money demand' (Goldfeld and Sichel, 1990, p. 349). By the early 1990s, researchers concluded that in most industrialized countries the relationship between monetary aggregates and GDP had broken down: 'Once viewed as a pillar of macroeconomic models, it is now widely regarded as one of the weakest stones in the foundation' (Boughton, 1991).

As a result, most researchers have abandoned the ambition of finding a generally applicable measure of the money supply or a general explanation of the anomaly of an unstable velocity. The instability of velocity and the money demand function meant that central banks were not able to keep monetary aggregates 'under control'. The British government, in 1980 and 1981 still insisting that achieving the sterling M3 target was 'the absolute centerpiece of policy' (Goodhart, 1989a) had to abandon targets entirely by the mid-1980s. In the US, the Federal Reserve 'de-emphasized' M1 targeting in 1982 and abandoned formal targeting altogether in 1987.[6] Today, virtually all central banks monitor a large number of deposit aggregates, but often make clear that they give them a minor role in their policy-making.

Federal Reserve researchers resigned themselves to the fact that 'there is still no definitive answer in terms of all its final uses to the question: What is money?' (Belongia and Chalfant, 1990, p. 32).

Alan Greenspan, the Chairman of the Board of Governors of the Federal Reserve System, recently went on record with this assessment of the state of affairs:

> We have had an extraordinary difficulty in trying to find the right proxy to measure money per se, and none of these various measures – M2, M3, MZM – as best we can judge, seems to have the characteristics necessary for moneyness... as a consequence... we have not found, at least for the time being, money supply useful.[7]

Thus not only the challenge to solve the enigma of the velocity decline (and thus breakdown in the money demand function) remains to be solved, as Goodhart (1989a) emphasized: 'The breakdown of existing econometric relationships, e.g. in the form of demand-for-money functions... can be easily retold. What remains much harder is to explain just how, and why such breakdowns occurred' (p. 298). Even harder still seems the issue of identifying the type of money that is useful for analysts and policy-makers, and that has the 'characteristics necessary for moneyness', in Greenspan's words. Indeed, the question he seems to be asking is: 'Just what is money?' And this from the one whom many thought would know best.

The findings reported in this chapter are devastating for mainstream macroeconomics. The single pillar of all macroeconomic theories, the stable relationship between money and the economy, does not exist. Thus with one stroke it becomes clear that none of the mainstream macroeconomic theories are useful in explaining economic reality, let alone provide reliable policy advice. Worse, when it comes to empirical applications, economists and central bankers appear to have resigned themselves to the fact that they cannot even answer the question 'What is money?'

8
The Enigma of Japanese Asset Prices

Japanese asset prices have recorded significant declines since the late 1980s. The Nikkei index of 225 average stock prices dropped from a peak of ¥38,916 on 29 December 1989 to ¥7862 on 11 March 2003, a drop of 79.8%. Land prices also dropped sharply: since the first half of 1992, land prices have dropped relentlessly, usually falling at a double-digit pace. The semi-annual index of commercial land prices in the six major cities stood at 104.5 in the second half of 1990. By the first half of 2002 it had dropped to 15.9, the same level it had in the second half of 1979 (the figures had become so low that the statisticians decided to switch the base year). Peak to trough, this amounts to a fall of 84.8%. There have been many attempts at explaining such extraordinary and prolonged falls in asset prices. The only sensible explanation, however, remains that asset prices had simply been too high in the first place. Indeed, most observers recognize now that the recession of the 1990s has its roots in the events of the 1980s, especially its asset markets.[1]

That, however, leaves us with the enigma of explaining just why asset prices rose so extraordinarily during the 1980s. Figure 8.1 shows indices for GDP and consumer prices, with 1955 rebased to 100. Compared to this, the value of stocks listed on the Tokyo Stock Exchange are shown, as measured by the Nikkei index, and commercial real estate prices in the six major cities. As can be seen, there was an enormous expansion in the nominal stock of irreproducible assets, mainly land. While the consumer price index rose by less than 500% between 1955 and 1989, land prices increased by more than 5000% over the same period. The biggest rises took place in the late 1980s. We also notice that the volume of asset transactions expanded rapidly during the second half of the 1980s.

Due to its extraordinary appreciation, in 1991 land occupied an immensely large portion of the private sector net worth. According to the National Income Accounts, land wealth occupied 70% of Japan's total net worth, while it made up only about 25% of US net worth (Bradford, 1990).

134

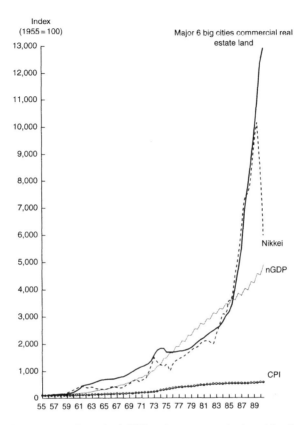

Figure 8.1 Comparison of nominal GDP and consumer, stock and land prices
Source: Japan Real Estate Institute; Nikkei Shinbun; Cabinet Office, Government of Japan.

In 20 years, total private sector land wealth multiplied by a factor of 14, rising from ¥14.2 trillion in 1969 to ¥2000 trillion in 1989. While there appeared to be a stable relationship of 1 : 1 between land value and GDP in several industrialized countries, the Japanese land value was twice as large as GDP in 1977 and by 1989 had reached a multiple of five (see Figure 8.2).

Table 8.1 compares a breakdown of tangible Japanese assets with those of the US at the end of 1988. The dominance of land in the Japanese case becomes apparent.

This meant that in 1989 all of Japan's land was valued at approximately four times the value of all property of the entire United States of America – despite the fact that Japan's land area is only 4% of that of the United States (one-twenty-fifth). An often quoted calculation at the end of the 1980s was that when the Imperial Palace garden was valued at the going prices of its

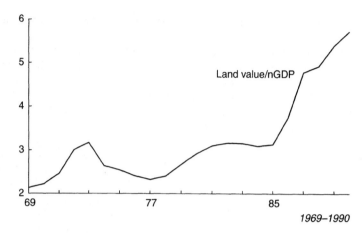

Figure 8.2   Land value/GDP ratio
Source: Cabinet Office, Government of Japan.

Table 8.1   Tangible assets as a percentage of GDP in the US and Japan in 1988

	US	Japan
Inventory	0.19	0.18
Houses, factories	1.61	2.20
Net external assets	−0.10	0.10
Land	0.67	5.15
Net national assets	2.70	7.63

Source: Nomura Research Institute, Tokyo.

central Marunouchi location, it was worth as much as all the property of the state of California, or all of Canada.

How do economic models explain the enormous rise of Japanese asset prices during the 1980s? Several researchers applied traditional asset pricing models to Japanese stock prices, such as French and Poterba (1991). Such asset pricing models use standard portfolio theory explanations, usually relying on interest rates as a key explanatory variable. However, they had to conclude that traditional models could not explain the surge in stock prices. Similarly, land prices had appreciated to an extent that defied economic reasoning and constituted a major puzzle. Noguchi (1990) found that land prices were detached from their theoretical value, imputed by mainstream asset pricing theory (see also Noguchi, 1992). Asako (1991) estimated that Japan's land price rise was too large even to qualify as a 'rational bubble'.

Despite the failure of standard asset pricing theory to explain asset prices in Japan – and many other countries during times of such a bubble – experts can still frequently be heard in the media asserting that the Japanese bubble in stock and land prices was due to excessively low interest rates. But the careful empirical studies cited above have demonstrated that this is not the case. Real and nominal interest rates did not fall significantly enough to be able to explain such enormous asset price rises. Most of all, the experience of the 1990s soundly rejects any attempt at explaining asset price rises of the 1980s with interest rates: short-term interest rates, as measured by the official discount rate, stood at a low of 2.5% from 1987 to 1989. That, many experts still claim, was what created the great Japanese asset price bubble. But if this was true, then the late 1990s should have seen an asset price bubble about 2500 times larger than the bubble of the 1980s: short-term interest rates fell to 0.001% – a two-thousand-five-hundredth of the rates recorded in the late 1980s. And there was no sign of an asset price bubble during the 1990s. Quite to the contrary, as we noted above, asset prices kept falling throughout the 1990s, with land prices falling still even in 2004.[2] While real interest rates did not fall quite as dramatically, they also fell below their levels of the 1980s. Thus it is once again clear that standard theories, and especially interest-rate-based explanations, fail to explain major events.

Other attempted explanations, such as that land prices were due to potentially higher Japanese 'land productivity', could not be empirically supported and were indeed contradicted by the fact that land was not mainly traded as a factor of production, but as an asset traded for speculative purposes (National Land Agency, 1990).

Economics could not explain the rise of asset prices during the 1980s in the second largest economy of the world. One could argue that Japan's asset price 'anomaly' was a special case. However, the puzzle of significant asset (especially real estate) price appreciations that went beyond the predictions of standard economic models also occurred in other countries. The literature increasingly is forced to deal with the mysterious phenomenon of 'asset inflation' or 'asset price bubbles', which seem quite frequently recurring events. These have been witnessed in most Scandinavian countries, in many Asian countries, in the UK and the US, among others – and usually with devastating consequences.[3] At the time of writing, the governor of the British central bank had just warned about UK house prices, which appear to be among the highest in the world. Indeed, the *Guinness Book of Records* entry for the most expensive housing transaction will now be held by a London property – the previous record was written by a property deal in Hong Kong in 1997 – at the peak of its housing bubble and just before a major collapse.

The literature has not explained the causes of these asset price bubbles. In each case, researchers tended to propose *ad hoc* explanations and relied on special factors to justify these mysteries that standard economic theory could not explain. However, such explanations lacked empirical support, and they failed to provide a general explanation of asset price bubbles – which is what we should be looking for. Thus the mystery of Japanese asset price movements remained unsolved.

9
The Enigma of Japanese Capital Flows in the 1980s

Another major 'anomaly' that economic theories had not been able to explain concerns Japanese capital flows in the 1980s and early 1990s. While capital flows are determined independently of the current account, balance of payments equilibrium implies that capital outflows counter-balance current account surpluses. These may either take the form of 'autonomous' capital flows (traditionally classified as long-term capital flows) or 'accommodating' capital flows (the short-term inter-bank capital flows). During the 1970s, the autonomous long-term capital outflows roughly matched the current account surplus (Figure 9.1).[1]

This meant that Japanese foreign currency earned from exports was 'recycled' back into the world in the form of Japanese foreign investment. In the 1980s, however, autonomous long-term capital outflows expanded faster than the current account surplus, by far exceeding it in size and preceding it in timing. Thus the Japanese basic balance was almost persistently negative in the 1980s.[2] While there was a capital inflow of US$2.3 billion in 1980, in 1982 US$15.0 billion was exported in long-term capital from Japan. Capital outflows accelerated, to reach a peak in 1987, when the long-term capital balance reached a historic record deficit of US$136.5 billion, exceeding the current account surplus by US$49.5 billion.

During the 1980s, Japanese indirect and direct foreign investment reached vast proportions and came to dominate world financial markets. Japan's share of net long-term capital outflows among the G7 countries plus traditional capital exporters Denmark, the Netherlands, Switzerland and Saudi Arabia rose from a quarter in 1982 to nearly 90% in 1987. In 1989, more than half of all foreign direct investment by these countries came from Japan. By that time Japan had become the biggest net creditor nation on record, easily surpassing previous US or OPEC surpluses at their peak.

Some readers will remember the significant impact this Japanese money was having on the world. Financial or real assets, including art objects and other valuables all over the world suddenly seemed to become the target of

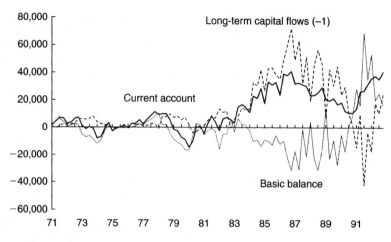

Figure 9.1   Japanese current account, long-term capital flows and the basic balance
Source: Bank of Japan.

Japanese buyers that appeared to have infinitely deep pockets. There were high-profile purchases, such as the Rockefeller Center, Columbia Pictures or Pebbles Beach Golf Course, but also many less well-known acquisitions of companies or real estate. California, Hawaii, Australia and the UK seemed particularly attractive to Japanese investors. Many factories were opened in Scotland, Wales and northern England.

This historic expansion of Japanese capital exports was, however, followed by an historic collapse: in 1991, virtually within the short period of one quarter, Japanese net capital exports suddenly vanished and the world's largest creditor nation turned into a net importer of capital. By 1993, as the current account was still heading for record highs, commentators complained that Japan's surplus was not fully 'recycled' through the long-term capital account.[3] Japanese money was in full-blown retreat. Many of the expensively-bought properties, company stakes and even factories were sold off or closed during the course of the 1990s.[4]

How could this extraordinary development of Japan's long-term capital account be explained by economic theory? Conventional portfolio balance approaches to the determination of long-term capital flows centre their explanation on the differential between expected foreign and domestic returns, changes in risk perception and risk aversion (see Branson, 1968). These effects, in practice often focusing on interest rate differentials and exchange rate expectations, are responsible for the stock adjustment of an aggregate international investment portfolio.

Although the extraordinary development of Japanese capital flows should have attracted widespread interest, surprisingly little work has been done on Japanese capital flows in the 1980s and early 1990s. What is more, the few existing studies mostly exhibited a remarkable lack of empirical success, despite the fact that none takes account of the precipitous collapse of foreign investment from 1990 onwards – which is even harder to explain. In the words of Balassa and Noland (1988), 'Econometric models of Japanese portfolio investment that emphasise the role of interest rate differentials, exchange risk, etc., have not been particularly successful in explaining the rapid growth of capital outflows' (Kawai, 1987; Ueda, 1987). Ueda (1990) and Kawai (1991) attempt to explain the foreign portfolio investment share of total financial assets. However, they did not find great empirical support.

Often, Japanese capital outflows increased, although the interest rate differential or its change would have indicated a reduction. During time periods when the yen appreciated significantly and consistently, investors continued to increase their overseas assets, thus incurring fairly immediate foreign exchange losses. Japanese capital flows seemed to defy economic rationality.

Other economists made recourse to *ad hoc* explanations, such as financial deregulation, the relaxation of capital controls and 'globalization' of Japanese financial markets as a reason for the surge in Japanese capital outflows. Indeed, exchange controls were gradually relaxed, starting with a major revision of the foreign-exchange law in December 1980 and proceeding with continuing relaxations of the foreign-asset ceilings which the authorities granted institutional investors. While this development may have played a role, it could only have been a minor one: Koo (1991) pointed out that the large Japanese institutional investors, such as pension funds and life insurance companies, persistently maintained foreign asset weights well below the statutory maximum ceilings. Moreover, explanations involving foreign asset ceilings say nothing about the underlying cause of observed capital flows.

While the surge of Japanese capital outflows remained an enigma to economic theory, the sudden and precipitous withdrawal of Japanese money from the rest of the world, as occurred in 1991 and 1992, could only dumbfound the theorists further. Using conventional economic theories and approaches, the movement of Japanese long-term capital flows in the 1980s and early 1990s remains a major mystery that has not been explained.

Once again, we find that Japan is not the only country that throws up such an enigma for standard theories. Already in decades before did international capital flows surge to such an extent that they seemed to defy economic logic. The two most gregarious examples are US capital outflows in the 1960s, and US capital outflows in the 1920s. The anomaly of US foreign investment in the 1960s was dubbed '*le défi américain*' at the time by French commentators who felt that US money was buying up important European assets and corporations. These capital flows also have not been explained empirically by traditional models. Again, an answer to these puzzles is required, and one that is general enough to explain not only events in Japan, but also, for instance, US capital flows in the 1960s. Mainstream theory offers no such answer.

10
The Enigma of Japanese
Bank Lending

Standard economic models assume that banks are financial intermediaries and as such rationally maximize their profits by minimizing risks and maximizing returns from asset allocation of their portfolio. Many economists have been arguing that the lending behaviour of banks during the 1990s has been in line with these models. Banks, it was argued, were not able to locate enough low-risk borrowers, so that overall credit growth failed to materialize. While there has been a dearth of empirical studies, it is conceivable that some empirical support could be found for this argument. Nevertheless, this explanation can only ever be a partial answer, since the true cause remains unexplained: why were there not enough low-risk borrowers?

Models of bank behaviour find it far harder to explain the development of bank lending during the 1980s. Bank lending rose by 9% year on year on average for every year during the second half of the 1980s. Especially bank lending to the real estate sector increased rapidly, rising by an annual average growth rate of 19% year on year between 1986 and 1990. Also lending to the construction sector and non-bank financial institutions rose rapidly. As a result, the share of bank lending to these three sectors (soon to be dubbed the 'bubble' sectors) more than doubled from 12% in the late 1970s to 28% in 1990. Its growth rate is shown in Figure 10.1.

Many commentators argued that such rapid bank lending growth was due to low interest rates, based on the mainstream interest rate theory. However, we have already found that careful international studies have rejected the 'liquidity effect', whereby low interest rates are supposed to be associated with high monetary growth and vice versa. As we saw in Chapter 6, Leeper and Gordon (1992) failed to find evidence for the liquidity effect and instead found that both causation and correlation were contrary to standard theory.

For our purposes, a simple scatter plot and time series graph will do to test the 'interest rate theory' of bank lending. Figure 10.2 shows the scatter plot between year-on-year growth of bank lending and the nominal short-term prime lending interest rate, in order to examine the nature of their correlation

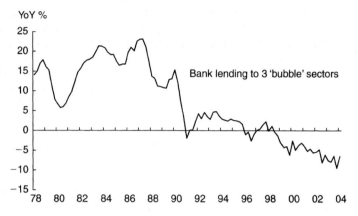

Figure 10.1   Annual growth rate of bank lending to the real estate, non-bank financial and construction industries

Source: Bank of Japan; Project Research Center.

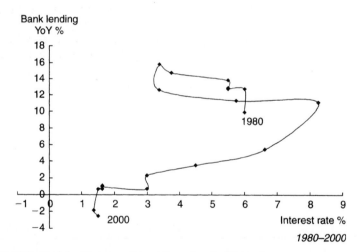

Figure 10.2   Bank lending growth and the prime lending rate

Source: Bank of Japan.

(to maintain clarity, only the annual averages are shown). As can be seen, over the 1980s and 1990s, bank lending was in no particular relationship with interest rates, certainly not a clear inverse relationship as mainstream theory proclaims. During the 1980s, bank lending growth varied little, remaining in the narrow band of between 10% and 16% year-on-year growth. However, interest rates varied between 3% and 8%.

The experience of the 1990s demonstrated that far lower interest rates could not stimulate bank lending to the contrary, during the 1990s there appeared to be a positive relationship between bank lending growth and nominal interest rates. In other words, higher interest rates seemed associated with higher bank lending growth and lower rates with lower growth.

We must conclude that, similar to Leeper and Gordon's (1992) finding on interest rates and money supply, there is little empirical support linking bank credit growth negatively with interest rates. It almost seems as if loan growth occurred irrespective of interest rates. Moreover, as we already pondered, if interest rates explained bank lending, then why did banks not lend more during the 1990s, when interest rates were far lower?

Similarly, in terms of timing we find little evidence that interest rate changes occur before significant changes in the pattern of bank lending. Figure 10.3 shows the time series graphs for the same data. Bank lending growth accelerated in 1985, before lending rates fell. Similarly, bank lending growth decelerated in 1987, although lending rates had not risen yet. Indeed, since the peak in 1987, bank lending growth seems to have decelerated, irrespective of what interest rates have done since. If anything, one could even hypothesize that interest rates follow bank lending (similar to our earlier finding that interest rates follow economic growth).

Considering bank lending and other interest rates, such as the call rate or long-term bond yields, it is also empirically difficult to establish a negative correlation between interest rates and bank lending growth. Figure 10.4 plots the growth rate of bank lending (of the four main bank types, namely

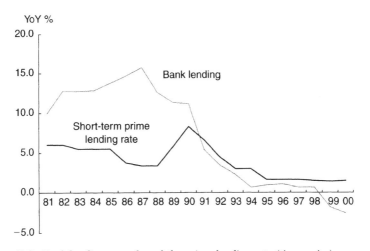

Figure 10.3 Bank lending growth and the prime lending rate (time series)

Ten-year JGB yield %

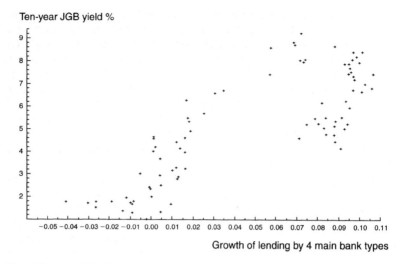

Figure 10.4   Bank lending and long-term nominal interest rates

Overnight call rate % (u/c)

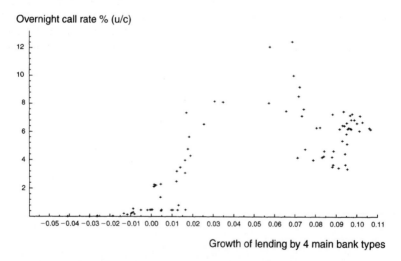

Figure 10.5   Bank lending and short-term nominal interest rates

city banks, trust banks, long-term credit banks and regional banks) against the ten-year benchmark government bond (JGB) yield during the 1980s and 1990s. Figure 10.5 does the same against the uncollateralized overnight call rate. As can be seen, there is little evidence of a negative correlation.

Attempts to sustain the argument by using real interest rates appear more promising, but also fail, as deflation was also recorded during the second half of the 1980s. Thus even real interest rates (both long and short) have declined significantly during the 1990s without a commensurate increase in bank lending. Thus the same kind of positive correlation between bank lending growth and interest rates is also found when considering real interest rates (calculated by subtracting consumer price inflation from nominal interest rates). This is illustrated in Figure 10.6, where bank lending growth and real call rates are shown in a scatter plot.

These findings suggest that the standard interest rate theory faces some fundamental problems, despite its predominance in textbooks, the financial media and statements by central bankers. Furthermore, it means that we have not yet found the actual factor that determines bank lending, for if rates follow lending, then they cannot at the same time cause it.

Others have attempted to explain parts of bank lending with the rising land prices of the 1980s (Yoshino, 1991; Shimizu, 2000).[1] Indeed, there is empirical support for a link between land prices and bank lending (see Yoshino, 1991; Werner, 1992, 1997d; Shimizu, 2000). However, there is doubt as to Shimizu's claim that causation runs unilaterally from land prices to bank lending. He reports some evidence that loan growth variables also have an effect on land prices (Shimizu, 2000, p. 88). Moreover, Shimizu finds that during the 1990s the claimed causal relationship between land prices and bank loans 'disappears'. Most of all, any argument that explains bank

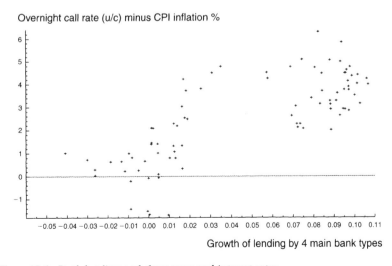

Figure 10.6 Bank lending and short-term real interest rates

lending with land prices must also provide a convincing rationale for the determination of land prices. Shimizu leaves this issue open, except for the somewhat inconsistent admission that bank lending may also be a factor.[2]

The surge of bank lending during the 1980s was not clearly explained by traditional theories. It is yet another enigma that requires explanation. And as in earlier cases, we also find parallels in other countries. In both Korea and Thailand, among others, bank lending to the real estate sector, as well as overall bank lending rose rapidly during the first half of the 1990s. It was difficult to explain bank behaviour with traditional variables, such as interest rates. What is the solution to this puzzle?

11
The Enigma of Banking and its Recurring Crises

During the 1990s, many economists have argued that Japan possesses too many banks. The financial press has referred to both Japan and Germany as seriously 'over-banked' economies, with the helpful advice that banks should be merged, sold to foreign investors or closed down. However, in order to come to this conclusion, it is necessary to understand the actual role of banks in economies. While the layperson may assume that economists have long solved this issue, in fact the very existence of banks has remained an enigma according to the mainstream theories.

Those economics textbooks that actually still feature banks (many don't), represent them as financial intermediaries which are not different from others, such as stockbrokers or capital market participants (see, for instance, Miller and VanHoose, 1993). Their function, we are told, is to intermediate between savers (depositors) and investors (borrowers). This is usually represented as shown in Figure 11.1. With banks being considered mere intermediaries, funding from banks is commonly called 'indirect financing', while funding from the capital markets is considered 'direct', as the buyers of debt or equity papers effectively lend directly to the firms that borrow. An increase in this so-called direct financing is said to constitute 'disintermediation', since the alleged intermediary function of banks is not required.

Given such a view of banking, it becomes difficult, however, to explain why banks exist at all, or why they should be different from other financial intermediaries. This may also explain why economists have not spent much time researching banks: firstly, they do not exist in many deductive theories and, according to these theories, should not exist in reality; and secondly, according to these theories banks should become extinct soon, since increasing deregulation and liberalization of financial markets and the resulting 'disintermediation' renders them even more obsolete. As a result, the latest textbooks in monetary economics tend to leave out banking entirely (see, for instance, Walsh, 2003).

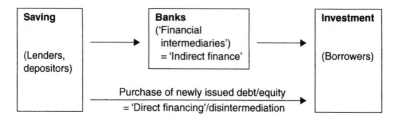

Figure 11.1　The textbook representation of banks as mere intermediaries

Yet despite the frequent predictions by deductivist economists that banks will disappear, they continue to play a substantial role in virtually all economies of this world. So how can their existence be explained?

According to the textbook by Blanchard and Fischer (1989), the notion that there is something about banks that makes them 'special' is a 'recurrent theme'. To explain their existence, it is indeed necessary to identify a special feature that only banks can perform. Fama (1985) conducted empirical research on CP and CD markets and concluded that the banking industry must have some monopoly power compared to other financial institutions. But what is it that makes banks special and gives them such power?

Many theories of financial intermediation try to account for the existence of institutions that take deposits and issue funds to firms through the occurrence of transaction costs and asymmetric information. Economists have postulated that due to these, funding in borrowers and lenders' portfolio are imperfectly substitutable. But as we saw in Chapter 3, the Japanese experience contradicts such arguments: a credit crunch existed, although many non-bank financial intermediaries, including from abroad were theoretically able to step in. As we saw, the 'credit channel' or credit rationing views that small firms are credit rationed, remain empirical concepts in search for a simple and compelling explanation why this should have such a large impact on the economy. Indeed, as Allen and Santomero (1997) have pointed out, there is evidence that transaction costs and asymmetric information have declined over recent decades, yet intermediation has increased: 'New markets for financial futures and options are mainly markets for intermediaries rather than individuals or firms. These changes are difficult to reconcile with the traditional theories.'

Sheard (1989), Aoki (1994), Okazaki and Okuno-Fujiwara (1999), among others, argue that banks may be able to engage in closer monitoring of companies. This is said to have led to the development of bank-centred finance and corporate government structures, which allegedly reduce the cost of financial distress (Hoshi, 1994) or share risk (Sheard, 1994). However, researchers such as Caves and Uekusa (1976), Agarwal and Elston (2001) and

Fohlin (1999) have found little empirical support for these postulated features of banks. Others have found that such considerations were irrelevant in the actual decision-making process that led to the introduction of bank-centred economic structures in Japan (Werner, 2003d).

Kashyap et al. (1999) conclude that despite much theoretical and also empirical analysis, so far the literature has not yet adequately explained why the two commercial banking activities of deposit-taking and lending are conducted by one institution carrying out both functions 'under the same roof'.[1]

Put simply, economists cannot explain why banks exist or why only they apparently possess some special quality that gives them monopoly power over certain markets. The investigative researcher, in other words the inductivist, would take this challenge as encouragement to spend more time on researching banks, and how they operate and function, in order to find out just why they do exist – which we will do in the following chapter.

The enigma of the recurring banking crises

Given that economists know so little about banks, it is perhaps less surprising that they also have had difficulties in explaining why banks repeatedly become the centre of major banking and financial crises that have engulfed a large number of economies.

Systemic banking sector crises, involving significant corporate and financial distress and economic dislocation have occurred in many countries during the past quarter century. Caprio and Klingebiel (1999) identified 93 countries in which a systemic financial crisis occurred during the 1980s and 1990s, of which five were in industrial countries and the remainder in the developing world. Well-known examples include the crises among Scandinavian countries in the 1990s, the prolonged Japanese crisis of the 1990s, the Mexican crisis of 1994, the so-called Asian financial crisis involving Thailand, Korea, Indonesia and Malaysia, and crises in transition economies.

A common feature of financial crises has been that they typically resulted in large-scale resource misallocation and deadweight losses to society. This takes the form of non-performing loans (NPLs), bankruptcies, deteriorating economic performance, unemployment and a high fiscal burden (the latter often as the result of the post-crisis reform policies). In Scandinavia, for instance, loan losses incurred by banks in Finland, Norway, and Sweden amounted to 4.2–6.7% of GDP in 1991/92 (Sheng, 1996). Primary bad debts in the banking system exceeded 25% of total loans in Japan in the 1990s (Werner, 1999h) and amounted to as much as 55–60% in transition economies (Sheng, 1992). Wealth losses, including the subsequent loss of GDP growth, often reaches vast proportions, such as almost 30% for Chile in 1982, or the even larger cost of Japan's 'lost decade' of the 1990s. Table 11.1 compares key features of the Scandinavian and Mexican crises with that of the East Asian countries in 1998.

Table 11.1   Common features of systemic banking crises

Country	Crisis year	Fiscal cost (% of GDP)	Peak NPLs (% of loans)	Real GDP growth (%)
Finland	1992	11.0	13	−4.6
Indonesia	1998	50.0	65–75	−15.4
Korea	1998	37.0	30–40	−10.6
Malaysia	1998	16.4	25–35	−12.7
Mexico	1995	19.3	30	−6.2
Philippines	1998	0.5	20	−0.8
Sweden	1992	4.0	18	−3.3
Thailand	1998	32.8	33	−5.4

Source: Figures and definitions from Claessens et al. (2001).

It is frequently argued that banks' tendency to 'borrow short' and 'lend long' is a cause for crises. It is referred to as a 'term mismatch' or 'maturity mismatch'.[2] It is apparent that bank assets tend to be less liquid, and therefore banks face a solvency crisis if a large part of the liabilities is suddenly withdrawn. A number of studies have pointed out that this is a cause for crises, such as Kindleberger (1978), Minsky (1982), Hinds (1988), Davis (1989) and Sundararajan and Balino (1991). The international organizations have thus argued that crises can be avoided by reducing the reliance on banking systems entirely, and instead relying on bond markets.

Although there has been a variety of policy responses to these crises, in the majority of cases, post-crisis policies centred on banking sector restructuring. This has been especially the case when funding from international organizations was involved, since the usual bank reform package is a staple component of IMF 'conditionality'. However, it is also often part of post-crisis reforms implemented independently by domestic governments (such as in the case of Japan or Sweden). Such bank sector reform is here defined as a package of microeconomic, institutional and regulatory reforms aiming at addressing problems in the banking sector and restoring its solvency and health.[3] While the declared goal of banking reforms is the restoration of the health of the banking system in order to revive overall economic activity, more often than not these goals were not achieved and the adopted policies seem to have worsened both the state of the banking sector and the economy.

The enigma of the link between finance and growth

Although much has been written about financial crises, little work has been done about the precise link between bank sector reform and macroeconomic performance and what type of coordinated policies are most desirable from a social welfare cost–benefit perspective. In the words of Claessens et al. (2001): 'In spite of much analysis, the tradeoffs along these dimensions are still not well known, leading at times to conflicting policy advice and possibly larger than necessary economic costs' (p. 2). Some studies do recognize a linkage between bank reform and macroeconomic performance and the need for some form of policy coordination (such as Claessens et al., 2001). Despite the fact that much of the bank reform literature fails to deal adequately with the reasons for the development of banking crises in the first place (again, see Claessens et al., 2001, for an example), the issues involved are represented as being almost intractable and ultimately the precise nature of the link between bank restructuring and macroeconomic performance remains unspecified.

While such a link is frequently observed and commented on – whether in the context of the Asian financial crisis of 1997/98, the Latin American crisis of the present, the 1990s or the 1980s, or the US bank crisis of the late 1980s – its precise nature remains unclear. Meanwhile, apart from the crisis and bank reform literature, there is a growing body of work that recognizes a potential link between the state of the banking sector and overall macroeconomic stability. Recent research such as reviewed in IBRD (2001) and Vittas et al. (2002) suggests a significant correlation between the 'real sector' of the economy and the performance of the financial sector. Levine and Renelt (1992), Faruqi (1994) and Levine (1997) argue that the development of the financial sector is associated with stronger real sector performance. Such findings are consistent with earlier theoretical and empirical models that link finance to economic development, including Gurley and Shaw (1955, 1960), Goldsmith (1969), Shaw (1973), McKinnon (1973) and Fry (1978, 1980, 1984). Just like the crisis and bank reform literature, the more general finance literature and the 'finance and development' literature have failed to render the link between the financial sector and macroeconomic performance explicit. Since textbooks treat banks as mere financial intermediaries, akin to mutual funds and capital markets, it is thought that investors should be able to raise funds in the capital markets.

The only reason cited in the finance literature why there could be a special link between banks and macroeconomic performance is the so-called 'credit channel' or 'credit view' approach, which assumes capital market imperfections that render borrowing from banks imperfectly substitutable with so-called 'direct financing' in the capital markets (see, for instance, Kashyap et al., 1993).[4] If evidence for such imperfect substitutability of bank funding with other forms of financing is found, for instance in the form of a credit crunch, then this is considered confirmation of the view that the capital market structure is not efficient enough and, like the banking sector, requires structural change and reform.[5] Thus when banking sector reform further reduced the supply of bank loans in developing countries, exacerbating the economic and financial crisis, this was frequently interpreted as proof of how inefficient, backward and underdeveloped the financial sector was and just how badly broad and far-reaching financial sector reforms were needed. This often strengthened the conviction of researchers that no further analysis of the causes of banking crises (and their mysteriously frequent occurrence) is necessary – for the very fact that the systems are in crisis is seen as evidence of their inefficiency.

The banking sector and its recurring crises thus adds another major enigma to our list of puzzles to be solved. Furthermore, while empirical literature in this area has found a link between finance on the one hand and economic growth and development on the other, the finance theories have also not provided conclusive insights into the specific nature of this link and the specific role played by banks in it.

Part III
Explanations: Applying the New Paradigm

Knowledge and wisdom in economics

What is the quest that economists have embarked upon? If it is to find knowledge about how the economy works, and to gain wisdom about how economies should be operated, then how should they go about it? Looking up these two words in the *Oxford English Dictionary*, we find:

knowledge
● **noun 1** information and skills acquired through experience or education. **2** the sum of what is known. **3** awareness or familiarity gained by experience of a fact or situation. (*Compact Oxford English Dictionary*)

wisdom
● **noun 1** experience and knowledge together with the power of applying them critically or practically. (*Concise Oxford Dictionary of English*)

The very meanings of these words give us important information about how one should acquire knowledge and wisdom concerning the economy. Two of the three definitions of knowledge refer to the inductive research method when it comes to gaining primary knowledge, namely the acquisition of information and skills through experience of reality, and the awareness or familiarity gained by experience – this is a general description of what amounts to empirical research in our context. The third definition, the sum of what is known, would normally also derive from inductive learning, as Mill (1834) showed. However, if universities and centres of learning teach exclusively a body of deductive economics that places low priority on experience and empirical evidence, then this so-called 'sum of what is known' may end up being based largely on deductive, theoretical reasoning. In this case, with few 'reality checks', there is no guarantee that the 'sum of what is known' will amount to much. Modern mainstream equilibrium economics can at best lay claim to only one of three definitions of knowledge.

Meanwhile, knowledge only forms one part of wisdom. Wisdom, according to the Oxford dictionary, is the combination of experience (which is named first), knowledge, and critical and practical application. Therefore we find that the very meanings of the words 'knowledge' and 'wisdom' suggest that researchers should adopt the inductive research methodology. A purely deductive methodology may produce experts who are very clever, but lack relevant knowledge and have no wisdom at all.

Paradigm shift

Thomas Kuhn (1962) argued in his account of the growth of scientific knowledge that researchers operate within generally accepted 'paradigms'. The process of shifting to a new, more advanced paradigm is not necessarily smooth, as the old paradigm is supported by vested interests. Nevertheless,

Kuhn argues that shifts to a new paradigm tend to happen when the received theory or approach, consisting of a set of assumptions and procedures, suffers from an increasing number of what he calls 'anomalies' – facts that the old paradigm is unable to explain. The initial reaction by defenders of the old paradigm is to patch up the received theory through *ad hoc* assumptions or adjustments. However, as the number of inexplicable facts rises, the call for a new paradigm becomes louder. Eventually the old theory is replaced by a new paradigm which must fulfil the requirement of explaining at least as much as the previous approach, and in addition also accounts for the many 'anomalies' of the old paradigm. Similarly, Lakatos (1970), who suggested the concept of scientific research programmes that are based on a hard core of provisionally accepted assumptions, argues that a research programme should be rejected, if another programme can explain everything its rival can explain, but also those facts the rival could not (see Backhouse, 1985, or Hay, 1989, for a discussion of economic methodology). Such 'encompassing' is indeed the test for any new approach that wishes to replace the old. Nevertheless, Lakatos also provided an insightful description of the strategies pursued by supporters of the 'old paradigm' in order to 'protect' their 'core' beliefs against contrary empirical evidence.

Anomalies and enigmas

We have seen that there are many puzzles and anomalies that current economic theories cannot explain. If these instances involved a country of the size of the Principality of Liechtenstein or Panama, they might easily be dismissed by defenders of orthodox economics as mere exceptions that prove the rule. However, they involve the second largest economy in the world. Furthermore, they are found in many other economies as well.

Part II of this book has introduced some of the more egregious 'anomalies' that standard economic theories could not explain. Japanese asset prices could not be explained by standard theories, and neither could Japanese capital flows. A ten-year recession with more than 5 million unemployed, as happened in Japan from 1992 onwards, has remained a mystery and made sport of the neoclassical contention that the economy always operates at full employment. References to long-run equilibrium wore thin after a few years. Similarly, the structural policy advice derived from new classical theories failed to pass the test of reality: there is no evidence that structural changes have helped in the short term or the long term, or that they were actually the cause of the recession.

Keynesian, fiscalist and monetarist advice did not fare much better: the monetary transmission mechanism via interest rates appeared to have broken down. The 'liquidity trap' argument failed to explain why this situation came about and the policy advice to boost the economy via fiscal spending has also not resulted in the desired outcome. Since the stability of velocity was the foundation of all the major macroeconomic theories, its collapse brought them down with it.

Indeed, there is international evidence that interest rates are not the key explanatory variable that mainstream theory makes them out to be. In empirical work, interest rate variables often lack explanatory power. And as we saw, when there is a correlation between interest rates and economic growth, it is more likely to be a positive one. Furthermore, interest rates appear to follow economic activity, not lead it. This suggests quite a different world from the one that we are daily being presented with by central bankers who make announcements about their interest rate policies.

Given this state of affairs concerning present-day macroeconomics, many researchers have called for 'an alternative paradigm' (Judd and Scadding, 1982; Gordon, 1984; Roley, 1985; Spindt, 1987). These calls for a 'new paradigm' have become much louder since then, thanks to the work by Joseph Stiglitz and associates (see Stiglitz, 2001; Stiglitz and Greenwald, 2003). Nothing less is needed: these facts suggest that the edifice constructed by millions of pages of macroeconomics books and articles in learned journals is not built on firm foundations. This also means that economists should be open-minded about alternative approaches that may be able to explain the anomalies of the old. Indeed, the slow but steady rise of non-mainstream theories over the past 20 years, including institutional economics, experimental economics and psychological economics, suggests that momentum is building up in favour of a paradigm shift. What, then, would be the key features of an alterative approach?

The return of inductivism

We found that the main macroeconomic theories have two features in common, apart from their insufficient empirical track record. Firstly, they share the deductive research methodology which does not primarily base the development of theories on empirical observation, but instead emphasizes axioms and theoretical postulates that may be far removed from reality. The predominance of this methodology is virtually unique among the academic disciplines. Secondly, they are based on the traditional quantity equation linking money to the economy.

There are good reasons why the natural sciences are based on the inductive research method. Of course, the inductive research method does not exclude deductive processes. In fact, inductivism uses deductive logic, but it places priority on empirical data and has sequenced research tasks such that empirical work is allowed to lay the foundation for the development of theories, which are then also tested, suitably modified and applied to reality. Such an approach meets the criteria for gaining knowledge and wisdom far better than deductivism, which has dominated economics in the English language. Nevertheless, if deductive mainstream economics had been empirically successful, one might have wished to tolerate its unusual methodology. However, the fact that major challenges exist to the fundamental tenets of macroeconomics means that the deductive approach cannot be sustained.

This is not to say that deductive, mainstream economics has not served any purpose. As we saw in the Prologue, it has taught us many things, including how highly unrealistic the theoretical environment must be in order to obtain market clearing and a situation where government intervention in markets will always be inefficient. Furthermore, mainstream economics has developed a rich tool-kit for the economic sciences, which will prove useful also for the new paradigm. Also, it has proven far more fruitful in microeconomics and applied disciplines, including finance. Thus there can be no doubt that mainstream economics has advanced knowledge. However, economists should aspire to acquiring a degree of wisdom.

The empirical approach of a new paradigm requires data. By the time data becomes available, it is about the past. Thus history provides the data set upon which theories should be built. The solutions offered in this part of the book are the result of years of conducting empirical research according to the inductive methodology, and the desire to explain the true cause of things, as best as possible, without being beholden to any preconceived idea or ideological blinkers.

12
Solving the Enigma of Banking and Money

To solve the enigma of why banks exist, and to understand their role in the economy properly, it is necessary to find out what makes them special and why others, for instance brokers or non-bank intermediaries, cannot easily perform the same functions. Fama (1980) argues that one of the two main functions of banks is the provision of transactions and accounting services. Together with the central bank, they serve as the settlement system of non-cash transactions in the economy. This has long been recognized, such as by Schumpeter (1912, 1917/18), who describes the banking system as the 'central settlement bureau, a kind of clearing house or bookkeeping center for the economic system' (1934, p. 124). Thus to him banks and the central bank perform the function of a 'social accounting and clearing system' of the economy.[1] This feature must indeed be important, since non-cash transactions constitute the majority of all transactions in the economy. It is also what banking systems have usually had in common over the past 5000 years. In Japan, transactions amounting to about 70% of annual GDP are settled through the banking system (and thus through the central bank) every single day.[2] Thus the volume of annual transactions in Japan amounts to over ¥100,000 trillion. Notes and coins amount to an average outstanding balance of ¥62.1 trillion.[3] This means that less than 5%, most likely between 1% and 2%, of all transactions takes place in cash.[4] The rest is settled as non-cash transfers. Since even non-bank financial institutions, such as credit card companies, ultimately settle their accounts through the banking system, virtually all non-cash payments are settled in the accounts of banks (and the central bank).[5]

The accounting and settlement feature alone is not sufficient, however, to explain the pivotal role banks have been playing in economic systems – after all, there are specialized accounting firms, and bookkeepers, or scribes, have existed outside the banking system for thousands of years. As Fama (1980), suggests, this first feature is likely to become important due to its interaction with a second feature, so that together a unique combination comes about. What is this second feature?

161

In search of the second key feature of banks

Fama's (1980) answer is that banks are special, because they combine this accounting and transaction role with portfolio management services. Goodhart (1989b) notes that 'it is this joint role that is often held to give a special character to banking and to require special treatment for banks through the establishment of a Central Bank' (p. 181). However, he points out that 'in their role as portfolio managers, banks have much in common with other intermediaries acting in this capacity' (p. 181). In this sense, Fama's proposed second feature is not 'special'. Neither does the combination of the two features produce anything that cannot be or is not offered by other service providers. We must therefore look for another special feature that may interact with the accounting and settlement function to produce a unique quality. The mainstream literature, but even more recent approaches such as the 'credit view' or information economics, has failed to provide conclusive answers.

The appropriate methodology to solve this puzzle is the inductive method and empirical research. Thus a closer look at the history of banking becomes necessary. If this yields an important feature of banks that, together with their accounting role, makes them 'special', then this explanation should also account for the observation that banks tend to flourish with economies and that banking sector growth tends to be correlated with economic growth and expansion. Further, in many countries banks appear to be doing so well that they become major owners or controlling forces in key industries (such as J. P. Morgan in US history, or German, French and Japanese banks in their respective economies).

The reality of banking

Mainstream economics and finance books give the impression that historically, early societies moved from barter to commodity money, and then to precious metals and coins. Banking and other financial institutions and financial instruments are often treated as a recent phenomenon. Coined money, whether made from precious or base metals, is usually considered the starting point for models of money and the economy. These models were updated to account for central banking by simply replacing coined cash or precious metals with paper notes issued by the central bank. In line with this view, many modern theories emphasize 'cash' and 'narrow money' indicators, even though cash transactions account for a small percentage of all transactions (usually less than 5%). It is with such analysis in mind that the 'quantity equation' was developed, linking such cash money to economic activity.

Banks were thus of secondary – or no – interest to economists. They were usually described – if mentioned at all – as devices to economize on cash, providing services as financial intermediaries and thus merely working as tools to increase the efficiency of the ultimately money-based economic system. Fisher (1926) incorporated banks in his quantity equation, but distinguished between 'primary money' and bank deposits or deposit notes, which are 'not money' (p. 11). Keynes (1930) and others proceeded to aggregate 'money proper' and 'bank money', in the form of deposits. As a result, mainstream textbooks have treated banks until this day as intermediaries that facilitate the exchange of goods and services, but that do not through their activity have a systematic effect on prices or quantities in the economy. Schumpeter's observation of over half a century ago still holds:

> Even today, textbooks on Money, Currency, and Banking are more likely than not to begin with an analysis of a state of things in which legal-tender 'money' is the only means of paying and lending. (Schumpeter, 1954, p. 717)

From such analysis also springs the implicit suggestion that coined money came first, and banks were developed later. But such explanations could only become the perceived wisdom, because economists were not sufficiently engaged in empirical research. Today historians have demonstrated – though little-known to most economists – that banking came about much earlier, and credit transactions most likely preceded the development of money: 'banking operation...preceded coinage by well over a thousand years, and so did private banking houses by some hundreds of years' (Davies, 1994, p. 49).

Banking was widespread throughout Mesopotamia in the third millennium BC. Metal coinage was only to be developed much later and elsewhere, in the seventh century BC.[6] Banking thus was a complete substitute for coinage in Sumeria and Babylon, which were basically bank-based credit economies.[7] What is meant with banking here is not some rudimentary Stone Age type of conception, but the very same type of banking transactions that modern banks engage in: deposit banking, unsecured and secured loan operations, bank transfers, giro settlement of debts, bill discounting, foreign exchange – these banking operations are recorded on thousands of cuneiform clay tablets.[8] Babylon was the flourishing banking centre of the region, with advanced financial markets, including financial products such as futures, and legislation regulating financial transactions.[9] Temples, royal palaces and private firms operated banks, which were at the heart of the economy. Bankers' activities extended beyond taking deposits and lending money at interest to include trade, mining, production and tax farming (the purchase of tax collection privileges from the government, whereby the collectors were remunerated by any excess takings). Bankers funded governments and military campaigns.

The Athenian economy of classical Greece was also characterized by flourishing deposit banking houses at least since the fifth century BC (Cohen, 1992).

In Ptolemaic Egypt 'payments were effected by transfer from one account to another, without money passing' (Rostovtzeff, 1941, quoted by Davies, 1994, pp. 52ff). Papyri served for bookkeeping and receipt issuance. The bank books distinguished credit and debit entries.[10] A central bank was established in Alexandria. Next, 'Rome and Constantinople became the main inheritors of the banking wisdom of the ancient world' (Davies, 1994, p. 91). Banking has existed in Rome since at least 310 BC. Wax-covered writing tablets served as deposit or loan receipts and the collateralization of land to secure loans played an important role. With bankers becoming influential senators and vice versa, links to the political leadership were apparent and controversial – Julius Caesar was involved in banking himself (Andreau, 1999).[11] Between the third and sixth centuries AD banking houses are known to have existed in Europe in the form of deposit-taking silversmiths (Andreau, 1999). Meanwhile, bankers have been instrumental in the rapid economic development of China since the Song Dynasty of the tenth century. The Mongolian empire spread advanced banking practices across much of Euroasia. Finally, over the past millennium, banking dynasties have played a major and well-documented economic and political role in the whole of Europe. To name a few, there were Italian bankers who at one stage dominated European banking, influential banking houses in the Low Countries, and even organizations such as the Knights Templar who engaged in sophisticated, international banking activities, beginning in the eleventh century. Bills of exchange were 'discounted' by banking houses to circumvent the ban on charging interest (usury). In England, an ancient form of issuing receipts were the wooden 'tallies', eight- or nine-inch-long sticks carved from hazel, with notches to mark different amounts. They acted as bills of exchange and stimulated banking activities for centuries.[12]

Wars were often funded by banks, whether it was William of Orange's invasion of Britain or Napoleon's international campaigns. Indeed, a cursory survey of the history of banking appears to coincide with the history of the rise (and fall) of advanced economies and empires. There are few advanced civilizations that did not use credit systems. Sparta appears to have been one such exception, which perhaps contributed to the rivalry perceived by banking-dominated Athens. In almost all cases, these banking systems led to the development of economies dominated by non-cash and non-money transactions. Petty transactions for day-to-day expenses by the ordinary population were usually conducted with the use of commodity money or cash, as they are today. But these amounted to a small fraction of total transaction values.

Banking, we thus find, has been at the heart of human economic activity for thousands of years. It has also been an important aspect of the political economy, and via its link to warfare contributed to reshaping world history. Given these facts, we should expect banking to either constitute the crucial link between the monetary/financial side and the 'real economy' or at least provide a major illumination of it. So why have banking activities been neglected for so long by economists?[13] When banks were analysed, they were viewed merely as extensions of the 'money'-based structures postulated by deductive theory. In Schumpeter's (1954) words:

> The huge system of credits and debits, of claims and debts, by which capitalist society carries on its daily business of production and consumption is...built up step by step by introducing claims to money or credit instruments that act as substitutes for legal tender and are allowed indeed to affect its functioning in many ways but not to oust it from its fundamental role in the theoretical picture of the financial structure... The legal constructions, too ... were geared to a sharp distinction between money as the only genuine and ultimate means of payment and the credit instrument that embodied a claim to money. But logically, it is by no means clear that the most useful method is to start from the coin...in order to proceed to the credit transactions of reality. It may be more useful to start from these in the first place, to look upon capitalist finance as a clearing system that cancels claims and debts and carries forward the differences – so that 'money' payments come in only as a special case without any particularly fundamental importance. (p. 717)[14]

To identify the other special feature of banks, we need to research how banks came about. While so far too few clay tablets have been found or translated to answer this question in the case of the first banking systems in Babylon, we can use the case study of more recent introductions of banking systems, such as the development of the goldsmith bankers in London. Since they were banks in every sense, the key empirical features of their development should lend themselves to a degree of abstraction and generalization.

Chinese paper money

However, first a brief look at an alternative financial system will be useful, in order to put banks into sharper contrast. This is the monetary system of the Mongol Empire, including China, as it is described in the thirteenth century. Marco Polo was a trained merchant, and his description of Kublai Khan's financial system is highly illuminating. The Khan's government issued paper money, which was legal tender. It appears that the majority of transactions were actually transacted through this paper money. In this case, it is apparent that the definition for money in any quantity equation would be the stock of paper money issued by the government's mint. Thus the government was directly in control of the money supply and could stimulate demand by creating more paper money, or slow the economy by taking paper out of circulation. This was done through 'open market operations', which are also described by Polo. The description is well worth citing at length:

It is in this city of Khan-balik that the Great Khan has his mint; and it is so organized that you might well say that he has mastered the art of alchemy. I will demonstrate this to you here and now. You must know that he has money made for him ... out of the bark of trees – to be precise, from mulberry trees (the same whose leaves furnish food for silkworms) ... all these papers are sealed with the seal of the Great Khan. The procedure of issue is as formal and as authoritative as if they were made of pure gold or silver. On each piece of money several specially appointed officials write their names, each setting his own stamp. When it is completed in due form, the chief of the officials deputed by the Khan dips in cinnabar the seal or bull assigned to him and stamps it on the top of the piece of money so that the shape of the seal in vermilion remains impressed upon it. And then the money is authentic. And if anyone were to forge it, he would suffer the extreme penalty.

Of this money the Khan has such a quantity made that with it he could buy all the treasure in the world. With this currency he orders all payments to be made throughout every province and kingdom and region of his empire. And no one dares refuse it on pain of losing his life. And I assure you that all the peoples and populations who are subject to his rule are perfectly willing to accept these papers in payment, since wherever they go they pay in the same currency, whether for goods or for pearls or precious stones or gold or silver. With these pieces of paper they can buy anything and pay for anything ...

Several times a year parties of traders arrive with pearls and precious stones and gold and silver and other valuables, such as cloth of gold and silk, and surrender them all to the Great Khan. The Khan then summons twelve experts, who are chosen for the task and have special knowledge of it, and bids them examine the wares that the traders have brought and pay for them what they judge to be their true value. The twelve experts duly examine the wares and pay the value in the paper currency of which I have spoken. The traders accept it willingly, because they can spend it afterwards on the various goods they buy throughout the Great Khan's dominions ...

Let me tell you further that several times a year a fiat goes forth through the towns that all those who have gems and pearls and gold and silver must bring them to the Great Khan's mint. This they do, and in such abundance that it is past all reckoning; and they are all paid in paper money. By this means the Great Khan acquires all the gold and silver and pearls and precious stones of all his territories ... And all the Khan's armies are paid with this sort of money. I have now told you how it comes about that the Great Khan must have, as indeed he has, more treasure than anyone else in the world. I may go further and affirm that all the world's great potentates put together have not such riches as belong to the Great Khan alone. (Polo, 1987, pp. 147ff.)

Marco Polo's description must have seemed exaggerated to his fellow Europeans at the time, but we now know that he was giving what amounts to a fairly precise description of the monetary system prevailing at this time in the Mongolian Empire. Even his estimation of the Khan's wealth as far exceeding that of his counterparts in the rest of the world might well have been accurate. The government in the Mongolian Empire could not only control nominal economic growth, but also allocate resources at will. According to descriptions of the Chinese economy at the time, it was flourishing.

At the time, European kings and princes had far less control over the economy. This is because the rulers did not understand the true nature of money and therefore never realized that they could issue paper money. Instead, they believed that money had to be in the form of gold or other precious metals. The problem was that in this case it is impossible for the government to control the money supply at will and allocate resources. Rulers spent significant resources on alchemy, in an attempt to produce gold. While they failed, this delivered positive side effects by advancing chemistry. It also demonstrates that rulers did seek to exert power over the economy through the control of the money supply. But they failed and thus European governments never gained nearly as much control over the economy as Kublai Khan's government enjoyed.

The alchemy of banking

This was also largely the situation in England in the seventeenth century. Precious metals and coins made thereof were considered the only form of money. However, it was a time of war, lack of security, plague and fire. In this time of insecurity, luxuries were less in demand. Thus also 'the ordinary demand for goldsmiths to make objects of gold and silver for the customers had ... practically ceased' (Davies, 1994, p. 250). However, there was demand for another activity the jewellers could offer: dealing in precious metals and originally focusing on turning them into handcrafted jewellery; they naturally had stocks of precious metals, and the necessary safes and private security staff – if not small private armies – to protect their property. Dealing in gold and silver, they were already independently wealthy and thus considered trustworthy. Therefore the general public began to use 'goldsmiths' safes as a secure place for people's jewels, bullion and coins' (Davies, 1994, pp. 249ff.). This storage and safekeeping business generated small fees. When gold was deposited with a goldsmith, he would write a receipt to certify that it was in his custody, which would be presented in case of withdrawals. As this practice became widespread, depositors would soon begin to pay for purchases by handing over their deposit receipts, and thus transferring the ownership of their gold to the seller. To facilitate such cashless transactions, the use of unnamed deposit receipts became more widespread. The diary of Samuel Pepys mentions his sending of a deposit note to his father of over £600 in 1668. The deposit receipts had become paper money.

However, this European form of paper money was crucially different in its function and implication from the paper money used in Polo's time in China: it was issued not by the government but by a private group of businessmen. Since most crafts in medieval times were organized in trade guilds, at their regular meetings the goldsmiths must have discussed the phenomenon of substantial amounts of gold remaining deposited with them without being regularly withdrawn, as the deposit receipts were becoming generally accepted means of payment. This opened up further business opportunities for the goldsmiths: the gold, instead of lying idly in their vaults, could be lent out at interest. For the goldsmiths, the interest revenues were pure profits, for which they did not have to labour particularly hard. They merely needed to secure sufficient collateral, such as real estate or other property and ensure enforcement (either of debt servicing or repossession of the collateral). Further, if the goldsmiths cooperated with each other, they could minimize the risk of being unable to meet unexpected withdrawals.

Lending at interest is an attractive business model, because of the common practice to compound the interest. In the case of other businesses, revenues are directly proportional to the provision of goods and services, and hence to costs (though usually at a declining rate). When lending at interest, the revenue stream can rise exponentially, without the provision of any new goods or services, and hence without further costs.[15] For instance, the borrower of a ten-year interest-only mortgage of £100,000, compounded at a fixed annual interest rate of 8%, will have paid back a total of £221,964 at the end of the ten years. In the case of a 30-year interest-only mortgage, the amount will be £1,093,573. If the interest is 10% per annum, the borrower, though having only ever received £100,000, will ultimately have to pay back £1,983,740.[16]

Such calculations, using the well-known compound interest formula, are usually considered too simple to even feature in any economics or finance book. As a result, even economics graduates are not rarely surprised when confronted with the results of compound interest. Considering Table 12.1, it becomes apparent why none less than a Baron Rothschild is said to have called compound interest the 'eighth wonder of the world'. Interest rates of 40% or higher often apply in the case of consumer loan companies, and it is apparent why such companies can have high profit margins. Compound interest also explains why developing countries find it difficult to escape from their debt burden and why many NGOs and NPOs are lobbying for cancellation of Third World debt: for years, many developing countries have

Table 12.1 Compound interest: examples

Borrowed amount: £100,000

Total required repayment: mortgage with monthly downpayments on principal

Fixed interest (%)	5 years	10 years	20 years	30 years
5	113,227	127,279	158,389	193,256
6	115,997	133,225	171,943	215,838
7	118,807	139,330	186,072	239,509
8	121,658	145,593	200,746	264,155
9	124,550	152,011	215,934	289,664
10	127,482	158,581	231,605	315,926
15	142,740	193,602	316,029	455,200
20	158,963	231,907	407,718	601,567
30	194,120	316,341	601,603	900,122
40	232,510	407,976	800,304	1,200,006

Total required repayment: interest-only mortgage, monthly compounding

Fixed interest (%)	5 years	10 years	20 years	30 years
5	128,336	164,701	271,264	446,774
6	134,885	181,940	331,020	602,258
7	141,763	200,966	403,874	811,650
8	148,985	221,964	492,680	1,093,573
9	156,568	245,136	600,915	1,473,058
10	164,531	270,704	732,807	1,983,740
15	210,718	444,021	1,971,549	8,754,100
20	269,597	726,826	5,282,753	38,396,396
30	439,979	1,935,815	37,473,797	725,428,367
40	715,198	5,115,083	261,540,751	13,383,141,853

Note: The calculation can be done on many websites, such as www.bloomberg.com/analysis/calculators/mortgage.html. Also note that there are many flexible-rate mortgages, and lenders tend to charge further fixed fees, as well as require life insurance premiums, and so on.

been transferring wealth to the bankers, not to pay back the much smaller original principal, but merely to service part of the compounded interest.

Analysing the implications of the loaning of gold that had been entrusted to goldsmiths for safekeeping, we note three major consequences:

1. From a legal perspective, the goldsmiths committed fraud. Their deposit receipts guaranteed that the gold was deposited with them. The depositors and their counter-parties relied on the assurance that the gold was held in deposit. Yet this was no longer true.
2. A business model came about, whereby potentially exponential revenue growth could be generated by some entrepreneurs with disproportionately few inputs required.
3. New purchasing power was created. While the receipts for the gold were used to purchase goods in the economy, the gold itself, when lent out, provided someone else with additional purchasing power that had not previously existed. The total amount of purchasing power in the economy increased. The goldsmiths had expanded the money supply. However, unlike in China, where the government made the decision over creation and allocation of purchasing power, in Europe it was a private group of businessmen. Though unknown to the public, the goldsmiths' actions affected everyone: their creation of purchasing power, their expansion of the claims on limited existing resources, their 'issuing of more tickets to the game' (to use one of Schumpeter's expressions), could not fail to affect the entire economy.

Yet this was only the first stage. The goldsmiths must have quickly noticed that their business model, though already attractive, could still be enhanced substantially. The goldsmiths most likely experienced a continuous demand for loans, as the possibility to command resources was attractive to many people, businesses and the government. Since it would not be wise for the goldsmiths to lend out too much of their deposited gold, they soon realized that they could continue to expand their lending business, earn interest and interest on interest, and potentially even increase their stock of gold, if they gave their borrowers deposit receipts instead of gold. In other words, borrowers were not given bullion, but merely deposit receipts – which they then could use as money.[17]

When this happened, four things occurred:

1. The number of claims on resources, the money supply, increased further. This created a larger potential for economic booms or inflation of consumer or asset prices. It also created a larger potential for crises when depositors would demand their money back simultaneously.[18]
2. The fraud became more substantial, as the impression of a deposit was given when actually the borrower had not deposited any money. Legally,

such deposit receipts were faked documents. Due to imperfect information, however, the general public was unaware of the facts.

3. The potential for exponential profit growth rose, as the goldsmiths did not have to draw down any resources when they 'lent', but instead issued a piece of paper by the stroke of a pen. Furthermore, while it did not cost them anything to issue such paper, the borrowers were required to pay back in full what the goldsmiths had not owned (ideally, in precious metals). Thus goldsmiths could simply 'print' money and with it obtain real purchasing power. If borrowers failed to stick to their loan schedules, the goldsmiths could proceed to foreclose on them and repossess the collateralized assets.

4. Banking was born: the same process describes the activity of present-day commercial banks: 'some ingenious goldsmith conceived the epoch-making notion of giving notes not only to those who had deposited metal, but also to those who came to borrow it, and so founded modern banking' (Withers, 1909, p. 20; quoted by Davies, 1994, p. 251).

Modern banking

It is evident why the goldsmiths chose to pursue this business model in preference to their more cumbersome craft of creating jewellery. They became wealthier, more influential and henceforth would be known as bankers. This is not just meant allegorically, but quite literally.

While we are all used to financial systems with central banks, in most countries there were no central banks until recently (for instance, until 1913 in the US). Before central banks acquired their recent monopoly over the issuance of paper money, private sector banks issued paper money. They did this apparently in receipt of the deposit of 'cash', but since the majority of the money supply consisted of bank money, this meant merely other deposit receipts from other banks or bank transfers from other accounts. So how could the total amount of paper money increase? Only when the banks did what they liked to do best, and what indeed remains their main business: when they extended a loan. In that case, the borrower would receive a fictitious deposit receipt or deposit entry in their bank accounts, although no deposit had been made. This describes the activity of banks until this day. The introduction of central banks has also not changed this, although it has made it far harder for observers to detect the actual activity of banks: while banks nowadays do not issue paper money, they still create the bulk of all money in the economy (since paper money is a diminishing percentage of all transactions). They still do what the goldsmiths did: pretend a borrower has deposited money and by so doing encourage others to accept the pretended money. The banks' business model works, since the majority of transactions are settled through the banking system. The enormous degree of discretionary power enjoyed by the creators of money, and hence issues such as equity, transparency, accountability and social responsibility are hardly ever discussed, because the general public, like most economists, are not aware of the reality of banking.

We conclude that bankers had managed to do what kings, emperors and alchemists had failed to do – they were creating money. They had found the philosopher's stone.[19] Since they created the money (that is, paper money in the form of deposit receipts) when extending loans, they simultaneously created credit and money.

Credit creation through the ages

The London goldsmiths were, of course, by far from the first to conceive this epoch-making (and fraudulent) notion of extending more receipts than had ever been deposited, thereby expanding the money supply. Temptation is likely to have overcome entrepreneurs in many other, similar businesses, whenever deposits were made and receipts were issued, and where these receipts had become generally accepted.

A similar process occurred centuries earlier with the habit by bankers of 'accepting' bills of exchange issued by merchants and businessmen. Prohibited to charge interest, they 'accepted' these bills of exchange, but at a 'discount', that is, the issuer had to pay back 100, but would only receive, for instance, 70. This amounted to charging interest. The rates were often high, as the interest was commonly charged per month. John Law reported in 1717 that 'the bills of exchange of the most creditworthy merchants of the Kingdom were commonly discounted at the rate of 4 per cent per month which amounted to 48 per cent per year' (quoted by Murphy, 1997, p. 156). Since the bills were used as paper money, the bankers effectively issued new paper money when they extended a loan by 'discounting a bill'.

Many of the clay tablets found in Mesopotamia and issued some 5000 years ago are in fact deposit receipts. Were only as many receipts issued as underlying deposits (of grain, precious metals, and so on) had been made? Or did the Babylonian bankers issue more receipts, since the cost of producing a clay tablet was negligible, but the returns from extending loans this way and thus creating money 'out of nothing' were substantial? Trade was conducted, whereby traders did not have to carry precious metals, but signed tablets, letters of credit – 'the ancient equivalent of a paper currency' (Woolley, 1936). Thus we also have to expect that Babylonian banks created money.

The same applies to the clay moulds that archaeologists have found in ancient Greece, of which 'it can be conjectured that such pseudo-currencies of baked clay moulded from existing types [of money] had a fiduciary circulation' (Lenormant, 1878, Book II, Tome I, p. 216; quoted by Astle, 1975). Clay tablets, wax tablets and papyri served as deposit certificates, bills of exchange, letters of credit, or cheques in the Greek, Egyptian and Roman eras. A 'credit system developed in Greece as in other parts of the ancient world long before the adoption of coinage' (Einzig, 1948, p. 225). Einzig points out that even when silver 'was used in many instances as standard of value ... it was not actually employed in payments' (1948, p. 206). The Greek bankers (*trapezitae*)

> acted as money lenders both on a small and a large scale. Finally, they received money on deposit. People placed their money with them for safe custody, partly to facilitate the management of it. The depositors, according to their convenience, either drew out sums of money temselves, or commissioned their banker to make payment to a third person. In this line the business of the banks was considerable. (Seyffert, 1904, p. 91)

According to scholars of ancient Rome, banking was conducted by *argentarii* and *nummularii*, who engaged in 'all the activities that go with banking business' (Mommsen and Marquardt, 1887/88). More directly, *Harper's Dictionary of Classical Literature and Antiquities* points out that the '*argentarii* made payments for persons who had not deposited any money with them: this was equivalent to lending money; which in fact they often did for a certain percentage of interest ...' (Peck, 1965, p. 1598). Thus the 'money lenders' frequently referred to in historical texts, often by historians or archaeologists not necessarily familiar with the credit and deposit creation function of banks, or the biblical account of the money lenders in the Temple in Jerusalem, are likely to have referred to bankers that created money.[20]

In the case of the early Chinese paper money of the tenth century, it is documented that private bankers issued such 'uncovered' deposit receipts and hence simply printed money (Tullock, 1957; Davies, 1994; Kagin, 2002). When wooden tallies became widespread as a money substitute in England, soon more tallies were created and brought into circulation. This led to an 'enlarged total of credit' and 'effectively increased the money supply beyond the limits of minting'. The 'fictitiously swollen loans' earned interest to the bankers (Davies, 1994, pp. 149, 151). Bills of exchange became widespread as *de facto* paper money, facilitating international transactions, but also to disguise domestic loans at interest (and thus circumvent usury laws). Italian (Lombard) bankers created money through the issuance of bills and deposit receipts. Since about the twelfth century it became common that in this way 'large amounts of "fictitious" bills were issued which either were simply domestic deals masquerading as foreign or simply dealing in credit without real goods or services being involved' (Davies, 1994, p. 156). The Fuggers and other banks flourished in continental Europe in the fifteenth and sixteenth centuries, acting as bankers to the Emperor. The Bank of Amsterdam was founded in 1609, followed by a large number of banks in Holland, Germany and Sweden, and the Bank of England in 1694, with the right to issue its own bank notes. 'In general, it may be said that the private banks were the main agents responsible for the increase in the quantity ... of money' (Davies, 1994, p. 552).

Before the (fairly recent) introduction of central banking, bank notes – as the name still indicates – were issued competitively by commercial banks. Such private paper money (dominant in the US until 1913, when the central bank was founded) was issued newly, when a borrower received a loan. This meant that a deposit receipt was issued 'fraudulently', as no deposit had taken place. Sometimes these bank notes would still have inscriptions alluding to their original function as deposit receipts. Thus many people, including many economists today, believed that these bank notes were issued when a deposit was made. That was not the case, as in this case the total amount of paper money in circulation could not increase, as merely a transfer of existing purchasing power would take place. For a net increase in bank notes in circulation, bank loans had to be extended. Or, to put it the other way around, bank loans were paid out with newly printed money.

Today's common definition of the money supply as the various M deposit receipts is likely to derive from this link to 'deposit notes' issued by banks. Economists like Fisher and Brown (1911), Philips (1920), Keynes (1930) and others therefore believed that narrow money was cash, while broader money measures could be constructed using statistics for bank deposits. Unfortunately, as we saw, these do not have a convincing empirical record.

The most important feature of banks: credit creation

Many economics textbooks that mention banks still acknowledge that they can 'create credit'. However, it appears that the original meaning of this expression has been lost. Those textbooks and authors that mention the words credit creation now give it quite a different meaning. Proponents of the present-day 'credit view' define credit creation as 'the process by which saving is channeled to alternative uses' (Bernanke, 1993, p. 50). To Bernanke, 'credit creation' is therefore the 'diversion' or transfer of already existing purchasing power. This is also the understanding of the concept by economists from other persuasions, including monetarists like Meltzer (1995). They all therefore agree in classifying banks as mere financial intermediaries, providing services similar to and in parallel with non-banks and capital markets (as shown in Figure 11.1 earlier).[21] Clearly, thus defined, credit creation would not be a unique feature of banking. Proponents of the credit view consequently also argue that credit aggregates are *not* to be considered an 'independent causal factor affecting the economy'; rather,

> credit conditions – best measured, by the way, by the external finance premium and not the aggregate quantity of credit – are an endogenous factor that help shape the dynamic response of the economy to shifts in monetary policy. Thus the theory has no particular implications about

the relative forecasting power of credit aggregates. (Bernanke and Gertler, 1995, pp. 43ff.)

The representation of banks as mere intermediaries is perpetuated by the explanation of credit creation in textbooks, which depict it as a process of successive lending of already existing purchasing power by intermediating banks. Figure 12.1 reproduces the textbook representation of credit creation: Bank A receives a new deposit of US$100. If the reserve requirement is 1%, textbooks say that the bank will lend out US$99, and deposit US$1 with the central bank as reserve. The US$99 will, however, be deposited with another bank, Bank B, which will also be able to lend out 99% of that amount (US$98.01), and keep 1% as reserve. This process continues until in the end a total of US$9900 has been lent out. Textbooks represent credit creation as successive financial intermediation. According to this description, a single bank is unable to create credit.

While even this description does conclude that the overall banking system creates money, credit creation seems to be the result of a diffuse process, in which money 'circulates' in the economy (in line with the concept of 'velocity' in the quantity equation). Most of all, we are told that each bank can only lend 99% of the money deposited with it. This renders banks similar to fund managers who lend out savings deposited with them and thus they are considered mere financial intermediaries. Thus Bernanke's understanding of credit creation as the (successive?) 'channelling of savings' to investors is not far-fetched and most economists do consider banks merely an alternative channel to capital market or other intermediation.[22]

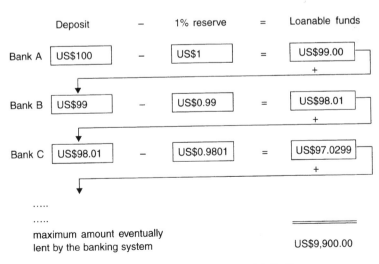

Figure 12.1 The textbook representation of money multiplication

Phillips' (1920) 'money multiplier' concept, linking cash and reserves to bank deposits (the money supply), has not helped in resolving this misunderstanding. However, Goodhart (1989b) has clarified that the multiplier identities suffer from a 'lack of any innate theoretical, or behavioural, content' (p. 133) so that accounts of the underlying dynamic processes based on them 'are at best misleading and often wrong'.[23]

Given our empirical observation of banks, such as the London goldsmiths, we conclude that the textbook representation of the actions of each bank is inaccurate (Figure 12.1). Firstly, the frequent description of banks' activity as 'lending' is misleading. The definition for this word according to the *Oxford English Dictionary* is as follows:

lend
• **verb** (past and past part. **lent**) 1 grant to (someone) the use of (something) on the understanding that it shall be returned. 2 allow (someone) the use of (a sum of money) under an agreement to pay it back later, typically with interest. (*Compact Oxford English Dictionary*)

As can be seen, the standard use of the concept of lending implies that an item is physically removed from use by A and instead transferred to the use by B. Lending thus describes a transfer, a diversion of an existing commodity to the exclusive use somewhere else. Given the laws of physics, this usage is only natural. However, the credit extended by banks does not remove purchasing power or claims on resources from anywhere else in the economy. Therefore, strictly speaking, it cannot be described as 'lending'. Banks do not lend money, they create it. Meanwhile, 'credit creation' does not refer to mere 'financial intermediation', as many recent authors have argued. According to the *OED*:

creation
• **noun** 1 the action or process of creating. 2 a thing which has been made or invented, especially something showing artistic talent. 3 (**the Creation**) the creating of the universe regarded as an act of God.

create
• **verb** 1 bring into existence. 2 make (someone) a member of the nobility. — ORIGIN Latin *creare* 'produce'. (*Compact Oxford English Dictionary*)

The word 'creation' refers to 'the act of creating' or something that 'has been made or invented'. To create, in turn, is defined as to 'bring something into existence'. If the savings already existed, their transfer could not possibly be called 'credit creation'. Indeed, the etymology of the term 'credit creation' reveals quickly that it originally referred to the new creation of credit (or money) that did not exist before. Instead of referring to the transfer of already existing purchasing power, as Bernanke describes it, many authors recognized that it described the ability of each individual bank to create money 'out of nothing'.[24]

In line with this alternative view, a more accurate presentation of credit creation can be shown in Figure 12.2, which depicts the balance sheet of a bank that receives a new deposit of US$1, recorded as a new liability of the bank. Instead of lending out US$99, as the textbooks tell us, the bank will use the US$100 as reserve with the central bank (entered as asset on its balance sheet). The US$100 can now become the 1% on the basis of which the bank can lend out 99 times as much. Thus this very first bank can grant a new loan amounting to US$9900. The moment the loan is granted, the bank simultaneously increases its assets by US$9900 (the amount of the loan, which is an asset for the bank) and its deposits by US$9900 – the person or company who receives the loan of US$9900 will actually obtain a book entry of US$9900 in his or her deposit account – money that can now be spent on transactions. The money the bank has created, US$9900, is 99% of the increase in the bank balance sheet (US$100 new deposit plus US$9900 in loans/deposits).[25] Thus the reserve requirement is met.

Contrary to the standard depiction of the credit creation process in most textbooks, each individual bank creates credit and money when it extends a loan. The original deposit of US$100 becomes the 1% reserve on the basis of which loans 99 times as large can be granted by the same bank. Credit creation has 'lengthened' the bank's balance sheet.

Balance sheet of Bank A

Step 1 Deposit of US$100 by customer at Bank A

Assets	Liabilities
	US$100

Step 2 US$100 used to increase the reserve of Bank A

Assets	Liabilities
US$100	US$100

Step 3 Loan of US$9,900 granted, by crediting borrower's bank account with deposit

Assets	Liabilities
US$100	US$100
+	+
US$9,900	US$9,900

Figure 12.2 A more accurate representation of credit creation

The crucial question is: 'Where did the US$9900 come from?' The money was not withdrawn by the bank from other uses. It was not diverted or transferred from any other part of the economy. Most of all, although it is shown as a deposit, it was not actually deposited by anyone. The bank simply created the money by writing the figures into its books and the customer's account book. In effect, the bank pretends that its borrower has made a deposit that was not actually made. Unlike the textbook representation, we see that each individual bank can thus create money when it extends a loan. *Showing this truth in textbooks would not only be more memorable, but it would also teach students about what banks really do: they create money out of nothing. The bank just pretends it has the US$9900, credits someone's books with them, and nobody knows the difference.*

In the words of Schumpeter (1954),

this alters the analytic situation profoundly and makes it highly inadvisable to construe bank credit on the model of existing funds being withdrawn from previous uses by an entirely imaginary act of saving and then lent out by their owners. It is much more realistic to say that the banks 'create credit', that is, that they create deposits in their act of lending, than to say that they lend the deposits that have been entrusted to them. And the reason for insisting on this is that depositors should not be invested with the insignia of a role which they do not play. The theory to which economists clung so tenaciously makes them out to be savers when they neither save nor intend to do so; it attributes to them an influence on the 'supply of credit' which they do not have. The theory of 'credit creation' not only recognizes patent facts without obscuring them by artificial constructions; it also brings out the peculiar mechanism of saving and investment that is characteristic of fully fledged capitalist society and the true role of banks in capitalist evolution. (p. 1114)

Wicksell (1898) also knew that each individual bank could create money:

The banks in their lending business are not only not limited by their own capital; they are not, at least not immediately limited by any capital whatever; by concentrating in their hands almost all payments, they themselves create the money required ... (Wicksell, 1907, pp. 214–15)

In a pure system of credit, where all payments were made by transference in the bank-books, the banks would be able to grant at any moment any amount of loans at any, however diminutive, rate of interest. (Wicksell, 1907, p. 215)

Hahn (1920) emphasized that each bank can create money 'out of nothing' and pointed out the macroeconomic consequences. Schumpeter (1912) referred to this creation of new money as being equivalent to the issuance of new 'tickets' to a game. According to him, the banker is 'not so much primarily a middleman in the commodity "purchasing power" ', but instead he is 'a *producer* of this commodity'. Banks issue additional claims on existing resources. *Bank credit creation does not channel existing money to new uses. It newly creates money that did not exist beforehand and channels it to some use.*

This process was more obvious in the time when there was no central bank with a monopoly on the issuance of paper currency – such as until 1913 in the US. As Goodhart (1989c) stresses, in those days the main liabilities of banks consisted not of deposits, but issued bank notes. The latter increased on a net basis only when more loans were granted. Thus the loans were effectively paid out by printing bank notes.

What makes this 'creative accounting' possible is the other function of banks as the settlement system of all non-cash transactions in the economy. If they so wish, they can extend loans to agents not in the form of withdrawals of funds from elsewhere in the financial system, but by creating the accounting fiction that the borrower has deposited sums with the banking system. Since banks work as the accountants of record – while the rest of the economy assumes they are honest accountants – it is possible for the banks to increase the money in the accounts of some of us (those who receive a loan), by simply altering the figures. Nobody else will notice, because agents cannot distinguish between money that had actually been saved and deposited and money that has been created 'out of nothing' by the bank.[26]

This, then, is also a major distinguishing feature between credit creation in the banking system and the debasement of coinage that was implemented by monarchs in their attempts to increase the money supply: debased coins can be checked and identified as such by experienced traders or professional assayists. However, bank credit creation is impossible to distinguish from 'legitimate' deposits, especially when the majority of transactions already takes place in a cashless form via the banking system.

We conclude that the feature of banks as creators of credit (what could equally be called their ability to 'create money') is what renders them special. This feature also explains why bankers quickly became powerful and influential, and could easily expand into various industries, quickly becoming the core of a network of affiliated companies that they either founded or bought up (life is much easier when one has a licence to print money).

Thanks to the special ability of banks to create credit, clear statistical demarcations between various forms of fundraising can now be drawn, and an accurate description of the 'money supply' found. Only the central bank (usually allowed to engage in banking business) and banks can create new credit and money and use it to settle transactions directly via the main settlement system of the economy. This differentiates them both on the microeconomic and the macroeconomic level from other agents and renders funding from banks and the central bank 'imperfectly substitutable'.

Thus when analysing the economy, banks and the central bank need to be considered separately from others. Government banks, when as usual funded from the Treasury, non-bank financial intermediaries (such as leasing firms, life insurers, mutual funds), households, corporations and the government itself all have one thing in common: they cannot (legally) fulfil this function of banks and the central bank.[27] While banks are credit creators, other financial institutions are financial intermediaries. In this, macroeconomic, sense bank credit can never be perfectly substitutable with intermediated loans. Moreover, in this sense a 'bank credit channel', defined by the creation of new credit, must not only exist, but must also dominate other transmission channels. Banks therefore also cannot but play the pivotal role in every economy.

The example of Figure 12.2, however, remains an example: for in actual practice, banks are rarely, if ever, limited in their lending by the reserve requirement. As Goodhart (1989c) has argued, central banks that set targets for inter-bank interest rates will supply any necessary amount of reserves to banks so that at the time of the monthly deadline for reserve requirements to be met, short-term interest rates do not rise precipitously. This raises issues for monetary policy, namely how bank credit creation can be most effectively controlled, especially when we recognize the existence of imperfect information.

Further, the fact that banks do not have money, but create it, explains why financial fragility is such a major issue in the banking sector. To be able to consider the issue of banking crises, how to respond to them and how to avoid them in the first place, it will next become necessary to render explicit the link between banking and the macroeconomy. This, indeed, should solve the enigma of the link between money and the economy.

13
Credit, Money and the Economy

Having identified the key feature that makes banks unique, it is now time to re-examine the link between the tangible economy and the monetary or financial part of the economy. In order to identify where possible errors could have been made in the construction of the edifice that is mainstream macroeconomics, it is necessary to return to first principles. As we saw, the various theories all rely on the quantity equation MV = PY. The textbooks consider it an identity that is true by definition and requires little further discussion. Handa (2000) writes that MV = PY

> is an identity since it is derived solely from identities. It is valid under any set of circumstances whatever since it can be reduced to the statement: in a given period by a given group of people, expenditures equal expenditures, with only a difference in the computational method between them. (p. 25)

However, is this actually true? Following the inductive method, it is of interest how this equation came about. We find that a quantitative link has been proposed between money and the economy for hundreds of years, if not much longer. A quantity relationship was mentioned by ancient Chinese classical scholars (von Glahn, 1996), Spanish scholastic writers of the Salamanca School (Humphrey, 1997), and many others (including Locke, Hume, Cantillon and Ricardo). A modern version very close to the present quantity equation was presented by Fisher and Brown (1911), who cited Newcomb (1885), as follows:[1]

(1)   MV = PT

where M stands for the quantity of money in circulation (and thus used for transactions), V for the transactions velocity, T for the number of transactions and P the price paid per transaction.[2] The idea was that the total value of transactions (PT) must be as large as the money used to pay for these transactions. Fisher had the concept of species in mind as money M, and realized that the total volume of transactions was much larger than the stock of gold or precious metals. Thus like other economists at the time, he felt that banking or other financial innovations served to economize on this stock of gold. Thus some kind of 'multiplier' was necessary – the number of times one unit of gold money M was used for transactions during the period of observation. This is velocity V.

There was an important drawback of Fisher's equation. When attempting to employ statistical data to apply it in practice, data for M and P could be found. V was the residual, thus data on T were necessary. But they did not exist. However, national income accounts were being compiled and became increasingly reliable. According to the national income accounts we can express essentially the same aggregate figures either as national income, output or expenditure. Thus Pigou (1917) and many of his colleagues at Cambridge University argued that the stock of money should be proportional to 'total nominal expenditures', which could be represented by GNP. Many Cambridge economists therefore replaced PT with PY, yielding the most widely-known formulation of the quantity equation:[3]

(2) $MV = PY$

As a result to this day most economists have been using this income version in their work, although the original quantity equation is all about transactions. Influential postwar studies relying on this income version include Friedman and Schwartz (1963), Goldfeld (1973, 1976), Judd and Scadding (1982) and Laidler (1985). Today, it is considered the quantity equation or 'equation of exchange', which textbooks describe as being true by definition or 'valid under any set of circumstances whatever'.

However, is it always quite so valid? It is only accurate, if and only if

(3) $PY = PT$

that is, if all transactions are as large as nominal GDP, or, to put it differently, if only transactions take place that are represented by nominal GDP. When considering growth rates, it would be necessary for GDP-based transactions to be a constant proportion of total transactions. However, it is not clear that GDP accurately reflects all transactions. A long list of literature has recognized that asset transactions are substantial, yet are not included in the GDP statistics: Fisher and after him Keynes suggested distinguishing between transactions arising from the sale or purchase of finished goods and services (which can be measured by GDP) and financial transactions that are not related to national income. Fisher (1926) distinguished between income and financial transactions, Keynes (1930) between 'industrial' and 'financial' transactions. Theoretical and empirical work using this distinction includes

Selden (1956), Spindt (1985), Cramer (1986), Stone and Thornton (1987), Niggle (1988) and Allen (1989). The UK's Central Statistical Office (CSO, 1986) argued that the total value of transactions should be used in the quantity equation, while GDP was merely a subset of transactions involving final output (as quoted by Howells and Biefang-Frisancho Mariscal, 1992). It can therefore be said that the need to distinguish between GDP-based transactions and non-GDP-based transactions is well-established (see also Werner, 1992, 1997d).

Yet the mainstream use of the quantity equation has remained confined to nominal income. An important example is Gowland (1985), who recognizes the greater accuracy of total transactions in the quantity equation, instead of nominal income. However, as Friedman (1956), he argues that for the equation of exchange to be 'economically useful' (p. 24), nominal income should be employed, not total transactions. In the words of Howells and Biefang-Fisancho Mariscal (1992):

> It is not the lack of transactions data, nor the stability of the PT/PY multiple that requires us to focus on PY. It is that in the end we are primarily concerned with the relationship between money and final output – its magnitude or average price. Thus, we make the assumptions (whatever, and however justified, they may be) necessary to convert the quantity theory into a theory of the determination of nominal income. (p. 369)

Solving the enigma of the 'velocity decline'

The problems arising from the implicit assumption that nominal GDP (that is, PY) can be used to represent total transaction values (PT) are obvious. GDP transactions are a subset of all transactions. The mainstream quantity equation (2) that uses income or GDP to represent transactions will thus only be reliable in time periods when the value of non-GDP transactions, such as asset transactions, remains constant (thus dropping out when considering flows). However, when their value rises, this will cause GDP to be an unreliable proxy for the value of all transactions. In those time periods we must expect the traditional quantity equation, MV = PY, to give the appearance of a fall in the velocity V, as money is used for transactions other than nominal GDP (PY). This explains why in many countries with asset price booms economists puzzled over an apparent 'velocity decline', a 'breakdown of the money demand function' or a 'mystery of missing money' – issues that severely hampered the monetarist approach to monetary policy implementation.

Spindt (1985), Allen (1989, 1994), Howells and Biefang-Fisancho Mariscal (1992) and Werner (1992, 1997d) explicitly argue that the widely observed velocity decline is not due to 'disintermediation', financial innovations or structural issues such as deregulation, as the literature has argued, but instead is the result of an increase in transactions that are not part of GDP (see also Akabane, 1997). Besides financial transactions, the majority of real estate transactions are equally not part of the GDP statistics (Werner, 1992).[4]

The UK's CSO regretted that accurate figures for total transactions were not available. Occasionally, Japan's former Economic Planning Agency had calculated such transactions series. For instance, in 1991 the EPA published its estimates of economic transactions. It noted a remarkable surge in financial and real estate transactions during the second half of the 1980s. This already proves that it will be necessary to disaggregate the above equation of exchange into transactions that are part of GDP (which we can call 'real transactions') and those that are not ('financial transactions'). But these figures are not available on a frequent basis, such as quarterly, as would be necessary to conduct research on Japan during the 1980s and 1990s.

There is an agency that has access to the majority of the transactions data even on a daily basis: the central bank. As Bank of Japan Governor Matsushita reminds us:

> a large part of the daily transactions of households, firms and investors are settled by means of funds transfers and remittances between banks. In turn, banks' balances are settled across their accounts held with the Bank of Japan. In other words, the majority of transactions conducted throughout the country is eventually concentrated and settled at the Bank [of Japan]. As a result, the amount settled across the current accounts at the Bank [of Japan] totals more than ¥300 trillion per day. This means that an amount equivalent to approximately 70 percent of Japan's annual GDP is transferred each day through the accounts at the Bank [of Japan]. (Matsushita, 1996, p. 7)

Unfortunately, the central bank does not make any of this invaluable data accessible to the public, despite the virtually zero cost of publication (all the figures are already online on the central bank's settlement computer system and could be published almost instantaneously on the internet).

Some researchers have used proxies. Keynes (1930) and Selden (1956) suggested the use of the total value of cheque clearings. Spindt (1985) used data on the debits to various money accounts. Howells and Biefang-Frisancho Mariscal (1992) used aggregate monthly data on inter-bank and inter-branch payments provided by the Association of Payments Clearing Systems (APACS) in the UK. They found that the velocity on financial transactions was actually stable, but that the increase in financial transactions over the 1980s explained the apparent decline in the income velocity of the traditional quantity equation.

A disaggregated equation of exchange

Given the insufficient empirical record of the traditional equation of exchange, it is desirable to modify it to bring it in line with the empirical record, while rendering the old version a special case, true under certain circumstances. Let us recall that the original transaction-based equation of exchange states that

> the amount of money changing hands to pay for transactions during a given time period must be equal to the nominal value of these transactions.

Following the traditional way of formulating this (though replacing Fisher's T with the slightly more intuitive notation Q for the quantity of transactions) we get:

$$(4) \quad MV = PQ$$

where MV now does not stand for an arbitrary measure of the money supply, but the total amount of money actually changing hands as part of transactions, while PQ stands for the value of these same transactions.[5] Next, a disaggregation into GDP-based transactions and those not part of GDP is necessary.

Theoretically, we can of course disaggregate the transaction data in any way we wish.[6] It will become an empirical issue whether we can find good statistical data to proxy the theoretical breakdown. As discussed, and following Werner (1992, 1997d), we choose to break both sides of (4) down: on the one hand, into money used for transactions that are part of GDP ($M_R V_R$) and those that are not (called $M_F V_F$); and on the other hand, the value of transactions that are part of GDP ($P_R Q_R = P_R Y$), and those that are not ($P_R Q_R$):[7]

$$(5) \quad MV = M_R V_R + M_F V_F$$
$$(6) \quad PQ = P_R Q_R + P_F Q_F$$

At the same time, equations (6) and (7) must also hold:

$$(7) \quad M_R V_R = P_R Q_R$$
$$(8) \quad M_F V_F = P_F Q_F$$

Since we defined $P_R Q_R$ as the value of all GDP-based transactions, we also know that the following equation holds, where P_R stands for the GDP deflator and ($P_R Y$) stands for nominal GDP.

$$(7') \quad M_R V_R = P_R Y$$
$$\text{with} \quad V_R = (P_R Y)/M_R = \text{const.}$$

With a stable 'real' velocity of money, V_R, the effective amount of money used for GDP transactions during any period of time ($M_R V_R$) must be equal to nominal GDP. Meanwhile, the amount of money effectively used for non-GDP transactions will be equal to the value of these non-GDP transactions.

Growth and the disaggregated quantity equation

In most circumstances, researchers are interested in dynamic situations, where economic growth takes place. By definition, for economic growth to take place, the value of economic transactions during one time period must exceed that of the previous period of comparison. Considering therefore net changes in variables over the observed time period (for instance, the first quarter of this year compared to the first quarter last year), we obtain:

(9) $\Delta MV = \Delta(PQ)$

This merely restates that an increase in the value of transactions (and hence economic growth) can only take place if there has been an increase in the amount of money used to conduct these transactions. Dividing both the change in the amount of money used for transactions and the change in the value of transactions into those that are part of the GDP definition (ΔM_R and ΔQ_R) and those that are not (ΔM_F and ΔQ_F), we obtain:

(10) $\Delta MV = \Delta M_R V_R + \Delta M_F V_F$
(11) $\Delta(PQ) = \Delta(P_R Q_R) + \Delta(P_F Q_F)$

At the same time, equations (12) and (13) must also hold:

(12) $\Delta M_R V_R = \Delta(P_R Q_R) = \Delta(P_R Y)$
(13) $\Delta M_F V_F = \Delta(P_F Q_F)$

We can say that the rise (fall) in the amount of money used for GDP-based transactions is equal to the rise (fall) in nominal GDP. Similarly, the rise (fall) in the amount of money used for non-GDP transactions is equal to the change in the value of non-GDP transactions.

The definition of M

It now becomes necessary to find that measure of ΔMV, the rise (or fall) of the net amount of nominal money effectively used for all transactions, which is correct given the reality of our bank-based monetary systems. This is an area where many misunderstandings exist. As we saw, Fisher, Keynes and most postwar researchers used deposit aggregates ranging from M0 to M4. However, even without empirical testing we must expect this approach to suffer from a number of problems.

Firstly, the quantity equation defines M as that purchasing power which is actually exerted when transactions take place. Therefore a quantity relationship between prices or GDP and money should more precisely refer to that part of the money supply that becomes effective purchasing power. Traditional money supply measures, such as M1, M2 or M3, mainly refer to money deposited with banks. Thus the M measures of the money supply constitute subsets of private sector savings. They must therefore be disqualified for use in our equation of exchange, since they mainly measure money that, at the moment of measurement, is *not* used for transactions. At any moment in time, this is merely potential, not effective purchasing power. Thus what central banks announce on a monthly basis as the so-called 'money supply' should more accurately be described as a savings supply. For our purposes we therefore are still in need of an accurate measure of the increase in actual purchasing power that is used for transactions.

Secondly, defining money by certain private sector assets, such as deposits, creates the identification problem recognized by Friedman (1956) that 'there is no hard-and-fast line between "money" and other assets'. Since none of them is at any moment in time directly used for purchases, but merely represents potential purchasing power, there is no *a priori* theoretical reason why not increasingly broader definitions of private sector assets should be used to define M. Time deposits, CDs, bonds and perhaps even real estate could be defined as money in this view. Once any specific definition has been decided upon, M measures of the money supply are then susceptible to shifts of private sector assets into or out of this measure. For instance, if savers withdraw money from postal savings accounts and place it in current accounts with banks, narrow measures of the money supply may rise. This may give the appearance of increases or reductions in the 'money supply', when actually no macroeconomic change in the amount of purchasing power or transactions in the economy has taken place. In Japan, the widely-used deposit measure M2 + CD does not include private deposits with the postal savings system. Any shift of private deposits from banks to postal savings accounts has therefore tended to slow the growth of the 'money supply' defined by M2 + CD and any reverse shift suggested faster 'money supply' growth.

Thirdly, using the traditional definition of money as cash or deposits, it remains practically impossible to implement a disaggregation of the money by the use it is put to. As Milton Friedman (1956) noted, 'dollars of money are not distinguished according as they are said to be held for one or the other purpose'.

There is, however, an alternative definition of M without these problems. This is the definition that is suggested by the inductive research method, which yields the finding that in an economy with a banking system, the amount of money actually used for transactions can only increase when, as we saw, banks create new credit. This means that bank credit creation should have a direct impact on transaction volumes, demand, and hence also prices. This has been recognized by Pollexfen (1697), Law (1720) and Thornton (1802), among others, but failed to become the mainstream view due to the erroneous fixation on legal tender or metallic money. Henry Thornton, in his classic *The Paper Credit of Great Britain* (1802), observed that new money created by banks enters the financial markets initially via an expansion of bank loans, increasing the supply of loanable funds.[8] Schumpeter (1954) points out that these authors recognized that in their economic effect, money (traditionally measured) and bank credit could be identical:

As soon as we realize that there is no essential difference between those forms of 'paper credit' that are used for paying and lending, and that demand, supported by 'credit', acts upon prices in essentially the same manner as does demand supported by legal tender, we are on the way toward a serviceable theory of the credit structure ... (pp. 718ff.)

This recognition that credit may have the same economic effect as money was a major breakthrough, because legally money and credit are quite different constructs:

And this is why Thornton's perception of the fact that the different means of payments may, on a certain level of abstraction, be treated as essentially alike was a major analytic performance, for the mere practitioner will in general be impressed by the technical differences rather than by the fundamental sameness. (Schumpeter, 1954, p. 719; italics in original)

The link between credit and the macroeconomy has not been commented upon much in the twentieth century, although at its beginning this theory was widespread enough to warrant the following entry in the *Encyclopaedia Britannica* (1910–11 edition):

The immense growth of credit and its embodiment in instruments that can be used as substitutes for money has led to the promulgation of a view respecting the value of money which may be called the Credit Theory. According to the upholders of this doctrine, the actual amount of metallic money has but a trifling effect on the range of prices, and therefore on the value of money. *What is really important is the volume of credit instruments in circulation.* It is on their amount that price movements depend. Gold has become only the small change of the wholesale markets, and its quantity is comparatively unimportant as determinant of prices. (italics added)

An explicit link between bank credit creation and macroeconomic activity was made by Hahn (1920). But despite these early insights and occasional bursts of research focusing on credit, its role has remained too small in mainstream theories. According to Schumpeter (1954),

> it proved extraordinarily difficult for economists to recognize that bank loans and bank investments do create deposits. In fact, throughout the period under survey they refused with practical unanimity to do so. (p. 1114)

Schumpeter notices the even greater curiosity that those economists that seemed to have recognized it at one stage, then completely abrogated the idea a few years later: Keynes recognized the function of banks as creators of credit in his 1930 *Treatise*, but the

> deposit-creating bank loan and its role in the financing of investment *without any previous saving up of the sums thus lent* have practically disappeared in the analytic schema of the *General Theory*, where it is again the saving public that holds the scene. Orthodox Keynesiansim has in fact reverted to the old view ... Whether this spells progress or retrogression, every economist must decide for himself. (Schumpeter, 1954, p. 1115; italics in original)

In the postwar era, Britain's Radcliffe Report (1959) emphasized credit conditions, as well as Gurley and Shaw (1960).[9] However, credit creation was not an explicit feature rendering banks unique in these theories. Further, the Hicksian IS-LM analysis, dominant in the postwar era, leaves out any role of banks, and has therefore contributed much to the neglect of bank credit and its role in the macroeconomy. Further, the deductive methodology has been a fundamental stumbling block, as it minimized empirical input. Gertler (1988) argues that the methodological approach of deducing macroeconomic frameworks from first principles – the 'micro-foundation' – favoured the emphasis on money, not credit. However, with the breakdown of the traditional monetarist 'money demand function' and the instability of velocity, the focus has increasingly shifted back to credit aggregates. Empirical evidence has so far been supportive of monetary economic models that emphasize credit, instead of deposit aggregates.[10]

In Thornton's days, specie was still used as money, but was already 'small change'. In our day and age, only created instruments serve to pay for transactions. They are brought about in the banking system, including the central bank, through the process of credit creation. Therefore we must recognize this reality by measuring M in the equation of exchange appropriately with a variable for credit creation (denoted ΔC). In order to clarify this and avoid confusion, we change notation from the traditional 'M' to 'C':[11]

(14) $CV = PQ$
(15) $CV = C_R V_R + C_F V_F$
(16) $PQ = P_R Q_R + P_F Q_F$
(17) $C_R V_R = P_R Q_R$

Since we defined $P_R Q_R$ as the value of all GDP-based transactions, we also know that the following equation holds, where P_R stands for the GDP deflator and $(P_R Y)$ stands for nominal GDP.

(17') $C_R V_R = P_R Y$
       with $V_R = (P_R Y)/C_R = \text{const.}$

(18) $C_F V_F = P_F Q_F$
       with $V_F = (P_F Q_F)/C_F = \text{const.}$

For growth:

(19) $\Delta CV = \Delta(PQ)$
(20) $\Delta CV = \Delta C_R V_R + \Delta C_F V_F$
(21) $\Delta(PQ) = \Delta(P_R Q_R) + \Delta(P_F Q_F)$

At the same time:

(22) $\Delta C_R V_R = \Delta(P_R Q_R) = \Delta(P_R Y)$
(23) $\Delta C_F V_F = \Delta(P_F Q_F)$

Solving some puzzles

Defining money

Our simple model of disaggregated credit already has a number of implications and offers solutions to some problems identified earlier in the literature. Firstly, we find that the problems of the traditional approach in measuring the money supply can be solved by this focus on credit creation:[12]

1. Credit creation measures only purchasing power that is actually used for transactions at the time of measurement – which is what the equation of exchange requires, and deposit aggregates cannot deliver. Credit always represents *effective* purchasing power, as borrowers take out loans to engage in transactions.

2. There is no doubt about where credit creation starts or stops – thus accurate and clear-cut measures of the effective 'money supply', namely credit creation, can be found. To be clear, only the net creation of new purchasing power is part of the definition. Thus what is often termed 'credit', for instance, the issuance of corporate debt or government bonds, does not in itself constitute credit creation, as in these cases existing purchasing power is merely transferred between parties.

3. Importantly for our disaggregated quantity equation, credit creation can be disaggregated, as we can obtain and analyse information about who obtains loans and what use they are put to. Sectoral loan data provide us with information about the direction of purchasing power – something deposit aggregates cannot tell us. By institutional analysis and the use of such disaggregated credit data it can be determined, at least approximately, what share of purchasing power is primarily spent on 'real' transactions that are part of GDP and what part is primarily used for financial transactions.

Multiplier analysis

The credit creation model also puts to rest the multiplier analysis, which has increasingly lost support: there is no concept of a money multiplier in this framework, since we measure the final product of bank credit creation. The money multiplier was an *ex post* attempt to link narrow money measures to broader deposit aggregates – little more than a scale factor, void of any behavioural meaning.

'Direct' and 'indirect finance'

The finance literature has discussed the difference between funding from banks and funding from capital markets from the viewpoint of the firm. It has become established practice to refer to bank loans as 'indirect finance' and borrowing from the capital markets as 'direct finance'. These labels are based on the erroneous definition of banks as mere financial intermediaries. However, banks and capital markets are different in one crucial aspect: when banks lend, new purchasing power is created that did not exist before. When firms raise money in capital markets, no new money is created. It merely represents a diversion of already existing purchasing power. Thus the labels of bank lending as 'indirect finance' and capital market funding as 'direct finance' are at best misleading. If anything, from a macroeconomic viewpoint, bank lending should instead be referred to as 'direct finance', since firms receive money directly from the creator of purchasing power. Borrowing money in the capital markets is a round-about and indirect way of receiving money, since it was originally created by the banks or the central bank and only diverted via the capital markets.

Financial disintermediation

Debates about 'financial disintermediation' can also be put in perspective. The trend towards 'disintermediation', that is, increasing corporate finance through bond issuance instead of borrowing from banks, may be a much more mixed blessing than has previously been recognized. For one, it is clear that banks should not be expected ever to become extinct (except by direct government policy to eliminate them): they have a monopoly power among private sector institutions that capital markets can never approach – they can create money 'out of nothing'. When firms increasingly desert banks in order to borrow 'directly' in the capital markets, banks will not close down, but they may end up lending to other, often lower-risk borrowers (such as consumers or speculators). The latter obtain the newly created money. But money is fungible. As it finds its way into the capital markets, the firms that issue bonds will ultimately receive some of it. However, such a process is far more indirect in the true sense of the word, and increases banks' risk, and hence overall systemic risk. Thus disintermediation may not be a desirable development, from the perspective of financial and economic stability.

Savings and growth

Without fully reflecting the implications of credit creation, macroeconomic theories were doomed to misunderstand also other concepts, such as the role of savings and the determinants of growth. Most of modern economics assumes – and policy-makers cite regularly – the idea that there is a given amount of savings that poses a physical limit for the total amount of money that can be raised by firms and hence invested. In reality, savings are not limited at any moment in time. They are not a constraint on loans or investment. Occasionally economists worry about a 'savings shortage' or 'capital shortage', which they feel is holding back growth. There is no such thing. Savings do not impose a limit on economic growth. If more money is required for investment, banks can simply create it.[13] Thus savings do not have to precede investment. To the contrary, investment is funded by credit creation, which will create nominal income growth and also increase savings.[14]

Endogenous money

As we have seen, there is a school of thought that argues that money, defined as deposits, is endogenous. In the present framework, money (defined as deposit aggregates) is always endogenous – namely to the creation of credit. As we saw, the amount of deposits can only increase if banks create new credit. The more interesting question is whether credit creation is endogenous or exogenous. Thus what requires further examination is the issue of causality. Many proponents of endogenous money also argue that credit is endogenous – as Wicksell argued in the nineteenth century. Is this true? To find an answer about how the credit market is determined, it is useful to consider in general how market outcomes come about.

Market rationing and disequilibrium economics

We have seen that the mainstream approach makes a large number of assumptions. On the basis of these, it is concluded that markets are in equilibrium (the Walrasian outcome). One of the necessary assumptions is perfect information. The inductive methodology can be used to identify whether an economy can be characterized by perfect information. For this, a few basic empirical tests can be conducted. Firstly, one can test whether in the economy in question money exists. Should there be no money in an economy and instead all transactions take place by barter, then this would be consistent with the assumption that there is perfect information. If money does exist and is commonly used, then this is evidence that information, for instance about the multiple coincidence of wants, is imperfect. As a result, barter will be cumbersome, and therefore money is used as medium of exchange.[15] Secondly, one can empirically test the degree of perfection of information by analysing whether a significant amount of economic activities exist in the economy that thrive on imperfect information. If they do, this is evidence that information cannot be perfect – otherwise these industries could not possibly exist. A third empirical test can be conducted easily by any reader of this book. If the reader is currently reading this book or has read any other books or newspapers then this can be considered *prima facie* evidence that the reader does not yet know everything that is worth knowing, and hence suffers from imperfect information.

Conducting these empirical tests, what can we conclude about the availability of information in virtually all economies in the world? Money exists in almost all economies. Sizeable industries exist that are based on providing information services, namely banking, broking, real estate, advertising, consulting, employment agencies, media and communications businesses, and so forth. In most industrialized countries these account for substantial proportions of GDP. None of these industries should exist, if information was really perfect. Thus we can report the results of our empirical tests: information is not perfect. Imperfect information appears to be pervasive.

This has major implications for Walrasian models of market clearing – the foundation of most economics textbooks, where an equilibrium is determined through movements of prices to the level that equalizes demand and supply. If we relax the assumption of perfect information or the presence of an all-knowing price-setting auctioneer, we find that there is no guarantee that any market will clear. Market clearing would be merely by chance. The probability of disequilibrium is therefore far likelier than equilibrium.

What happens when markets do not clear? They are rationed and thus not determined by prices, but quantities – namely according to the short side principle: whichever quantity of demand or supply is smaller determines the market outcome. Since we must expect virtually all markets to be rationed, prices cannot be the key variables that theoretical textbook economics make them out to be. Instead, quantities are more important. A quite different kind of economics is required to understand the real world, namely disequilibrium economics. Since the majority of all recent writings in economics are based on equilibrium economics, it is fair to say that the majority of economics is irrelevant as a description of how economies work and for the purpose of formulating suitable policy advice. Instead, we need to acknowledge and utilize the insights by such pioneers of disequilibrium economics that have proposed models with non-Walrasian outcomes, but have remained largely ignored by mainstream economics, namely Barro and Grossman (1976), Malinvaud (1977), Muellbauer and Portes (1978), Quandt and Rosen (1986) and Benassy (1986) (see also Clower, 1965). Disequilibrium economics is clearly more relevant to the real world.

The determination of the credit market

We can now proceed to apply this finding of the pervasiveness of market rationing to the credit market. Since due to imperfect information also the credit market will be rationed, it will be determined by the quantity (according to the short principle), and not the price. This explains the empirical fact that interest rates have not been very useful as explanatory or predictive variables of either economic activity or, indeed, money and credit growth.

Next we need to determine which of demand and supply is more likely to be the 'short' quantity, that is, whether the credit market is more likely to be demand- or supply-rationed. The question is whether the credit supply is more important (in which case credit would be exogenously determined by the credit creating institutions) or whether credit demand is more important (in which case credit would be endogenous).

Those who argue that credit is endogenous in effect make the case that banks cannot create too much credit (for instance, so that inflation is created), 'because there is a market mechanism that induces banks to supply just the amount of money that the public wants to hold' (Glasner, 1992, p. 869). In the words of Tobin (1963): 'For bank created money, there is an economic mechanism of extinction as well as creation, contraction as well as expansion. If bank deposits are excessive relative to public preferences, they will tend to decline; otherwise banks will lose income' (p. 278). Black (1972) concurred: 'If a bank issues money to make a loan to one person and that money is more than the public wants to hold at equilibrium interest rates, then it will simply be used to pay off another loan, at the same bank or at another bank' (p. 812) (all three quotes from Dalziel, 2000, p. 379). Although the creation of deposits is endogenous to credit creation in a technical sense, the argument here is that demand for deposits determines the supply of deposits. The main function of banks is to supply deposits in this view. Banks supply just the right amount of credit in order to supply the amount of deposits that is demanded. Hence in this view the supply of credit is endogenous to the demand for deposits. In the limit, the banking system would always supply as much credit and thus deposits as are demanded at whatever interest rate is determined by the central bank.

However, this school makes several unrealistic assumptions. Firstly, it assumes that the demand for money or credit is similar to the demand for apples or oranges, namely that it is finite. Tobin and authors with a similar view had a stable, downward-sloping demand function for deposits (the 'money demand function') in mind. This ignores the unusual feature of credit or money: while the demand for goods and services may be finite (as increased amounts, beyond a certain level, also tend to create disutility), this is not the case with money. As Stiglitz and Weiss (1981) have pointed out, the legal construct of corporate entities with limited liability of directors creates an asymmetric incentive structure, where directors who borrow money to build up their business may gain much if they succeed, but their downside will be limited if they don't (their personal wealth will remain untouched). If they succeed, they may be the next Bill Gates. If they fail, they will lose their paid-in equity capital, but not more. The actual demand for credit is therefore always relatively large (even if from crank entrepreneurs with high-risk ideas). Faced with the reality of many high-risk borrowers and imperfect information about their true intentions or the viability of their projects, banks would be unwise to raise interest rates until credit demand equals supply. Adverse selection and moral hazard would raise the banks' default risk: to equalize the strong credit demand with credit supply would produce extremely high interest rates, which would force the sensible borrowers out of the market and leave banks with the high-risk borrowers. As a result, banks would not maximize their profits, as non- performing loans would be substantial. Given this reality, rational, profit-maximizing banks will maintain interest rates far below the equilibrium level and instead ration credit (see also Keeton, 1979).[16]

Put simply, since demand for money or credit is very large (perhaps infinite), the supply is the short side, which determines the market outcome. This means (a) that the market for credit is determined by the quantity of credit supplied by the creators of credit, and (b) those suppliers – mainly commercial banks – make allocative decisions about who will obtain loans and who will not. As Blanchard and Fischer (1989) point out, if credit rationing exists 'it is possible that the interest rate is not a reliable indicator of the impact of financial variables on aggregate demand. It is quite likely in that case that quantity variables, such as the amount of credit, have to be looked at in appraising monetary and financial policy' (p. 479). Figure 13.1 shows a representation of the aggregate bank credit supply. Based on Stiglitz and Weiss (1981), the curve is assumed to be continuous (using assumptions that we do not require in our framework) and backward-bending around the level of interest i^* at which the banking system in aggregate maximizes

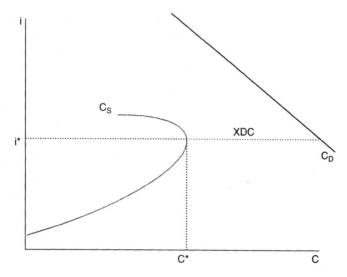

Figure 13.1   An example of credit market disequilibrium

profits. As discussed, banks in this model balance the revenue effect from higher interest rates against the losses due to bankruptcies that are likely to rise with interest rates (as the sensible projects become fewer and the riskier projects increase). Beyond i* higher interest rates have a net negative effect on bank revenues and hence banks do not wish to raise rates beyond this point.

The aggregate demand for credit is deliberately shown far removed from the supply curve, though this is likely to be an understatement of actual aggregate loan demand. In practice it is likely to be so large as to be 'off the chart'. Banks will set interest rates based on their profit maximization at i* and supply a quantity of credit C* to the economy. Since aggregate credit demand is far larger than supply of credit, the difference represents the excess demand for credit (marked XDC). In reality, there need not be a continuous aggregate credit supply curve.

Solving the enigma of interest rates

There has been ample empirical evidence that banks ration credit. This includes the studies we have already cited in Chapter 3 when we discussed the credit view and credit rationing approaches. As Keynes (1930) once put it, there is always a 'fringe of unsatisfied borrowers'. In the case of Japan, we saw in Figure 10.2 that bank lending and lending rates were not in the type of clear-cut negative correlation postulated by mainstream theory. This is in line with our theory of a rationed credit market. Even the call market, where short-term credit is supplied between banks and the central bank, appears to be a market that is not in equilibrium: Figure 13.2 shows the quantity of credit supplied by the Bank of Japan and the call rate.

The central bank could set interest rates at virtually any desired level and supply the desired amount of funds (on occasion vastly positive, as in March 1998, and on occasion significantly negative, despite the same or even lower interest rates, as in 1999). Short-term interest rates can thus be determined separately, and usually in reflection of (that is, following) economic growth. That was also what we saw from Figures 6.1 and 6.2, which suggested that central banks move short-term interest rates following economic growth – higher after growth has accelerated and lower after it has decelerated. Finally, the enigma of the link between interest rates and economic activity can be explained by our model: interest rates are not the primary variable determining the credit market or economic growth, but the quantity of credit. The link between the quantity of credit and growth will be examined further in Chapter 15.

We conclude that the likeliest assumption concerning the determination of the credit market is that it is supply-determined.[17] Anyone who has ever applied for a bank loan and was turned down can confirm that banks do not always lend to everyone who wants to borrow, and thus loan demand is likely to be larger than supply.

As discussed, the traditional credit view approach remains insufficient to explain why bank credit rationing should have macroeconomic outcomes.

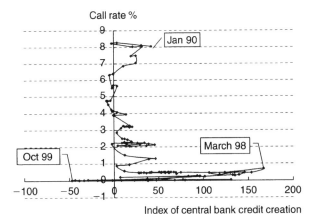

Figure 13.2   Bank of Japan credit creation and the call rate

Source: Profit Research Center Ltd.

The current literature maintains that the Stiglitz and Weiss (1981) case is 'not sufficient to establish a binding finance constraint on the macrolevel' (Trautwein, 2000, p. 157). There are two reasons for this: the standard literature, including the credit view approach, considers banks mere financial intermediaries. As a result, even if we recognize credit rationing by banks, there is no reason why other financial intermediaries should not step in to make up for the lack of bank credit supply. Secondly, some economists argue that the existence of rationing means that banks are not able to expand credit, even though they may wish to do so.

However, in reality banks are special, as they are (together with the central bank) the only financial service providers that can create new purchasing power out of nothing. Thus if banks ration credit, this certainly will result in macroeconomic credit rationing, since the total amount of credit creation constitutes the overarching budget constraint on the entire economy which is quantity-rationed by it. This is clear from equations (17') and (22), for nominal GDP.

Secondly, the argument that credit rationing means that banks cannot lend does not follow, either from Stiglitz and Weiss (1981) or in our framework. What a model with excess loan demand establishes is that the credit supply is not endogenous to credit demand. How precisely banks determine the supply of credit and to which other variables outside the model credit may be endogenous is an issue we will not address here, but return to in a later chapter, when we discuss the puzzle of Japanese bank lending in the 1980s. But even if credit is endogenous to other variables that are outside the model (such as central bank behaviour or the amount of bad debts) then this does not change the fact that, as far as our model is concerned, credit supply determines the credit market and hence economic activity. The supply of credit constitutes a binding finance constraint on the macroeconomy, while at the same time further bank credit expansion is possible in principle.[18]

We conclude that we must expect causation to always run from the credit variable (C) to the transaction variable (PQ) or its components. Muellbauer and Portes (1978) have shown how rationing in one market leads to rationing in others. Credit rationing by the banking system in aggregate will also lead to rationing in other markets. With rationing, quantities become the most important macroeconomic variable, delivering exogenous budget constraints to any microeconomic market. In terms of the structure of economic models, this clearly favours a top-down approach, where a macro foundation is imposed on micro models. Micro-foundation-based macro models suffer from the fallacy of composition and fail to take the binding macro constraint imposed by the quantity of credit creation into consideration.

Thus pulling together the various strands of relevant literature, we obtain the following picture: by virtue of the credit creation process, money is endogenous to credit. By virtue of the limited liability of directors and the unique nature of money, there is always some demand for credit. Due to imperfect information, banks ration credit and the credit market does not clear and is determined by the quantity of credit supplied by banks (and the central bank). By virtue of the special nature of banks as creators of credit, the quantity of credit supplied becomes the ultimate budget constraint on economic activity.

A final point on the argument whether the credit market is demand or supply determined: We also need to remind ourselves that the conditions for endogeneity are more stringent than those for exogeneity. This is due to the difference in status – power, if one wants to put it this way – between a bank and a loan applicant. The ultimate decision about a loan is made by the bank. Thus a rejection of the thesis of exogeneity is harder, because banks (and/or the central bank) may on occasion voluntarily decide to accommodate demand for loans more than on other occasions. Thus examples of apparently endogenous credit may still be consistent with the exogeneity proposition. However, to reject the hypothesis of endogeneity, we only need to provide evidence that banks do not always lend to everyone as much as is demanded. This would demonstrate that the credit market is rationed.

Some implications

Our framework settles the dispute about the question whether there has been a credit crunch in Japan (or other countries) at one time or another. If a credit crunch is defined as credit rationing, then it always exists. The issue becomes one of ascertaining the degree of rationing.[19] Moreover, our framework settles the question of whether there is a 'credit channel' of monetary transmission. There is, by virtue of the nature of the credit creation process. Indeed, it is the main transmission channel.

More importantly, the debate about government intervention versus free and unimpeded markets receives a decisive jolt in favour of intervention, once we admit that markets do not generally clear. For all the theoretical proofs that government intervention disturbs the perfect free market equilibrium becomes irrelevant. Since the markets are nowhere as powerful and efficient as the mainstream economists have argued, the hurdle for government intervention to be at least as efficient as markets becomes much lower. It still remains true that stupid government intervention will not be good. However, we will see that clever government intervention can beat the less impressive reality of many market outcomes, especially that type of government intervention which uses market mechanisms, focuses on indirect intervention in the form of the conscious design of incentive structures and concentrates direct intervention on the credit markets, by directing credit to highly productive uses. Since the invisible hand is shown to be especially powerful in the theoretical models that focus on static allocation of given resources and even in those theoretical models has difficulties dealing with the dynamics of economic growth, it is not surprising to find that in a non-fiction world with the pervasiveness of rationed markets, government intervention is especially powerful in enhancing economic growth.

A quantity theorem of disaggregated credit

Having settled the issue of the definition of money to be used in the equation of exchange – it must be credit – our knowledge of the causation between credit and other variables delivered behavioural relationships. We can thus now restate our disequilibrium model of disaggregated credit more clearly, placing the endogenous variables on the left-hand side of the equation:

(14′) $PQ = CV$
(17″) $P_RQ_R = C_RV_R$
          with $V_R = (P_RY)/C_R = \text{const.}$
(18′) $P_FQ_F = C_FV_F$

Thus the two key equations of our model can be restated as follows:

(22′) $\Delta(P_RY) = V_R\,\Delta C_R$
(23′) $\Delta(P_FQ_F) = V_F\,\Delta C_F$

This basic model, which remains largely unrestricted by assumptions, can now also be used to answer the many puzzles of Japanese macroeconomic performance – and indeed the macroeconomic puzzles encountered in many other countries.

14
Explaining the Velocity Decline

Our framework solves the enigma of the velocity decline that was observed in many countries during the 1980s, including Japan. The apparent decline in velocity is simply due to the fact that the equation of exchange has been erroneously defined. Researchers assumed that

(1) $MV = PQ$

can be proxied reasonably accurately by

(2) $MV = P_R Y$

However, this is true if and only if

(3) $PQ = P_R Y$

that is, all transactions for which money is used are part of and accurately measured by nominal GDP. This ignores the possibility that transactions that are not part of GDP, such as financial and real estate transactions, exist and may develop differently from GDP-based transactions. There is little empirical evidence that equation (3) can be considered to hold true. Instead, it is a special case that only applies when there are no real estate or financial transactions, or, in the case of changes, when these non-GDP transactions remain a constant proportion of all transactions. In general, we must expect that GDP-based transactions are a subset of all transactions. Thus instead of equation (3):

(4) $PQ \geq P_R Y$

If

(5) $C_F V_F = P_F Q_F \neq 0$

then equation (3) does not hold and

(6) $PQ \neq P_R Y$

If we then erroneously employ equation (2), then any increase in the supply of credit that is used for non-GDP transactions will affect the value of financial transactions, but need not affect the value of nominal GDP. Thus the velocity must fall, as it has been defined by the erroneous equation (2), here called V_M, with

(2′) $V_M = (P_R Y)/M$

In other words, we see that the reported velocity decline is not surprising in those countries where financial and real estate transactions increased disproportionately (due to a disproportionate rise in C_F). Indeed, declines of velocity V in equation (2′) were reported in those countries, where financial transactions increased and usually asset prices rose as a result. Both phenomena are due to an expansion in credit used for financial transactions C_F.

This can easily be seen when comparing the traditional 'quantity theory of money' velocity in equation (2′) (here called V_M) with our disaggregated credit velocities. Even if the real velocity V_R remained constant over the 1980s, the velocity of the traditional quantity theory of money, would give the erroneous impression that overall velocity has declined. Since a rise in total credit that is mainly due to an increase in financial transactions tends to increase traditional measures of the money supply M, but will hardly affect nominal GDP ($P_R Y$), V_M cannot remain constant: M rises, but $P_R Y$ does not. Hence V_M falls. However, real velocity V_R, or, indeed, the overall velocity of equation (1) need not decline. The observed velocity decline is merely due to the misspecification of equations (2) and (3), which neglect financial transactions. The framework of disaggregated credit thus explains the velocity 'anomaly'.

Empirical test

It is now straightforward to put this explanation of the apparent velocity 'puzzle' to an empirical test. We use the case of the velocity decline during the 1980s in Japan. First, let us recall our empirical finding of Chapter 7, where we saw that the traditionally defined income velocity, following equation (2′), showed a significant decline. This was true even for the most popular measure of the money supply, M2 + CD.

According to our disaggregated framework, this was to be expected. The first test of our model is therefore to see whether the correctly defined income velocity – what we call V_R, the velocity of real circulation – is also declining, or whether it is more stable, as we would expect. Since we know that the income velocity will be constant, as long as we find an accurate measure of C_R, credit in real circulation, this is in practice a test of our empirical proxies for C_R and C_F. We have therefore reached the point where we need to find accurate measures of disaggregated credit. How can this be done?

The identification of suitable empirical proxies for our disaggregation of credit into that used for GDP-based transactions and that credit which is not, requires some examination of the statistics on bank credit that are compiled by central banks. Since 1942, the Bank of Japan has published a detailed breakdown of credit by the industrial sector that receives the loans. These sectoral credit statistics were available on a monthly basis until April 1998, when the Bank of Japan stopped releasing them to the public. They are still available on a quarterly basis. Incidentally, the development of these statistics did not occur by coincidence: at around the year 1942, the Bank of Japan started using a model similar to our own, and employed direct controls over bank lending in order to manipulate the economy (more on this in Chapter 20).[1]

Analysing those figures, we need to identify which industries are likely to conduct transactions with the newly created credit that are outside the definition of GDP. We already have identified financial and real estate transactions as the main type of transactions that are not part of GDP. Transactions of this kind, which are not due to shifts of already existing purchasing power, but based on bank borrowing (and hence on a net addition in purchasing power) are mainly conducted by the real estate and construction sector and the non-bank financial institutions (such as brokers' margin loans, or loans passed on to the real estate sector). Nikkei Koshasai Joho (1991) and Werner (1991) identified loans to the real estate sector, construction firms and non-bank financial institutions (which mainly served as conduit for real estate loans) as speculative credit creation used for real estate transactions (later dubbed the three 'bubble sectors'). In addition, many loans to the service sector also ended up as purchasing power used for financial or real estate speculation. However, not the entire total of service sector loans are likely to be relevant. We will use the three 'bubble sectors' as our primary definition of C_F, and add the service sector as a fourth sector for purposes of comparison. The empirical test will reveal how accurate the definitions are.

With C_F determined and total credit C known, we can also calculate C_R. Using these figures, we first calculate a measure of the traditional velocity V_M of equation (2'). Concerning the empirical proxy for M, one could of course use any of the many deposit aggregates. For a fair comparison, we here use the most popular M2 + CD aggregate, whose movement is said to be most closely correlated with total credit C and whose absolute size is also most similar to the total of outstanding loans. Next, we can calculate the accurately defined income velocity derived previously, namely

(7) $V_R = (P_R Y)/C_R$

and compare the two measures of velocity.

Figure 14.1 shows the time series of both types of velocity. The traditional, wrongly defined income velocity V_M is seen to be falling by over 35% between 1979 and 2001. Using loans to the three 'bubble' sectors to proxy C_F, we obtain a more correctly defined income velocity, shown in the graph as V_R. As can be seen, it is not perfect – there is also a temporary decline of about 10% during the observation period. However, the velocity recovers and overall maintains an almost horizontal trend line. Clearly, some loans also to other sectors ended up being used for financial speculation and non-GDP transactions. Using loans to the service sector as the likeliest candidate, we calculated an alternative measure of the real circulation velocity V_R, called V_{R4}, and find that it remains almost perfectly constant throughout the 1980s, the time of the financial 'bubble'. However, it showed a temporary rise during the early 1990s (suggesting that not the entire rise in service sector loans was used for speculative purposes, thus implying that adding all four sectors is somewhat too broad a measure of the bubble sectors). In any case, it is clear that the phenomenon of a declining velocity is due to the lack of consideration given to financial transactions.

As the four-sector proxy appears too large, we continue to use loans to the three 'bubble' sectors as our main proxy for C_F. Figure 14.2 compares only

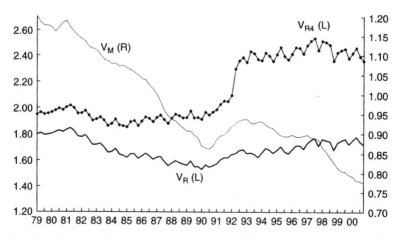

Figure 14.1   Old and new velocities V_M, V_R and V_{R4}

Sources: Cabinet Office, Government of Japan; Bank of Japan.

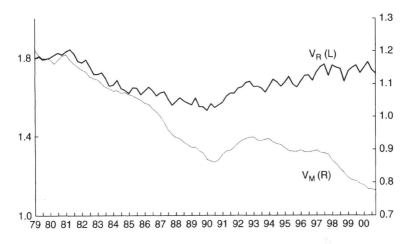

Figure 14.2 The old velocity V_M and the new velocity V_R

Sources: Cabinet Office, Government of Japan; Bank of Japan.

Table 14.1 Regression of V_M and V_R against trend

The estimation sample is: 1979 (1) to 2000 (4)   no. of observations 88

Modelling V_M *(nGDP/M2CD) by OLS*

Variable	Coefficient	Std. Error	t-value	t-prob.	Part. R^2
Constant	1.16934	0.009073	129.	0.000	0.9948
Trend	−0.00444243	0.0001771	−25.1	0.000	0.8798

$R^2 = 0.879783$ $F(1,86) = 629.4$ [0.000]**   Sigma = 0.042196   RSS = 0.153123447
log-likelihood = 154.703   DW = 0.0351   var(V_M) = 0.0144742

Modelling V_R *(nGDP/C$_R$) by OLS*

Variable	Coefficient	Std. Error	t-value	t-prob.	Part. R^2
Constant	1.70243	0.01727	98.6	0.000	0.9912
Trend	−0.000460290	0.0003371	−1.37	0.176	0.0212

$R^2 = 0.021224$ $F(1,86) = 1.865$ [0.176]   Sigma = 0.0803185   RSS = 0.55479184
log-likelihood = 98.0594   DW = 0.104   var(V_R) = 0.00644116

the old velocity V_M and the velocity V_R, based on subtracting the three bubble sectors from total credit.

We now proceed to a formal test of the time trend, using ordinary least squares (Table 14.1). Here it can be seen that V_M has a negative trend that is highly significant, while V_R has virtually no significantly correlated time trend – its trend is almost a horizontal line.[2] This supports the proposed framework of a dichotomous credit circulation and indicates that the proxies used to represent C_F and C_R are reasonably accurate.

We can conclude that we have solved the puzzle of the apparent velocity decline that has preoccupied many economists and researchers and that has demonstrated that there were fundamental problems with the traditional approaches to macroeconomics. In our new framework we recognize that the alleged velocity decline did not actually occur: it was merely due to the misleading definition of velocity, based on an inaccurate quantity equation, which neglects the possibility of a rise in 'money' used for financial transactions. The true income velocity identified by our model did not in fact decline. This also means that there is a stable link between the monetary side of the economy and the non-monetary, 'real' side. We can now use this link in order to solve the other enigmas that traditional approaches could not solve.

15
The Determinants of Growth

John Law, born in Edinburgh, the son of a goldsmith and banker, recognized the implications of the activities of banks and their link to the economy. He argued that wealth depends on goods and their trade 'and Trade depends on Money'. 'But only banker-created money ensures a sufficiently active supply' (Davies, 1994, p. 553, paraphrasing Law). 'By this Money the People may be employed, the Country improved, Manufacture advanced, Trade Domestic and Foreign be carried on, and Wealth and Power attained' (quoted in Davies, 1994, p. 553).

Indeed, we saw that growth of economic activity is only possible if more money is used for transactions. Since the majority of transactions is paid for by book money or bank money, such money must increase for growth to be possible. Thus the budget constraint on the amount of money available for new transactions is credit creation. Specifically, for nominal GDP growth to take place, necessary and sufficient condition is an increase in the amount of credit creation used for GDP transactions:

(1) $\Delta(P_R Y) = V_R \Delta C_R$

Before we move to test this model of nominal GDP growth, we need to address several other issues. Firstly, in our framework we have been primarily interested in nominal GDP. We have, so far, not been concerned with the distribution of this increase in nominal GDP between prices (the GDP deflator) and real output (real GDP) (since nominal GDP growth is the sum of inflation as measured by the GDP deflator and real GDP growth).

Potential output

If credit creation used for GDP transactions C_R rises, what will be the impact on prices P_R and real output Y? The answer depends on several factors, including the potential growth rate. Put simply, if actual growth approaches its maximum potential growth rate, further increases in credit creation will deliver actual nominal GDP growth, but also inflation. If actual GDP growth lags behind potential growth, there will be deflationary pressures. In general, potential output is the maximum possible output that can be achieved when (a) all resources (factor inputs) are fully mobilized (that is, when the quantity of factor inputs is maximized) *and* (b) when the productivity of their use is maximized (that is, maximum factor productivity). Thus:

(2) $Y^* = f(QFI^*; TFP^*)$

where Y^* stands for potential real output, which is a function of the quantity of factor inputs (QFI) and the quality of their use (total factor productivity, TFP). Potential output can also be considered akin to the aggregate supply of the economy.

Actual output, as we saw, is determined by actual demand, which is a function of credit creation. Much of the traditional growth theories or development economics have focused on potential output. In a world where we assume that actual output is always at potential this is of course sufficient. However, in reality, where there is imperfect information and the long list of standard assumptions does not hold, there is no reason why actual output can be expected to equal potential output. In the non-fiction world of disequilibrium economics, actual growth often falls short of the potential. We therefore need the kind of development economics that includes a realistic modelling of the reasons why actual growth may fall short of potential. Credit rationing and the subsequent quantity rationing of the entire economy supply a realistic answer.

The relationship between credit creation and economic activity can be illustrated by the following basic scenarios. We can consider the various scenarios easily, when expressing equation (1) in terms of percentage growth rates, abstracting from the velocity. In this case, actual growth is given by nominal GDP growth, which in turn is determined by the increase in credit creation for GDP transactions. The (seasonally) differenced natural logarithm of a variable is a close approximation of its percentage growth rate. Following the convention to denote natural logarithms with small letters, the percentage growth rate of C_R is written as Δc_R and equation (1) becomes:

(1′) $\Delta p_R + \Delta y = \Delta c_R$

The price impact of credit creation at full employment

If the economy operates at full employment of all factor inputs, then for given productivity any increase in GDP-based credit creation C_R must raise prices. This is the special case which classical and neoclassical economists focused on, by assuming that it will always apply. Using (1′), it can be represented as follows:

If $\qquad$ $Y^* = Y = $ constant
and $\qquad$ $\Delta c_R > 0$
then with $\qquad$ $\Delta y = 0$
we obtain $\qquad$ $\Delta c_R = \Delta p_R$

In this case, with output already operating at maximum capacity, new credit creation will push up only prices. A 5% increase in (GDP-based) credit creation will result in a 5% increase in prices. As the entire increase in real circulation credit C_R is reflected in an increase in the GDP deflator, real GDP Y will remain unchanged.

The price impact of credit creation below full employment

If actual output is below potential output, then in principle there is no reason for increases in credit creation used for GDP transactions (Δc_R) to produce inflation. In this case, our disequilibrium model reads as follows:

If $\qquad$ $Y^* > Y$
and $\qquad$ $\Delta c_R > 0$
then with $\qquad$ $\Delta p_R = 0$
we obtain $\qquad$ $\Delta c_R = \Delta y$

This means that when not all resources are fully mobilized, or when there are productivity gains, one yen in new credit creation used for GDP transactions may result in one yen in new real output and income – without inflation. The increase in nominal GDP (PY) will be entirely due to rises in real GDP (Y). This case of underutilization of factor inputs (and thus unemployment, idle factories, and so on) of course describes Japan's situation during much of the 1990s.

Speculative credit creation

If banks create new purchasing power and lend it for financial transactions, including stock and real estate transactions (C_F), then the amount of output will stay unchanged, since this does not lead to the production of new goods or services. However, this will not lead to consumer price inflation even when output is at the full employment level, since the extra purchasing power is not used to lay claim on output that is part of GDP. However, the newly created purchasing power is used for financial transactions, whose nominal value must rise. This is, at least in the short-term and certainly in the case of fixed assets, such as real estate, likely to result in asset price rises. Thus:

If $Y^* = Y = $ constant
and $\Delta c_F > 0$
such that $\Delta c_R = 0$
we obtain $\Delta c_R = \Delta p_R = \Delta y = 0$

However,

$$\Delta p_F + \Delta q_F = \Delta c_F$$

Speculative credit creation may therefore result in asset price inflation, while output and prices may not be affected. This case will be examined more closely in the following chapter.

Further disaggregation of credit creation

Consider again an economy at full employment. Modern economics neglects the possibility that increases in credit remain without inflation, and instead result only in real economic growth, even when there is full employment of factor inputs. Proponents of the real bills doctrine presumably tried to describe this case, but their attempts were misunderstood (or too clumsy).[1] To analyse this case we need to remind ourselves that we can easily disaggregate credit further than we have done so far. We have split credit creation into that new purchasing power used for non-GDP transactions, and credit used for GDP or national income-based transactions (C_F and C_R). However, we can split national income Y further into its components, enabling us also to disaggregate the use of GDP-based credit C_R further.

All this seems unfamiliar to economists that are only used to Walrasian-style equilibrium economics, where continuous functions and well-behaved models mainly deal with prices. However, as we saw, such economics belongs to the world of fiction. The reality is governed by disequilibrium economics, and this means that in practice we are dealing with often 'lumpy' quantities. Let us therefore break nominal GDP into its income components (here considering a closed economy):

(3) $PY = C + I + G$

where C, I and G stand for nominal consumption, nominal private-sector investment and nominal government spending. Likewise, we can now disaggregate credit used for GDP transactions C_R further into credit used for consumption, credit used for investment, credit used for government expenditure (our model can be easily extended for an open economy by adding net exports

NX, with exports being exogenous and imports a function of income; however, for expositional purposes we will ignore net exports). Hence:

$$(4) \quad C_R = C_C + C_I + C_G$$

For which type of economic activity newly created credit will be used is an important question that will affect the potential growth rate and thus establishes a direct link between credit creation and potential growth. It will also affect the determination of prices.

Consumptive credit creation

If banks create new purchasing power and lend it for consumption purposes (C_C), then the amount of output will stay unchanged, since consumption does not lead to new output of goods or services. Thus when output is at or close to the full employment level and more purchasing power is created through 'consumptive credit creation', more transactions will take place, chasing a given amount of output. This consumptive credit creation C_C will then translate into higher consumer goods prices. This is a restatement of the slightly less specific first case above. Thus:

If $Y^* = Y = \text{constant}$
and $\Delta c_C > 0$
such that $\Delta c_R > 0$
we obtain $\Delta c_R = \Delta p_R$

A 5% increase in consumptive credit creation will push up consumer prices by 5%. The rise in total real circulation credit C_R will push up the GDP deflator proportionately. Consumptive credit creation is therefore inflationary.

Productive credit creation and the theory of economic development

If, however, the banks (or their regulatory authority) can ensure that new credit creation is used specifically for that type of activity that will enhance the potential growth rate, such as for productive investment, then even with output at the full employment level, additional credit creation may remain non-inflationary and result in higher output – beyond the former full employment level.

In effect, the allocation of credit organizes and mobilizes the factors of input, which may boost the potential growth rate. Moreover, as Schumpeter (1912) described, credit allows the implementation of research and development, which can result in the invention of innovations and new technologies. New technologies – in effect recipes to combine given inputs in a new way that produces a product which is valued highly by buyers – enhance total factor productivity. Credit can also enable entrepreneurs or firms to implement new technologies. This means that both the mobilization of factor inputs and total factor productivity can be enhanced through the clever direction of credit to productive uses. Since the credit market is always rationed and supply-determined, banks are already engaged as allocators. They have the power to discriminate, and this can be harnessed to benefit economic growth. Credit creation fulfils the crucial (but neglected) function of organizing inputs to enable the production of new products, and at the same time creates the income to enable consumers to buy the product.[2] Thus it is possible (but not necessarily always the case) that the following functions will hold true:

(5) $QFI = g(C_I; ...)$

(6) $TFP = h(C_I; ...)$

In other words, the creation of new credit for productive investment C_I ('productive credit creation') may help mobilize factors of production that the borrowing firm would otherwise not have been able to mobilize (boosting QFI), while at the same time it may allow the invention of new recipes and their implementation (raising TFP). These new technologies may therefore increase the potential growth rate. Thus even when the economy is in a situation where actual output is at the full employment level it is possible for new credit creation to be non-inflationary and instead boost growth further, namely by raising the full employment level of output through the implementation of new technologies.

A dynamic disequilibrium model is necessary to represent this process. To keep it as tractable as the above relationships, we make a number of simplifying assumptions, for instance that the boost to potential output (in money terms) is as large or larger than the cost in terms of productive credit creation ($\Delta Y^*P_R \geq \Delta C_R$). This is a plausible assumption, since new technology is characterized by increasing returns to scale and has other unusual features and positive externalities which traditional economics models cannot deal with well – but which sit comfortably with our framework (some of these features of technology are that it is a non-rival, non-exclusive, reproducible good to which the second law of thermodynamics does not apply; because it is pure knowledge, code that can be stored, accumulated, reused without diminishing and without limiting the simultaneous use by others). Moreover, we assume that the full employment level of output allows for frictional or natural unemployment, which provides enough leeway for the temporary mobilization of resources without immediate inflationary pressure. We further assume that credit creation takes one time period to affect nominal GDP (either prices or output), just as the implementation of new technologies takes one time period:

(7) $\Delta p_{Rt+1} + \Delta y_{t+1} = \Delta c_{Rt}$

(8) $Y_{t+1}^* = f(QFI_t^*; TFP_t^*)$

Thanks to the productive credit creation C_I in time period 1, the rise in nominal output PY (due to greater C_I and C_R) is matched by higher real output in period 2, made possible due to the productivity gains implemented due to credit creation C_I. During this time period 2, prices would rise in reaction to the increased purchasing power created in time period 1, if output had not increased. However, this incipient rise is neutralized and price pressure disappears in the second time period, as potential output has risen. Thus:

Time period t:

$$Y_t^* = Y_t$$

and $\quad \Delta c_{Rt} = 0$

Time period t + 1:

$$\Delta c_{It+1} > 0$$
so that $\quad \Delta c_{Rt+1} > 0$

but since in the previous period there was no increase in credit, we obtain

$$\Delta p_{Rt+1} = 0$$

and $\quad \Delta y_{t+1} = 0$

Time period t + 2:

$$\Delta tfp_{t+2} > 0 \text{ (due to } \Delta c_{It+1} > 0)$$

so that $\quad \Delta y_{t+2}^* > 0$ (according to equation (6); with $\Delta Y^* P_{Rt+2} \geq \Delta C_{Rt+1}$)
and $\quad \Delta y_{t+2} > 0$
with $\quad Y_{t+2}^* \geq Y_{t+2}$
then $\quad \Delta y_{t+2} = \Delta c_{Rt+1}$
and $\quad \Delta p_{Rt+2} = 0$

Although the economy initially already operated at the full employment level, an increase in productive credit creation increased productivity and thus boosted output without stirring inflation. It is possible to create more credit (and thus also increase the money supply) in an economy that is already at full employment without inflation, if this new credit creation is used for activities that enhance the maximum potential and actual output.

This is what German economists, including Schumpeter (1912) referred to frequently in the late nineteenth century and the first half of the twentieth century, when they suggested that 'productive credit creation is non-inflationary' (see Werner, 2003d, 2004b).[3]

> Banks do not, of course, 'create' legal-tender money and still less do they 'create' machines. They do, however, something – it is perhaps easier to see this in the case of the issue of banknotes – which, in its economic effects, comes pretty near to creating legal-tender money and which may *lead* to the creation of 'real capital' that could not have been created without this practice. (Schumpeter, 1954, p. 1114; italics in original)

This suggestion was dismissed by classical economists, dominant especially in the UK, who based their models on the reality-challenged axiom of equilibrium economics. They could not accept the possibility that an increase in credit could be the force that would allow an expansion of output beyond the old potential output.

Further disaggregation of investment credit

To maximize economic growth, a further disaggregation of nominal investment I into different types of investment, and hence a further disaggregation of C_I may be called for. For instance, it will make a difference to economic growth, whether new claims on finite resources are created by banks and handed over to those who use it for investment in research and development, investment in the application of research results, or investment in the replacement of machinery, and so on. Thus a further disaggregation could attempt to classify investments into those in low-value-added industries and those in high-value-added industries, and so on. Clearly, our model raises the need for much further research into methods to identify different levels of productivity of investment projects *ex ante*.

Credit allocation and direction of credit

In our model of non-Walrasian rationing market outcomes there is no indication that the market, left to its own devices, will allocate credit in the way that is optimal for overall social welfare. Since the credit market is supply-determined and the decision about whether and how much to lend and who to lend to is entirely made by the banks, a crucial public goods function that affects the entire economy is performed by them. They not only create most of the purchasing power in the economy, they also decide about who will use it for what purposes. A rationed market means that some loan applicants are accepted, while others are rejected. There is no guarantee that the choice made by individual banks is consistent with the allocation that would maximize social welfare. Given the pervasiveness of imperfect information, it would be a mere coincidence if the banks' decisions were welfare optimal. Indeed, the incentive structure of loan officers may produce behaviour that is oriented towards other goals than what would be in the interest of the overall population (for instance, they may favour large-scale firms in established industries, as this may minimize risk to their own job security, or real estate speculators, expecting high profits).

Thus there is a case for government intervention at various levels: firstly, the government can intervene to implement an institutional design for the banking system, which will give loan officers incentives that will align their individual behaviour more with the social welfare goal. Secondly, the government or other delegated authority (such as the central bank) may enhance welfare by intervening in the decision-making process concerning the decision of how much to lend in aggregate (that is, how much total credit should be created) and who to lend to (which industrial sector, and so on). This can take the form of either formal or informal direction or 'guidance' by the central bank of private sector bank lending, whereby the central bank calculates by how much total credit creation should increase in the economy (quantitative credit controls) and whereby it decides how the increase (or decrease) in credit creation will be allocated across different industries and sectors of the economy (qualitative credit controls), while purely unproductive credit (for consumptive or speculative purposes) is suppressed.[4]

We would expect a natural tendency of central banks to engage in such guidance and direction of credit, if our model is indeed a realistic description of the world. Central banks would be expected to have experienced that the credit market does not clear and that there is therefore scope for welfare-enhancing intervention through sectoral guidance of bank credit.

Thus at this stage we can already conduct a preliminary empirical test of the accuracy of our above disequilibrium model. The hypothesis is that there should be evidence that many central banks have engaged in direct credit controls. The fact is that precisely such credit controls have been implemented by most central banks all over the world. Credit controls have at one stage been used by, among others, the Bank of England, the Bank of France, the Bank of Japan, the Bank of Korea, the Bank of Thailand, the US Federal Reserve, the German Reichsbank, the Austrian National Bank, the Reserve Bank of India, the central banks of Malaysia, Indonesia, Taiwan, China and several dozen central banks of developing countries. Finally, even the IMF has throughout its existence engaged in 'direct guidance' of bank credit to specific sectors of the economy. It turns out that most fast-growing economies have relied on fairly formalized procedures of credit control in order to enhance economic growth (more on this in Chapter 20).

Polak (1997) describes a typical IMF exercise in 'financial programming' of the kind that the Fund has regularly implemented in numerous countries over the past decades. According to Polak, information about credit creation in a client country is disaggregated by IMF staff, and the specific allocation of credit creation to different parts of the economy is made subject to IMF conditionality. Credit creation for 'non-productive expenditures' receives the IMF's 'frowning' and is dealt with through the enforcement of 'financial restraint' (p. 9), that is, credit rationing. Much more evidence can be gleaned from the (often confidential) structural adjustment programmes implemented by the IMF all over the world in over 100 instances over the past 50 years.

If this is the case, why have central banks and the IMF not openly admitted their *de facto* belief in disequilibrium economics? Central banks and the IMF have spent considerable resources on supporting esoteric Walrasian equilibrium economics by hiring many expensive economists and funding their publications. Their revealed preference in terms of their actions (as opposed to their official publications in economics) does not conform with their proclaimed economic orthodoxy concerning the assumptions about market clearing (but they make sense in the real world with disequilibrium economics). It would appear that the IMF uses such mainly neoclassical models as a political tool to justify, or cover up, what is *de facto* direct intervention by a bureaucracy. While this in itself is contradictory, it is likely that the IMF has refrained from admitting publicly its belief in more realistic, quantity-based and credit-focused models, as it may undermine its political agenda of enforcing predetermined, market-oriented structural adjustment programmes that tend to force open the markets of developing countries for the benefit of foreign investors. As a result, both the IMF and most central banks have played down the importance of credit controls in many official publications. Even when credit controls exist, their existence has frequently been denied (see Chapter 20, or Werner, 2003c).

Developing countries have often been more open about the use of directed credit. This may be, because the consequences of our model of productive credit creation for developing countries are far-reaching: the model shows that it is possible to create high real economic growth with low inflation, if a regime of directed credit can be implemented, whereby credit for unproductive use is restricted and is only extended for productive use. Ideally, it would be used to either purchase and implement or develop technologies that are new to the country in question. This is of course what the early pioneers of our model said they were trying to do, especially Hjalmar Schacht of the German Reichsbank. The German case may be an exception among industrialized countries, since the Reichsbank repeatedly and publicly attempted to explain its belief in the importance of 'productive credit creation' (see Werner, 2003d). Schacht had a significant impact on Keynes, who greatly admired his financial policy skills (Skidelsky, 2000). He was a popular adviser with many developing countries in the postwar era. The German example had an especially profound impact on East Asian economies, including Japan, Korea and Taiwan (see Werner, 2003c, 2003d). Thus it was not surprising that the IBRD's (1993) study of the East Asian 'Economic Miracle' concluded that intervention in the direction of credit has played a substantial role in achieving superior economic performance.[5] By properly implementing the model described in this book, virtually any developing country can boost its real economic growth rate – and can advance development, without relying on foreign investment.

Economic growth and foreign investment

Foreign direct investment as well as the borrowing of foreign currency (foreign portfolio investment) is usually considered an important policy for developing countries to enhance economic growth and boost development. However, thanks to our framework we see that welcoming foreign investment is neither a necessary nor a sufficient condition for economic growth.

If funds are necessary to mobilize domestic resources, then these can be created 'out of nothing' through the costless process of credit creation. Why borrow from abroad and pay back interest and the principal in foreign currency, when one can create the money for free at home? After all, the foreign banks are also merely creating the money 'out of nothing' through the process of credit creation. Of course, certain foreign purchases may be necessary. But these can be kept to a minimum and in line with export earnings.

Apart from usually being unnecessary, foreign investment has a number of disadvantages: firstly, foreign investors are primarily oriented towards their own interests, and these are unlikely to coincide with the national interest of the developing country. Secondly, foreign ownership of real assets, such as land and factories, implies foreign control – including over the allocation and disposal of profits, as well as the decision when to close local factories and pull out. Thirdly, foreign investment may be encouraged by a developing country in order to enhance technology transfer and the level of know-how at home. However, few studies of technology transfer have shown that much technology is actually transferred to developing countries. In the real world of imperfect information, technology is protected know-how that firms are reluctant to share. Thus there may be cheaper and more efficient methods to transfer technology, not related to foreign investment. Fourthly, foreign debt, usually in foreign currency, needs to be serviced, and the principal ultimately paid back. This imposes additional costs and currency risk. With many development countries suffering from structural trade deficits (since they mainly export low-value-added goods, whose long-term relative prices tend to fall, while importing high-value-added goods, whose relative prices tend to rise), their currencies tend to depreciate, thus raising their real debt. Together with the compound interest, an escalating debt trap quickly develops. None of these problems occur, if the developing country understands the macroeconomic realities shown by our model and acts accordingly.

A key example of wholly unnecessary foreign investment is Thailand or Korea in the mid to late 1990s. On pressure from the US Treasury, the IMF and their central banks, both countries liberalized their capital flows. The central banks then took policies to encourage borrowing from abroad, namely to reaffirm publicly their determination to maintain the dollar pegs, while raising domestic interest rates above US dollar rates. Companies in both countries reacted rationally by borrowing significant sums from foreign investors, despite the fact that both countries had substantial savings and functioning banking systems that could have created this money domestically. When the foreign investors decided to cancel their loans at short notice, large-scale bankruptcies were triggered and foreign investors could acquire assets and market shares that earlier they could only dream of.

Meanwhile an example of successful technology transfer is Japan, which achieved it by sending students and apprentices abroad, and by inviting foreign experts to Japan to transfer their knowledge. This method does not generate the type of kickbacks or windfall gains that foreign investment may generate in the short term for a small group of locals, and it may take a little while to reveal its fruits. But empirical evidence shows that this method has been successful in transferring only technology, without also inviting foreign control and draining domestic resources. With many developing countries the problems are, however, more basic, as they are not even mobilizing given domestic resources properly, and neither do they make sufficient use of the technology that is already available and which thus does not need to be paid for in foreign currency.

Explaining Japanese nominal GDP growth in the 1980s and 1990s

We now proceed to test the validity of our model of nominal GDP growth, as represented in equation (1) in the case of Japan. We have already identified suitable empirical proxies for C_R and C_F in the previous chapter. We can therefore now run an econometric test in order to determine the explanatory power of ΔC_R in accounting for the movement of $\Delta(P_R Y)$.

However, simply estimating (1) would imply a weak test of our model, since we would allow our theoretical knowledge to bias our choice of variables. We therefore adopt the Hendry methodology of sequential downward reduction from a general model to its parsimonious form (see Hendry and Mizon, 1978; Hendry, 1979, 1986, 1987, 2000). According to this methodology, a large number of potentially relevant explanatory variables are used in the regression, of which our *ex ante* favoured explanation is only one. Then an iterative procedure is used in order to eliminate explanatory variables sequentially, each time running the regression again. The elimination procedure followed here was to drop the variable whose t-statistic was the most insignificant, until one ends up with only the significant variables.

Tests for the validity of these restrictions are conducted in order to confirm whether the new parsimonious forms are admissible. Then a battery of tests is performed on the remaining regression, including unit root tests, tests for normality and the dynamic long-run equation. This approach provides a stricter empirical test of a model, since it does not give any advantage to the model possibly favoured by the researcher and instead lets the data speak.

We thus formulated a general empirical model of nominal GDP, with a general lag structure, based on quarterly statistics:

$$(9) \quad \Delta GDP_t = \alpha_j + \Sigma\beta_j\Delta GDP_{t-j-1} + \Sigma\gamma_j\Delta C_{Rt-j} + \Sigma\delta_j\Delta WPI_{t-j}$$
$$+ \Sigma\phi_j\Delta M2 + CD_{t-j} + \Sigma\omega_j\Delta M1_{t-j} + \Sigma\rho_j\Delta HPM_{t-j} + \Sigma\tau_j\Delta call_{t-j}$$
$$+ \Sigma\varphi_j\Delta JGB_{t-j} + \Sigma\lambda_j\Delta ODR_{t-j} + \varepsilon_t$$

All variables are in seasonal log differences, with

GDP = nominal GDP
C_R = credit used for GDP transactions
WPI = wholesale price index
M1 = money supply M1
M2+CD = money supply M2 + CD
HPM = high powered money
call = overnight uncollateralized call rate
JGB = ten-year JGB yield
ODR = official discount rate

As above, C_R is defined as bank credit creation, excluding lending to the real estate, construction and financial sectors.[6] Since the quarterly data exhibit strong seasonality, we calculated the seasonally differenced logarithms of the data series (with the exception of interest rates). Next we test for stationarity, employing the augmented Dickey Fuller test. Unit roots were detected in the seasonally differenced series, but not after further differencing. The original level data, with the exception of interest rates, are found to be I(2), or, more precisely, SI(1,1). Visual inspection of the seasonally differenced logarithms suggests a low probability of a spurious regression, as the trends do not seem to diverge. Formal cointegration tests are shown below.

We show no preference for any of the potential explanatory variables or lags and reduce down by sequentially dropping the variable that is least significant, using the PC-Give 10.0 software, which is ideal for downward reductions of the Hendry-type. The final parsimonious model resulting from this process was as follows:

$$(10) \quad \Delta GDP_t = \alpha + \beta_1\Delta GDP_{t-1} + \gamma_0\Delta C_{Rt} + \gamma_3\Delta C_{Rt-3} + \varepsilon_t$$

This is, of course, the empirical formulation of equation (1). Key regression results of the parsimonious model are shown in Table 15.1. The progress

Table 15.1 Parsimonious model of nominal GDP growth

Modelling ΔnGDP by OLS

The estimation sample is: 1984 (1) to 2001 (1)

	Coefficient	Std. Error	t-value	t-prob.	Part. R^2
ΔnGDP	0.411	0.103	3.99	0.000	0.197
Constant	0.509	0.200	2.54	0.013	0.090
ΔC_R	0.283	0.082	3.45	0.001	0.155
ΔC_{R_3}	0.178	0.098	1.83	0.072	0.049

Sigma	1.043	RSS	70.654	
R^2	0.887	$F(3,65) =$	169.5[0.000]**	
log-likelihood	− 98.724	DW	2.04	
no. of observ.	69	no. of parameters	4	
mean(ΔnGDP)	3.410	var(ΔnGDP)	9.033	

AR 1–5 test:	F (5,60) = 1.274 [0.287]
ARCH 1–4 test:	F (4,57) = 0.666 [0.618]
Normality test:	$Chi^2(2)$ = 4.029 [0.133]
hetero test:	F (6,58) = 1.082 [0.384]
hetero-X test:	F (9,55) = 0.933 [0.504]
RESET test:	F (1,64) = 0.020 [0.888]

Solved static long-run equation for ΔnGDP:

	Coefficient	Std. Error	t-value	t-prob.
Constant	0.863	0.289	2.99	0.004
ΔC_R	0.782	0.059	13.3	0.000

Long-run sigma = 1.769

ECM = ΔnGDP − 0.863 − 0.782*ΔC_R;
WALD test: $Chi^2(1)$ = 176.03 [0.000]**

Analysis of lag structure, coefficients:

	Lag 0	Lag 1	Lag 2	Lag 3	Sum	SE(Sum)
ΔnGDP	− 1	0.411	0	0	− 0.589	0.103
Constant	0.509	0	0	0	0.509	0.2
ΔC_R	0.282	0	0	0.178	0.461	0.083

Tests on the significance of each variable:

Variable	F-test	Value	[Prob.]	Unit-root t-test
ΔnGDP	F (1,65) =	15.911	[0.000]**	−5.726**
Constant	F (1,65) =	6.461	[0.013]*	
ΔC_R	F (2,65) =	17.137	[0.000]**	5.545

Tests on the significance of each lag:

Lag 1	F (1,65) = 15.911 [0.000]**
Lag 3	F (1,65) = 3.341 [0.072]

Tests on the significance of all lags up to 3:

Lag 1–3	F (2,65) = 21.362 [0.000]**
Lag 2–3	F (1,65) = 3.341 [0.072]
Lag 3–3	F (1,65) = 3.341 [0.072]

report shows that the null of the restriction is not rejected and thus the downward reduction is valid. We confirm the restrictions by testing for omitted variables.

The long-term static solution is presented, as well as formal tests for co-integration: as expected, nominal GDP growth and credit creation used for GDP transactions appear to be cointegrated. The final parsimonious form seems well defined and without visible problems. Tests for the significance of the parameters find joint significance. The dynamic analysis results show that the long-run coefficient of C_R is well determined and significant at the 1% level, rejecting the null that it is zero. The error terms are found to be normal: the Durbin-Watson statistic is close to 2, indicating that the null hypothesis of no autocorrelation of residuals fails to reject. Moreover, Breusch-Godfrey's LM test failed to reject the hypothesis of no autocorrelation. Tests for autoregressive conditional heteroscedasticity (ARCH) failed to reject the null of no ARCH. The null hypothesis of normality of errors failed to reject by Jarque Bera statistic test, thus no skewness and kurtosis problems exist. The null of no heteroscedasticity in the disturbance term, as tested by White's heteroscedasticity test fails to reject, indicating unconditional homoscedasticity of errors. The functional form also appears without problems, as the RESET test of functional form misspecification failed to reject the null that the model is correct, indicating that the model is correctly specified and no variables are omitted. Finally, the goodness of fit is satisfactory. In summary, the final empirical relationship (10) passes all standard tests without visible statistical problems.

Possible objection

The main theoretical objection to the above finding could be based on the argument that credit may be endogenous to nominal GDP. To address this objection, the following statistical tests were conducted: firstly, a Granger 'causality' analysis, using significance of autoregressive-distributed lags as well as linear restriction tests was conducted. Secondly, assuming the endogeneity of credit due to contemporaneous feedback, instrumental variables were used for the regression. Thirdly, and most substantially, the regressions of nominal GDP on credit and vice versa were tested for their behaviour during a period when a structural break may have occurred (namely the early 1990s, when the asset 'bubble' burst and both credit and GDP growth dropped sharply, while many relationships in the economy changed significantly). The behaviour of both regressions during this period should yield strong evidence concerning their direction of causation.[7]

We find that the explanations of nominal GDP advanced by traditional models, such as high powered money, money supply, short-term interest rates or long-term interest rates, all drop out of the empirical model as insignificant. Lowering (or raising) interest rates does not have any significant impact on economic growth. What remains is the variable that our model had indicated as being most important: credit creation used for GDP transactions. The model is robust and well defined. The findings suggest that our theoretical model is a useful description of reality. For illustration purposes, Figure 15.1 plots the growth rates of C_R against nominal GDP. As can be seen, once we have filtered out credit for financial transactions C_F, we find a stable relationship between that 'money' (that is, credit C_R) that enters the real economy and nominal GDP.

These strong results were also robust over different time periods.[8] Running the model only for the 1990s finds that it is robust. Indeed, the diagnostic tests appear equally strong, if not stronger than for the entire 20-year period. The 1990s thus do not represent an anomalous period in our model (while this seems to be the case for many other models or alternative theories). We have found a model that can account for Japanese nominal GDP without break during this 20-year time period – and we have demonstrated that the 1990s are no exception.

Tests for Granger causality were conducted between ΔnGDP and ΔC_R by an autoregressive-distributed lag model (Table 15.2). They were confirmed with linear restriction tests. It is found that credit cannot be omitted from an autoregressive-distributed lag model of nominal GDP growth, while nominal GDP can be omitted from such a model of credit creation. The direction

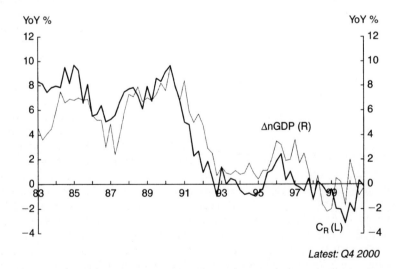

Figure 15.1   Japanese nominal GDP and credit creation used for GDP transactions
Sources: Bank of Japan; Cabinet Office, Government of Japan.

Table 15.2   Granger-causality test between credit ΔC_R and ΔnGDP

The sample is: 1984 (1) to 2001 (1)	
Autoregressive-distributed lag model of ΔC_R	
5 lags	$F(10,58) = 101.5\ [0.000]$**
Granger-causality test for adding	
ΔnGDP to ΔC_R	$F(5,58) = 0.31889\ [0.8997]$
Linear restriction test on all ΔnGDP	LinRes $F(1,58) = 0.154607\ [0.6956]$
Autoregressive-distributed lag model of ΔnGDP	
5 lags	$F(10,58) = 48.32\ [0.000]$**
Granger-causality test for adding	
ΔC_R to ΔnGDP	$F(5,58) = 4.5762\ [0.0014]$**
Linear restriction test on all ΔC_R	LinRes $F(1,58) = 16.3228\ [0.0002]$**

of Granger 'causation' between credit creation in the 'real circulation' and nominal GDP growth was found to be unidirectional: while past values of credit creation are significant in forecasting nominal GDP, past values of GDP are not significant in forecasting credit creation.

Using instrumental variables to account for potential simultaneous feedback, a similar result is found as with ordinary least squares. Furthermore, the strongest test for causality is an analysis of potential structural breaks. Thus regressions of nominal GDP on credit C_R and of credit C_R on nominal GDP were tested for their behaviour during a period when a structural break is likely to have occurred (namely in and around the year 1991, when both credit and GDP growth dropped sharply and Japan's economy moved relatively swiftly from 'boom' to 'bust'). Parameter constancy tests of both regressions during this period will yield strong evidence concerning their relative merit and thus the direction of causation.

Specifically, two types of tests for parameter stability were conducted. The first involved dividing the sample into two sub-samples, from 1982:Q1 to 1990:Q4 and 1991:Q1 to 2001:Q1, reflecting the observation of a likely structural break in early 1991. Firstly, recursive estimation was used to produce one-step parameter constancy forecast tests (forecasting eight quarters) for the whole period and two sub-samples. This was used to compare the parameter constancy of the two directional hypotheses (credit as explanatory variable versus nominal GDP as explanatory variable). The estimations with credit as explanatory variable fared better and produced more stable parameters in *ex post* forecasts, as is especially clear from the Chow tests in the second sub-sample. Secondly, and perhaps most reliably, a recursive estimation yielded the PC-GIVE graphics tests, namely the recursive one-step residual tests, the one-step Chow tests, the breakpoint Chow tests and the forecast Chow tests. The regressions with credit as explanatory variable perform well. This is not true for the regression of credit on GDP: this relationship broke down. If the fundamental (structural) relationship is better described by credit as explanatory variable of nominal GDP, then it should survive with sufficient parameter stability any regime shift, as it should be a process-generating independent relationship. Conversely, if there is no fundamental relationship in this direction of causation, then parameters would become unstable during periods of regime shift. Such a regime shift occurred in 1991. While the relationship with credit as explanatory variable remained reasonably stable, this is not true for the hypothesized relationship with credit as dependent variable, regressed on nominal GDP. The latter broke down. The evidence is therefore relatively clear-cut.

Thus all the above tests favour the hypothesis that causation runs from credit to nominal GDP and not inversely, which is also in line with the findings from the Granger 'causality' and instrumental variable tests.

Hendry and Richard (1983) have identified the criteria that should be observed when selecting an empirical model out of the many possible models. Firstly, a model must be data-coherent, which means it should explain adequately existing data. For this purpose, the model should have a good fit and the error term should not have any serious statistical problems. In particular, there should not be any autocorrelation problems so that a functional misspecification can be ruled out. Secondly, the regressors should be exogenous. The Granger causality tests indicate that C_R may be strongly exogenous to nominal GDP. Further, as we would expect from our theoretical analysis, and as we will see in Chapter 18, it is 'superexogenous'.[9] Thirdly, the model should be able to forecast well outside the sample period. Ideally, the model should be tested against data that was not available when the model was constructed. Since the model was constructed in the early 1990s (see Werner, 1992, 1997d), the present tests already constitute such a test. Further, the model was used for real out of sample forecasts throughout the 1990s.[10] Fourthly, the functional forms used should be data-admissible. This is the case. Fifthly, the model should be consistent with one of the competing economic theories. While it is not consistent with mainstream theory, it is consistent with the disaggregated credit theory presented here. Sixthly, the model should encompass all models previously presented by investigators, by being able to explain the findings of previous researchers. The result suggests that the traditional macroeconomic theories, relying on interest rates and 'money supply' variables, are encompassed by our disaggregated credit model. We already saw that our model explains the 'velocity decline' phenomenon that has afflicted the previous theories. Finally, the models should be parsimonious: 'a simple explanation of the data should always be preferred to a more complicated explanation. In a regression context, this implies that, other things being equal, an equation with few variables should always be preferred to an equation with more variables' (Thomas, 1997, p. 363).

In conclusion, the disaggregated credit model solves the puzzle of why Japanese nominal GDP growth suddenly fell after 1991: credit growth collapsed. It also explains why interest rate policy could not help: interest rates drop out as explanatory variable and thus have no direct bearing on growth. Necessary and sufficient condition for larger nominal GDP growth is an increase in credit creation.

16
The Cause of the Asset Price Bubbles and Banking Crises

We find that the average length of aggregate asset price booms in the eighteen industrial countries we study has increased from 1.3 years in the 1970s to 3.5 years in the 1980s and 4.4 years in the 1990s.

Our search for stylised facts with regard to asset price boom episodes, by construction, cannot say much about the role of monetary policy in responding or even triggering asset price booms. Monetary policy is clearly endogenous so that the issue of causality is not addressed.

(Detken and Smets, 2004)

As we saw, asset price bubbles and subsequent busts have been observed in many countries across the world, including Japan in the 1980s and 1990s. Usually, neither the surge in asset prices nor the subsequent fall can be explained by standard economic models. Banking crises have happened in over one hundred countries in the past half century, usually following a period of financial boom. Many of the policies, especially those adopted by the IMF in such post-crisis countries have focused on raising bank stability by tightening up loan procedures, bank supervision and capital adequacy. These policies had a significant negative impact on macroeconomic performance, which was not explained by standard theory.

These enigmas can be solved with our model, whose relevant equations are restated:

(1) $CV = C_R V_R + C_F V_F$

(2) $C_R V_R = P_R Y$

(3) $C_F V_F = P_F Q_F$

(4) $\Delta(P_R Y) = V_R \Delta C_R$

(5) $\Delta(P_F Q_F) = V_F \Delta C_F$

When credit creation expands, but is mainly channelled into the financial circulation C_F, total credit C in equation (1) rises. However, because credit used for GDP-based transactions C_R does not increase, *ceteris paribus* there will be no rise in the GDP deflator P_R or real GDP (leaving $P_R Y$ unchanged), but according to equation (5), the value of asset transactions is likely to rise, which usually is reflected at least partly in rising asset prices. In other words, in times when banks lend heavily for speculative purposes, such as the margin lending of the 1920s in the US, the property lending of the 1980s in Scandinavia and Japan, or that of the 1990s in many Asian countries, as well as the real estate lending presently in the UK, asset price inflation is likely to occur. Meanwhile, consumer prices may hardly rise. This is precisely what was observed in the major cases of asset price inflations, and it is readily explicable in our framework.

However, this dichotomy often puzzles economists used to models based on perfect information and Walrasian market equilibrium. In reality, with pervasive quantity-rationing, there is nothing surprising about it. The same is true for the valuations of asset prices resulting from this process. Since such asset price inflation is driven by the creation of new purchasing power, irrespective of fundamentals, it is not surprising that the higher asset prices cannot be explained by fundamentals, such as traditional asset pricing models using the net present values of discounted future income streams. Thus the appearance of asset price bubbles is not an 'anomaly' but a result that is to be expected when C_F rises significantly.

The type of asset whose price is boosted through credit creation may vary. In many cases it may be real estate. In the UK experience of the 1980s (as again today), a speculative bubble in the housing market was triggered by competition among banks to extend mortgages to individuals. The share of mortgage loans out of total loans rose sixfold from 1980 to 1984 alone (Drayson, 1985). In terms of our model, new credit creation entered not only the financial, but also the real circulation, as speculators were mainly individuals, not firms (as in the case of Scandinavia and Japan in the 1980s). Their increased purchasing power reduced savings, boosted consumption and thus pushed up consumer prices. It also produced a balance of payments deficit, as the domestic economy was not able to satisfy the increased demand produced by excess credit creation.

Collateral and the fallacy of composition

Banks tend to extend loans with real or financial assets as collateral. This way, they take a low risk when they pretend a borrower has deposited money and they credit the sum of the loan in his or her deposit account through the entry of the figures. If the borrower cannot service the loan sufficiently, the bank can 'call' the loan by foreclosing on the borrower, who may lose the collateral (or more). In the past it was often the practice to use all available assets as collateral, including the physical body of the borrower, who would on default be sold into slavery. This practice has not entirely disappeared, as in countries such as China or even Japan, the second richest country in the world, lenders have on occasion demanded body parts, such as kidneys or eyeballs, as collateral.

Table 12.1 gave some examples of the effects of compound interest. The rapidly spiralling debt of high-interest loans (while the banker has not offered any new services) explains why borrowers that are charged high interest rates of about 40% or more (the so-called 'sub-prime loan market') will quickly be driven into default, thus forfeiting their collateral (perhaps the house they are living in). Sometimes lenders may even expect that the borrower will be unable to service the spiralling loan costs, but will nevertheless extend loans if assets of interest exist that can be collateralized and then seized. This practice is called 'predatory lending' and has been a consistent feature in the history of banking.[1]

When banks engage in asset collateralization, each individual bank tends to assume it cannot influence the price of the collateral asset. However, banks suffer from the fallacy of composition. If a large proportion of a country's banks engage in increased real estate-related lending, the increase in the value of real estate transactions is likely to be reflected largely in higher prices, according to equation (5), as the real estate market is more illiquid than other markets. Thus real estate prices will be pushed up by the very action of rising bank lending. In the short term, rising asset prices create capital gains for the borrowers and render banks' loan books technically sound, thus further encouraging increased loan extension. The consequence is a substantial externality in bank behaviour, since each individual bank fails to take the aggregate effect on overall real estate prices, and hence on its own portfolio, into consideration. A real estate 'bubble' is the likely result.

If the quantity of assets available on the market is fixed and the number of transactions also remains unchanged (in actual fact the number of transactions is also likely to rise), we can simplify equations (3) and (5). We thus replace Q_F with the fixed stock of assets A. Taking differences, we obtain the case where all increases in credit creation for real estate transactions are translated into higher real estate prices.

(3') $C_F V_F = P_F A$

(5') $\Delta P_F = (V_F/A) \Delta C_F$

If we wish to assume market clearing, the collateralization of assets by lenders would provide an alternative rationale for the credit market to be supply-determined: if banks wish to expand their loan books (due to exogenous factors such as regulation or market-share competition), banks will be able to do so through an expansion of asset collateralizing loans, which push up the price of the collateral. This would produce a kind of 'Say's Law of credit', where speculative credit supply creates its demand via appreciating collateral values.

One reason why banks can expand collateralizing loans almost always is their benchmarking behaviour, which tends to produce similar lending strategies (thus we find banks lending in unison to the same sector). Another is that the assessment of the loan/valuation ratio is ultimately done by the banks themselves. Collateral values, in turn, influence the demand for speculative loans. Hendry (1984), Muellbauer and Murphy (1989) and Muellbauer (1992) have argued that increased availability of bank loans which collateralize assets is a main factor in the rise of those asset prices. Muellbauer (1992) has pointed out that rises in the loan/valuation ratio greatly magnify the rate of return on the collateral. Thus as banks raise expected returns on speculatively holding or purchasing the collateral asset, demand for speculative lending will rise. In the 1980s, banks focused on real estate collateralization. In the 1920s in the US, they engaged in margin lending, using stocks as collateral. The outcome is the same: the price of the collateralized asset is driven up, which facilitates further loan growth.

However, in aggregate, bank lending for unproductive purposes can usually not be recovered, since the only source of income are the capital gains that are only sustainable while such bank lending increases. As soon as bank lending for speculative purposes slows, asset prices fall. This damages speculators, and hence banks, because loans become non-performing. Thus banking systems are prone to credit cycles that affect macroeconomic stability.

Asset price collapses, banking crises and recessions

Instances of asset inflation are not welfare optimal. For one thing, it cannot be considered efficient nor equitable when new claims on finite resources are created by banks and then granted to a specific group of individuals who use them purely for speculative gain, without adding to productivity or output. Moreover, the extension of speculative loans and asset-collateralizing loans creates negative externalities in the economy and thus directly affects others. If house prices are driven so high that they are beyond the reach of first-time buyers, this can affect the quality of life of entire communities. In England, many cities are unable to attract sufficient numbers of welfare workers, teachers or firemen, as they cannot afford to live in them on their salaries. High real estate prices in city centres may increase commuting times and hence shorten the time available for family or leisure.

The externalities in the banking system are also significant: as banks become overextended to borrowers who have not invested the newly created money productively, our theory of productive credit creation tells us that, in aggregate, such loans cannot be paid back (only 'productive' loans will be non-inflationary and only 'productive' loans will produce goods and services of value, thus producing income to service the loans). As a result, systemic risk increases.

Bank lending for speculative purposes C_F is only viable as long as banks continue to increase such lending. It seems a reasonable assumption that

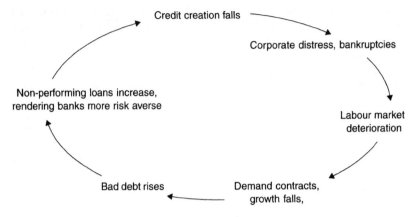

Figure 16.1   The vicious cycle of a credit crunch recession

banks will not continue to increase their speculative lending C_F into eternity. We thus consider what happens when at some stage (perhaps again induced by a regulatory shock, such as a change in the monetary policy of the central bank) C_F falls. According to equation (5), asset prices will fall. This will then reduce collateral values and bankrupt the first group of speculative borrowers who were seeking merely capital gains. Their default will create bad debts in the banking system. This in turn will raise banks' risk aversion and reduce the amount of credit newly extended. This further reduces asset prices (equation 5), which increases bankruptcies. The process can easily make banks so risk averse that they also reduce lending to firms for productive purposes, in which case GDP growth will also fall (equation 4). Such credit crunches have been observed in many cases, including the US.[2] This exacerbates the vicious cycle, since with less economic growth, corporate sales and profits decline. As more firms become unstable, bad debts increase further (see Figure 16.1).

How to prevent banking crises

To understand how to prevent banking and financial crises, their causes must be understood. Banking crises are always preceded by what is afterwards regarded as 'excessive lending'. The question is therefore to identify just what constitutes 'excessive', for at the time most bankers would argue that their lending was principally sound. According to our credit theory, we find that the main factor determining 'excessive' lending is whether lending is used for 'productive' or 'unproductive' purposes (Werner, 1992, 1997d).

The most frequent form of 'unproductive' lending is lending for non-GDP transactions, namely speculative lending for financial transactions (ΔC_F). Usually this takes the form of loans secured with assets as collateral (such as real estate loans or margin loans).

Empirically, two causes for the rise in C_F can be observed. Firstly, in several important countries that subsequently faced large-scale banking crises and macroeconomic instability, bank credit growth for speculative purposes rose sharply in the preceding period, because the central bank used informal and extra-legal 'moral suasion' to encourage banks to increase lending. This was the case, among others, in Thailand and Korea.[3] Secondly, in several countries that later faced banking crises, rapid expansion of bank credit was preceded by deregulation of the banking sector. This was the case in countries as diverse as Argentina, Brazil, Chile and Mexico (during the 1970s) and Sweden, Norway, Denmark, the UK (during the 1980s). There is an *a priori* reason why banking sector deregulation may cause a subsequent expansion in credit creation. In general, any market that is operated as a cartel is characterized by stable market shares among the cartel members. If a regulatory shock is applied to the players through the abolition of the cartel and introduction of competition, the players are likely to respond by initially focusing their optimisation behaviour on market-share competition, even at the short-term neglect of profit maximization (as such behaviour maximizes long-term profits). In order to gain market share, the players will reduce the price of their products, often even in the form of subsidizing them (dumping). Assuming standard price-elasticities of demand, *ceteris paribus* the total amount of products sold in a post-deregulation market must be larger than the number of products in the pre-deregulation state.

Applying this analysis to banks, we notice that in the pre-deregulation state, the credit market resembles that of a cartel. The product of the banks are loans. In order to gain market share in the post-deregulation environment, banks will have a lowered risk aversion and a larger appetite to extend loans. They may lower prices or simply reduce their credit rationing. The total amount of loans in the post-deregulation environment will be larger, while their quality will tend to be lower. If the pre-shock steady state t was characterized by total credit growth being in line with GDP (thus credit for financial transactions being negligible), the post-deregulation $(t + 1)$ environment will be characterized by positive credit creation used for speculative purposes. Whether induced by direct central bank 'guidance' or due to increased competition among banks, the result is as follows:

(6) $\Delta C_{Ft+1} > 0$

and hence

(7) $\Delta (P_A A)_{t+1} > 0.$

A similar effect as deregulation can result from increased competition from international banks or innovations in financial products offered by invest- ment banks that compete with bank loans.

An early warning indicator of the build-up of systemic risk in the banking system is the ratio of loans for non-GDP-based transactions to total loans, C_F/C in our notation. This ratio increased significantly in most countries that were subsequently struck by banking crises due to increases in credit for financial speculation.

If this ratio has risen significantly (based on historical experience of the country in question), then there is a high likelihood that this country will suffer from a major banking, and possibly also economic, crisis.

The call for banking sector reform usually takes place during such a credit crunch cycle. Without taking account of this phenomenon, bank restruc- turing is likely to exert further detrimental influence on macroeconomic stability.

Banks' power of credit creation constitutes a public goods function, while each individual bank does not consider public welfare. Credit creation for speculative purposes is not socially optimal, as it constitutes a misuse of limited resources for unproductive purposes. Moreover, bank lending for speculative purposes usually sows the seeds of a systemic crisis. Nevertheless, banks may at times engage in it in the pursuit of the profit motive. Thus it is clear that from a social welfare perspective, such loans should be restricted. Thus there is a justification for some kind of government intervention in the credit market.

Banking crises can be prevented by monitoring of the ratio of speculative loans to total credit (C_F/C) and directly intervening in the banking system to suppress a rise in C_F when necessary.[4] This avoids the financial crises, and hence the cause of bad debts and banking problems. Once bad debts are on the rise, some form of crisis is inevitable, if not countered by suitable poli- cies (see below).[5]

The creation of the Japanese bubble

Based on our model, the Japanese 'asset bubble' of the 1990s is immediately recognized as being due to excessive credit creation for non-GDP transac- tions, driving up asset prices. Once credit creation tightened, it was clear that excess lending had to turn into bad debts, resulting in a credit crunch and subsequent recession (see Werner, 1991, 1992). Falling credit creation implies that the total amount of transactions in the economy must shrink. As also bank lending for GDP-based transactions declines (according to equation (4)), the economy must contract due to reduced purchasing power for transactions. This creates unemployment and deflation, increases bank- ruptcies and in turn exacerbates the bad debt problem. As banks are rendered more risk averse, their supply of credit falls further. Based on our framework, an early warning of the impending banking crisis was possible. Moreover, it was possible to predict that neither increases in high powered money, nor the money supply, nor reductions in interest rates, nor fiscal stimulation were necessary or sufficient to stimulate the economy. The sole necessary and sufficient condition for a recovery has been an expansion in net credit creation.[6]

Figure 16.2 shows the dramatic rise of the proportion of bank loans which ended up in real estate-related transactions (loans to real estate, construction and non-bank financial institutions), the ratio of C_F to total credit. With such a rise in C_F/C, the increasing credit creation for speculative purposes expanded the financial circulation and nominal asset transactions values rose. This was reflected both in an increase in the number of transactions and prices. Meanwhile, consumer price inflation remained remarkably low, at times even registering deflation, despite double-digit credit-money growth rates.

The extent of the problem and the degree of fragility of the Japanese banking system can also be judged from Figure 16.2, indicating the large share of speculative loans in banks' portfolios. Since such loans are not linked to the creation of output and services, they cannot draw on non-speculative income streams. Speculative income streams to service these loans are

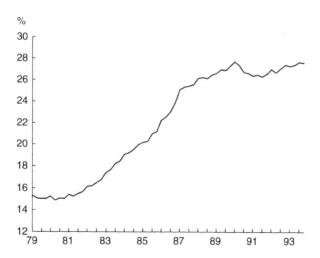

Figure 16.2 The ratio of speculative loans to total loans (C_F/C) in Japan
Source: Bank of Japan.

dependent on asset price rises, which in turn are dependent on the extension of more of these loans. Thus as soon as they fall, so do asset prices. The speculative loans will then turn into bad debts, damaging the banks and rendering them more risk averse. In this situation, a recession is likely, as reduced credit in real circulation tends to reduce real economic activity.

Moving to the empirical test of equation (5), we focus on the real estate market to represent non-GDP based transactions. Since land values dominated all other net worth in the Japanese economy, land was the asset class used to collateralize loans by banks, and since the real estate market was at the core of the propagation of the asset market 'bubble' in the 1980s, we think it is reasonable to focus on an empirical test of land prices as the proxy for P_F.

Since the speculative boom was concentrated on commercial land in the six major urban areas and rural land prices remained little affected by the land 'bubble', we use the bi-annual commercial land price data from the Japan Real Estate Institute on the six cities to proxy P_F. We use Bank of Japan sectoral loan data on credit to the real estate sector – the majority of speculative loans and most closely related to land transactions – transformed into biannual data, to represent ΔC_F. Using year-on-year percentage changes, adding a lag structure to account for partial adjustment dynamics and reducing to the parsimonious form, we obtain the following empirical model:

(8) $\Delta P_F = \alpha + \beta \Delta P_{Ft-1} + \gamma_1 \Delta C_{Ft-1} + \gamma_5 \Delta C_{Ft-5} + \varepsilon_t$

This turns out to be the empirical formulation of equation (5). We conduct the same statistical tests for significance, normality, model specification and causality as discussed above (see Table 16.1).

Again, the tests are supportive and show that equation (8) is well-defined, with high significance of the coefficients, normality of the error term and no omissions of variables. The test of direction of causation between credit creation extended to real estate firms and land prices finds that real estate lending Granger-causes land prices at the 1% significance level, but there is no causation the other way. The strength of the correlation is clearly visible (see Figure 16.3, which shows actual variables).

The finding is robust also over longer time periods. Figure 16.4 shows real estate lending of Japanese banks and nationwide land prices since 1971.

As can be seen, the bank lending data precedes the movements of real estate prices. Virtually all peaks and troughs of the lending series occur well in advance of similar peaks and troughs of the price data. The result is not ambiguous, even when using eye inspection. It is difficult to argue that real estate related lending, moving often over a year ahead of the price changes, has no impact on price developments in the real estate market.

Table 16.1 Empirical model of Japanese real estate prices

Modelling ΔP_F by OLS

The sample is: 1982 (2) to 1993 (1)

Variable	Coefficient	Std. Error	t-value	t-prob.	Part. R^2
Constant	-19.112	3.6015	-5.307	0.0000	0.6101
$\Delta P_{F\_}1$	0.55314	0.097790	5.656	0.0000	0.6400
$\Delta C_{F\_}1$	1.1366	0.17688	6.426	0.0000	0.6964
$\Delta C_{F\_}5$	0.44489	0.16932	2.628	0.0171	0.2772

$R^2 = 0.94852$ F (3, 18) = 110.55 [0.0000] $\sigma = 4.73678$ DW = 1.91
RSS = 403.8680302 for 4 variables and 22 observations

Dynamic analysis:

Solved static long-run equation:

$\Delta P_F =$ -42.77   +3.539 ΔC_F
(SE)   (8.112)   (0.4705)   WALD test Chi^2 (1) = 56.574 [0.0000]**

Tests on the significance of each variable:

Variable	F (num, denom)	Value	Probability	Unit Root t-test
ΔP_F	F (1, 18) =	31.966	[0.0000]**	-4.5695**
Constant	F (1, 18) =	28.161	[0.0000]**	-5.3067
ΔC_F	F (2, 18) =	20.65	[0.0000]**	5.4688

Tests on the significance of each lag:

Lag	F (num, denom)	Value Probability
1	F (2, 18) =	125.9 [0.0000]**
5	F (1, 18) =	6.9041 [0.0171]*

Test of error term normality:

Resid. autoregression: F (4, 13) = 1.26113 [0.3343]
Error autocorrelation:
(lags 1–3):   Chi^2 (3) = 2.1896 [0.5340]; F-form (3, 15) = 0.55265 [0.6542]
ARCH (lags 1–2):   Chi^2 (2) = 4.0682 [0.1308]; F-form (2, 14) = 1.7875 [0.2035]
Normality: Chi^2 (2) = 2.1916 [0.3343]
Heteroscedastic error: Chi^2 (6) = 4.3609 [0.6280]; F-form (6, 11) = 0.45325 [0.8285]

Test of functional form:

Chi^2 (9) = 5.5072 [0.7880]   and F-form (9, 8) = 0.29682 [0.9555]
RESET F (1, 17) = 4.3978 [0.0512]

Granger-causality test between ΔP_F and ΔC_F:

The sample is: 1982 (2) to 1996 (1)

Autoregressive-distributed lag model of ΔP_F on ΔC_F:
(autoreg.: lags 1–5, distributed: lags 0–5)   F (11, 16) = 73.1939 [0.0000]**
Granger-causality test for adding ΔC_F to ΔP_F: F (6, 16) = 7.3362 [0.0007]**

Autoregressive-distributed lag model of ΔC_F on ΔP_F:
(autoreg.: lags 1–5, distributed: lags 0–5)   F (11, 16) = 12.9867 [0.0000]**
Granger-causality test for adding ΔP_F to ΔC_F: F (6, 16) = 1.9163 [0.1398]

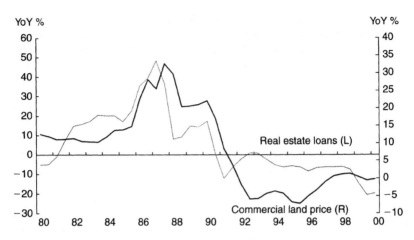

Figure 16.3   Real estate lending and commercial land prices (six major cities)
Sources: Bank of Japan; Japan Real Estate Institute.

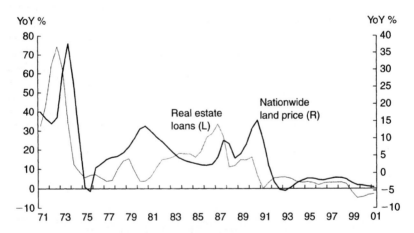

Figure 16.4   Real estate lending and nationwide land prices
Sources: Bank of Japan; Japan Real Estate Institute.

Thus we have found empirical support for the relationship postulated in
(3) and (5) that maintains that credit creation used for financial transactions
will lead to rises in asset prices. The 'anomaly' of the Japanese asset price
bubble is explained both theoretically and empirically by the new approach.
The main determinant of Japanese land prices in the 1980s has been real

estate-related bank lending. This is in contrast to the mainstream literature, which has not been able to find determinants of land price rises or has found, as in Hutchison (1994), that, using the traditional deposit-money-based approach, there is 'little evidence that monetary factors have played a significant *systematic* role in land price fluctuations in Japan' (Hutchison, 1994, p. 80; italics in original).[7]

Some policy implications are that governments and central banks would be well-advised to monitor and keep in check 'speculative' credit creation C_F. If, for instance, banks increasingly lend for real estate investment purposes, extend margin loans or lend to hedge funds, purchasing power entering the financial markets is increasing, which will tend to push up prices of the assets concerned. However, such asset price rises are not sustainable and hence threaten the stability of the financial system and the economy.

How can the authorities keep speculative lending in check? Since in our world of imperfect information and market disequilibrium interest rates are not likely to be useful as a policy tool to manipulate the quantity of credit, direct forms of intervention in the credit market – for instance, through credit controls or 'guidance' of bank lending – are called for. Arestis and Sawyer (2003b) have indeed advocated selective credit controls for this purpose. These will be examined in Chapter 20. They may provide a lesson presently relevant for the UK housing sector.

Our finding also raises new questions. What caused bank lending for financial transactions to rise so significantly in Japan during the second half of the 1980s? Whatever the cause, it was responsible for the creation of the bubble and thus also for the banking and economic crisis of the 1990s. We will examine this question in greater detail in Chapter 20. Before then, we can solve a few more enigmas with our approach, including the question of suitable post-crisis banking sector reform policies, and the determinants of Japanese capital flows.

17
The Determinants of Japanese Capital Flows in the 1980s

We saw that the movement of Japanese long-term capital flows in the 1980s and early 1990s has remained a mystery according to standard explanations.[1] Indeed, very few researchers even tackled the problem. One of the few is Ueda (1990), whose regression has a disappointing fit and is not subjected to the standard tests. The only paper that successfully explains Japanese long-term capital flows in the 1980s and early 1990s has done so by moving beyond the traditional portfolio models by incorporating, more or less *ad hoc*, a variable that represents the Japanese asset price bubble: in a portfolio model of capital flows, of the Kouri and Porter (1974) type, price variables, such as interest rates, had little explanatory power, while land-related credit creation, which was suspected to be fuelling the land price boom in Japan, was strongly significant (Werner, 1994a). However, this attempt to reconcile traditional models with reality did so with great difficulty: the key variable of the portfolio model is not a price, but a quantity. Moreover, this quantity – land-related credit – is not a private sector asset, but a liability. This raises questions about the applicability of the portfolio model approach altogether, which so far has been the theoretical underpinning of capital flow studies.

But this finding resembles another. In the 1960s, US money seemed to be flooding the world, especially Europe, triggering fears of *le défi américain*.[2] Since the US dollar was the anchor of the Bretton Woods fixed exchange rate system, some observers argued that US capital flows might be due to 'excessive credit creation' in the US. Charles Kindleberger (1966) relayed this suspicion as follows:

A favourite European banking view is that the capital outflow from the USA is the result of excessive credit creation in the latter. It is sometimes said that the USA exports inflation, although it is not explained how it happens that the USA has lower rates of increase in prices and money supply than European countries. (In one view, the USA has no inflation because it exported it to Europe!) ... John Exter of the First National City

Bank of New York has gone so far as to say that a dollar in credit creation is a dollar of capital outflow. (p. 216)

Did the US simply print dollars and then go out and buy up the world in the 1960s? Indeed, is this perhaps also what happened in the case of Japan during the late 1980s? Kindleberger dismissed such a link. Indeed, it was never put to a serious econometric test or embedded in a theoretical model. However, our model of disaggregated credit may enable us to do so now.

Of course, the international financial system was different by the 1980s: flexible exchange rates meant that it was up to the markets to recognize 'excessive credit creation' and respond to it with a depreciating currency. However, this presupposes knowledge of the fact. With low inflation and high productivity growth, many observers were unaware of the excessive creation of new purchasing power in the Japanese banking system, which was used to purchase financial assets.

Foreign assets constitute one part of all available financial assets. Thus the link that we observed between credit creation for financial transactions C_F and the value of financial transactions may also be observable in the case of foreign investment.

Open economy extension of credit model

Our basic model of disaggregated credit can be extended for open economies to take account of international capital flows. Foreign assets constitute one component of a diversified asset portfolio.

We divide total financial wealth W into domestic and foreign assets:

(1) $W = F + D$

In general, changes in the total amount of F can be due to two factors: firstly, the stock adjustment, which means that at any given portfolio size W, the share of the portfolio held in foreign assets, F/W has increased. Secondly, the flow adjustment, which means that foreign investment F may increase even if the share of foreign assets F/W is unchanged, as long as the total portfolio size W has increased.

In notation, F must be the foreign asset share F/W times the size of the portfolio:

(2) $F = (F/W)W$

We can now differentiate this to separate the two flow and stock adjustment effects:

(3) $\Delta F = \Delta(F/W)W + \Delta W(F/W)$

In other words, the change in the stock of foreign assets ΔF is composed of the change in the foreign asset share $\Delta(F/W)$ (the stock adjustment) and the change in wealth ΔW (the flow adjustment).

So far, empirical research on Japanese foreign investment has focused on the stock adjustment. The flow adjustment has been neglected, thus implicitly assuming that $\Delta W = 0$. Such studies (Ueda, 1990; Kawai, 1991) thus tested whether the stock adjustment could explain Japanese foreign investment. However, these stock adjustment factors (changes in international interest differentials, exchange rate expectations, and so on) were not empirically successful. A number of writers have also criticized the mainstream capital flow models and their undue emphasis on stock adjustment and interest differentials, thus neglecting the importance of flow adjustment and overall portfolio growth (see Willett and Forte, 1969; Floyd, 1969; Niehans, 1984; Werner, 1994a).

Indeed, Koo (1991) found that Japanese institutional investors were not raising the share of foreign assets significantly, despite substantial capital outflows. We thus focus on the opposite hypothesis, namely that the stock adjustment was not substantial, and proceed to examine how much foreign investment can be explained by the flow adjustment alone.

This may also be what events surrounding US capital flows in the 1960s were suggesting: due to credit creation, total wealth W increased, resulting in capital outflows purely due to the flow adjustment effect.

Since the real circulation of credit creation is confined to the domestic real economy, funds for net foreign investment (both 'direct' and 'portfolio' investment) derive from the financial circulation.[3]

We therefore focus on the flow adjustment (also called wealth effect) and consider the impact of a rise in the available purchasing power for financial transactions. We assume, therefore, that the share of foreign assets in Japanese investors' portfolios remains the same:

(4)   F/W = constant

and thus

(5) $\Delta(F/W) = 0$

To simplify, we can rename the (here constant) foreign asset share F/W:

(6)   F/W = constant $\equiv$ k

Substituting (5) and (6) into (3) we obtain a model of international capital flows purely due to flow adjustment:

(7) $\Delta F = k\Delta W$

The increase in wealth ΔW, which is available for new investment in the portfolio, corresponds to credit creation used for non-GDP (thus mainly asset) transactions C_F. The link to our disaggregated credit model is therefore straightforward:

(8) $\quad \Delta W = \Delta C_F$

Substituting in (7) yields our simplified model of capital flows, which focuses exclusively on the flow adjustment (and hence is only applicable in time periods when flow adjustment is dominant over stock adjustment):

(9) $\quad \Delta F = k\Delta C_F$

In the pure case, and in the short-term abstracting from any stock adjustment due to other, standard stock adjustment factors, net capital outflows are directly proportional to excess credit creation entering the financial circulation. Excess credit creation in the financial circulation expands the total national financial portfolio.

In the words of Willett and Forte (1969): 'Thus as portfolios grow over time, the absolute amount of capital placed abroad would increase even though relative interest incentives remained the same' (p. 247).

Similarly to the 'diffusion of specie' of classical writers, in a world with high capital mobility, increased speculative credit C_F is unlikely to remain restricted to domestic financial assets, but is likely to be reflected in increased foreign investment as well.

This framework provides a theoretical explanation of the 'anomaly' of Japanese capital flows in the 1980s and early 1990s: with the rise of credit creation in financial circulation, capital would be expected to flow out of Japan, irrespective of interest rate and exchange rate movements. It would also support the 1960s suspicion about US capital flows: in the extreme case, with a high foreign asset share k, it might even approximate what John Exter said, when he claimed that 'one dollar in credit creation leads to one dollar in capital outflows'.

Once again, we note close affinities of our quantity-based approach with the IMF's own model, notably its so-called monetary approach to capital flows and the balance of payments (Gordon, 1977; IMF, 1977; Polak and Argy, 1977).

Explaining Japanese capital flows

It is now time to proceed to an empirical test of our model and to see whether we can solve the enigma of enormous Japanese net long-term capital outflows in the 1980s and their dramatic collapse in the early 1990s.

According to equation (9), in an open economy without capital controls, excess credit in the financial circulation should produce a proportionate accumulation of foreign assets. Thus in time periods when C_F becomes significant in size compared to C_R, we would expect that ΔC_F has explanatory power in estimating net long-term capital flows.

Figure 17.1 portrays Japanese net long-term capital flows, the variable we are attempting to explain, and plots them next to the changes in bank lending to the real estate industry, our main proxy of ΔC_F. A strong correlation over the entire observation period cannot be overlooked by mere eye inspection. Indeed, the robustness of this link was demonstrated after 1990, when the sudden contraction of credit C_F virtually stopped net long-term capital exports. It is notable that the correlation also holds in the 1970s.

Of course, land-related credit creation does not necessarily imply that those real estate companies which borrowed from banks were also the foreign investors. Credit money is fungible and a rebalancing of accounts means that some investor will eventually purchase foreign assets with this extra purchasing power – in practice these were to a great extent large-scale institutional investors, banks and other financial institutions (but also real estate and financial arms of Japanese corporations). Their assets expanded as credit money was rapidly being created by the banks.

In order to rigorously establish (9) also relative to an alternative model, we once again adopt the impartial econometric modelling methodology of proceeding from 'general to specific' of Hendry and Mizon (1978) and Hendry (1979). We include the type of explanatory variables that a general macroeconomic portfolio model proposed by Kouri and Porter (1974) would

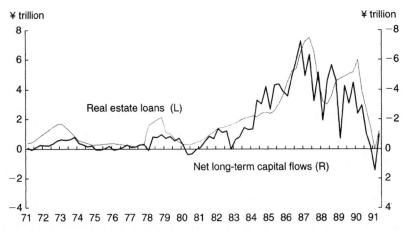

Figure 17.1 Japanese net long-term capital outflows and banks' real estate loans
Sources: Bank of Japan; Ministry of Finance.

suggest, including domestic and foreign interest rates, bond holdings, traditional 'money supply' measures and the exchange rate. As in Werner (1994a), ΔC_F is thus initially only one of many explanatory variables. We add a lag structure to account for partial adjustment dynamics, but unlike in Werner (1994a), we then reduce to the parsimonious form, consisting only of those variables whose coefficients are significant. This form is then subjected to rigorous testing.

The final result of this testing procedure, the parsimonious empirical model which resulted from the downward reduction, is shown in equation (10):

$$(10) \qquad \Delta F = \alpha + \beta \Delta F_{t-1} + \gamma_0 \Delta C + \gamma_1 \Delta C_{t-1} + \varepsilon_t$$

We find that all other arguments, used in the traditional portfolio model, including exchange rates and interest rates, drop out due to lack of significance. Equation (10) turns out to be the empirical formulation of equation (9), after lags are added to model dynamic adjustment. We conduct the same statistical tests for significance, normality, model specification and causality as discussed above (see Table 17.1). ΔC_F is highly significant and the model accounts for about 80% of variations in Japanese capital outflows. Again, all tests are supportive and show that equation (10) is well-defined, with high significance of the coefficients, normality of the error term and no omissions of variables. In particular, tests of the direction of causation found that ΔC_F Granger-causes ΔF at the 1% significance level, but there is no causation in the other direction. Our results were robust over different time periods.[4]

What is more, the empirical model obtained when sequentially reducing a more general empirical model to the parsimonious form – the independent product of a 'general-to-specific' modelling methodology – coincides with the relationship predicted by our theoretical model. Thus excess credit creation also accounts for the anomaly of Japanese foreign investment during its surge in the 1980s and the collapse of the early 1990s, just as our model of disaggregated credit would suggest. For countries and time periods when C_F is rising significantly compared to C_R, our model is preferable to the traditional capital flow theories that are based on stock adjustment. The more traditional portfolio model based on interest rates and exchange rates is encompassed by the disaggregated credit model.

We conclude that the open economy version of the disaggregated credit model also found significant empirical support. Japanese capital outflows during the 1980s can also be explained by excess credit creation that entered the financial circulation and that was diffused around the world in the form of foreign investment.

Japan in effect created much money that was not backed by real economic activity and used it to 'go shopping' in the world. Many foreign observers were not aware of this, perhaps because, using the traditional monetary approach, they relied on consumer prices as an indicator of monetary policy.

Table 17.1 Parsimonious empirical model of Japanese foreign investment

Modelling ΔF by OLS with ΔC_F

The sample is: 1981 (1) to 1991 (1)

Variable	Coefficient	Std. Error	t-value	HCSE	Part. R^2
Constant	−1654.7	2159.6	−0.77	572.2	0.0156
ΔF_1	0.43487	0.10735	4.051	0.08845	0.3072
ΔC_F	0.81664	0.19144	4.266	0.12826	0.3297
ΔC_{F_1}	0.637109	0.23360	2.727	0.126691	0.1674

$R^2 = 0.871632$ F (3, 37) = 83.744 [0.0000] σ = 6881.24   DW = 2.12
Variance instability test: 0.199019; joint instability test: 0.763375
Information criteria: SC = 17.9328; HQ = 17.8265; FPE = 5.19711e + 007

Dynamic analysis:

Solved static long-run equation:

$\Delta F =$ 　　−2928 　　+2.572 ΔC_F
(SE) 　　(3902) 　　(0.2872)
WALD test Chi^2 (1) = 80.226**

Tests on the significance of each variable:

Variable	F (num, denom)	Value	Probability	Unit Root t-test
ΔF	F (1, 37) =	16.409	[0.0003]**	−5.2643**
Constant	F (1, 37) =	0.58709	[0.4484]	−0.76622
ΔC_F	F (2, 37) =	14.393	[0.0000]**	5.1189

Tests on the significance of each lag:

Lag	F (num, denom)	Value	Probability
1	F (2, 37) =	34.069	[0.0000]**

Test of error term normality:

Resid. autocorrelation (lags 1–3): Chi^2 (3) = 3.055 [0.5340]; F-form (3, 34)
　　　　　　　　　　　　　= 0.91245 [0.4452]
ARCH (lags 1–3, res. scaled): Chi^2 (3) = 0.1121 [0.1308]; F-form (3, 31)
　　　　　　　　　　　　　= 0.030574 [0.9927]
Normality: Normality Chi^2 (2) = 0.59454
Heteroscedastic errors: Chi^2 (6) = 9.141 [0.6280]; F-form (6, 30) = 1.4346 [0.2344]

Test of functional form:

RESET test: RESET F (1, 36) = 1.1063 [0.2999]
Functional form: Chi^2 (9) = 11.195; F-form (9, 27) = 1.1268 [0.3785]

Granger-causality test between ΔC_F and ΔF:

The sample is: 1981 (1) to 1991 (1)

Autoregressive distributed lag model of ΔF on ΔC_F:
Granger-causality test for adding ΔC_F to ΔF: F (5, 34) = 3.6642 [0.0093]**

Autoregressive distributed lag model of ΔC_F on ΔF:
Granger-causality test for adding ΔF to ΔC_F: F (5, 34) = 1.1655 [0.3462]

Without consumer price inflation, they did not recognize the expansive monetary policy.

The French raid on Fort Knox in perspective

These findings may also apply to the US in the 1960s. Excess credit creation in the US would also be reflected in increased foreign investment, according to our model. However, the Japanese case is more surprising than the US case, because in the 1960s the US dollar was effectively the world's currency, and thus additional creation of dollars could be expected to be diffused around the world, without any adjustment in exchange rates – until the world rebels. When France decided to convert US dollars into gold at the official fixed price, as the Bretton Woods system formally provided for, the US had to make the decision whether to make good on its promise to redeem the excessively created dollars into gold, or whether it should break its promise – and with it bring down the Bretton Woods System of fixed exchange rates. France proceeded to demand conversion of dollars into gold, in an episode later called the 'French raid on Fort Knox'. The US leadership decided to break its promise. It 'closed the gold window'. With this, the fixed exchange rate system had ended, and currencies started to float – for the first time without any link to gold.

However, this new world of floating fiat currencies places a great burden on the foreign exchange markets: if a country decides to create more purchasing power than is backed by real economic activity, it now is the task of the foreign exchange markets to recognize this and respond by selling enough of this currency to reduce its value. The Japanese experience demonstrates that even the yen–dollar foreign exchange market, the most liquid market in the world, may be inefficient, for apparently market participants were for years unaware of the Japanese excessive credit creation.

When the US tried to create new money out of nothing and buy the world, France called the US's bluff. It seems that nobody called Japan's bluff during the 1980s. The Plaza agreement of September 1985 succeeded in raising Japan's exchange rate politically. Thus Japan succeeded, for a time, in creating money and buying foreign assets. The world seems to have suffered from 'yen illusion'. When financial credit creation stopped abruptly in 1989, capital outflows also came to a halt and even reversed. The enigma of Japanese capital flows is solved.

18
Why Fiscal Policy Could Not Work

Japanese fiscal expenditures were substantial during the 1990s, but did not achieve the desired effects. Even the crowding out effect due to higher interest rates, which the literature recognizes, could not be observed. Since these findings discredit the Keynesian analysis and more recent, related theories, including the IS-LM model, it may be necessary to revisit the type of literature that was prevalent before the Keynesian fiscal multiplier analysis was proposed.

> Before Keynes, it was commonplace that government spending and taxation were powerless to affect the aggregate levels of spending and employment in the economy; they could only redirect resources from the private to the public sector ... The Keynesian demonstration ... changed all this ... The old view that government spending simply crowded out private spending was banished. (Blinder and Solow, 1973, p. 319)

A main representative of this 'pre-Keynesian' literature was Irving Fisher's (Fisher and Brown, 1911) model, which does not rely on the monetary transmission through interest rates and, ironically, also Keynes' own (1930) version of it in his *Treatise on Money*. Instead of interest-rate-based crowding-out, the Fisher model relies on direct quantity-based crowding-out of private demand, due to increased claims on limited stocks of money by the government. Thus, unlike Ricardian equivalence, it was not dependent on deliberate actions by private sector consumers – instead, private demand was forced to shrink, whether consumers liked it or not.

In 1929, Keynes argued that stimulatory fiscal expenditure should be funded by monetary expansion (Klein, 1968). Crucially, Keynes emphasized (in 1929) that the central bank could negate the effect of stimulatory fiscal policy and therefore 'ensure that the expenditure financed by the Treasury *was* at the expense of other business enterprise' (Keynes, 1932, p. 126).

Since Keynes' (1936) *General Theory*, this view has been neglected. Even monetarist models adopted the Keynesian argument of an interest-based investment function and thus came to rely on interest-based crowding-out of private demand. However, some of Friedman's writings indicate that he continued to sympathize with Fisher's quantity-based crowding-out: 'I regard the description of our position as "money is all that matters for changes in *nominal* income and for *short-run* changes in real income" as an exaggeration but one that gives the right flavor of our conclusions', he said as late as 1970 (Friedman, 1970, p. 217). Handa (2000, p. 365) reports:

> On the transmission mechanism from money supply changes to income changes, Friedman supported Fisher's direct transmission mechanism – from money supply changes directly to expenditures changes – over the indirect one – from money supply to interest rates to investment – in Keynesian and IS-LM models.[1]

This direct transmission of money to the economy and consequent quantity-based crowding-out of fiscal expenditure was also supported by the so-called 'St. Louis monetarists' (Handa, 2000: 370). They argue that government spending financed by bonds must be ineffective, because the money supply is left unaltered. Empirical evidence in support of this contention has been provided by Andersen and Jordan (1968), Andersen and Carlson (1970) and Keran (1969, 1970).

Using the Cambridge version of Fisher's (Fisher and Brown, 1911) equation of exchange, which Keynes initially agreed with, we can quickly see why fiscal policy that is not monetized cannot be effective:

(1) $PY = MV$

When considering changes (so that the constant velocity drops out), we can rewrite this to state that nominal GDP growth is proportional to money supply growth:

(2) $\Delta(PY) = V\Delta M$

It follows that any exogenous increase in a component of nominal GDP (such as in G) cannot affect total nominal GDP, if the money supply remains unaltered: with $\Delta M = 0$, and breaking down nominal GDP (PY) into nominal consumption c, nominal government expenditure g, nominal investment i and nominal net exports nx, we obtain:

(3) $\Delta M = 0$
(4) $\Delta(PY) = \Delta c + \Delta i + \Delta g + \Delta nx$
(5) $\Delta g = -(\Delta c + \Delta i + \Delta nx)$

Equation (5) indicates that, following Say's Law, each dollar of additional government spending must crowd out exactly one dollar of private spending. The change in government expenditure Δg is countered by a change in private sector expenditure of equal size and opposite sign. Thus the level of aggregate income will be unchanged and the multiplier for bond-financed government spending is zero. Notice that this conclusion is not dependent on the classical assumption of full employment. Instead of the employment constraint, the economy can be held back by a lack of money. Fiscal policy can thus crowd out private demand even in the context of less than full employment. Furthermore, the original formulation of Fisher, favoured also by Friedman, does not include interest rates and thus does not require crowding out via higher interest rates. Instead, the direct quantity effect of the government using up money that will not be available for spending by the private sector is sufficient. Equation (5) shows that without an increase in the money supply, a rise in government expenditure must result in an equal reduction in private demand, leaving nominal GDP unaltered and fiscal policy completely ineffective. As Milton Friedman put it:

> The quantity theory implies that the effect of government deficits or surpluses depends critically on how they are financed. If a deficit is financed by borrowing from the public without an increase in the quantity of money, the direct expansionary effect of the excess of government spending over receipts will be offset to some extent, and possibly to a very great extent, by the indirect contractionary effect of the transfer of funds to the government through borrowing ... If a deficit is financed by printing money, there will be no offset, and the enlarged stock of money will continue to exert an effect after the deficit is terminated. What matters most is the behavior of the stock of money, and government deficits are expansionary primarily if they serve as the means of increasing the stock of money; other means of increasing the stock of money will have closely similar effects.[2]

However, we saw a formidable obstacle to utilizing this analysis for the Japanese experience of the 1990s: the traditional quantity equation approach suffers from the empirical obstacle that velocity has not been constant and the previously stable relationship between M and PY 'increasingly came apart at the seams during the course of the 1980s' (Goodhart, 1989a). It is therefore time to apply our disaggregated credit model to the problem of fiscal policy ineffectiveness.

Correctly defining the previous 'ΔM' in the equation of exchange as credit creation ΔC and disaggregating, we obtain the properly defined (and stable) relationship:

(6) $\Delta(P_R Y) = V_R \Delta C_R$

Breaking nominal GDP growth into its components,

(7) $\Delta(P_R Y) = \Delta c + \Delta i + \Delta g + \Delta nx$

substituting equation (6) and solving for growth in domestic demand $\Delta(c + i + nx)$ we obtain:

(8) $\Delta(c + i + nx) = V_R \Delta C_R - \Delta g$

whereby the coefficient for Δg is expected to be approximately -1. In other words, given the amount of credit creation produced by the banking system, an autonomous increase in government expenditure g must result in an equal reduction in private demand. As the government issues bonds to fund increased fiscal stimulation, private sector investors (such as life insurance companies) that purchase the bonds must withdraw purchasing power elsewhere from the economy. With an unchanged national income pie (whose growth is restricted by ΔC_R, the total amount of new purchasing power created – the overarching budget constraint on the economy), any increases in government spending must shrink the private sector share of the pie. The same applies (more visibly) to tax-financed government spending. With unchanged credit creation, every yen in additional government spending reduces private sector activity by one yen.

This resurrects the conclusions of the 'pre-Keynesian', or 'early Keynesian' or perhaps 'proto-monetarist' Fisher model: neither lowering interest rates is useful (as it does not increase the supply of credit from risk-averse banks), nor increasing fiscal stimulation (as pure fiscal policy does not create credit). In this framework, fiscal policy cannot affect nominal GDP growth, if it is not linked to an increase in credit creation.

We observe a different kind of crowding out than postulated by Keynesian or Ricardian models: Unlike the Keynesian interest-rate-based crowding-out, and like Ricardian equivalence, it is quantity-based and does not require any particular movement in interest rates. It therefore fits the observation of the 1990s that interest rates did not rise. Unlike Ricardian equivalence, it does not depend on restrictive assumptions about unobservable expectations and their formation. Moreover, it does not operate via a change in household savings. Instead, crowding-out occurs due to the lack of new purchasing power supplied by the financial system (credit creation). This therefore fits the observation that savings did not increase in proportion to increased government spending.

Empirical test

We can test the fiscal policy ineffectiveness proposition of equation (8) by using our empirical model of nominal GDP growth of Chapter 15, and its equation (10), which is here reiterated as equation (9):

(9) $\Delta GDP_t = \alpha + \beta_1 \Delta GDP_{t-1} + \gamma_0 \Delta C_{Rt} + \gamma_3 \Delta C_{Rt-3} + \varepsilon_t$

We disaggregate contemporary nominal GDP (ΔGDP_t) into domestic and private demand, as above:

(4') $\Delta GDP_t = \Delta(c_t + i_t + nx_t) + \Delta g_t$

Substituting this into equation (9) and solving for non-government demand, we obtain the empirical model:

(10) $\Delta(c_t + i_t + nx_t) = \alpha + \beta_0 \Delta g_t + \beta_1 \Delta GDP_{t-1} + \gamma_0 \Delta C_{Rt} - \gamma_3 \Delta C_{Rt-3} + \varepsilon_t$

If there was complete quantity crowding out, due to lack of credit creation, then a regression would yield the following coefficient for government expenditure:

(11) $\beta_0 = -1$

The results of our regression are shown in Table 18.1.

We found that the coefficient for government expenditure (β_0) is -0.974. Rounding to one digit, we obtain:

$\beta_0 = -1.0$

More formal linear restriction tests are conducted to see if the null hypothesis that $\beta_0 = -1.0$ can be rejected. The results are presented in Table 18.2.

As can be seen, the linear restriction F-test fails to reject the null hypothesis that $\beta_0 = -1.0$ (probability: 85.5%). These findings suggest that for every yen in government spending that is not monetized (that is, not supported by suitable monetary policy or other credit creation), private demand shrank by one yen. The empirical evidence supports the contention of the pre- and early Keynesian economists that an economic recovery and fiscal stimulation require monetary expansion, here defined as credit creation.

Importantly, this finding holds not only for the 1990s, which appeared to pose a particularly large challenge to traditional theories. The above tests were conducted for the longer time period, including much of the 1980s. Thus again it is seen that the experience of the 1990s was not an exception. This finding strengthens confidence in the credit model, as it appears to be a general model that can account for a variety of economic circumstances, including the more extreme 1990s. Testing separately only for the 1990s, the same result of complete fiscal policy ineffectiveness was found. The 'early Keynesian' or 'proto-monetarist' model, in modified form, appears to fit the

Table 18.1 Estimation results of private demand model

Dependent variable: $\Delta(c_t + i_t + nx_t)$

The estimation sample is: 1983 (1) to 2001 (1)

	Coefficient	Std. Error	t-value	t-prob.	Part. R^2
Constant	440.286	244.6	1.80	0.076	0.046
Δg	−0.974	0.140	−6.94	0.000	0.415
$\Delta nGDP\_1$	0.476	0.098	4.85	0.000	0.257
ΔC_R	0.085	0.031	2.75	0.008	0.100
ΔC_R_3	0.059	0.036	1.64	0.105	0.038

Sigma	1231.87	RSS	103190221
R^2	0.832	$F(4,68) =$	83.97 [0.000]**
log-likelihood	−620.482	DW	2.03
no. of obs.	73	no. of param.	5
mean $\Delta(c_t+i_t+nx_t)$	2441.51	$var\Delta(c_t+i_t+nx_t)$	8.39605e + 006

AR 1–5 test:	$F(5,63)$	= 1.214 [0.313]
ARCH 1–4 test:	$F(4,60)$	= 0.605 [0.661]
Normality test:	$Chi^2(2)$	= 5.672 [0.059]
hetero test:	$F(8,59)$	= 1.990 [0.064]
hetero-X test:	$F(14,53)$	= 1.772 [0.068]
RESET test:	$F(1,67)$	= 0.199 [0.657]

Solved static long-run equation for $\Delta(c_t + i_t + nx_t)$:

	Coefficient	Std. Error	t-value	t-prob.
Constant	440.286	244.6	1.80	0.076
Δg	−0.974	0.140	−6.94	0.000
$\Delta nGDP$	0.476	0.098	4.85	0.000
ΔC_R	0.144	0.029	4.93	0.000

Long-run sigma = 1231.87
ECM = $\Delta(c_t + i_t + nx_t)$ − 440.286 + 0.974*Δg − 0.476*$\Delta nGDP$ − 0.144*ΔC_R;
WALD test: $Chi^2(3)$ = 334.98 [0.0000]**

Tests on the significance of each variable:

Variable	F-test	Value [Prob.]
Constant	F (1,68)	= 3.239 [0.076]
$\Delta nGDP$	F (1,68)	= 23.512 [0.000]**
ΔC_R	F (2,68)	= 13.189 [0.000]**
Δg	F (1,68)	= 48.223 [0.000]**

Table 18.2   Linear restriction test of ineffectiveness hypothesis

Test for linear restrictions (Rb = r): R matrix					
Const	ΔnGDP_1	ΔC_R	ΔC_{R-3}	Δg	r vector
0.000	0.000	0.000	0.000	1.000	−1.000
LinRes	F(1,68) = 0.0335743 [0.8552]				

Japanese experience of the 1980s and 1990s well, in preference to alternative explanations.

Possible objection

There is a possible objection to this empirical finding: causality may run from private demand to government spending, not the other way round. While we are here suggesting that increased government expenditure has crowded out private expenditure through laying claim on the limited amount of credit available, this objection argues that government expenditure may have *responded* to declines or rises in private demand, in order to maintain stable growth. If true, this would mean that t-statistics and other diagnostics would become unreliable.

There are two responses to this objection. The first takes the form of statistical tests, the second of logic. An instrumental variable regression was run, assuming the endogeneity of government expenditure to private demand due to contemporaneous feedback. Government expenditure lags were used as instruments. The coefficient for contemporaneous credit is smaller, although the standard error is only marginally larger. The value for sigma is almost unchanged, while the value for the reduced form sigma is not substantially higher. The specification X-square test for independence (and hence validity) of the instruments and the errors fails to reject, and the diagnostic tests of error normality and specification yield similar strong results as the OLS regression. A graphic analysis of recursive estimation statistics finds reasonably stable parameters. Most importantly, while the coefficient for government expenditure has increased somewhat, the linear restrictions test of the null hypothesis that the coefficient of government expenditure is −1, again failed to reject.

Secondly, and most importantly, logic suggests that there are a number of serious problems with the argument that causality may run from private demand to government expenditure:

- Control exogeneity rests with government expenditure.
- For government expenditure to contemporaneously react to private demand, the government would have to have perfect knowledge of

current gross domestic expenditure, and be able to react during the same quarter, by adjusting government expenditure appropriately. However, GDP statistics are only available long after the end of the current quarter. Furthermore, government expenditure is the result of a somewhat complex bureaucratic procedure, which involves budgets drawn up by the Ministry of Finance and the government, which are approved by the Diet. There is no empirical evidence that this process has been fast enough to accommodate potential current-quarter changes in spending needs or that spending decisions by the various bureaucracies have been sufficiently coordinated and calibrated to counteract current-quarter private demand. More often than not, politicians and bureaucrats appear satisfied if they can respond within the same fiscal year to perceived changes in public spending requirements.

• If the government expenditure did not in fact crowd out private demand, as suggested by the credit model, but instead the government counteracted changes in private demand, then this argument would imply that government expenditure was, after all, largely effective in changing total output and employment. If that was the case, it remains to be explained why the government, apparently well-informed and infinitely fast in its short-term spending policies, did not use fiscal policy to achieve the declared government policy goal of stimulating an economic recovery, or the more modest goal of meeting its own official growth targets. If fiscal policy had the desired effects, as this argument suggests, and could counteract a change in private demand, then why did the government use it to create negative nominal GDP in 1998, 1999, 2001 and 2002?

It emerges that a large number of auxiliary assumptions – most of them highly implausible – are required to rescue this counter-argument. The fundamental principle of parsimony suggests that the proposed explanation should be considered preferable.

Policy implications

The tests confirm that for every yen in government spending that is not monetized (and hence not supported by credit creation), private demand must shrink by one yen. Fiscal policy was almost perfectly ineffective. This explains the finding we saw in Figure 2.1 of Chapter 2, namely that government expenditure and domestic demand appear to be moving in opposite directions. The empirical evidence supports our conclusion that an economic recovery can only take place, if there is an increase in credit creation. Neither interest rate nor fiscal policies can be expected to be useful. We have solved the mystery of the ineffectiveness of fiscal policy: it was not backed by increased credit creation, and hence quantity crowding-out reduced private demand one yen for each yen of fiscal spending.

The finding suggests that Japanese fiscal policy has been ineffective during the 1990s, because it was not supported by monetary policy. Ironically, this ineffectiveness finding may provide a strong case for using fiscal policy as an effective avenue for stimulating the economy, especially in times when bank credit is stagnating – fiscal policy, that is, which is appropriately coordinated with suitable monetary policy. The need for coordination of fiscal and monetary policy has been emphasized by economists such as Lerner (1943) or Wray (2001).[3]

Blinder and Solow (1973, p. 323) stated that there 'is no controversy over government spending financed by printing money. Both sides agree that it will be expansionary'. In the terms of our modified model this translates into the policy advice that the Japanese authorities needed to increase credit creation, in order to stimulate growth and also fund fiscal expenditure through credit creation.

Credit creation can be increased by a number of different policies: the central bank could act to increase credit creation by raising its net open market purchase operations. For instance, the Bank of Japan could have sufficiently increased its bond purchases (Werner, 1994b, 1995a, 1996a).[4] Policies to stimulate bank credit creation could also have been adopted. Here the central bank could have been more helpful, for instance by utilizing its unique status to solve the bad debt problem at zero cost to the taxpayer or society (by purchasing the bad debts at face value from all banks) (see Werner, 2003c). Given these findings, it appears central bank policy has not been as helpful as it could have been. The lack of incentives to coordinate monetary policy with the government's fiscal policy may be one of the disadvantages of central bank independence.[5]

How to render fiscal policy effective

Werner (1998b, 2000a, 2000d) has suggested a policy for governments to monetize fiscal policy even without cooperation from the central bank. The method renders fiscal policy effective, and would have worked also in the Japanese circumstances of the 1990s. As we saw, the majority of the Japanese public borrowing requirement has been covered through bond issuance. Without the cooperation of the central bank, money-financed fiscal policy is not an option. However, credit-financed fiscal policy is possible: the Ministry of Finance could cover the public sector borrowing requirement by borrowing from the private sector commercial banks. This would increase credit creation and stimulate the economy.

There are objections to this proposal. Hawtrey, before the Macmillan Committee of 1930, 'considered the "radical" idea of government spending out of new bank credit, but predicted that the result of such a policy would be inflationary, and a threat to the gold standard, thus forcing up the bank rate of interest and causing credit contraction. [It] ... would mean the end of cheap money for free enterprise' (Klein, 1968, quoted by Spencer and Yohe, 1970, p. 15).[6] However, Hawtrey's objection is predicated on the assumptions that (a) the market for credit is in equilibrium, so that interest rates respond proportionately to an increase in the demand for credit; and/or (b) that banks are merely financial intermediaries that cannot create new credit, so that any extension of bank loans to the government must be at the expense of bank lending to alternative uses. However, both assumptions do not hold: the theoretical and empirical literature has provided ample arguments for the case of a rationed credit market, whereby interest rates do not respond proportionately to changes in the demand for money. Furthermore, the institutional reality of banking systems allows banks to create new purchasing power without withdrawing existing purchasing power from other parts of the economy. Empirically, the Japanese example has also disproved Hawtrey's assumptions: using Japanese data, no evidence can be found that interest rates are in an inverse relationship with the quantity of bank loans extended. Furthermore, Japanese banks as of early 2005 had excess reserves of over ¥30 trillion with the central bank, and continued to reduce bank lending. They have ample opportunity to increase lending without withdrawing loans from current borrowers.

Thus the argument stands that funding of fiscal expenditure by borrowing from banks would increase credit creation and hence the total amount of purchasing power in the economy.[7] As a result, C_R in equation (6) or (10) above would rise, which would in turn boost nominal GDP. By shifting government funding away from bond finance and replacing it with borrowing from the commercial banks via simple loan contracts, credit creation will be stimulated.[8] Unlike bond markets, banks create new purchasing power when they lend. This means that overall economic activity can be boosted (via fiscal policy), without any quantity crowding-out that rendered fiscal policy ineffective during the 1990s.[9] Banks, though risk-averse due to their bad debts, would not mind lending to the government – a zero-risk borrower.

Although the central government funded parts of the 1998 budget from banks, this has remained negligible in absolute size. With the majority of bond issuance taken up by the non-bank private sector (which does not have the power to create credit), fiscal spending had to crowd out private activity.

Figures 18.1 and 18.2 are used to illustrate the difference between stimulatory fiscal policy – here the example of a fiscal spending package – funded via bond issuance taken up by investors, such as life insurers, and stimulatory fiscal policy that is backed by credit creation as suggested here.

When a fiscal expenditure package amounting to ¥20 trillion is funded by issuing bonds that are bought by private investors such as life insurance companies, ¥20 trillion in purchasing power are drained from the economy through bond issuance (and hence not used any longer for private demand or investments). Thus a gross stimulatory effect of ¥20 trillion together with a gross negative effect of ¥20 trillion delivers a net effect of zero: since

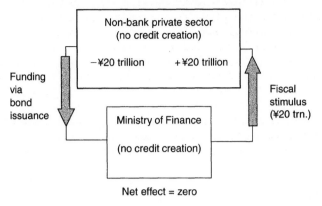

Figure 18.1   Fiscal stimulation funded by bond issuance

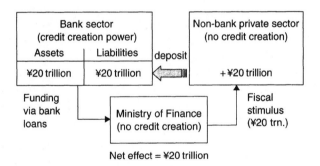

Figure 18.2   Fiscal stimulation funded by bank borrowing

credit creation did not increase, the national income pie could not grow (Figure 18.1). Hence any increase in the government share of the pie had to result in a reduction in the private sector share. A direct example of this effect is the behaviour of Japanese life insurance companies, which used to extend loans to small and medium-sized companies, but in the 1990s increasingly reduced such loans, and instead purchased government bonds or other assets.

If, however, the fiscal expenditure package of ¥20 trillion is funded not by bond issuance but by direct government borrowing from commercial banks, through the extension of loan contracts (which banks will be more than happy to provide: after all the government is the safest borrower), then bank assets increase by ¥20 trillion (Figure 18.2). This creates ¥20 trillion in new purchasing power that did not exist before. Simultaneously, the government's deposit account is credited with ¥20 trillion, which are used for fiscal expenditure. Even when the government withdraws these deposits, they will remain a deposit on the banks' balance sheet: the receivers of the funds will pay the money into their accounts with the banks. The net result: the same fiscal expenditure package of ¥20 trillion which had zero effect in the case of government bond finance will have a full effect of boosting demand by ¥20 trillion. The reason is that it was fully 'monetized', or, rather, 'creditized', since fully paid for with new credit creation. Since Japanese banks have been lending far less than reserve requirements allow them to, the latter would also not have posed an obstacle.[10]

Reviewing the options of funding deficit spending

Textbooks tell us that there are two options to fund a fiscal revenue shortfall: debt finance or money finance. In the former case, the government borrows from the private sector through bond issuance; in the latter, it either creates money directly, or borrows from the central bank, which pays by creating money.[11] The literature has always agreed unanimously that fiscal policy, if funded through central bank money creation, will be effective:

> There is no controversy over government spending financed by printing money. Both sides agree that it will be expansionary; but one group likes to call it fiscal policy, while the other prefers to call it monetary policy. Nothing much hinges on this distinction. (Blinder and Solow, 1973, p. 323)

Despite this rare unanimous agreement among economists, the possibility of money-financed fiscal expenditure has today virtually disappeared from the policy debate.[12] While this may reflect the changed institutional environment of the past decade or so, where central banks have become independent, this does not eliminate the possibility of voluntary central bank cooperation with government policy or the need by economists to analyse it.

There are therefore serious gaps in the coverage by mainstream economists of the possibilities open to governments to fund their public sector borrowing requirement. Although textbooks recognize two options to fund the borrowing requirement (bond issuance and central bank money creation), in practice economists have ignored one of them, and focused on the one that is least desirable: bond issuance renders fiscal policy growth-neutral due to quantity crowding-out. But there are two further options which do not suffer from such crowding-out that remain entirely ignored. One we have discussed above, namely the possibility to fund fiscal policy through bank credit creation via bank loans.

The most efficient way to fund fiscal expenditure

There is a fourth option of funding government expenditure which has also been ignored by most of the literature. The first three all share one common drawback: they create debt, which needs to be serviced through interest and interest on interest. In the case of most industrialized nations, but especially in the case of the US and Japan, these compound interest liabilities are substantial. They will have to be serviced by generations of taxpayers, while public expenditures (such as on public services, healthcare, education, and so on) will have to be cut in order to save money to be able to service the accumulated debt mountain. Economically, this is a highly inefficient, unproductive and inequitable allocation of resources.

There is an option to fund government expenditure, which has the advantage of no quantity crowding out, but also does not suffer from the disadvantage of incurring debt. It is thus the most desirable, efficient and equitable method: this is the option for governments to create money directly and use it to fund their expenditure, just as Kublai Khan did in thirteenth-century China, or as the US government did during several stages of its history. In these cases, no debt is incurred, and no interest liabilities weigh on future generations of taxpayers.

Indeed, the US Constitution, largely under the influence of Thomas Jefferson (an opponent of privately-owned central banks), explicitly reserved the right of money creation for the US government. Since the creation of the privately-owned Federal Reserve banks in 1913, this option was increasingly avoided, thus incurring significant government debt and substantial interest liabilities. One of the few presidents to challenge the *de facto* monopoly to create credit that the banking system and the Federal Reserve banks enjoy was John F. Kennedy, who ordered the issuance of 'United States Notes' in 1963 with one of his last executive orders (No. 11,110).[13] This government money had the same design as the more common 'Federal Reserve Notes', but instead was entitled 'United States Notes' (compare Figures 18.3 and 18.4). Further, it was only graced by the seal of the US Treasury, and did not have any seal linked to the Federal Reserve system. After Kennedy's death this practice has not been repeated. Since then, interest liabilities of the US population have mounted.

In line with this argument, Joseph Stiglitz has called for the Japanese government to issue government paper money.[14] In Japan, this policy was last implemented in the early Meiji era. To fund stimulatory fiscal policy through the issuance of paper money is economically more efficient than borrowing. In practice, the technique can still be improved upon, however: paper note issuance is somewhat cumbersome, carries (small) production costs and, most of all, is limited in potential maximum scope by the fact that only about 5% of all transactions make use of paper money. Therefore an improved version of this funding policy, which allows the government to

Figure 18.3 The standard Federal Reserve Note
The standard five dollar 'Federal Reserve Note' is entitled as such and carries the seal of the Federal Reserve system (on the left) and the seal of the US Treasury (on the right)

Figure 18.4 The United States Note
In 1963, President Kennedy ordered the issuance of government paper money, with the same design as the Federal Reserve Notes, but entitled 'United States Note' and bearing only the seal of the US Treasury (on the right)

create larger volumes of credit, would be for the Finance Ministry (or, in the case of the US, the Treasury) to institute credit creation on its own accounts, the same way that currently the central banks and the commercial banks create credit. This could be achieved if Milton Friedman's (1982) advice was heeded, which constitutes the culmination of his decades of research into the functioning and economic implications of the Federal Reserve system, namely to fold the functions of the central bank into the Treasury, by rendering 'the Federal Reserve a bureau in the Treasury under the secretary of the Treasury' (Friedman, 1982, p. 118).[15]

Conclusion

The proposed disaggregated credit creation model has provided an answer to the question why fiscal policy has appeared ineffective during the 1990s. The problem was the way this deficit spending was financed: among the four options available to the government, namely to create credit itself, borrow from banks through loan contracts, borrow from the central bank and borrow from the public (through bond issuance), the government has chosen the least efficient method, namely the latter. Bond issuance tends to crowd out private sector demand, as we demonstrated in the case of the 1990s in Japan, and thus render fiscal policy entirely ineffective in stimulating growth. Furthermore, it creates debt, and compounding interest liabilities.

Even without the right government policies taking place, the central bank could have created a recovery, as we will see in the next chapter. However, the government has also not adopted suitable policies to counter the lack of cooperation from the central bank. It could have (and still can) increase credit creation, and hence render fiscal policy effective, by switching its funding from bond issuance to loan contracts from commercial banks, or by adopting the more radical policy of issuing government money.

19
Monetary Policy in the 1990s and How to Create a Recovery

It has by now already been demonstrated that with the framework of disaggregated credit creation in a world of credit rationing the enigmas of monetary policy in the 1990s can be solved.

The ineffectiveness of interest rate policy

The familiar equation (1) indicates that even if interest rates were reduced to zero, no economic recovery would follow as long as bad debts prevent banks from lending and as long as the central bank does not increase its credit creation to compensate:[1]

$$(1) \quad \Delta(P_R Y) = V_R \Delta C_R$$

Nominal GDP is constrained by the net creation of credit. The ineffectiveness of interest rate policy *per se* is therefore not a phenomenon that occurs when interest rates have dropped to zero. It is a general phenomenon that is due to imperfect information and the quantity rationing that it entails, thus leaving no direct causal role for interest rates in the macroeconomic framework. This means that credit quantities should be used as the operational target of monetary policy.

The ineffectiveness of high powered money

If high powered money was equal to the net credit creation of the central bank, then the monetarist prescription to increase high powered money would be identical to one of the prescriptions of our model, namely to increase central bank credit creation in order to make up for a lack of bank credit creation. This should be done through direct injection of credit into the economy (since banks may not wish to borrow from the central bank). However, high powered money is not identical with central bank credit creation. As we saw in Chapter 7, high powered money (aka M0 or base money) is defined as the sum of notes and coins in circulation and banks' reserves with the central bank. The latter is not necessarily relevant for central bank credit creation, since an increase in banks' voluntary excess reserves with the central bank would constitute an increase in high powered money, but may not coincide with an increase in the central bank's credit creation or an increase in purchasing power in the non-bank economy. Concerning the former, the central bank can create credit in excess of the volume of notes and coins in circulation.

The ineffectiveness of deposit aggregates

We have seen that the breakdown of the correlation between broad 'money supply' deposit aggregates and nominal GDP in many countries, including Japan in the 1980s and 1990s, is due to (a) the violation of the assumption that Y represents all transactions in the traditional quantity equation (equation (2) in Chapter 13); and (b) the attempt to measure money that changes hands for economic transactions during a given time period by arbitrary deposit aggregates. Since there are many different ways of aggregating private sector assets, it is *a priori* not clear which subset of possible savings measures (for example, M1, M2, M3, M4, and so on) would accurately proxy the increase in purchasing power that is due to credit creation. Shifts in asset holdings (due to various factors, such as changes in institutional arrangements and regulations) across the definition domains of the various savings aggregates render any correlation with credit creation unreliable. Attempting to increase the growth of any arbitrary deposit aggregate is therefore neither necessary nor sufficient for an increase in economic activity.

Effective monetary policy to stimulate the Japanese economy

With the ability of banks to create credit severely impaired by bad debts, an economic recovery could be created by a policy of aggressive expansion of both central bank and bank credit.[2] Note that increases in lending by the formerly twelve government-owned financial institutions (such as the Japan Development Bank, Small Business Finance Corporation, and so on) do not create credit; neither does lending by non-bank financial institutions, such as life insurers. They are not client institutions of the central bank and merely act as financial intermediaries, similar to investment funds, but are not creators of new purchasing power. It is such a policy of broadly expanded credit creation that should be referred to as 'quantitative monetary easing', in line with the traditional Bank of Japan nomenclature (*ryouteki kinyuu kanwa*: see, for instance, Werner, 1995c). The policy adopted since March 2001 of increasing banks' reserves with the central bank cannot properly be called that, since it does not increase the quantity of credit creation.[3]

Expanding central bank credit creation

The Bank of Japan's argument that monetary policy is powerless with zero interest rates, as well as its explanation of how it has been conducting monetary policy hinges on interest rates being the only mechanism for transmission.[4] However, in our quantity-rationed framework we see that monetary policy does not mainly work via interest rates, but through straightforward quantity effects. Even the goal to prevent surges in call rates around the 15th of the month does not prevent the central bank from implementing exogenous monetary policy by increasing the amount of its credit creation (through increased asset purchases) (Werner, 1995c, 1996c, 1997a, 1997c, 1998a). Instead of high powered money, preferred by monetarists, a more useful operating target would be the net quantity of credit creation, measured by the sum of all central bank transactions, including those outside the money market operations.

Against the central bank's argument of money endogeneity and that 'Monetary policy cannot directly generate demand ...' (Hayami, 2001), it can be said that there has been excess demand for money (though largely from institutions and individuals that had no direct access to the 'closed' call market, where the 'open market' operations are concentrated, namely small firms and the government). Secondly, the central bank should conduct true 'open market operations', namely not just with the small number of participants in the practically closed call market, but directly with the non-bank sector of the economy (Werner, 1995c, 1996a, 1996c, 1997a, 1998a).[5] Thirdly, even if there was no demand for money, the central bank could simply create more credit and inject it through its purchase operations, which would increase demand and stop deflation. These purchases could be of financial assets (bills, government bonds, corporate bonds, equities, foreign exchange, preferred bank stocks; the bad debts of the banks at face value) or real assets (real estate, creating 'Bank of Japan parks' in Tokyo). The central bank can also create credit by directly lending to the corporate sector (Werner, 1994b, 1995a, 1995c, 1996b, 1996c).[6] Since about 1998, these policy recommendations have been seconded by many others.[7] Another obvious suggestion is to have the central bank create money and transfer it to each taxpayer in the country.[8] Unlike tax reductions, this present would constitute monetary policy and hence not crowd out private activity.

In general, the central bank should target its own and banks' credit creation in order to achieve a nominal GDP growth target.[9] We notice that this seems to have worked, whenever the Bank of Japan decided to (temporarily) increase credit creation: its significant expansion of credit creation in 1998 contributed to an economic recovery in 1999. Its substantial reduction in credit creation in 1999 choked off this recovery. Its significant expansion in credit creation from June 2001 onwards created a recovery in 2002 that took most economists by surprise.

Foreign exchange intervention

The Bank of Japan was largely sterilizing, at times even oversterilizing the foreign exchange intervention ordered by the ministry, such as in 1994 and 1995, 1999 and 2003. In order to increase credit creation, the central bank should not sterilize such intervention.[10] This argument is supported by Hamada (1999).

Expanding bank credit creation

For bank credit creation to rise, banks' risk aversion needs to be reduced, which can be done by writing off the bad debts. To do so, the banks require money. The question is therefore reduced to determining where this money should come from. A non-exhaustive list would be: the taxpayer/the government, the central bank and private investors. Concerning each source of money, many different schemes are possible, each time hinging on the issue of just how much money would be put up and what would be received in return. Any combination is possible, ranging from putting up enough money to make up for the book value (face value) of the loans, and obtaining nothing in return; to putting up less money, and getting much in return (including ownership of the bank). Since various interest groups (including the central bank) are involved, which scheme is chosen becomes a question of political economy.

Economists can, however, suggest the most efficient scheme from the viewpoint of the entire economy. This would be for the central bank, in fulfilment of its function, to solve the bad debt problem in the banking system at zero cost to society, namely by conducting a one-off purchase operation of all declared bad debts from the banks at the original book value.[11] The banks' balance sheets would immediately be among the strongest in the world and they could begin to engage in their normal credit business again. Unlike a fiscal bank bailout, this would not burden the taxpayer, and thus would also not crowd out the private sector. Moreover, it would be a 'free lunch', since there would be no cost to the economy. The central bank could simply keep those assets on its books at face value *ad infinitum*. Notice that, as with any other asset purchases by the central bank, it would not actually make a loss, since its fundraising costs are zero. As long as the market value of the assets was higher than zero, the central bank would still gain, as it purchases assets with some value, for money that it has just created for free. If the value of the assets drops to zero, the central bank would still have no loss, but would just break even with this transaction. While the central bank could freely choose to treat such transactions differently in its accounts, such that it would report a loss, there is no logical reason why it should do so (except as a sectarian political argument against conducting this transaction in the first place).

Other proposals to increase bank credit creation include the creation of profits through bond market operations, measures to introduce zero-risk borrowers to banks (government and central bank guarantees on loans to small and medium-sized enterprises, direct lending to the central government), and measures to relieve market pressure on banks (exemption from BIS capital adequacy; relaxation of accounting standards: on the latter, see, for instance, Werner, 1998g).

How to avoid moral hazard

It has been suggested that any such bank rescue operation should respect the moral hazard principle. Since a problem of the 1990s has been that banks have been shrinking credit creation, there can be little immediate concern that any action to help them would lead to excessive credit creation. More fundamentally, the idea of the moral hazard principle is that those responsible for costly problems should also bear the brunt of those costs, otherwise the wrong incentive structures would be created and problems might recur. The question is thus: who is responsible for the bad debt problem in the banking system? Whoever it is should bear the brunt of the costs of helping banks to become healthy again.

So far, the authorities and the Bank of Japan have argued that the taxpayer should foot the bill. Tax money has been used to recapitalize banks. However, there is no evidence that taxpayers have been responsible for the banks' problems. Thus these policies are likely to have created a moral hazard problem. Alternatively it has been argued that the banks or their shareholders should shoulder the costs. Friedman (2000) questions whether it is

> fair to treat Japanese banks as strictly private firms, whose shareholders and managers should appropriately be subject to market discipline when their institutions' affairs go badly? Under Japan's traditional system of administrative guidance of the entire financial sector ... perhaps the banks, in lending so aggressively against rapidly inflating real estate and equity values, were merely acting as agents of public policy. If so, then the conventional rationale underlying the argument for exposing these institutions and their managers to market discipline would not apply.

Indeed, to determine the best policy of avoiding moral hazard, it is necessary now to turn to the issue of responsibility for the bad debt problem in the banking system. For the 1990s the answer must be: the Bank of Japan.

Once the bad debt problem occurred, the central bank could have compensated for shrinking bank credit through a sufficient expansion in its own credit creation. Alternatively, the Bank of Japan could have solved the bad debt problem at zero costs to society by buying the bad debts from banks at face value. The Bank of Japan could have rendered fiscal policy effective, by monetizing government debt. Finally, the Bank of Japan could have omitted its sterilization of the significant foreign exchange interventions ordered by the Ministry of Finance, especially in 1994/95, 1999 and 2003. In all cases, the Bank of Japan chose not to.

In neoclassical economics, the principle of revealed preference is used to assess the intentions of agents, since often words can be unreliable or misleading. Using this approach to assess the policies of the Bank of Japan, we come to the conclusion that the Bank of Japan chose not to adopt the type of policies which would have prevented the long recession of the 1990s and which were in its power.

While the bad debts of the 1990s placed the burden of action on the central bank, they were themselves the result of events in the 1980s, when the Japanese financial bubble occurred. For a complete answer to the question of responsibility, it is therefore now necessary to solve the enigma of the determination of Japanese bank lending in the 1980s.

20
Monetary Policy in the 1980s: How Bank Credit was Determined

> What is it that monetary policy-makers do and how do they do it?
> The simple answer is that a central banker moves interest rates…
> (Cecchetti, 2000)

In Chapter 16 it was found that the strong growth in bank lending during the 1980s was the main cause of asset price movements in the 1980s and early 1990s. Further, in Chapter 15 it was shown that the weak credit growth of the 1990s was the cause of the recession. The weak lending of the 1990s was due to banks' substantial bad debts, which rendered them risk averse, thus increasing the always present rationing in the credit market. These findings motivate interest in the question why banks increased their lending so aggressively during the 1980s. Moreover, in the previous chapter the issue of how to avoid moral hazard was raised. Also for this purpose and the formulation of suitable policies it is necessary to identify the cause of the rapid bank lending of the 1980s and identify those who are responsible for it. It is this question that will be examined in the present chapter.

In Chapter 10 it was found that traditional explanations of bank lending, specifically the interest rate argument, do not work. Thus traditional theory has not been able to provide an answer to the question why Japanese banks expanded bank lending so aggressively during the mid to late 1980s.

It can in general be stated that there is a large number of potential factors that influence aggregate bank lending. Other frequently cited factors include the partial deregulation of interest rate controls and international capital flows during the 1980s. However, to avoid fruitless searches, deductive logic suggests that a priority of ranking of potential explanatory variables can be established. The rational investigator would start by seeking to refute the most plausible explanation first. This ranking of explanations would thus be guided by the degree of complexity of explanations. Those arguments that require fewer assumptions must by the principles of logic be considered more plausible and thus should be tested first.

267

Central bank policy as explanation

In most countries, the single most important factor influencing bank behaviour is the central bank. It is therefore sensible to start research into the determinants of bank lending by an examination of central bank monetary policy implementation. Most of the literature on central bank policy emphasizes the three standard tools with which a central bank can influence monetary policy: the formal regulatory tool (such as changes in the reserve requirement), the price tool (such as the discount rate) and the quantity tool (such as the supply of reserves to the banking system via open market operations or lending). The operational procedures of these instruments are relatively well-researched, and they have not yielded new insights into the causes of the rise in real estate-related lending during the 1980s in Japan.

Informal 'guidance' of bank lending

However, there are other monetary policy tools that have been employed in many countries in the past, yet which remain under-appreciated by the economic literature. Monetary authorities in many countries are known to have used 'informal', that is unofficial and extra-legal regulatory tools, such as direct control of the quantity of bank credit. This has been widespread in developing countries, but also the developed ones: 'Most industrialized countries outside of North America imposed direct controls over the volume of bank lending for some, often most, of the time from 1945 till the 1980s' (Goodhart, 1989b, p. 157). Depending on the country, this has variously been christened 'credit controls' (US, UK), 'lending ceilings', 'corset' (UK), '*encadrement du crédit*' (France), '*Kredit-Plafondierung*' (Germany, Austria), 'credit planning scheme' (Thailand), or, in the case of Japan and Korea, 'window guidance' (see Goodhart, 1989b; Bredemeier, 1972; and the literature cited below).

There is broad agreement in the literature about the role and importance of direct credit controls in Japan before the 1980s. Researchers agree that bank credit growth was successfully controlled by the central bank through the use of this tool. We summarize the literature only briefly here (for more details, see, for instance, Patrick, 1962; Yoshino, 1962; Suzuki, 1974; Kure, 1973, 1975; Horiuchi, 1980).[1] The so-called 'window guidance' loan controls consisted of regular meetings with monitoring and feedback. Essentially, the central bank told the private banks on a quarterly basis by how much they were to increase their lending. Overshooting as well as undershooting the quota was strictly forbidden and punished. The central bank first decided the desired overall economy-wide increase in bank lending (on a year-on-year basis, recalculated and announced as quarter-on-quarter absolute loan increase quotas), then allocated the increase to individual banks on a pro rata basis. Since bank officials came to the Bank of Japan to be told virtually over the counter (the 'teller window') by its Banking Department about their loan quota allocations for the following quarter, this procedure came to be referred to as 'window guidance' (*madoguchi shidō*).[2]

Direct controls over the loan books of private banks remained unofficial, without legal foundation and were conducted largely in secrecy (Patrick, 1962). Such controls were not fully consistent with the OECD requirement of market orientation. Despite their widespread use also in other countries, Japan had come under political pressure by the early 1960s to liberalize its markets. Thus the Bank of Japan has always downplayed their role.[3] Moreover, throughout the postwar era, the Bank of Japan switched between open recognition of the existence of window guidance, official denial and phases where such guidance was supposedly abolished – only to be reintroduced soon with more wide-ranging scope. Since April 1973 it has been imposed on all client institutions of the Bank of Japan that create credit. Since life insurance companies and other non-bank financial institutions do not create credit, window guidance has never covered them.[4]

Once the banks had submitted detailed lending plans, the Bank of Japan would analyse them according to the use of the loans, such as by sector of the economy or by size of company (Patrick, 1964). The official Bank of Japan view was that '[window guidance] is employed to regulate the total amount of commercial bank credit and is not a tool for the qualitative control of lending' (Bank of Japan, 1973, p. 159). However, if it was deemed necessary, it actively 'guided' the credit allocation among the various categories. Consumer goods and service industries were generally considered 'luxuries' that Japan could not afford and therefore received fewer allocations. The Bank of Japan gave preference to loans to export businesses, while importers would also be disadvantaged (Patrick, 1962). Qualitative window guidance suppressed real estate-related loans in the late 1970s (Nikkei, 1979). Therefore it is apparent that the credit controls always had an important qualitative element and served not only to ration but also to allocate credit in the economy.

The decision about how much bank loans should increase was taken explicitly with economic growth targets in mind. Kure (1975), formerly a member of the Bank of Japan, explains in his informative work that first a 'suitable' nominal GDP growth rate was decided and then the aggregate bank loan growth quota was set at about the same growth rate. In terms of the location of decision-making power, Patrick (1962) finds that window guidance 'is rather free of Ministry of Finance interference because the process of establishing ceilings poses a number of technical problems and because the details of the operations are kept quite secret' (p. 143). The key decision-maker concerning the credit control policy was found to be the Director of the Banking Department (*Eigyō kyokuchō*) of the Bank of Japan.

The literature is in agreement that window guidance was 'effective' in controlling credit aggregates of those institutions that were subject to the credit controls (see, for instance, Patrick, 1964; Kure, 1975). Compliance was assured by the monopoly power of the central bank to impose sanctions and penalties, such as cutting rediscount quotas, applying unfavourable conditions to its transactions with banks or reducing the next window guidance quotas. Moreover, in the postwar era large city banks were borrowing heavily from the central bank. This rendered them even more dependent on the Bank of Japan, who used the allocation of its direct lending in support of its policy.[5]

Some researchers, as well as the Bank of Japan, have argued that controls or 'guidance' on private bank credit have merely constituted a 'supplementary instrument for monetary control', with discount window lending and open market operations in securities markets having served as the 'primary instruments' (Hoshi et al., 1991; Suzuki, 1974; Bank of Japan, 1987; Calder, 1993). However, Kure (1975) found that from 1955 until the early 1970s, whenever monetary policy has tightened, a tightening of the credit growth ceilings preceded changes in other monetary policy tools. According to Patrick (1962), window guidance was the main policy tool which rendered other policy tools mere support mechanisms: Banks and the central bank first agreed on new lending plans; if these would push the total loan balance beyond the maximum that was possible with the given reserve requirement, then the Bank of Japan would lend the banks money as reserves. Horiuchi (1980) concluded that 'when one studies in detail the concrete process of monetary policy operation, one can't help gaining the impression that "window guidance" is more than just a supplementary tool augmenting other policy operations, but the "leading actor" of the monetary policy of our country' (p. 146).

It can be concluded that the practice of directed credit was well-established and sophisticated in its application. This may be surprising from the viewpoint of traditional macroeconomic models, where interest rates are the most important variable. However, in a more realistic world of imperfect information and consequent market rationing, the quantity of credit becomes the most important macroeconomic variable. Further, as we saw in Chapter 15, the sectoral allocation of credit is crucial for the determination of economic growth, and the distribution between real growth and inflation (of consumer or asset prices). It is therefore not surprising that the Bank of Japan has used window guidance throughout the postwar era. Window guidance determined Japanese bank credit growth, which in turn determined nominal GDP growth. Thanks to the sectoral allocation of loans via window guidance to productive investments, the high growth of the 1960s was achieved, with only modest inflation. The Japanese 'economic miracle' occurred to a large extent due to this mechanism of credit control.

'Official history' of window guidance since 1982

While a relatively large (though little known) literature exists on window guidance before the 1980s, there is little detailed empirical research about the actual conduct and role of window guidance in the crucial 1980s. Dotsey (1986), an economist from the Federal Reserve Bank of Richmond, who was invited to the Bank of Japan to study its operating mechanisms and compare them with those of the US central bank, concluded that 'although there are some interesting differences, the two central banks' daily operating procedures are very similar. Both monetary authorities basically use the inter-bank market interest rate as their policy instrument' (p. 105). Since he saw no theoretical reason for 'moral suasion', apparently he also saw no need to study the question of their existence empirically. Hoshi et al. (1991) state in their paper on window guidance: 'After 1982 and until 1989, window guidance played an insignificant role in the conduct of monetary policy' (p. 9). They do refer to statistical evidence, which we will examine more closely later in this chapter. However, Hoshi et al. present no independent research into the question of whether window guidance was actually abandoned.

Rhodes and Yoshino claim, without presenting supportive empirical evidence, that window guidance functioned 'to supplement conventional monetary policy instruments' (1999, pp. 167ff.), while the discount rate and the call rate were 'the two primary tools of monetary adjustment' (p. 168).

Indeed, it appears that the view that credit controls were unimportant in the 1980s is based primarily on official pronouncements by the Bank of Japan itself: in December 1981, the Bank of Japan announced the abolition of credit controls with effect of January 1982. The central bank said it would not set loan growth limits for banks any more. Rather, it would 'respect' the banks' lending plans. Again, in 1984, the central bank announced the '*de facto*' abolition of window guidance (Nikkei, 1984a, 1984b, 1985). In 1986, a Bank of Japan official is quoted in the *Nihon Keizai Shinbun* (Nikkei) as saying that the central bank 'currently is not doing window guidance' (Nikkei, 1986). In 1988, the Bank of Japan claimed that since 1982 there has been no window guidance in 'a narrow sense', as deregulation of interest rates, disintermediation and liberalization have rendered this policy tool less effective. The Bank also says that in the future it will depend even less on window guidance (Nikkei Kinyū, 1988). In December 1988, the Bank of Japan even produced an important empirical study that denies the fundamental reason for credit controls, by arguing that credit aggregates as such were not especially useful in explaining economic activity.[6]

In a report published by the Bank of Japan in March 1991 in English, it is argued that 'in line with the trend of financial deregulation, window guidance has no longer been applied in its original form of credit control since 1982, when the Bank of Japan stopped giving individual banks instructions with respect to their lending plans' (Bank of Japan, 1991b, pp. 21f.).[7] Soon after the publication of this report, the Bank of Japan announced in July 1991 that window guidance would be abolished with immediate effect (once again).

Empirical evidence on the practice of window guidance 1982–91

The official Bank of Japan explanation that window guidance was not an important policy tool in the 1980s needs to be substantiated by empirical evidence.[8] Simply assuming that the Bank of Japan has actually ceased using window guidance, because it says so, and because in the 1980s it has increasingly had other tools at its disposal, is not the same as ascertaining through empirical research whether window guidance existed, and if so, what role it played. Scepticism about the official view seems justified for several reasons:

1. the very nature of window guidance as an informal, extra-legal policy tool that is based on moral suasion and secrecy implies that it is less likely to be fully disclosed in official statements;
2. since Japan has joined the OECD, it has been obliged to reduce direct economic controls and adopt a market-oriented economic system. Direct credit controls have been criticized by the US. Especially since the 1980s, authorities have thus had a political incentive to downplay direct controls and emphasize market mechanisms;
3. window guidance has a pre-1980s track record of being officially declared 'abolished', although *de facto* it either continued unofficially and/or was reinstituted officially again soon after;[9]
4. the fact that it was abolished (again) in 1991 suggests that it did exist in a meaningful way in the 1980s – only existing procedures can be abolished;
5. credit aggregates have proven to be the cause of the economic boom of the 1980s and the long recession that followed afterwards. Anybody involved in the determination of these credit aggregates can be presumed to have an incentive to downplay such involvement and degree of control;
6. finally, some noted scholars of monetary policy in Japan have already concluded that the Bank of Japan has purposely 'misled' the public about the use of its monetary policy tools in a different context before.[10]

When there is reasonable doubt about the validity of official descriptions of institutional arrangements it is scientific practice to establish the facts by way of fieldwork. Eye-witness accounts can be derived by

1. secondary testimonies, that is, quotations from individuals involved in window guidance that have been reported by reliable sources, and

2. primary testimonies, that is, eye-witness accounts gained directly by the researcher during interviews conducted specifically for that purpose (for more on field research and interview methodology in the social sciences; see, for instance, Whyte, 1988).[11]

In order to prevent bias or error, and to obtain an independent 'control' source of information, we decided to utilize both secondary and primary testimonies. Among the primary testimonies we also obtained a 'control' check by independently interviewing both eye-witnesses of the window guidance procedures who were employed by the Bank of Japan and those who were employed by private sector banks. Finally, we conduct statistical tests of the relevance of window guidance, and specifi-cally of the hypothesis that a change took place in the Bank of Japan's operating procedures in 1982, rendering window guidance ineffective or irrelevant.

Secondary sources

The most widely read and most highly respected daily newspapers that focus on economic and financial matters in Japan are the *Nihon Keizai Shinbun* (commonly known as Nikkei) and its sister publication, the *Nikkei Kinyū Shinbun* (the Nikkei Financial Daily). Their reporting of facts and quotations by officials is generally considered reliable. There is no reason to suspect significant bias or inaccuracies in our context.[12] A search for the keywords *'madoguchi kisei'* ('window regulation') yielded 107 articles in the Nikkei papers from 1980 to 1992. A search for the keywords *'madoguchi shidō'* ('window guidance') yielded 53 articles over the same time period. In many of these articles, Bank of Japan officials, but also private bank officers, are quoted, either with their names being mentioned or as unnamed 'sources', mainly from the Banking Department of the Bank of Japan.[13]

In these articles we found evidence that during the 1980s window guidance continued virtually unchanged and thus played a much larger role than is officially acknowledged by the Bank of Japan. Table 20.1 summarizes key passages abridged from selected articles in chronological order.[14]

The secondary sources provide a relatively consistent picture of the continuation of window guidance and, indeed, its expansion to include special types of loans, such as 'impact loans'. Based on the secondary testimonies, window guidance appears to have existed throughout the 1980s until 1991, when our observation period ends. It appears to have taken virtually the same form as before the 1980s and it appears to have been of significant impact on bank loan aggregates. Finally, several secondary sources suggest that the Bank of Japan was monitoring the composition of loan aggregates and was aware of the increase in credit creation for real estate-related lending.

274

Table 20.1 Secondary sources on the existence of credit controls in the 1980s

Date	Information concerning the existence of 'window guidance' (abridged)
Dec. 1981	A 'new style window guidance', tantamount to abolition, is being introduced by the Bank of Japan, in which it will 'respect' the lending plans of banks. Referred to as 'the loosest regulation since 1945'. However, Bank of Japan officials are quoted as stating that window guidance is 'not abolished' ... 'there is the intention to control lending via direct daily contact with private sector financial institutions'. (Nikkei, 1981)
Sep. 1982	Despite the official Bank of Japan claim that all bank lending plans are being 'respected', voices from the top city banks complain that 'the lending plans of the individual banks are not being respected enough' and banks are not allowed to compete freely. If lending plans were fully accepted, competition among banks would increase and the ranking of banks would change. However, the ranking remained unchanged. The Bank of Japan engaged in 'adjustment' of the banks' lending plans. (Nikkei, 1982a)
Oct. 1982	The Bank of Japan 'adjusts' the lending plans it receives from the banks, so that they differ from the original proposals. (Nikkei, 1982b)
Oct. 1986	As a result of window guidance, lending plans are in similar proportion in the various bank groups. For example, when the largest, DKB, gets an increase of 120, then the other large city banks (Fuji, Sumitomo, Mitsubishi, Sanwa) obtain 100. (Nikkei, 1986)
Oct. 1987	Because window guidance was tightened, banks are extending more 'impact loans' [foreign-denominated loans swapped back into yen-loans] in order to circumvent the tight window guidance loan quotas. (Nikkei Kinyū, 1987)
Mar. 1988	Window guidance loan quotas for Q2 1988 are being tightened, because the Bank of Japan thinks that loan demand for real estate investment and 'zai-tech' [financial] speculation has peaked. The central bank shows itself aware of the fact that the fastest growing segment of bank lending was real estate and zai-tech. (Nikkei Kinyū, 1988a)
	Control over impact loans is tightened, with city banks forced to reduce impact loans by 25% year-on-year in Q2 1988, because according to the Bank of Japan impact loans are mainly connected to real estate speculation and zai-tech speculation. (Nikkei Kinyū, 1988b)
Jun. 1989	The central bank tightened its lending quotas to banks for Q3 1989. (Nikkei Kinyū, 1989)

Table 20.1 Continued

Date	Information concerning the existence of 'window guidance' (abridged)
Sep. 1990	'Window guidance is a powerful tool for adjusting monetary quantity ... The Bank of Japan says "We will at least tighten [the guidance] beyond the [previous] quarter". Until now, whenever the actual year-on-year loan growth has not reached the regulated quota, the Bank of Japan had reduced the next quota by the amount that was not used up. That resulted in the problem that every bank struggled hard to use up its loan quota, even if this was unreasonable. From now on, the Bank of Japan is studying to abolish this procedure ...' (Nikkei, 1990)
Feb. 1991	On the occasion of the official abolition of window guidance, Nikkei Kinyū (1991a) explains that so far window guidance controlled every bank's lending increases and that the Bank of Japan for a long time period also 'intervened' concerning the allocation of loans.
Jun. 1991	A bank officer from a 'high-ranking city bank' is quoted as saying that the side effect of the window guidance rule of loan increases was that banks increased lending even when there was no loan demand. And even when there was loan demand, they had to stay in line with other banks. (Nikkei, 1991)
	'There is no such system in other advanced countries that the central bank decides the quarterly loan growth increases. Because there is window guidance, even when banks make irresponsible loans, they justify them by saying "the BoJ said it's OK" ... Since window guidance is so non-transparent and irrational, it is natural that the Bank of Japan rushed to abolish it. However, overall, window guidance had a certain effect in controlling bank loans. There are also voices doubting whether the Bank of Japan would really give up such power ...' On the other hand, window guidance is useful when raising interest rates is hard to justify, for instance, in order to prevent a bubble. (Nikkei Kinyū, 1991a)
Jul. 1991	Discussing the abolition of window guidance, the Nikkei quotes Bank of Japan officials to the effect that the central bank 'will continue to monitor individual bank loan figures to see if lending is "sound" and will caution banks if it sees unsound lending'. This would imply that qualitative guidance would continue, but no quantitative guidance. (Nikkei, 1991)
	Tatsuya Tamura, the director of the Bank of Japan Banking Department, is quoted in the Nikkei Kinyū: 'When the banks put together their quarterly lending plans, they will from the third quarter this year onwards not receive our policy advice any more ... [However] in the future, hearings with the banks about their loan situation will continue'. Although window guidance

Table 20.1 Continued

Date	Information concerning the existence of 'window guidance' (abridged)
	was officially 'abolished' in 1982 already, 'a scheme continued until now such that policy guidance could be given'. Bankers fear that similar clandestine 'guidance' is likely to remain. (Nikkei Kinyū, 1991b)
	Others complain about 'headaches', because they don't know how to decide their lending plans from now on. 'So far, first the total credit amount was decided by the Bank of Japan credit allocation frame, then we decided about how to divide that quota', a bank officer is quoted. (Nikkei Kinyū, 1991b)

Primary sources

Primary source research took the form of conducting interviews with eyewitnesses. To prevent bias and check for consistency or contradictions, we interviewed not only some of those central bank officials that were personally involved in administering window guidance during the late 1980s, but also some of those private bank officers that were at the time counterparts to the central bank window guidance officials – in other words, members from both parties involved in the window guidance process. For our study, we interviewed twelve Bank of Japan officials in both tape-recorded and note-recorded interviews.[15] We also completed note-recorded interviews with six private bank officers from three different banks (as well as different bank types). As we will see, the testimonies of private bank officers fully confirmed the testimony obtained from Bank of Japan officials (as well as the secondary testimonies). Finally, as an additional control group, we conducted interviews with various members of the Ministry of Finance. They added little new information, but helped confirm the location of the window-guidance decision-making process. The interviews took place in 1992 and 1993 and referred specifically to the period of the late 1980s.[16]

The research findings from these primary sources are briefly summarized. It was found that window guidance must be considered the generic term for a process of informal but tight control of bank behaviour that includes daily and monthly hearings and quarterly meetings and whose key function consists of the imposition by the Bank of Japan of loan growth quotas on private banks.[17] We confirmed that window guidance was conducted without interruption during the 1980s, until at least June 1991. The quotas were binding, in the sense that procedures for punishing over- or undershooting existed. Banks virtually always fulfilled them.

The banks subject to window guidance during the 1980s were all the credit creating institutions.[18] Window guidance was never concerned with loans extended by trading firms, insurance companies or non-bank financial institutions. It was administered by the Banking Department of the Bank of Japan in Tokyo, as well as the branch offices of the Bank of Japan throughout the country.[19]

In the monthly 'hearings', or *'shikin kaigi'*, with the banks, officers explained their business plans in terms of incremental changes in deposits, loans and investments in stocks and bonds, so that Bank of Japan staff could monitor the smooth implementation of the quarterly loan quotas. 'Not too much guidance actually takes place' in these monthly meetings, but banks provide details about their loan portfolios, about their deposits and about their other investments in stocks and bonds (Bank of Japan official 5).

Indeed, banks gave 'every piece of information we have' to the Bank of Japan about the asset side of their balance sheets, with particular emphasis on bank loans (bank officer 3). Deposits were only of secondary interest during window guidance. The loan information was broken down into loans to each industrial sector of the economy, within which it was further broken down to the names and amounts of big borrowers (more than ¥100 million). All of these were subject to detailed scrutiny by the Bank of Japan officials concerned.[20]

Towards the end of the quarter, the Bank of Japan summoned the private bank representatives to its offices and announced to them the quarterly loan growth quotas that constituted the core of window guidance. The loan quota was decided by the Bank of Japan and presented to the banks in both year-on-year percentage growth and quarter-on-quarter absolute growth figures (Bank of Japan officials 5, 6). The quota was broken into monthly increments, which were also monitored.

> When the end of a quarter approaches, it becomes clear by how much the banks have increased loans so far. Thus around that time bank people come, for example towards the end of March, and talk to their counterparts here at the Bank of Japan ... They come to give reports. We actually call them. We ask them every month how much they have raised loans. If it looks that they have gone over the limit, we tell them: 'slow it down a bit'. (Bank of Japan officials 5, 6)

The individual loan growth quotas, called *waku* (literally, 'frame', just as the French term for credit controls – *encadrement* – or the German *Kredit-Rahmen*), were determined through a 'top-down' process. First, the Bank of Japan decided by how much (on an absolute year-on-year basis) the overall loan volume in the entire economy should increase in the coming quarter. These quotas would then be divided into incremental increases by bank type (city banks, trust banks, regional banks, and so on) and by individual bank

(Fuji Bank, Mitsubishi Bank, Sanwa Bank, and so on). Banks would then be told both year-on-year growth rates and quarter-on-quarter absolute increase amounts.[21]

The Bank of Japan was not just concerned with the total volume of bank loans, but also followed the allocation of funds in the economy closely. It knew not only which sectors received funds, but also the names of the major firms that did. As a bank officer put it, the Bank of Japan was interested to see 'where the money goes for what purpose' (bank officer 3). 'Window guidance is very detailed' (Bank of Japan official 5).

> We disclose every piece of information we have ... by economic sector, by company ... Thus we tell them: the real estate sector gets this and this much ... If one sector has a big weight, we give examples: this company and this project, to explain. (bank officer 3)

> The Bank of Japan asked how many loans for which industrial sector, how much for short-term, or long-term lending, how big is the scale of the borrowers, how many loans are demanded by the real estate sector, etc. Sometimes they ask the names of big customers, e.g. Matsushita, case by case. (bank officer 4)[22]

The private banks were excluded from the decision-making process: 'We don't know how the window guidance ceilings are decided' (bank officer 4).

For most banks, window guidance quotas were 'one way', without negotiations and 'like an order' (Bank of Japan official 7). The decision was apparently made exclusively at the Bank of Japan:

> First it was decided by which percentage the total loan volume in the country should rise ... The head of the Banking Department decides the total increase ... Then this was divided among the different types of banks and individual banks (*warifuri*) ... The department head decided over the *warifuri* ... The city banks are decided first. (Bank of Japan official 7)

> The loan growth increase quota handed out in the branches came from the BoJ headquarters, although that is not very detailed. For the city banks it is split up by bank, but for the secondary regional banks, the window guidance officers in the branches have to decide which specific bank lends how much. (Bank of Japan official 6)

> The overall window guidance credit growth limits were decided by the *chōsayaku* or *shingiyaku* [officers in the Banking Department] who consulted with the *eigyō kyokuchō* [director of the Banking Department]. The influence of the Ministry of Finance was indirect only. I have no knowledge of banks deciding for themselves. (Bank of Japan official 3)

> The decision about the official discount rate is totally different. This is decided by the Planning Department (of the Bank of Japan) after

collecting information from the Research and Statistics Department and the Banking Department. Then the Ministry of Finance is consulted ... Its influence is very strong ... Sometimes the Ministry of Finance cancelled [a change in] the discount rate. There is also a policy board, but in reality it is [decided by] the Bank of Japan Planning Department and the Ministry of Finance Banking Bureau together. But this is all quite secret. (Bank of Japan official 7)

It is not quite clear how the total country-wide loan growth increase is decided. They look at money supply, GNP, prices. But I don't know what they use. There is no decided formula. (Bank of Japan official 5)

The additional interviews with staff from the Ministry of Finance confirmed that window guidance was the exclusive domain of the Bank of Japan. The Ministry was kept in the belief that interest rates (over which it exerted some influence) was the Bank of Japan's main monetary policy tool. Since it was never informed about the role of window guidance, it never even attempted to interfere – just as Patrick (1962) had found for the earlier postwar period.[23]

It is found that the credit controls were highly effective during the 1980s. According to the Bank of Japan officials, banks virtually never exceeded the window guidance loan quotas set for them, as punishment would follow immediately.[24]

If they went over the maximum, then they would get a lower quota next time. But I have never heard of this. It virtually never happened. Window guidance has been very strictly observed. (Bank of Japan official 5)[25]

While banks virtually never exceeded their window guidance quotas, they also almost always had to use them up. Private bankers stated that they always fulfilled the quotas in the 1980s, but not always after the first oil shock, in the mid-1970s. (bank officer 3).

Banks always went to the maximum of the lending ceiling. The quota was supposed to be digested completely by the banks. If we go below it, our allotment will be decreased compared to our competitors. So we have to eat it all: it's an *o-bento* [lunch box] to be taken. (bank officer 2)

Indeed, the Bank of Japan used the same penalty for exceeding window guidance as for underutilizing it: if banks did not use up their loan growth allocation for more than one quarter, then the bank's future loan quotas would also be reduced.

I have reduced their quota [*waku*] because of this. Maybe not if it happens just once, but if it happens for two quarters, if they don't use it, well, we reduced their allocation. (Bank of Japan official 5)

Banks that wanted a bigger quota in the future had to avoid a penalty and demonstrate their 'strength' by always using 100% of the window guidance quota.

> If banks do not go to the limit and do not use up their quota, their loan growth ceiling will be reduced next time. This has been a problem in the bubble [period]...The maximum [loan growth quota] had been very high. Thus banks wanted to reach it, they tried all they could to fulfil it. Banks always strove to reach the maximum ... (Bank of Japan official 5)

This Bank of Japan testimony was confirmed by bank officers, who stated that often the quotas set by the Bank of Japan were considered too high by the banks. However, they had to comply with the guidance:

> In the bubble period, we wanted a certain amount [of loan increases], but the BoJ wanted us to use more than that. After 1985, the BoJ said: 'Use more!' Normally, we would not get as much as we want to use... Especially in 1986 and 1987, for about one year, the Bank of Japan said: 'Please use more, because we have a recession ...' Window guidance can be used not just to make borrowing smaller, but also to make it bigger. We actually thought: this is a little bit much. But we couldn't leave anything unused of the quota given to us. If we did, we could be beaten by other city banks who received a similar quota. Thus in order to keep the ranking [of banks] we had to use it all up ... Also, if we would get a reputation for being weak, we would get less in the future ... The Bank of Japan used the *yokonarabi ishiki* [desire to stay in line with others] so that the banks will always do what it wants. (bank officer 4)

> Window guidance was a burden for banks, because sometimes we had to do loans when we didn't need to and at other times less than we wanted to. (bank officer 5)[26]

The interviewees clearly considered credit controls the most effective and also the most important tool of monetary policy used by the Bank of Japan.

> Window guidance is more powerful than interest rates, more than the official discount rate. Because it works directly. (Bank of Japan official 5)

> Normally what is done is to change the official discount rate and window guidance together as a package. This is the most popular case. (Bank of Japan official 5)

> Window guidance is quite a strong regulation. Loans are the main business of banks. Thus this is the strongest regulation ... Window guidance is important, because loans are a big part of the money

supply ... If there are more loans then naturally, the deposits come back into the system. Since the loans have a very large effect on the money supply, their quantity decides the inflation rate. (Bank of Japan official 7)[27]

The official reasons given for the abolition of window guidance in July 1991 were mainly based on the claim that it had become increasingly ineffective due to financial deregulation. Given the above findings that window guidance did exist and was actually the most effective policy tool used by the Bank of Japan, the official reasons for abolition appear hardly credible. Our interviewees certainly did not feel that window guidance was abolished, because it did not work. However, they also could not provide other plausible reasons why window guidance was abolished in July 1991. Most said they were surprised by the decision to scrap window guidance.[28] No reasons were given to Bank of Japan window guidance officers (Bank of Japan official 5).[29]

Econometric evaluation

In the statistical part we first attempt to model bank lending by using a number of explanatory variables, including window guidance. We then test the properties of the model and check for statistical causality. Finally we test the hypothesis that a structural break occurred in the model in 1982, due to the alleged discontinuation of lending control procedures.

We use quarterly month-end bank loan balance statistics published by the Bank of Japan in its monthly reports to represent the dependent variable (bank lending). Based on our empirical fieldwork, we have the *a priori* expectation that the window guidance loan growth quotas, of which banks were notified in advance of the coming quarter, would turn out to be the most significant explanatory variable. We obtained data for the window guidance loan growth quotas from the Nomura Research Institute, Tokyo, which compiled it from information obtained directly from the Bank of Japan soon after the window guidance quotas had been made known to the banks at the end of each quarter.[30]

The data is available either separately for the four different types of banks (city banks, long-term credit banks, trust banks, regional banks) or for the total, consisting of approximately 120 banks.[31] The data series begins in 1974:Q1 and ends in 1991:Q2, when the Bank of Japan stopped announcing window guidance loan quotas. This provides us with 70 observations for each category. Here, we focus our research on the aggregate of bank lending by all banks, called 'D4LBL4' below.

The window guidance quotas were announced to the inquiring public in the form of quarter-on-quarter absolute increases in outstanding loan balances. Since these are unwieldy, and known to have been computed from what originally were year-on-year loan growth rates, we follow Horiuchi's

(1993) method for calculating the implicit window guidance loan balance targets, from which in turn growth rates can be calculated.[32]

Notice that the actual bank lending statistics are measured at the end of the quarter (and announced a further two months later), while the window guidance loan growth quota are announced at the end of the previous quarter. In other words, for any one quarterly period t, actual quarter-end figures would become available later than the end of t, while the window guidance loan quotas for period t would be announced at the end of t − 1, a little more than one quarter earlier.[33]

We adopt Hendry's inductive methodology of proceeding from the general to the specific model, as it is not only methodologically consistent, but also because it allows for the severest test of our obvious *a priori* expectations and presents the model of bank lending nested with alternative hypotheses (Hendry, 1979, 1986, 1987, 2000; Hendry and Mizon, 1978). Since the general model is sequentially reduced to the parsimonious form it is not influenced by our preconceptions.

Thus we add other potential explanatory variables that could influence our dependent variable according to rival models. These were: consumer prices (as measured by the CPI), the overnight call rate (uncollateralized), the official discount rate (ODR), money supply (as measured by the most widely used M2 + CD aggregate), nominal GDP, and finally the window guidance bank lending quotas.[34]

To allow for partial adjustment dynamics, we add a general lag structure, formulating an autoregressive distributed lag (ADL) model. We then proceed to estimate an OLS regression of bank lending, using the seasonal differences (except interest rates). The tests on the significance of variables indicate that only window guidance is significant. We thus proceed to reduce down to the parsimonious form. All other independent variables are dropped. The progress report shows that the null of the restriction is not rejected. We confirm the restrictions by testing for omitted variables. We proceed with further downward reduction to obtain an initial parsimonious form. According to the diagnostics, the restriction is valid and the model is well defined, without visible problems. The long-term static solution is presented, as well as formal tests for cointegration: as expected, window guidance and bank lending appear to be cointegrated. However, the null hypothesis of the RESET test for functional form is rejected at the 5% level. Given the zero coefficient on the constant, this is likely to be due to the constant remaining in the model. After dropping it, the functional form is also acceptable. Table 20.2 shows the final results, here taking advantage of the longer sample length of the parsimonious form.

We notice that the window guidance coefficients basically add up to one. Window guidance single-handedly accounts for the vast majority of bank lending in a well defined unitary relationship. All other explanatory variables drop out as insignificant. The final parsimonious form shows no statistical problems. The equation seems well-defined and without visible

Table 20.2 Parsimonious model of bank lending

Modelling D4LBL4 by OLS

The estimation sample is: 1974 (4) to 1991 (1)

	Coefficient	Std. Error	t-value	t-prob.	Part. R^2
D4LBL4_1	0.241	0.064	3.78	0.000	0.188
D4LBL4_4	−0.228	0.090	−2.53	0.014	0.094
D4LWG	0.723	0.043	16.7	0.000	0.819
D4LWG_4	0.269	0.105	2.56	0.013	0.095

Sigma	0.003	RSS	0.00072
log-likelihood	283.508	DW	2.01
no. of observ.	66	no. of par.	4
mean (D4LBL4)	0.101	var (D4LBL4)	0.000

AR 1–5 test:	F (5,57) =	1.521 [0.198]
ARCH 1–4 test:	F (4,54) =	0.159 [0.958]
Normality test:	Chi^2(2) =	3.095 [0.213]
hetero test:	F (8,53) =	0.840 [0.572]
hetero-X test:	F (14,47) =	0.586 [0.862]
RESET test:	F (1,61) =	1.258 [0.267]

Solved static long-run equation for D4LBL4:

	Coefficient	Std. Error	t-value	t-prob.
D4LWG	1.005	0.004	240	0.000

Long-run sigma = 0.00344501

ECM =	D4LBL4 − 1.005 * D4LWG

WALD test:	Chi^2(1) = 57766.9 [0.000]**

Tests on the significance of each variable:

Variable	F-test	Value [Prob.]	Unit-root t-test
D4LBL4	F (2,62) =	11.777 [0.000]**	−8.454**
D4LWG	F (2,62) =	140.38 [0.000]**	8.4429

Tests on the significance of each lag:

Lag 1	F (1,62) =	14.326 [0.0003]**
Lag 4	F (2,62) =	3.3270 [0.0424]*

Tests on the significance of all lags up to 4:

Lag 1–4	F (3,62) =	19.192 [0.000]**
Lag 2–4	F (2,62) =	3.3270 [0.042]*
Lag 3–4	F (2,62) =	3.3270 [0.042]*
Lag 4–4	F (2,62) =	3.3270 [0.042]*

---

problems. Tests for the significance of the parameters find joint significance. The dynamic analysis results show that the long-run coefficient of window guidance is well-determined and significant at the 1% level, rejecting the null that it is zero. The error terms are found to be normal: the Durbin-Watson statistic is close to 2 (also with constant), indicating that the null hypothesis of no autocorrelation of residuals fails to reject. Moreover, Breusch-Godfrey's LM test failed to reject the hypothesis of no autocorrelation at the 5% critical level. Tests for autoregressive conditional heteroscedasticity (ARCH) failed to reject the null of no ARCH at the 5% level. The null hypothesis of normality of errors failed to reject by Jarque Bera statistic test at the 5% level, thus no skewness and kurtosis problems exist. The null of no heteroscedasticity in the disturbance term, as tested by White's heteroscedasticity test fails to reject at the 4% and 1% critical levels, indicating unconditional homoscedasticity of errors. The functional form also appears without problems, as the RESET test of functional form misspecification failed to reject the null that the model is correct at the 5% level, indicating that the model is correctly specified and no variables are omitted. In summary, there is no discernable statistical problem.

Instead of showing the actual and fitted curves (which are virtually indistinguishable), Figure 20.1 shows the original series of the window guidance and bank lending data. Eye inspection reveals that the above statistical findings should not surprise. In fact, the two original variables appear to be almost identical over this time period.

In order to provide information about the breakdown of these lending aggregates by the various bank types, Table 20.3 lists the year-on-year percentage growth rates of the actual loan increases, summarized annually by type of bank, as well as the total, and compares this with the window guidance loan growth quotas. As can be seen, both growth rates are very similar.

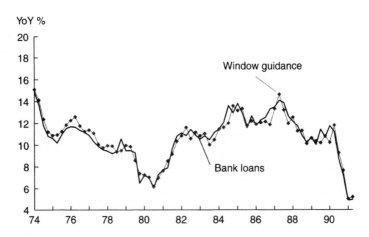

Figure 20.1   Central bank credit controls ('window guidance') and actual bank lending three months later

Source: Bank of Japan; Nomura Research Institute.

Table 20.3 Window guidance loan growth quota (WG) versus actual loan growth, 1974–91 (YoY%)

	City banks		Regional banks		Trust banks		Long-term credit banks		Total	
	WG	Actual	WG	Actual	WG	Actual	WG	Actual	WG	Actual
1974	11.81	11.86	14.88	14.74	21.54	10.50	12.86	13.01	13.21	12.78
1975	10.41	10.38	12.01	12.00	15.88	5.32	11.39	11.51	11.21	10.80
1976	11.03	11.00	12.52	12.42	19.65	8.53	12.31	11.96	11.95	11.45
1977	9.34	9.13	11.74	11.69	20.14	12.69	10.24	10.16	10.56	10.16
1978	8.86	9.00	10.59	10.89	19.15	13.82	8.14	8.07	9.67	9.64
1979	7.84	7.72	10.69	10.85	15.69	9.29	7.23	7.25	8.93	8.68
1980	6.33	6.62	7.82	8.00	6.90	1.13	6.56	6.81	6.85	6.86
1981	8.31	8.80	9.15	9.18	16.55	11.45	8.59	8.85	8.91	9.02
1982	10.42	10.75	10.59	10.36	25.49	22.82	10.54	10.71	11.04	11.07
1983	10.02	10.37	9.44	9.49	27.36	26.66	10.37	10.22	10.58	10.74
1984	11.50	11.64	11.45	12.12	29.08	29.42	10.50	10.87	12.17	12.52
1985	13.15	13.37	9.84	9.70	26.46	24.71	11.62	12.81	12.63	12.75
1986	13.64	14.19	6.94	6.73	23.9	28.00	11.80	12.01	11.99	12.48
1987	13.97	14.53	10.50	10.23	23.53	21.45	11.77	13.03	13.30	13.54
1988	11.73	11.70	11.02	11.46	9.98	7.72	10.91	10.94	11.31	11.26
1989	10.00	10.28	12.27	12.86	9.19	6.45	9.31	9.93	10.49	10.69
1990	9.39	9.64	11.59	11.51	5.69	2.68	9.21	9.61	9.74	9.70
1991	5.83	5.94	5.45	5.64	-4.03	-8.64	6.02	5.96	5.11	4.92

As our field interviews showed, window guidance loan growth quotas were met fairly closely by the banking system. This applies to the entire 1980s. The direction of 'Granger causation' between window guidance loan quotas and actual bank lending is tested by an autoregressive-distributed lag model on the SI(1,1) series. We find that window guidance cannot be omitted from an autoregressive-distributed lag model of bank lending, while bank lending can be omitted from such a model of window guidance. Thus there appears to be unidirectional 'Granger causality' from window guidance to bank lending.

In conclusion, the empirical relationship explaining bank lending in Japan, including the period of the 1980s, passes the standard tests at highest significance levels and without visible statistical problems. The relationship is strong enough to be visible without statistical techniques. Moreover, 'causality' runs unidirectionally from window guidance to lending. We appear to have identified an explanation of bank lending which is least contradicted by the empirical record. Bank lending in Japan in the 1970s, 1980s and the beginning of the 1990s was determined by the credit controls operated by the Bank of Japan.

Tests of the discontinuation hypothesis

Next we are interested in testing the hypothesis that the window guidance monetary policy procedures were changed and that, as the Bank of Japan claimed, 'window guidance has no longer been applied in its original form of credit control since 1982, when the Bank of Japan stopped giving individual banks instructions with respect to their lending plans' (Bank of Japan, 1991b, pp. 21f.). While some researchers have found partial evidence for the continuation of window guidance in the 1980s (Rhodes and Yoshino, 1999), others, namely Hoshi et al. (1991), have argued that a close match between actual bank lending and window guidance during the 1980s can be attributed to 'lending programs of financial institutions having been accepted completely' by the Bank of Japan (p. 9). This reflects the Bank of Japan's claim that, since 1982, it merely 'respected' the banks' lending plans, without the type of interference in bank lending that characterized pre-1982 credit controls.

We note that the two other sources of empirical evidence, namely secondary and primary eye-witness testimonials have already strongly rejected this theory. However, we can also use statistical techniques to test it. To do this, we divide our data sample into the first sample period, which runs from 1974:Q1 to 1981:Q4, and the second period, from 1982:Q1 to 1991:Q2. If commercial banks really had 'leeway and flexibility … for adjusting credit' since 1982, as the Bank of Japan claims, this should be reflected in a structural break in the relationship between window guidance and bank lending. We therefore use various tests to probe this.

To begin with, we simply calculate the average percentage gap between the window guidance loan quota and the actual bank lending observed three months later. Hoshi et al. (1991) seem to believe that if a loosening and *de facto* abolition of window guidance had happened during the 1980s, as the Bank of Japan claims, this should result in a closer fit between window guidance quotas and the actual bank lending observed over three months later. It is difficult to follow their logic. Logic suggests that if window guidance had become non-binding and 'flexible', banks would be less concerned about meeting precisely the loan growth quotas that had been set three months earlier. Surely, if the threat of harsh punishment for non-compliance before 1982, when credit controls are known to have existed with full force, produced a certain error margin between window guidance and actual lending, then the change in procedure claimed by the Bank of Japan in 1982 must be expected to increase that error margin, as banks feel less obliged to stick to a previously agreed quota and as the central bank is less concerned about enforcing window guidance (thus also less likely to impose painful sanctions for non-compliance). To sustain the theory that the window guidance quota was voluntary under these circumstances would require a significant number of additional assumptions (including perfect foresight by the banks over a period of more than three months), and thus becomes less compelling. As a result, our *a priori* expectation is that the error margin between window guidance quotas and the final outcome should show an increase in the period after 1982, if window guidance was less important, as the Bank of Japan or Hoshi et al. claim.

The error margin, as measured by the mean absolute percentage error between window guidance target of the new loan balance and actual result was 0.19% before 1982. During the second period since 1982:Q1 it amounted to only 0.13%. This suggests that window guidance had not become any less stringent. It is evidence against a structural break towards loosening or abolition in 1982.

As part of the window guidance procedures, the Bank of Japan would raise bank lending of the different bank types (such as city banks, regional banks, and so on) in similar fixed proportions. This basically constituted a cartel of the loan market, because it fixed the market shares of the bank types in the credit market and maintained the pecking order. If the hypothesis is true that window guidance was not binding in the 1980s, then the rankings of the different bank types should have changed or at least moved more significantly during the 1980s. The market shares are shown in Figure 20.2 and Table 20.4. As can be seen, the shares hardly moved. At the end of 1981, city banks had a loan market share of 52.3%, regional banks 31.8%, trust banks 3.7% and long-term credit banks (LTCBs) 12.2%. This was virtually identical to the shares recorded at the end of 1974 (54.2%, 29.5%, 3.9% and 12.4%, respectively). But it was also very similar to those at the end of 1991 (53.4%, 29.3%, 5.6% and 11.8%, respectively). As a result, the rankings also

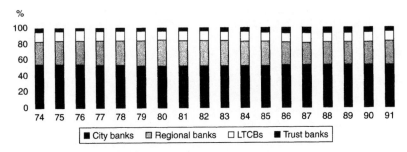

Figure 20.2   Loan market shares of the various types of banks

remained completely fixed, both in the 1970s and the entire 1980s (Table 20.5). We must conclude that there was no noticeable structural break. Market shares and rankings remained frozen. This suggests that window guidance continued unchanged in the second sample period.

Next we test for Granger 'causality' once again, but this time both sample periods separately. Of course, with shorter observation periods, the overall strength of causality is bound to fall, compared to the previous Granger-causality test of the entire period. The interesting question, though, is whether 'causality' from window guidance to lending is weaker in the 1980s than in the earlier sample period. As can be seen, window guidance (WG) unilaterally Granger-causes bank lending (LOANS) in both periods. The results are presented in Table 20.6. This shows that little has changed in the 1980s in the strength or direction of causation, which runs virtually equally strongly from window guidance to bank lending in both periods.

More formal tests for a structural break can be conducted with the graphics tests provided by PC-GIVE for recursive estimations, which allow tests for parameter constancy (Figures 20.3 and 20.4).

These recursive breakpoint tests all indicate that a structural break did indeed occur during the observation period, but not in 1982. A break seems to have occurred in the second quarter of 1978. We know, however, that this coincided with a period of window guidance tightening, which was widely reported in June 1978 (Nikkei, 1978a, 1978b, 1978c). Thus, the only structural break we can identify is towards tightening (and at a different time than indicated by the Bank of Japan).

Specific tests of the hypothesis that a structural break occurred in 1982: Q1 can be conducted using a Chow Breakpoint F test, as well as Dummy Variable Analysis. The results of the former are shown in Table 20.7: both fail to reject the null hypothesis of parameter stability and thus do not find evidence for structural change. Considering the above evidence and our simple mean error figures, it must be concluded in summary that most likely no

Table 20.4 Shares of total bank lending by type of bank

%	1974	1975	1976	1977	1978	1979	1980	1981	1982	1983	1984	1985	1986	1987	1988	1989	1990	1991
City banks	54.2	54.0	53.8	53.3	53.0	52.5	52.4	52.3	52.1	52.0	51.6	51.8	52.6	53.1	53.3	53.1	53.1	53.4
Regional banks	29.5	29.8	30.1	30.5	30.9	31.5	31.8	31.8	31.6	31.3	31.2	30.3	28.8	27.9	28.0	28.5	29.0	29.3
Trust banks	3.9	3.7	3.6	3.6	3.8	3.8	3.6	3.7	4.1	4.7	5.3	5.9	6.7	7.2	6.9	6.7	6.2	5.6
LTCBs	12.4	12.5	12.6	12.6	12.4	12.2	12.2	12.2	12.2	12.1	11.9	11.9	11.9	11.8	11.8	11.7	11.7	11.8

Table 20.5 Market share ranking by type of bank

	1974	1975	1976	1977	1978	1979	1980	1981	1982	1983	1984	1985	1986	1987	1988	1989	1990	1991
City banks	1	1	1	1	1	1	1	1	1	1	1	1	1	1	1	1	1	1
Regional banks	2	2	2	2	2	2	2	2	2	2	2	2	2	2	2	2	2	2
LTCBs	3	3	3	3	3	3	3	3	3	3	3	3	3	3	3	3	3	3
Trust banks	4	4	4	4	4	4	4	4	4	4	4	4	4	4	4	4	4	4

Table 20.6   Granger-causality test of SI(1,1) variables

Pairwise Granger-causality tests

Sample 1
Sample: 1974:Q1 1981:Q4
Lags: 5

Null hypothesis:	Observs.	F-stat.	Prob.
WG does not Granger-cause LOANS	31(16)	21.268	[0.0000]**
LOANS does not Granger-cause WG		1.9998	[0.1335]

Sample 2
Sample: 1982:Q1 1991:Q2
Lags: 5

Null hypothesis:	Observs.	F-stat.	Prob.
WG does not Granger-cause LOANS	38(27)	6.9128	[0.0003]**
LOANS does not Granger-cause WG		0.95351	[0.4638]

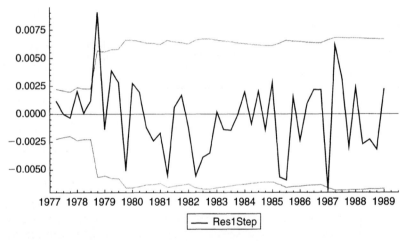

Figure 20.3   Recursive one-step residuals (+/–2 SE)
Testing recursively for residual behaviour, it is found that a structural break may have occurred in 1978:Q2.

structural change took place in 1982, and if one did take place, it was one of stricter enforcement of the window guidance policy and not one of abandoning the procedure. Window guidance continued to determine bank lending during the 1980s. If anything, window guidance became stricter and more effective in the 1980s, since the error margin between the loan quota and the actual bank lending three months later shrank marginally in the 1980s.[35] This finding contradicts the claims by the Bank of Japan about

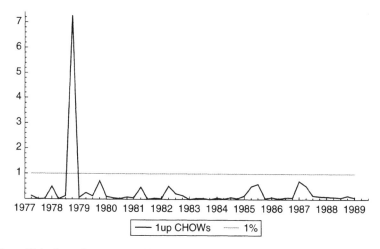

Figure 20.4   Recursive one-step Chow tests
Recursive one-step Chow tests also indicate that a structural change might have occurred in 1978:Q2.

Table 20.7   Tests for structural break in 1982:Q1

Chow Breakpoint Test		Dummy Variable Analysis	
F-Statistic		Tests of model reduction/omitting dummies:	
F (5,56) =	1.7169	F-Statistic	Probability
1% critical F (5,60):	3.34	F (2,59) = 0.63354	[0.5343]
5% critical F (5,60):	2.37		

window guidance in the 1980s. It also contrasts with Rhodes and Yoshino's (1999) claim that the 'near perfect compliance' of the pre-1982 period 'appears to have weakened in the post-1982 period, particularly in the last 4 years of the program' (p. 175), which is likely due to problems with their study.[36]

Conclusion

In this chapter, empirical evidence from (a) secondary sources, (b) primary eye-witnesses (fieldwork) and (c) statistical data series was utilized in order to answer the question why Japanese banks lent so aggressively during the 1980s. The testimonies from primary Bank of Japan and private bank sources were consistent with each other, and also consistent with the secondary sources. Moreover, the econometric evidence confirmed the fieldwork research. It appears that the main variable explaining bank lending in the 1980s and early 1990s was the credit controls operated by the central bank. Specifically, it was possible to establish that:

1. direct credit controls existed throughout the 1980s until at least 1991. This means that bank lending, and thus also the excessive credit creation of the 1980s bubble was determined by the Bank of Japan;
2. the loan plans by the banks were not merely sanctioned by the Bank of Japan. Rather, the Banking Department of the Bank of Japan decided and administered credit growth quotas at its discretion. Separately it was confirmed that the Ministry of Finance was not involved in the credit control procedures or the setting of the loan growth quotas;
3. the Bank of Japan punished banks for overshooting or undershooting of the loan growth quotas; it was also aware that rank-competition of banks meant that they would strive to fulfil and not undershoot loan growth quotas even without punishment procedures;
4. the credit controls took the same form as in the pre-1980s period (except that they were even more comprehensive, because impact loans were included). In other words, during the 1980s window guidance was the main, as well as the most effective tool of central bank policy employed by the Bank of Japan. Interest rates were at best a 'supplementary' tool;
5. as before 1982, the Bank of Japan was aware of the increase of loans to the real estate, construction and non-bank financial institutions, that is, the speculative credit creation that was identified as the cause of the bubble and subsequent recession.

We have established that the Bank of Japan's window guidance determined bank credit. This is consistent with earlier findings, such as Patrick's (1962).[37] The problem was not that bank lending was out of control. To the contrary, it was controlled almost perfectly by the Bank of Japan's window guidance. Instead, the problem was the policy taken by the Bank of Japan in setting those loan growth quotas. Since the Bank of Japan chose far larger quotas than banks thought necessary, compliance with window guidance meant that banks were forced to peddle their loans to real estate speculators. The Bank of Japan appeared to have been aware that its credit controls were sharply raising the allocation of new money to the real estate sector, thus pushing up real estate prices.

The window guidance loan quotas set by the Bank of Japan were inappropriate, if the policy was to avoid a major banking and economic crisis. This raises the question of just how the Bank of Japan chose to set its window guidance. The frequently cited external political pressure, such as in the form of the Plaza Agreement or the Ministry of Finance policy pressure to reduce the official discount rate, remain insufficient as explanations. To the contrary, during our interviews with Bank of Japan staff, it was pointed out that window guidance was the ideal tool to *avoid* the creation of a bubble when interest rates were set too low (during the 1950s and 1960s, when Japan's GDP grew at double-digit rates, interest rates were also set at artificially low levels. At the same time, window guidance was used to curtail the quantity of credit and avoid an economic boom).

In the words of one of our interview subjects:

> The Bank of Japan has promoted loan expansion in the bubble period ... My own opinion is: when one reduced the interest rate and *reduced* the window guidance loan growth limit, then with this policy-mix, the bubble would not have developed. But in reality, interest rates were reduced and window guidance was very relaxed. Thus the money supply rose by 10%, up to 13%. The question why they didn't close the window guidance more is extremely puzzling ... All the banks tried to use their loan growth quota until the maximum and did all they could to give out loans. But the loans did not go to normal corporations, such as steel, automobile, but instead to construction, non-bank financial institutions [which engaged in real estate speculation]. This became the bubble. (Bank of Japan official 5)[38]

The private sector bankers confirmed this assessment:

> I worried a lot about the policy of the authorities ... If they had taken a little tighter policy in the window guidance, this kind of phenomenon, the bubble, would have been prevented ... If the Bank of Japan had wanted to tighten, it would have achieved a lot. (bank officer 2)

Policy implications

The findings have policy implications and raise further questions. For one, there are legal issues. The Bank of Japan has not only misguided the public about the actual conduct of its policies. It has also circumvented the supervisory role of the Ministry of Finance, to whom it was legally required to report to. Until 1 April 1998, the Bank of Japan Law stipulated that monetary policy was in the hands of the Ministry of Finance.

Our findings also cast new light on the recent change in the Bank of Japan Law to grant greater legal powers to the central bank with even fewer provisions for accountability.[39] The main argument in favour of greater central bank independence was that the bad performance of the Bank of Japan was due to its lack of independence. However, contrary to perceived wisdom, the Bank of Japan already possessed a high degree of *de facto* independence concerning its key policy tool, the quantity of credit creation. This independence has not prevented the enormous swings of the business cycle over the past decades. To the contrary, lack of transparency and lack of meaningful accountability concerning its clandestine 'quantitative' monetary policy appear to have been the very reason why the Bank of Japan could embark on policies that created the bubble and the recession. Had the window guidance control mechanism been more widely known to the public in the 1980s, it is possible that a stricter monitoring of this policy tool through outside checks and balances could have prevented the creation of the bubble. The problem was not too little independence, but too much.

Returning to the issue raised at the end of the last chapter, namely how post-crisis banking policies should be designed in order to avoid moral hazard, and who should pay for any costs that result from the clean-up of the banking system, the findings make it clear that this should not be borne by the taxpayers, but also not by the banks or their shareholders. Responsibility for the creation of the bubble of the 1980s, thus also for the bad debts of the banking system of the 1990s, and indeed the long economic slump that began in 1992, lies squarely with the Bank of Japan. This strengthens the case that any policies to deal with the bad debts and stimulate an economic recovery should also be paid for by the Bank of Japan. Thus the central bank could have purchased all bad debts of the banks at face value, thus eliminating them at no cost to society, as well as monetize fiscal stimulation or the recapitalization of banks.

Any deeper probing into responsibility and the question why the window guidance quotas were so large cannot avoid the identification of those Bank of Japan officials who decided the nationwide window guidance loan growth aggregates. According to the eye-witness accounts, these were the head of the Banking Department and the deputy governor (Werner, 2003c). Toshihiko Fukui was director of the Banking Department from 1986 to 1989. He was the right-hand man of his mentor Yasushi Mieno, who was deputy governor and between 1989 and 1994 was governor of the Bank of Japan. Following Mieno, Fukui became the highest-ranking Bank of Japan officer appointed from inside the bank, when he became deputy governor from 1994 to 1998, and governor since March 2003. Both have placed the blame for the creation of the bubble on the private sector (Bank of Japan, 1992a). Fukui has demanded that private sector bank leaders 'take responsibility' for the bad debt problem (Fukui, 2002).

Since it appears that monetary policy during the late 1980s was determined by the same two individuals that determined the disastrous policies of the 1990s, the public deserves to know more about their true policy intentions. Why, for instance, has the Bank of Japan consistently failed to stimulate the economy sufficiently during the 1990s, despite ever-widening deflation, weak growth and rising unemployment?

Part IV
The Goal of Macroeconomic Policy

It is purpose of this part to discuss macroeconomic policy and its goals. Again, the inductive method is used, which means we first analyse what empirically has actually been the goal of macroeconomic policies. Next we apply our findings and our disaggregated credit model to the question of what macroeconomic policy should aim at, and how it should achieve these aims.

A major policy concern in Japan, but also in many other countries, including a large number of developing countries, has been the issue of banking sector reform. Since in our framework this is identified as being intrinsically linked with macroeconomic performance, we first examine banking reform – how it has empirically been conducted, and how it should be conducted according to our framework. After this, fiscal, structural and monetary policy are examined. The final two chapters are dedicated to the question of how macroeconomic policy should be designed and implemented, and the challenge of furthering a new paradigm in economics.

21
Banking Reform

Under the active 'guidance' of the IMF and the World Bank, far-reaching banking reforms have been implemented in several dozens of countries during the postwar era. These were not seldom part and parcel of broader structural adjustment programmes. However, the banking reforms have often not had the declared impact of improving social welfare, but instead produced adverse results. Przeworski and Vreeland (2000) found that the effect of participation in IMF programmes is to lower growth rates for as long as countries remain under a programme. Furthermore, the fact that banking crises have often recurred even in countries that have implemented IMF-guided banking reforms indicates that these reforms failed to address some fundamental problems with the operation of the banking system. It is thus necessary to re-examine the topic of banking reform in the light of our approach.

Traditional approach to post-crisis banking reform

Reform usually follows crisis. This also holds true for banking reform. Thus much of the literature on bank reform takes a banking crisis as the starting point of their analysis on how to deal with it (see, for instance, Claessens et al., 2001). Such an approach means, however, that the cause of banking crises is not directly addressed. Yet there are sound reasons why any analysis of post-crisis banking reform must take the crisis and its causes as the starting point. Firstly, only a thorough understanding of the causes of an event enables the formulation of a complete set of policies on how to deal with it efficiently. Secondly, post-crisis policies need to avoid creating new problems in the future, such as moral hazard. To avoid moral hazard, an understanding is required of the location of responsibility for the initial problems. Thirdly, in order to prevent the recurrence of crises, prevention policies must be taken; again, this is only possible, if the causes are understood.

The traditional approach to banking sector restructuring, as detailed, for instance, in the Letters of Intent to the IMF (see Government of Thailand, 1997, 1998, 1999; Government of Korea, 1997, 1998, 1999, 2000) commonly applies comparative static analysis by comparing a post-crisis banking system with its pre-crisis state or with an ideal state derived from international 'best-practice'. Since this assessment is done in the midst of or early aftermath of a crisis, it is not surprising that it is found that capital adequacy ratios are too low, that the supervisory regime had been too lenient, that accounting standards for non-performing loans are too lax and that implicit government guarantees of bank solvency and deposits had created moral hazard. Consequently, the restructuring programmes commonly seek to correct these problems by demanding:

1. an increase in the capital adequacy ratio; and/or adoption of Basle capital adequacy framework;
2. a tightening of accounting standards for non-performing loans;
3. an abolition of the implicit government guarantee of bank solvency by allowing banks to fail or forcing mergers, takeovers or acquisitions of banks, usually by 'foreign strategic partners' (in IMF parlance);
4. the introduction of an independent policy regime for monetary, banking and regulatory policies that implements the above measures;
5. involuntary exit of the bank management;
6. injection of tax money to support write-offs of bad debts;
7. foreclosure on borrowers whose loans were written off and distressed sale of their assets.

What is the expected impact of these measures on the lending attitude adopted by bank loan officers? Everything else being equal, it would be surprising to find any that become less risk averse. The Basle capital adequacy framework alone tends to induce a policy to shrink the loan book of banks. This means that the loan officers will likely reduce the quantity of loans extended and increase credit rationing. As overall credit creation contracts in the economy, economic growth is likely to decelerate, following our familiar equation linking credit creation to nominal GDP growth:

(1) $\Delta(P_R Y) = V_R \Delta C_R$

As we saw in Chapter 16, a vicious cycle is likely to develop of shrinking lending, reduced demand, increasing bankruptcies, growing non-performing loans, increased risk aversion of banks and shrinking lending. A full-blown recession may ensue which could last for many years and, depending on the degree of shortfall between nominal GDP and the potential growth rate, may involve disinflation or deflation (as in the case of Japan).

Policy-makers often point at the bad debts as the root problem and attempt to tighten the regulatory environment surrounding bank lending. However, it is necessary to distinguish two types of bad debts. Type I bad debts, or the primary bad debts, are those that were incurred due to excessive lending for speculative purposes. Since lending for such purposes usually declines with the onset of the crisis, their size is limited and can be estimated. In Japan, we have documented that the financial 'bubble' of the 1980s was mainly due to excessive bank lending for speculative and non-productive investment. The majority of these primary bad debts derive from the bank loans to real estate, construction, and non-bank financial institutions between the end of 1985 and the end of 1993, extended under instructions by the Bank of Japan. Since the beginning of the 'bubble' is commonly put in 1986, and since such loans did not increase significantly after about 1993, their total scale can be estimated by making the conservative assumption that all net new bank lending to these three sectors between 1 January 1996 and 1 January 1993 will eventually become unrecoverable. Allowing for some further bad debts resulting from lending to other sectors, one obtains a primary bad debt estimate of ¥80–90 trillion (see Werner, 1998a, 2003c).

However, by early 2002, Japanese banks had been writing off a total of ¥80 trillion in bad debts. This means that most of the Type I bad debts have been eliminated. Yet bad debts remained high (according to official figures, amounting to ¥40 trillion in early 2002). This is therefore due to Type II bad debts, or secondary bad debts. These are not the result of the pre-crisis lending. Instead, they are the result of the recession that was induced by the banking crisis and subsequent decline in credit for GDP transactions (equation (1)). While the size of Type I bad debts can be fairly accurately measured (since their maximum size is limited), this is not the case with Type II bad debts. Their scale is contingent on the state of the economy. However, without suitable intervention from the authorities, there is nothing banks can do to extricate themselves from the vicious credit crunch downward spiral identified in Chapter 16. The recession will trigger second-round and third-round bad debts, as even the healthiest companies will find it hard to secure sales and profits in an environment of shrinking demand and falling prices. The longer the suitable policy response is delayed, the larger the Type II bad debts will become (with the only theoretical limit being the total outstanding loan balance, when bad debts would have reached 100% of all loans).

It is necessary to analyse the above banking sector reform policies of tighter capital adequacy, prudential, supervisory and accounting standards, as well as the threat of regulator-determined exit, before the background of such dynamics. It follows immediately that such policies will be useful when implemented well before the occurrence of a banking crisis, indeed before the speculative lending that precedes it. In other words, such policies are useful for limiting excessive credit creation and the bad debt problems that may follow.

The timing of such policies is therefore crucial. If they are introduced too late, namely when the event that they are meant to prevent (excessive amounts of unproductive credit creation) has already occurred and a banking crisis has already begun, they do not have a salutary effect on the banking system and the economy. Instead, they compound the problems. There is no doubt that such policies have a negative impact on bank credit growth, and hence act pro-cyclically, worsening both the state of the economy and, ironically, the state of the banking system.

The minimum risk-weighted capital-asset ratio of 8% that was introduced by the Basle Committee on Bank Supervision is a case in point. It was decided upon in July 1988, but despite thus being known as the 1988 Basle Accord, it was only implemented at the end of 1992, at a time when the bank loan cycle in several countries (Sweden, Norway, Finland and Japan) had turned down. There is evidence that the introduction of the BIS rules compounded the boom-bust cycle by first giving banks incentive to increase credit creation too much (as Japanese banks were allowed to count equity holdings as part of their capital), and then giving them incentives to reduce it when the economy was in recession. Basle II sets out to improve various inadequacies of the first Basle Accord. However, there are reasons to believe that its pro-cyclical nature has not changed and may even get exacerbated. *Ceteris paribus*, fewer bank loans will improve a bank's capital adequacy ratio. However, as variously discussed, each bank's loans impose an externality on the economy in the sense that collectively bank lending affects economic growth. Thus if all banks attempt to improve their Basle ratios by reducing bank lending, they will find that this is not possible: through the feedback loop between bank lending and the economy, as seen in our equation (1), an aggregate reduction in lending will shrink economic growth, and hence cause a deterioration in borrowers' (and thus banks') balance sheets. If pronounced, it will lead to bankruptcies, and thus bad debts, which in turn will worsen capital adequacy ratios. If this encourages banks to double up their efforts to reduce assets, the process will continue.

Thus if wrongly handled, the introduction of stringent capital adequacy rules may trigger a similar vicious cycle as the one experienced in periods after a rapid expansion in non-productive lending.

The reason why this negative feedback loop between either post-crisis reform policies or a general tightening of international capital adequacy standards is not recognized explicitly in the literature, is that the mainstream literature fails to recognize the unique nature of banks as creators of credit. Since mainstream theories and models consider banks mere financial intermediaries, their function can easily be substituted by other intermediaries, including the capital market in general. Thus a reform policy-induced bank credit crunch does not affect the economy negatively, it is argued, if capital markets are in place. Since this often is not the case in developing countries, bank reform is usually accompanied by reform of capital markets (as in the case of post-crisis Thailand, Korea and Indonesia), in the expectation that increased financial intermediation via the capital markets will compensate for reduced bank lending.

However, this expectation is erroneous, as it neglects the fact that bank lending cannot be substituted by capital markets or non-bank financial intermediaries, since only banks (and the central bank) create credit. Thus non-bank financial institutions and capital markets can merely divert existing purchasing power. Only banks can create new purchasing power. However, as we saw from our model, economic growth requires the creation of new purchasing power.

Thus even in reasonably advanced economies with developed capital markets, such as the US, a credit crunch is likely when bank lending shrinks. The microeconomic reason is that the main customers of banks, small and medium-sized firms, cannot access capital markets as easily as they could previously obtain bank funding. But the macroeconomic reason is that even if small firms could indeed borrow from capital markets, a reduction in bank credit would have a negative impact on the economy, since it reduces the amount of purchasing power circulating in the economy, the money supply, and hence economic activity.

In the case of Japan, Thailand, Korea and Indonesia, the central bank and/or the IMF implemented the traditional set of banking restructuring policies at a time when banks were burdened with large-scale bad debts. As a result, credit creation slowed further and even turned negative.[1] Macroeconomic stability suffered further. Hence banking sector reform that is implemented in times of banking crises must be classified as *adverse banking sector reform*. While it may be aimed at positive long-term goals, it is not congruent with the macroeconomic policy of creating an economic recovery. By worsening the macroeconomic situation, even the goal of banking sector stability moves further out of reach, as the deteriorating economy once again hurts the banks in a negative feedback loop.

Growth-consistent banking reform

An alternative approach to banking sector reform, here called *growth-consistent banking sector reform* aims at satisfying the simultaneous objective function of creating an economic recovery and restoring the health of the banking system. To achieve this goal, the sequencing of policies, as well as the method of funding the costs is of importance.

The policies of growth-consistent bank restructuring can be divided into three different implementation phases. In Phase 1, credit creation is expanded by making use of central bank credit creation. This can be achieved by central bank purchases of (a) private sector assets (preferably purchases of the banks' bad debt, real estate collateral of bad loans and preferred stocks issued by banks to fund recapitalization) and (b) government debt, either in the primary or secondary market. The latter monetizes fiscal policy, and hence avoids crowding out of private sector activity due to increased government spending.[2]

In Phase 2, bank credit creation (for productive and non-speculative purposes, that is, C_R) should be expanded. To do this, direct and indirect policies can be implemented. The direct policies include halting all bond issuance by the government and shifting fundraising for the entire public sector borrowing requirement to direct borrowing by the government from banks in the form of standard bank loan agreements. By shifting public sector borrowing from bond issuance to borrowing from banks, crowding out of private sector activity is minimized: as we saw in Chapter 18, selling bonds to the non-bank private sector amounts to a zero-sum game, while borrowing from banks results in credit creation (a positive-sum game), that is, the increase in purchasing power in the economy (and hence, according to equation (1), increased economic activity).

Another policy is to issue government guarantees to banks for bank loans to firms/industrial sectors that are most severely credit-constrained and would use the newly-created money not for speculative purposes. In most countries, loans to small manufacturing firms are an obvious example, as these firms tend to be severely credit rationed, usually even in the best of times. Due to the positive feedback loop between credit, economic activity and hence the state of borrowers' balance sheets, suitably executed policies of issuing government guarantees on bank loans are likely never to incur substantial liabilities: as the government guarantees loans to small firms, for instance, for productive investors, each loan carries a certain default risk. But as consequently total lending increases, and hence economic activity expands, borrowers' balance sheets improve, hence reducing their risk of default. Thus the vicious cycle between credit reduction, economic growth and bad debts identified in Chapter 16 is turned into a positive feedback loop. Hence the actual net costs of such a policy are likely to be zero or negative, especially since an economic recovery increases fiscal revenues. Thus suitable government policies to increase productive credit creation, even if initially involving gross costs or potential liabilities, are likely to result in far larger gross gains for the government.

The indirect methods to increase banking sector credit creation focus on reducing banks' risk aversion via changes in the regulatory environment. This can include the temporary or partial suspension of the Basle capital adequacy requirement and the introduction of new, lenient capital adequacy rules, policies to reduce bad debts (write-offs, sales, provisions funded by public money, preferential tax treatment, bank profits, issuance of preference shares, and so on). Such a proposal should not be considered unorthodox. The Basle capital adequacy has a purpose, namely to strengthen the soundness of banking systems and to achieve overall financial stability. Thus once the feedback loop between bank lending and the economy, and hence financial stability is recognized, it becomes apparent that capital adequacy rules may become counterproductive, and thus their suspension may achieve the goal they originally set out to achieve.

Once the initial phases of such growth-consistent bank reform have been completed (approximately six to nine months after the start of the crisis) and macroeconomic stability is ensured, the tightening of the regulatory environment and banks' loan procedures can take greater precedence. This is the main goal during Phase 3, during which the banking sector incentive structure is reshaped such that in the long run (by a future target date) banks are required to implement all the international best-practice prudential rules and supervisory structures, ideally in a phased manner.

Should external stability (that is, currency stability) be an important issue, then, like banking sector restructuring, it should not receive precedence over the goal of macroeconomic stability. Countries with stable economic growth are less likely to succumb to currency crises than countries that are in the grips of recession. If necessary, curbs on short-term capital account transactions via reregulation, as were implemented by Malaysia and Chile, are recommended. The potential costs of these policies is likely to be smaller than the large cost of achieving external currency stability and banking sector restructuring by reducing domestic credit creation and therefore creating high unemployment and long-term social costs of a scale that is hard to quantify. The results of the Malaysian approach of dealing with the Asian crisis attest to this. The IMF has admitted this years later, though without visible effect on its policy advice.[3]

Why are the lessons not learned?

Although many authors (such as Claessens et al., 2001) suggest that the issues involved in dealing successfully with banking crises are 'complex', the framework presented in this book is not intractable. Indeed, the problem of lending-induced boom and bust cycles has recurred for several centuries and by now it is a familiar spectacle. The fruits of traditional, adverse banking sector reform are also well-documented, such as in the case of Thailand and Korea. Moreover, after severe international criticism the IMF reversed its policies of tight credit ceilings in these countries from 1999 onwards. Yet countries that attempted similar policies as proposed here, such as Malaysia, suffered severe international criticism, while policy-makers in many countries with banking crises appear to continue to favour traditional, growth-adverse banking reform. In Japan, for instance, where the almost ten-year-old recession had already bankrupted 193,000, mainly small and medium-sized companies, it was proposed in late 2002 that tax money be used to help banks write off bad debts, in return for foreclosing on large-scale borrowers.[4] Leading finance experts argued as late as 2004 that Japan required more bankruptcies, not less.[5] One of the new questions raised in this chapter is therefore just why the lessons do not seem to get learned. Imperfect information, especially on behalf of the experts, and especially concerning the facts of credit creation, accounts for much of the answer.

However, the incentive structure may also be such that interested parties may have little desire in 'learning the lessons'. Here we may note a few observations concerning the issue of 'who benefits' from traditional banking reform. International rating agencies usually take an increase in foreign ownership as a positive sign.[6] International organizations actively encourage foreign takeovers of indigenous banks in developing countries as part of structural adjustment programmes.

How is such increased ownership of the domestic financial system justified? Corsetti et al. (2001) argue that 'significant ownership of the domestic financial system by foreign banks could help prevent currency and financial crises, and/or help reduce the impact of a crisis on the economy', because

> direct ownership of a fraction of the domestic financial system by foreign banks may have positive stabilizing effects. In addition to enhancing competition, efficiency, and to bringing new managerial skills and banking knowledge, international banks may provide specific benefits in periods of crisis.

The benefits are, according to Corsetti et al., that foreign banks would 'follow an arms-length approach, rather than relationship banking; and they may be less exposed to political pressure to provide direct lending'. Also, 'foreign ownership of banks operating domestically may reduce the need for central banks in emerging market [sic] to provide a safety net, by performing as lenders of last resort' (Corsetti et al., pp. 23ff.).

Both the theory proposed in this book, as well as the empirical record of countries where foreign ownership of banks has become substantial – notably Argentina – reveals such arguments as unconvincing. The ownership of banks is not a variable in our model of the creation of banking crises and also does not feature in the list of suitable counter-policies. There is little reason to argue why foreign banks would exert a 'positive stabilizing effect', as Corsetti et al. claim. The explicit or implicit claim that 'foreign' banks, meaning banks from industrialized countries such as the US or Europe, have superior risk management, credit analysis skills or 'managerial skills and banking knowledge' is not supported by evidence. Perhaps Corsetti and colleagues (one of whom is a US Treasury official and another works at the New York Federal Reserve Bank, which itself is owned by Wall Street banks) had the superior managerial skills and banking knowledge of leading foreign bank J.P. Morgan in mind, when it engaged in its large-scale lending to Enron? The empirical record supports the argument that financial crises can happen, and have happened, in any country, even industrialized countries, whether it be the US, Sweden or Japan.

As to the argument that foreign banks may be less exposed to political pressure to provide lending, it is based on the unsubstantiated implicit assumption that the banking crises were caused by political pressure on lending. In the case of Japan, as we saw in the previous chapter, the pressure came from the central bank. Misguided lending quotas that were part of central bank credit controls were also instrumental in the propagation of the Asian crisis (Werner, 2000c). In these cases, foreign pressure groups, including the IMF and the US Treasury, shared part of the responsibility.[7] As to the argument that foreign ownership of banks will mean that domestic central banks would not have to act as lenders of last resort, it assumes that domestic subsidiaries of foreign banks will be supported by unlimited supplies of liquidity from overseas headquarters (an assumption not backed by empirical evidence) and even then could only hold if 100% of domestic banks had been sold to foreign banks. It is, of course, contradicted by Argentina's recent experience.

Despite the absence of empirical support for the claim that foreign ownership of banks is a helpful policy, it has been forcefully advanced by the IMF during its intervention in its East Asian client countries. The 'Letters of Intent' directly required disposal of banks to 'foreign strategic partners' and focused on such issues as changes in laws to allow foreign investors to take over local banks or purchase local real estate (see Werner, 2000a) or 'improvements' in the bankruptcy code to facilitate liquidations and takeovers. Since the above reasons cannot rationally support the demand to increase foreign ownership of local banks, further research is needed on what other motivations could exist to explain the IMF's insistence. Stiglitz (2002) controversially concludes: 'Looking at the IMF *as if* it were pursuing the interest of the [US] financial community provides a way of making sense of what might otherwise seem to be contradictory and intellectually incoherent behaviors' (p. 209; italics in original). His book, and his allegations against the IMF, have attracted much attention and stirred controversy.

It is noteworthy that international organizations appear aware of just what provides the main opportunity for increasing foreign ownership and implementing deep changes in the structure of other countries. World Bank staff argue that '[a] crisis can be a window for structural reform', and it can 'be an opportunity to reform the ownership structure in the country' (Claessens et al., 2001, p. 13). The view that a crisis is 'an opportunity' or a 'window of opportunity' suggests that such crisis is, in some respects, to be welcomed.

It remains to be noted that exacerbating a crisis either through lack of action or through active, anti-growth policies *in order to* implement desired structural reforms and changes in the ownership pattern would constitute a Machiavellian and somewhat unethical way to approach financial crises. Whether this has indeed been the main reason why growth-consistent post-crisis policies have rarely been adopted is a topic that requires further research.

Banks have throughout history also rationally maximized their profits by engaging in what today is called predatory lending – lending with the aim of foreclosing on the borrower in order to seize his/her collateralized assets. Banks can call loans in unison, thus shrink the money supply and create deflation and bankruptcies. In this situation it is easy for them to purchase assets cheaply, take over bankrupted firms and obtain economic control over many people. Given this significant and unique power of banks (to create money and lend it to borrowers of their choice, charging interest), there is a need for commensurate accountability and mechanisms that guarantee responsible behaviour. Thus a more useful form of banking reform should include improved processes according to which the allocative decisions of banks concerning their creation and distribution of new purchasing power are rendered transparent and subject to checks and balances that reflect the overall objective function of societies. Since, left to their own devices, banks will merely maximize profits (and hence engage in predatory lending or the creation of business cycles whenever possible), a well-designed form of government intervention is required to prevent at least the worst abuses of their monopoly power to create and allocate money.

22
The Goal of Fiscal, Structural and Monetary Policy

> ... a central banker moves interest rates in order to maintain steady real growth and stable prices.
>
> (Cecchetti, 2000)

> While destroying the high growth model, I am building a model that suits the new era. Now the fruits are beginning to show.
>
> (BoJ Governor Toshihiko Fukui, 2004)[1]

We have confirmed that the cause of Japan's recession has been the sharp reduction in credit creation that began in 1992 and was triggered by the bad debts in the banking system. We have also found that this was due to excessive loan growth quotas imposed on the banks by the Bank of Japan during the 1980s. Finally, we found that the problem of lack of credit during the 1990s could easily have been solved through monetary policy. Bad debts could have been taken off the banks' balance sheets without costs by the central bank. Even without bank lending, the central bank could have created a recovery a decade ago, by significantly increasing its own credit creation. In other words, Japan's recession of the 1990s has been the result of the Bank of Japan's policies.[2]

However, our research also raises a new question: if the solution to Japan's problems has been relatively straightforward, and could have been implemented in a costless fashion, then why has the principally responsible authority not implemented such or similar policies during the 1990s?

Prosecutors first establish responsibility and culpability. Incompetence may reduce the charge from premeditation to recklessness. So far, the central bank has not pleaded incompetence or insanity. If it did, it would have to build a case on ignorance of the key problem, namely that bad debts in the banking system would reduce credit creation. However, there is significant evidence that the central bank was aware of this problem. Firstly, the central bank's efforts over a decade to fend off suggestions to increase credit creation has led many observers to the conclusion that the central bank is making excuses to implement its predetermined policy.[3] Bernanke (2000) complains that 'in recent years BoJ officials have – to a far greater degree than is justified – hidden behind minor institutional or technical difficulties in order to avoid taking action' (pp. 158ff.).[4]

Secondly, the central bank has been competent enough to seek the advice of leading international monetary and financial experts throughout the 1990s. It has spent considerable resources on its visiting scholar programme and its conferences and seminars. Many have consistently criticized the central bank and clearly described how it could stimulate the economy. However, their advice has consistently been ignored. Hamada (2002), for instance, laments how the Bank of Japan invited leading economists from all over the world in 2000 to ask for their advice concerning the conduct of its monetary policy. 'It is a pity that [the Bank of Japan] has hardly made use of this advice' (p. 71).[5]

Thirdly, key Bank of Japan staff members have from very early onwards shown awareness of the crucial issues. Senior Bank of Japan staff showed familiarity with the credit shrinkage problem, as well as the possible solutions through the central bank.[6] The Bank of Japan's Sawamoto and Ichikawa (1994) do not deny that the central bank could have acted, but they argue that 'the basic principle is that overall monetary policy should not be turned into a bank rescue operation, except in very dire circumstances. At present, Japan is certainly not in such a situation' (p. 99).

The assessment of whether the situation is 'bad enough' to warrant more aggressive monetary stimulation clearly depends on the goal of monetary policy. This, then, becomes the next important question we must ask: Just what is the goal of monetary policy? Normally, observers tend to assume that central banks aim at low inflation and reasonable economic growth. However, there is evidence that the goal of Japanese monetary policy has been different.

The goal of monetary policy

Proponents of cyclical policies frequently assume that the central bank shares their desire for cyclical stimulation and besides avoiding inflation, aims at raising demand and lowering unemployment. There is, however, no evidence to infer such goals in the case of the Bank of Japan. Deputy Governor Yamaguchi (2001b) said: 'By and large, it might be true that, if a central bank continues purchasing all kinds of assets, almost by definition, inflation can be created in the end.' In other words, he agreed that a central bank can fight deflation by purchasing assets. In the same speech he pointed out that inflation can only come about after the economy has recovered. He therefore agrees that resources are unemployed and increased money creation would not directly lead to inflation, but first to a recovery.

Unfortunately, to create a recovery appears not to have been the goal of the central bank, as the deputy governor explained: 'However, our goal is not to cause inflation but to realize a sustainable growth.'[7] During the 1990s, central bank spokesmen have consistently repeated that the goal of monetary policy is to achieve 'sustainable growth'. Already in 1994, Governor Mieno (1994) said that 'the Bank of Japan will continue to do all it can to put the Japanese economy on the right track for a non-inflationary sustainable growth in the medium to long term' (p. 12).

The key to understanding the central bank's objective function is to understand what is meant by 'sustainable growth' and what kind of measures the Bank of Japan thinks are necessary to achieve it. It is tempting to interpret this to mean that the central bank wishes to stimulate the economy and engage in cyclical demand management. However, quite strikingly, the central bank has never clearly stated that it aims at doing that, nor has it taken policies to implement it in a consistent fashion. Quite to the contrary, the central bank has explained that 'sustainable growth' might require a short-term deterioration in the economy. In 1993, Governor Mieno indicated: 'As we pass through the current adjustment phase, the most important goal we have adopted for guiding policy management is not the attainment of short-term improvements in economic conditions, but the long-term objective of achieving non-inflationary sustainable growth without any bubbles' (Mieno, 1993, pp. 12ff.). How can 'sustainable growth' be achieved? The Bank of Japan has frequently said that it believes that the prerequisite for sustainable economic growth is 'structural reform' as the Bank of Japan's Shirakawa (2001) has stated, and as the central bank's spokesmen have increasingly openly indicated since about 1999.

Governor Mieno explained:

> In my description of how I would like the economy to look, you can see that there is a very close resemblance to the economy Japan was aiming at following the Plaza Agreement and during the subsequent period of the rapid appreciation of the yen. In hindsight, I feel that the structural transformation which Japan committed itself to at that time gradually receded into the background during the recent economic boom and the bubble phenomenon. Now, once again, Japan is becoming conscious of the need to implement such transformation ... I do wish to reiterate that it is very important that these medium- to long-term objectives [to implement a structural transformation] be kept in mind when managing the nation's monetary policy. (Mieno, 1993)

Given a choice between cyclical, short-term growth, and structural changes in the long run, which goal should be given priority? Many people, Governor Hayami admits, feel that 'bringing the economy back to the recovery phase of the business cycle is an important challenge'. But, like Mieno before him, he does not place priority on this goal: 'Furthermore, *it is more important* that Japan goes beyond this by regaining economic dynamism by steadily pursuing structural reform' (italics added).[8]

The Bank of Japan and its present or past staff have been the most consistent proponents of structural reform in Japan. The reports by commissions headed by former key Bank of Japan governors, namely the Sasaki Report of 1983 and the Maekawa Reports of 1986 and 1987, attracted much attention.[9] In terms of their content they reiterated many of the views of US trade negotiators. Somewhat less known, though closely resembling their content, are the frequent statements made by past or present Bank of Japan staff during the 1990s.

Their speeches and statements are remarkably consistent in arguing that the central bank had done all it could, and that instead it was up to the government to implement far-reaching structural reform.[10] The Bank of Japan's Okina (1999), for instance, warned:

> What monetary policy alone can do is limited ... the BoJ has taken the utmost efforts to promote monetary easing ... But monetary policy alone cannot guarantee a return of the economy to a sustainable growth path. To this end, it is essential to solve structural problems. (p. 181)

Another example is the Bank of Japan's Shirakawa (2001), who invokes Krugman's expectations-based analysis and poses that the effectiveness of monetary policy cannot be increased by a larger quantity of money injected, but by changing 'expectations resulting in the revitalization of economic activity'. In his view, positive expectations can be created only by structural reform, on which he offers some detailed advice.[11] Governor Hayami has said frequently that structural changes are necessary for an economic recovery. His deputies and colleagues have echoed this sentiment.[12] Deputy Governor Fukui argued in 1995 that for a recovery,

> there are several deep-rooted structural problems that must be solved ... To explain the viewpoint of the BoJ in extremely general terms, one must thoroughly deal with the competition-limiting environment that still remains in Japan's economy and society ...[13]

Bank of Japan spokesmen have not been shy to make detailed suggestions of 'needed' structural reforms.[14]

How can structural reform be achieved? Are structural reform not political goals, out of bounds and beyond reach of the central bank? The Bank of Japan does not think so. Shirakawa (2001) explains that, given the vested interests and political obstacles to such far-reaching changes, 'it is not easy to change the institutional framework and promote structural reform since it necessarily involves the vested interests of all the related individual economic agents' (p. 10). So how can monetary policy be helpful? It can be helpful, by not being helpful. Former Governor Mieno said that thanks to the recession everyone was becoming 'conscious of the need to implement such transformation'. Shirakawa (2001) said that 'further easing [of monetary policy] would not contribute to economic recovery, but would rather delay the progress of structural reform that is a prerequisite for sustainable economic growth' (p. 1). Okina (1999) asked:

Couldn't the current low interest rate policy cause some harm? The answer is yes. It could cause some harm ... low interest rates as a pain-reliever may induce a further delay in the progress of structural adjustment. When the economy recovers, non-performing loans could become collectable, excess inventories could be sold, and excess equipment could become operational. (p. 181)

Former Deputy Governor Yamaguchi said that 'monetary policies cannot replace structural policies', and that the Bank of Japan had faced the 'big dilemma' that monetary easing would produce a 'mitigation of immediate risks', which in turn would result in a 'delaying of adopting ultimate solutions'.[15] Present Governor Toshihiko Fukui said that

Considering the gap in supply and demand conditions in the economy, it's easy to think of a policy of decisive monetary easing ... But we must be wary of the risks associated with further easing, such as by purchasing more Japanese government bonds or setting inflation targets.

What are the risks?:

It's dubious to think that monetary policy alone could lead to a sustainable recovery ... As the financial markets tell us, what is also important are Prime Minister Koizumi's structural reforms ...[16]

According to prominent media reporting, then-Governor

Hayami is convinced that Japan needs to undergo radical corporate restructuring and banking reforms before it can recover – and that he has a duty to promote this ... Mr Hayami's passion for reform also has a flavour of austerity. On paper, most economists – and politicians – think it would be sensible to offset the pain of restructuring with ultra-loose monetary policy. But Mr Hayami fears that if he loosens policy too quickly, it would remove the pressure for reform.[17]

In his own words of May 2000: 'When the economy recovers ... it might well be the case that efforts for structural reform might be neglected due to a sense of security' (Hayami, 2000b, p. 8).

In other words, it must be concluded, as was done before (Werner, 1996b, 1996c, 1996e, 2001a, 2002b), that the central bank is aware that serious monetary stimulation would create a recovery, but it has chosen not to take such policies, because it would delay the structural reform agenda that it supports. Adam Posen of the Institute of International Economics agrees with this conclusion: 'Between a process of elimination, and careful reading of the statements of BoJ policy board members, I am led to the conclusion that a desire by the BoJ to promote structural change in the Japanese economy is a primary motivation for the Bank's passive-aggressive acceptance of deflation' (Posen, 2000, p. 22). Posen concludes that these are examples of a 'broadly held view at the bank'. So what is the policy intention of the Bank of Japan? 'The BoJ wants to use monetary policy to induce structural reforms ... It is clear that "creative destruction", invoked and praised repeatedly in [Bank of Japan Govenor] Hayami's speeches, is the motivating ideology' (pp. 205ff.).

Present Governor Toshihiko Fukui has on several occasions reiterated his conviction that the recession of the 1990s had to be prolonged, in order to pursue structural change.[18] In September 2004, he said during a public appearance, when asked by the audience about the dilapidated state of the banking system: 'While destroying the high growth model, I am building a model that suits the new era. Now the fruits are beginning to show.'[19]

All this may initially appear to be logically consistent for adherents of the real business cycle school. Given human nature, history appears to suggest that fundamental economic, social and political changes only happen in times of crisis. Monetary policy is capable of creating, exacerbating and prolonging crises. If the ultimate objective is a long-run structural reform agenda, then it may be rational from the viewpoint of the reformers, to use cyclical policies in order to implement it. In other words, if we agree with the Bank of Japan's structural reform agenda, then it might be tempting to feel that it is adopting the right policies.

However, this conclusion cannot follow. Firstly, the logic of the argument remains flawed: the Bank of Japan argues that stimulative monetary policies would be counterproductive to its long-term goal of structural change precisely because they would be effective in achieving their goal of creating a recovery. This recognizes that the economy *would* respond to cyclical policies, and hence admits that neoclassical or supply-side theories do not apply to Japan's economic situation. If such theories do not apply, then the long-term goal of structural change cannot be logically justified. In other words, by admitting that a short-term downturn may be necessary to implement structural changes, proponents of structural reform deprive themselves of their main argument for just why structural reforms are necessary. Those who agreed with structural changes, because they felt that the old system does not work, have been misled. The Bank of Japan effectively agrees with many of its critics that the economy, in an unreformed state, could have produced higher growth than has been the case for much of the 1990s. If this is the case, then just why did the Bank of Japan want to change Japan's economic structure at all? Higher growth cannot be the motivation.

Secondly, social welfare cost-benefit analysis is stacked against the Bank of Japan's large-scale live experiment. Cyclical policies aim at economic growth, hence at boosting the size of the national income pie. Structural policies aim at efficiency. While structural reform may indeed succeed in marginally increasing the efficiency of the economy, as measured by certain indicators, it seems clear that the enormous economic and social costs of the ten-year recession have greatly outstripped the potential benefits. To prolong the recession for sake of implementing structural change is like shrinking a cake to tiny size, only to be able to cut it up more easily.

There is therefore no good economic rationale for pursuing the types of policies that the Bank of Japan has pursued over the past decade. This leaves us with the fact that the decision about structural reform is ultimately a political one. Irrespective of the ultimate goal, the question here is whether the implementation of a long-term structural change agenda that affects income and wealth distribution, social and economic institutions and society in general is really the task of unelected central bankers. Nothing in the Bank of Japan Law, old or new, has ever awarded the central bank such a mandate. In Posen's (2000) words: 'no Japanese citizen elected the BoJ to pursue this policy of promoting restructuring, and in fact no elected official delegated this task to the BoJ or put the goal of "encouraging creative destruction" into its mandate' (pp. 206ff.). To create the public consensus for the 'need' for structural reform by purposely creating a recession must constitute an abuse of power.[20] Does the population really want to be manipulated in such a costly and dishonest manner?[21]

It must be concluded that we have empirically identified the goal of monetary policy in the 1990s. This was not to maintain a high factor utilization and stable economic growth, with stable prices. Instead, the central bank appears to have pursued other goals, namely what essentially amounts to a political agenda: to implement 'structural changes' in Japan and trigger policies of deregulation, liberalization and privatization.

Central banks and structural change

It would be reasonable to assume that the Japanese experience is an exception. Whether this is the case or not requires detailed research on other central banks and their monetary policies, as measured by the quantity of credit creation. Such research is beyond the scope of this book. However, it is of interest to ask a few questions and gather some stylized facts.

Consider Germany, the third largest economy in the world, as measured by GDP. Since January 1999, its central bank, the Bundesbank, has become

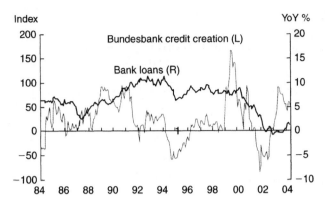

Figure 22.1   Bundesbank credit creation and bank lending in Germany
Source: Bundesbank.

part of the system of European Central Banks and thus its activities and monetary policy have become subject to the instructions of the European Central Bank. What have these policies been, when measured by the quantity of credit?

Figure 22.1 represents the quantity of credit created by the Bundesbank. While some of the transactions that make up this index may be 'endogenous', that is, demand-led, the total net amount is an exogenous policy variable, since the central bank can always engage in purchase or sales operations in the open market, and with this can make up for any endogenously triggered transactions in order to achieve any desired amount of overall net credit creation.

During 1999 and 2000, under the instructions of the ECB, the credit creation of the Bundesbank expanded significantly. While it is beyond the scope of this book to present more detailed econometric analysis of the relationship to growth in Germany, it can be noted that in these years the German economy grew satisfactorily. However, the ECB significantly altered the policy of the Bundesbank in 2001 and 2002. As can be seen, Bundesbank credit creation dropped precipitously in these years, switching to one of 'credit destruction', that is, a net withdrawal of purchasing power from the economy. Measured in terms of the quantity of credit, and not interest rates, monetary policy in 2002 became among the tightest in the history of the Bundesbank. As can be seen, bank credit followed, with a lag. Thus bank lending, still growing by almost 10% in late 2000, collapsed to zero two years later.

Figure 22.2 shows the correlation of the Bundesbank's credit creation with industrial production – a reasonable proxy for economic growth in Germany.

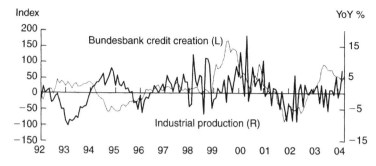

Figure 22.2 Bundesbank credit creation and economic activity
Source: Bundesbank.

In August 2001, German industrial production turned from growth to contraction. In December 2001, it fell by 8.7% year on year and contracted for much of 2002. Other indicators of the economy also deteriorated sharply during 2002, such as the IFO survey of business sentiment. Bankruptcies rose significantly, and the phenomenon of boarded-up shops in city-centre locations became widespread. With rising bankruptcies, unemployment also increased and for about two years it was very difficult for new university graduates to find jobs.

An informal straw poll of several bank loan officers at the time, conducted by the author, indicated that something akin to a 'loan stop' had been 'decreed' from bank headquarters concerning lending to specific sectors, including real estate, wholesale and retail, agriculture and farming, catering and various services. There was much evidence, widely reported in the press, that small and medium-sized businesses suffered from a 'credit crunch': loan supply was reduced beyond the level of previous years, thus cutting off many firms that had previously been able to receive funding (see also Werner, 2002e).

The decision about how much credit the Bundesbank should create was made in Frankfurt, but since 1999 by the ECB. How did the European Central Bank react to the recession in Germany, and to criticism that its policy was too restrictive? The President of the ECB, Wim Duisenberg, declared in 2002 that 'the liquidity situation is ample', 'financing conditions are favourable' and 'the monetary policy stance that we have is appropriate' (European Union, 2003). While according to Mr Duisenberg the policy of the ECB was not at fault, he saw the cause of the German recession elsewhere: European countries, including Germany, required a 'speeding up of structural policy measures which aim to increase productivity', by 'stepping up the pace of economic reform. This requires an acceleration and deepening of structural reforms in the labour, product and financial markets in order to provide economic agents with the proper incentives' (European Union, 2003). According to the *Financial Times*, the call for structural reform became the ECB's much-repeated 'monthly mantra' (Barber, 2001).

Duisenberg has been far from a lone voice at the ECB, whose leading figures appear to speak in unison, whether they hail from little Brittany or the northern permafrost fringes of Europe. According to ECB Executive Board member Sirkka Hämäläinen, criticism of ECB monetary policy was misplaced, despite the recession in large parts of the eurozone: 'The growth problems can not be solved by monetary policy or short-term macro-economic measures. They need far-reaching structural micro-economic changes.' Slow growth has been 'connected, inter alia, with the structural impediments and rigidities in the labour, financial and services markets' (Hämäläinen, 2003). Rather than treating such claims as hypotheses that require testing, ECB members appear convinced that they are axioms.

The new ECB President happens to hold the same personal opinion: 'the high rate of unemployment in the euro area ... signals a still insufficient flexibility of the euro area and thus the necessity of further substantial efforts with structural reform in labour markets in particular' (Trichet, 2004c). The current head of the ECB tells us that 'The case for decisive structural reforms is pressing ... By delivering the necessary structural reforms, I believe that governments and social partners could set in motion a virtuous circle of increasing confidence, favourable growth prospects and success in the reform process' (Trichet, 2004a). This has indeed become Trichet's much-repeated mantra: 'It is widely recognised that structural reforms are needed to improve the prospects of the euro area. Given that demographics in the EU are less dynamic than in other economies, including the US, the case for a decisive implementation of structural reforms is *even more* pressing' (Trichet, 2004b).

According to official central bank policy – managed through interest rates – there is no discrimination between member countries. However, when analysing the quantity of credit policies, even just those of the constituent central banks, a different picture emerges. While Germany was mired in recession, Ireland enjoyed economic growth at breakneck speed. Did this have anything to do with the more favourable credit policy (as measured by the quantity of credit), which the ECB lavished on Ireland? Not according to official ECB sources. Instead, Trichet informs us that it all had to do with the wisdom of the Irish government to implement deep structural reforms: 'Ireland's economic success can therefore be linked to the transformation of its labour market into a plentiful supply of competitively priced and quality labour resources' (Trichet, 2004b).

Trichet revealed himself to be a convinced 'supply-sider', just like virtually all central bankers (Trichet, 2004c). For a central bank that claims it must have independence so that its powers are not misused, the ECB has been surprisingly modest about the extent of its powers. Economic growth, for instance, has, according to Mr Trichet, little to do with monetary policy. Concerning the tight quantity of credit policy imposed on the Bundesbank in 2001 and 2002, Trichet claimed ignorance.[22]

In all cases, the European central bankers failed to cite any empirical evidence in favour of their claim that the weak economic performance of key European economies, especially the German one, was due to the economic structure. As discussed in Chapter 5, there are a number of conditions that must be met for a recession to be caused by the economic structure. These include full employment of factors of production, a shrinkage in the supply of factors of production, a fall in productivity of those factors of production that are employed, and so forth. Just as in Japan's case, there is no evidence that any of these conditions hold. Most of all, there has been ample evidence that the factors of productions have not been fully utilized, suggesting that demand-side policies – such as monetary policy – are at fault.

Is it conceivable that other central banks also aim at structural change?

The policies of the Bank of Japan and the ECB appear similar, with a striking coincidence of tight credit policy by the central bank and frequently repeated, though empirically unfounded, public claims that the recession was due to the economic structure – and thus deep reforms were needed.[23] Further parallels have also been found in several East Asian countries, especially in the case of Thailand, Korea and Indonesia during the time of significant monetary policy failure. The central bankers were quick to place the blame for the Asian crisis on 'structural problems' (Werner, 2003c).

Perhaps a different kind of central banker can be found in a neutral country such as Switzerland? Figure 22.3 shows the Swiss growth performance in recent years. In 2002, growth came to an abrupt halt. Industrial production shrank. In 2003, negative nominal GDP growth was recorded. The unemployment rate more than doubled between 2001 and 2003. The number of bankruptcies grew by over 20% in early 2003, reaching the highest level since 1996. Boarded-up shops and empty office space also became widespread in this Alpine nation.

Concerning the Swiss economic performance, the Swiss National Bank, Switzerland's central bank, gave no indication that monetary policy may have anything to do with it. Philipp Hildebrand, a member of its governing board, announced to the public that the cause of Swiss economic weakness was the 'structural straight jacket' of 'a web of regulatory hurdles' in many sectors. His policy advice: 'freeing up these sectors would ... raise economic growth' (Hildebrand, 2003). In other words, Switzerland's weak growth performance was due to structural problems which could be addressed by deregulation, liberalization, privatization and the introduction of shareholder-capitalism.

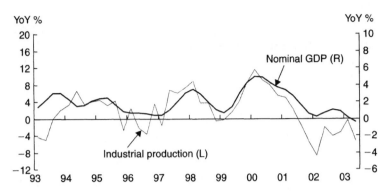

Figure 22.3   Recent Swiss economic performance
Source: Bundesant für statistik.

Meanwhile, according to Hildebrand, the recession was not all bad. Instead, he notes the 'welcome development' that, thanks to the crisis, 'difficult long-term problems which lie at the heart of our social contract are being openly debated'. While 'central banks have no ability to fine-tune the real economy', we learn that 'an important body of academic literature suggests that monetary policy has also become more effective as markets shed regulatory impediments' (Hildebrand, 2003). Given the underutilization of factors of production in Switzerland, the assertion by the central bank that the weak economic performance has been due to the Swiss economic structure, or that there is a need to implement structural reforms, remains without merit.

Meanwhile, measuring the quantity of credit created by the Swiss central bank, it emerges that it contracted by record amounts in 2002 (Figure 22.4). Can the argument that the Swiss central bank was not using all the means at its disposal in order to stimulate economic growth be dismissed? Meanwhile, is it possible that the Swiss central bank, as supporter of the political agenda of structural reform, may itself have been causally implicated in the propagation of the Swiss recession?

A cursory review of statements by central bankers all over the world – including many developing countries and emerging markets – will quickly yield the finding that they have much in common, no matter where spoken. Monetary policy is not powerful, and the burden of policy action rests with other players, whose foremost task is, according to the central bank, to implement deep structural changes. Analysing the precise details of these recommended structural changes, irrespective of country or continent, they seem to consist of the same set of policies that have been dubbed the 'Washington

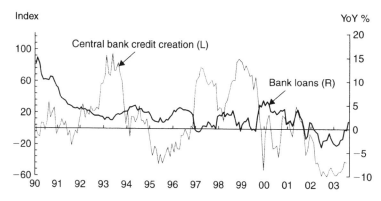

Figure 22.4 Credit creation in Switzerland
Source: Swiss National Bank.

consensus', as they have been advanced forcefully by the main Washington-based institutions, such as the Federal Reserve, the US Treasury, the IMF, the World Bank, the Inter-American Development Bank, and their various subsidiaries and satellites. As we saw in the previous chapter, international organizations such as the World Bank consider crises an 'opportunity' to implement 'structural reform' and 'transfer ownership'.

Every bureaucracy, including central banks, constitutes an interest group, and if the overall incentive structure within which it operates is not designed well, a gap is likely to unfold and gradually widen between the overall interests of society, and the sectarian interests of the bureaucracy itself. Again, the wisdom to grant independence to central banks, without commensurate checks and balances on their activities, is called into question.

Transparency of central bank monetary policy

The Bank of Japan, the ECB, and most other central banks, have consistently failed to discuss their quantitative policy in public. In a theoretical world of perfect information this would be justifiable. But in the world we live in there is no guarantee that interest rates and the quantity of credit offer the same signal or move in the way traditional theories predict. Much discussion and many research publications on interest rates have therefore ended up distracting public attention from the far more important issue of the quantitative credit policy of central banks. Since in rationed markets – as they exist everywhere and at all times – prices and quantities are not in a unique relationship, central banks are able to implement policies that are not recognized as such by the public, through their control over the quantity of credit. Thus the Bank of Japan has been lowering interest rates, while repeatedly claiming that it was taking all necessary steps to achieve an economic recovery – while it maintained an excessively tight monetary policy, as visible from the quantity of credit. This has helped it in advancing its structural reform agenda – a policy that is not an official part of the mandate of the central bank (or any central bank in the world).

Lack of true and meaningful transparency, especially concerning the quantity of credit, has enabled central banks to engage in such policies. In the case of the ECB, despite being one of the largest employers of economists and statisticians in the world, producing vast amounts of research, no publication has addressed the question why the quantity of credit creation of its constituent central banks – a policy variable – is so divergent. While Germany was thrown into recession, central banks of peripheral member countries were able to increase credit creation significantly. Does the ECB engage in structural policy? Does it engage in regional policy? And if so, how is such regional policy decided? It is not disclosed to the public, or parliaments.

Lack of disclosure by the ECB is not surprising: its statutes do not provide any incentives for transparency. While being known among economists as one of the world's most powerful and yet least transparent central banks, its President deals with this problem by merely asserting that there is no problem: 'The ECB is one of [the] most transparent central banks in the world and has helped define "the state of the art" of central banking in this domain', claims Trichet (2004d).

Meanwhile, if central banks are interested parties, then there is a need for more research into the degree to which their own economic research and publications have been influenced by their political agenda. Indeed, research is necessary in order to assess to what extent central banks have sought to and succeeded in influencing economic research produced by academic researchers, the content of textbooks used to teach at schools and universities, and the coverage received by central banks in the media. Some initial findings from Japan, reported in Werner (2004c), suggest that the extent of such activities may so far have been underestimated.

While the details of monetary policy implementation in European countries remain beyond the scope of this book, the focus on credit quantities sheds new light on the ECB and other central banks. More research is thus needed before we can dismiss the concerns raised in this chapter.

23
A New Kind of Economics

There are several criteria for deciding among competing theories. We already considered the more narrowly defined statistical criteria drawn up by Hendry and Richard (1983) in Chapter 15. Among their seven criteria, four are of broader significance and find application whenever scientists seek to choose between alternative theories.

The first and most important criterion for choosing between competing theories is the principle of parsimony. It is one of the fundamental rules of formal logic, which is associated with William of Ockham (1287–1347), the English philosopher and logician whose work became important for mathematics in the twentieth century. This is often put as *Pluralitas non est ponenda sine necessitas*. According to this rule, when choosing between competing theories that have similar explanatory power, the one is preferable that is simpler and hence requires fewer leaps of logic or the least restrictive set of assumptions. This simple principle cuts complex theories down to size, and it has become known as 'Ockham's Razor'. Earlier proponents include Aristotle in his *Physics*; a more recent proponent is Milton Friedman (1953), who pointed out that 'A hypothesis is important if it explains much by little' (Friedman, 1953, quoted by Thomas, 1997, p. 363).

We note that the model proposed in this book is parsimonious both in terms of the theoretical model and its empirical corroboration. The proposed theory does not require unrealistic assumptions, such as perfect information, complete and competitive markets, zero transaction costs, and so forth. The set of necessary assumptions is far smaller, and these are based on empirical observation, as scientific methodology requires. The model itself, including in its empirical formulation, is simpler than those of other theories. According to Ockham's Razor, even if our model could only explain as much as mainstream economics (and thus even if it failed to solve any of the enigmas and 'anomalies' of mainstream economics) it would be preferable to mainstream macroeconomic theories.

It may be noted here that this fundamental principle of logic does not seem to be well-known among economists. Many appear adherents of an opposite rule which claims that whichever theory is more complex and more difficult to understand must be preferable. Such an approach, however, leaves the realms of science and is more grounded in the principles of rhetoric, persuasion, if not manipulation (see McCloskey, 1987, 1994).

The second criterion to choose between competing theories is the ability to explain the data well, within a model based on sound empirical methodology. In Part III the proposed theory was tested and found supported by the data. The testing procedure adopted was Hendry's methodology, which could be called Ockham's Razor of econometrics, because a general statistical model, which should include explanatory variables from alternative models, is reduced down to the parsimonious form. Thus the criterion of empirical fit, when based on sound methodology, includes the requirement of encompassing. Already Kuhn (1962) and others have pointed out that any new theory that wishes to replace older ones must be able to explain the 'anomalies' the old theories could not explain, but also whatever they could explain. Following the Hendry general-to-specific methodology, our framework was tested together with the competing, traditional theories. In the process of dropping insignificant variables, the explanations of competing theories, such as interest rates and traditional 'money supply' measures dropped out. Our model thus has fit and also encompasses previous theories.

The third criterion is the ability to forecast, especially out of sample. This was also suggested by Friedman (1953). As noted in Chapter 15, the theory presented in this book was not developed with the hindsight of the experience of the 1990s, but at the beginning of the 1990s. The model's forecasting abilities have been tested repeatedly almost over the entire period of the 1990s, in the original meaning of 'forecasting'. For instance, already in the early 1990s the prediction was made that Japanese economic growth would slow significantly, based on the incipient bad debts that would render banks risk averse (Werner, 1991). In 1994 and 1995, it was argued that fiscal policy would crowd out private activity, that interest rate reductions, even to zero, would not stimulate the economy, and that credit creation was necessary and sufficient for a recovery (Werner, 1994b, 1994c, 1995a, 1995c, 1995d, 1996b). In late 1994 and early 1995 it was predicted that real GDP growth would accelerate sharply in 1996, recording about 4%, based on a (temporary) surge in bank lending (Werner, 1994c, 1995d). There are no competing models that recorded similarly accurate *ex ante* forecasts.

Based on these major criteria for selection between competing theories, the theory advanced in this book must appear preferable. Finally, it seems to be the only comprehensive approach that solves the major riddles surrounding Japan's economy.

Some implications

While the model has been tested for the Japanese case, it is also likely to apply to other economies, and other time periods. Since it has been founded on inductive research, based on the rich empirical facts of several thousand years of banking history, there is some confidence that it will stand the test of time and general application. Anecdotal evidence from many countries, especially in Asia and Europe, seems in line with model predictions. When the ratio of credit in the financial circulation to credit in the real circulation rises, the traditional monetary equation of exchange underpinning traditional macroeconomic theories cannot be accurate. In such time periods, a financial boom is likely, as asset prices are driven up by speculative borrowing on the back of collateralized assets. Similarly, the following period of asset price falls, caused by a reduction in credit creation from bad debt-burdened banks, disturbs the traditional quantity equation relationship. This explains why the traditional equation of exchange was not reliable in many countries in the 1920s and 1930s, and again in the late 1980s and early 1990s. Then the traditionally defined velocity of money declines and excess credit creation can 'spill over' as foreign investment. However, during time periods such as the 1950s, when in many countries credit was mainly channelled into the real economy, asset prices remained stable and the traditional equation of exchange was more likely to hold. The traditional model is thus but a special case of the more general disaggregated credit model.

Many of the implications of our findings have already been discussed. For instance, our approach casts doubt on the widespread emphasis of traditional economic theory on prices – such as interest rates. We found that key economic variables, namely nominal GDP, asset prices and Japanese foreign investment, could be explained almost single-handedly with quantity variables – mainly the quantity of disaggregated credit – while interest rates and exchange rates dropped out in parsimonious reductions as insignificant.

Our findings suggest that central bank targeting of credit aggregates is likely to be more successful than traditional monetary or interest rate targeting. They also indicate that further research into a more complex disaggregation of credit should prove fruitful. Further, given the importance of credit variables, they also call for comprehensive disclosure by central banks of timely and detailed high-frequency credit data. While central banks have such information available internally on a real-time basis, it often still takes several months, sometimes more than a quarter, until figures are released to the public, and then often only aggregate data lacking in detail.

The results imply for policy-makers that it is imperative to monitor the allocation of credit and intervene, if credit creation for unproductive, especially speculative purposes takes place to a significant degree. Once an asset bubble has occurred, excess credit creation must turn into bad debt that tends to cripple the banking system and create a credit crunch. There are policies that can be taken to prevent an incipient credit crunch from hurting the economy and to stimulate a fast recovery. Far better still, if the credit-driven boom-bust cycle can be avoided entirely. This can be done by using suitably designed direct intervention in the credit market in order to influence both quantity and allocation of credit and ensure that credit creation is mainly used productively. This ensures inflation-free, stable growth.

As we saw, our framework also indicates exciting opportunities for developing countries to achieve fast, non-inflationary growth. By ensuring that credit creation is mainly used for productive purposes, high real growth rates without inflation can be generated. As Japan's case of the 1960s demonstrated, even double-digit economic growth rates are possible. It is not a coincidence that Korea, Taiwan and, most recently, China, have been using credit controls and the selective allocation of credit as key policy tools. These produced high growth rates. With appropriate credit policies, the only limit to growth becomes the human creativity in inventing new ideas, new technologies and new recipes of organizing inputs. If there is much such creativity, very high growth is possible. This implies that some countries, especially the UK, have been growing below their potential: creativity and inventiveness is one of the hallmarks of Britain. However, entrepreneurs find it hard to obtain bank loans. Meanwhile, many banks prefer to lend for consumption or for speculative transactions in the real estate market or financial assets. Given the importance in creativity to provide the ideas that allow productive investments, our framework also shows that know-how, education and information are crucial for successful economic development – areas that were neglected in traditional theories, where agents were simply assumed to already know everything.

Non-fiction economics

The research programme of the macroeconomic role of credit in non-Walrasian, quantity-based models opens many avenues of promising work. What are some key features of this new kind of economics?

Most bookshops are divided into fiction and non-fiction sections. Novels are in the former, economics books in the latter. This seems to be a classification error. An objective scientific assessment would yield much doubt about whether current economics books constitute fact, not fiction. Over the past century, many economic theories have been based on assumptions that can only hold in a fictitious dream world. How this 'fiction economics' became the dominant paradigm in the world, followed and adopted by policy-makers and decision-makers worldwide, is another, enlightening story that requires detailed research. However, the intellectual justification and hence foundation for this fiction economics is known: it is the methodological approach to science called deductivism. Here, the researcher starts with assumptions that by assertion require no proof – axioms. Based on them, a theoretical structure is built, using the tools of logic. It may have little to do with reality. All this may be useful as abstract exercises in logic. However, these models are then used to provide policy recommendations which are applied to an entirely different and not demonstrably related world – reality.

The argument in defence of applying the dream-world models to reality was that any model has to simplify and thus some unrealistic assumptions are unavoidable. This, we were told, does not matter, as long as the result is useful and applicable to reality. In other words, as Milton Friedman argued, a model is acceptable if it works empirically (and, as Friedman demanded, if it can forecast reasonably accurately). However, we have seen in Part II that this justification cannot be sustained for mainstream economic theories. The old paradigm has failed by its own standards.

These standards have been too low: the deductive methodology adopted by mainstream economics is unscientific. The principle of 'choosing the scientific hypothesis which (currently) contains the least number of unproven assumptions' is known as Ockham's Razor, or, ironically for mainstream economists, the 'Principle of Economy'.[1] While it 'has become a basic perspective for those who follow the scientific method', much of mainstream economics happily violates it.[2]

According to Ockham, it is not permissible to build theories on assumptions that are neither self-evident nor based on empirical evidence.[3] Thus a new kind of economics, a reality-oriented, relevant and useful economics must be inductive. This means that its theoretical models must be firmly rooted in empirical facts and that it cannot be built on unrealistic assumptions.

If we consider the actual behaviour of natural scientists as indication of what constitutes scientific behaviour, we also have to conclude that deductivism cannot be scientific: most natural scientists follow the inductive methodology. They first seek an accurate description of reality and its facts. Based on the features of reality, a model is constructed. No doubt, in the process of building a model some simplifying assumptions are made (and deductive logic is also applied). However, these need to be in line with the facts. Based on such a reality-oriented model, policy conclusions can then be reached and applied.

The inductive approach also minimizes preconceptions. Scientists cannot afford to have preferences. A physicist cannot say: 'I really like the stability and simplicity of nineteenth-century energy physics, thus I will ignore all subsequent discoveries in quantum mechanics, with all its uncertainties.' If reality turns out differently, scientists will be eager to embrace it in their quest to utilize all facts and findings to push forward the frontiers of knowledge. Similarly, should we find something about economic reality that implies we have to let go of some dearly cherished theories or assumptions, then we must not be emotional about it, but pluck up the courage to face the facts. This is exciting, for we may enter a brave new world which may turn out quite differently from the one we would like to believe in.

A fundamental assumption of most macroeconomic models has been the assumption of perfect information. However, as we saw in the Prologue to this book, the imperfection of information is the very foundation of economic reality. The very existence of money is testimony to this fact. Yet Greenwald and Stiglitz (1986) showed that with imperfect information a Pareto efficient equilibrium cannot be expected.

Even more damaging is the fact that the model of Walrasian *tattonnement*, which produces an equilibrium and demand–supply balance, requires perfect information. This is the picture presented by the most famous diagram in economics, frequently used in the context of markets of all kinds, ranging from goods and services to labour and foreign exchange, namely that of the downward-sloping demand and upward-sloping supply curve. The variable that produces the equilibrium in this model is the price. However, to achieve this outcome, perfect information is required. If there is imperfect information, there is no guarantee that equilibrium will ever be obtained. It would be pure chance if demand equalled supply.

The implication is that in the 'real world' we live in, characterized by imperfect information, we cannot expect demand to ever equal supply. This has far-reaching implications, because the recognition of pervasive rationing and lack of market clearing would knock down a very fundamental pillar of modern, indeed much of twentieth-century economics. This may explain the extraordinary reluctance of economists even to consider this possibility. But if empirical research leads us to conclude that markets don't actually clear, then we must let go of theories that are based on market clearing.

The premise of much editorializing in the financial press that decisions should be 'left to the market' is based on the assumption that markets are efficient. But a precondition for efficiency is market clearing. Pervasive rationing means not only that markets are not efficient, they fail entirely – and operate quite differently from what mainstream theories hold.

Rationed markets are determined by quantities, not by prices (such as the interest rate). Thus when we leave the fictional world of perfect information, we obtain a new kind of economics, which is less centred on prices, but instead gives a bigger role to quantities. Among the more important quantities in a rationed world is that of the quantity of newly exerted purchasing power, which depends on the credit creation by banks and the central bank – another empirical fact of our world, which is ignored by neoclassical economics. Thus while the latest acclaimed neoclassical macroeconomics textbook is entitled '*Interest and Prices*', the new, reality-oriented kind of economics is likely to call a textbook '*Credit and Quantities*'.

The reality of rationing

Market rationing is such a large part of our daily lives that we don't even notice it any more – helping neoclassical economists in their agenda to 'assume it away'. The real estate market, for instance, is an important part of any economy. Yet it is based entirely on market rationing: since land cannot be moved, its supply in any one location is rationed. Further, the value of land crucially depends on regulatory decisions made by planning authorities: if it can only be used for agricultural purposes, its value will be a fraction of comparable land with permission to build large structures on. These planning decisions are not market outcomes. Such interventions, quantity allocations and rules are set by policy-makers, and market forces operate within these constraints. Thus it does not make sense to assume them away. Instead, efforts should be focused on determining the most efficient form of official intervention.

Many economists would admit that in the 'real world' many markets are rationed. But they will usually argue that at least financial markets are different: they are so liquid that they are not rationed, but in equilibrium. However, they usually only say this because they have not frequently traded financial instruments themselves. They therefore do not know what most fund managers are aware of: even if an order is issued to buy or sell a certain amount of government bonds at the price shown on the trading screen as the market price, it is not clear that the order will be executed. It may only be partially executed, or it may not be executed at all: each sell order requires a counter-party willing to buy exactly the same amount at the quoted prices.[4] Government bonds are usually represented as highly liquid markets in textbooks. But especially bond markets do not usually clear: there are no continuous demand or supply curves, because each bond is a separate product, and the supply and demand is limited. Astonishingly, the same also holds true for many currencies, despite the fact that the foreign exchange market is considered the most liquid in the world.

Walras, the classical economist who advanced the concept of market clearing, invoked the example of the auction and an all-knowing auctioneer to obtain market clearing. But even auctions do not normally produce true market clearing: there is no all-knowing auctioneer. Neither do all participants in auctions know everything that there is to know about the products at hand. Further, usually not all those who might be interested in the goods or services to be auctioned are even present at the auction: perhaps they simply did not know that a specific property or piece of art was going to be auctioned off. Certainly the expertise about antiquities, wine or precious metals is not equally distributed – this is why some are famous experts and others are not. If there was perfect information and no transactions costs, intermediaries and dealers could not make any money by going to auctions. As it is, only those 'in the know' go to auctions, and then these auctions are a contest of their wits and resources – some will be better informed than others and thus know whether a certain property or oil painting is worth a certain price or not. Often the badly informed may end up overpaying. Had they been fully informed, they might not have bought the painting at all. Thus there are market outcomes, but they are not equilibrium outcomes. The implication for auctions is that even these textbook examples cannot be said to be in equilibrium, as the very definition of such equilibrium requires perfect information.

Sometimes attempts are made to rescue the market equilibrium paradigm by arguing that perhaps in the past markets were rationed. But today, thanks to the internet and modern telecommunications technology, information flows have speeded up so dramatically that the assumption of perfect information is a close approximation of reality. Thanks to the internet, the perfect information paradigm has now become true. Thus, with (near-)perfect information, markets do clear, after all. This argument is, however, also far from the truth, thanks to the laws of biology, and the laws of thermodynamics: the fact is our lives are finite. Economists try to ignore this reality with 'overlapping generations models' or models of 'infinitely lived agents', but death remains an immovable certainty. Since the cost of gathering useful information is also paid in time, and time is an important cost factor for finitely-lived humans, market rationing is likely to be pervasive. The internet does not change this reality: the size of a computer screen is limited. So is the number of websites that can be displayed on it, and the time each user can spend in front of it.

The two most important rationed quantities are time and information. Money is a tool to organize and control resources, including labour, in order to mitigate these. With demand for money outstripping its supply, it is rationed itself. Rationing of time, information and money ensures that all other markets must also be rationed.[5]

Since even the most liquid financial markets or the proverbial auctions frequently do not clear, how can we possibly expect any other market to? If finite lives mean we must focus our attention on a limited set of activities (desires are unlimited, but time is not), and if lack of information means most activities require an investment in time, how can markets fail to be rationed? If equilibrium is the exception, not the rule, we need an economics that recognizes this reality.

The power of the allocators

Another important implication of market rationing is the dimension of economic power. Every market that is rationed gives the short side of supply or demand a type of power that does not exist in market-clearing economics: the power to allocate; the power to pick and choose. For instance, if there are more equally qualified applicants for one particular job than there are jobs, the selection committee can exert allocation powers in this rationed market. Often the section or department head in a company can pick and choose among the applicants. The actual decision may have little to do with market factors, but more with features that may personally endear the applicant to the selector – whether it is looks, personal connections, some inside knowledge, or an assessment of whether they will be personally useful to the selector. Clearly, the exercise of allocative power may bring with it perks, if only in the form of gratitude or loyalty to the selector.

Whenever a market is rationed, allocative power is exerted. The allocator can decide A or B or C, and the market has nothing to do with it. Discrete solutions are the outcome, not continuous curves and equilibrium points. Public announcements of job vacancies or public competitions may only provide a cover of openness and fairness, while the insiders at the firm or institution have long chosen their preferred candidate. Will the manager in charge of decorating a hotel let market forces decide the choice of materials, colours, furnishings? Or will it be allocative decisions based on her taste and artistic sense? Of the thousands of news items that newswires report on a daily basis, only a few hundred or even only a few dozen are reported the following day by the press and only a handful make it on TV. Somebody – usually a small number of senior editors – made a selection and allocation decision. As a result, many important news items never get reported, because the mainstream media have refused to cover them. Those who make these allocative decisions wield enormous power. They can say yes or no to a piece of news. Since we do not possess perfect information, but are dependent on the objectivity of the reporting services, our view of the world will be influenced, even manipulated, by the news reported in the media. This editorial power is not the power of the markets, but the power of a small number of individuals who select and allocate in rationed markets.

While the rhetoric is of a globalized world dominated by anonymous market forces which decide the flow of goods, services and capital across the globe, the reality is that the majority of trade flows are decided by planners – bureaucrats or bureaucrat-like managers at large-scale corporations – who make allocation decisions: large-scale corporations dominate international trade and much international trade takes place within these large global firms. This makes sense in a world of pervasive rationing, where practically all economic decisions are allocative decisions. These give power and control to the short side – not only to bureaucrats and managers. Even if it is a job applicant who receives several offers – she enjoys a power comparable to a Soviet-style apparatchik: a planning decision is made that is not determined by the invisible hand of market forces, but the visible decision-making power of the allocator.

The reality of 'market capitalism' is therefore that the market plays a much smaller role than is widely claimed. In truth, economic outcomes are not decided by markets, but by allocators. Reality may thus be far less 'fair' than the official rhetoric makes it out to be. Adam Smith argued for specialization and division of labour. This is indeed what we observe, and it makes sense. However, his argument was that this division of labour is based on individual talent. The cobbler is talented at cobbling shoes, thus he should focus on his area of 'comparative advantage'. Thus everyone's current job is justified by their area of advantage. The implication is that people should not covet jobs of others that seem more attractive: the impartial markets determined that the movie star got her job, because she is most talented, we are told.

However, there may be another reason why specialization and division of labour occurs: economies of scale. Almost all learning and production processes are characterized by increasing returns to scale and decreasing costs. This is another empirical reality of a three-dimensional world ruled by the laws of physics – but one often ignored by neoclassical economics. For instance, while volumes increase by the cube, the surface space (and thus cost) to cover them (with bricks, steel or glass) increases by the square. For any object whose size is increased without changing shape, the increase in volume is always greater than the increase in surface area. With a cube, by only quadrupling surface area, volume can be octupled. When increasing surface area ninefold, volume is increased twenty-sevenfold.[6] This means that the larger an object, the less surface area is needed relative to its volume. In terms of economics, this produces downward-sloping cost curves and helps explain why mass production tends to deliver lower unit costs. Yet for 'convenience', and perhaps in order to obtain desired results, economists prefer to assume constant or diminishing returns to scale and constant or increasing costs. Similarly, every job requires some initial investment in terms of learning, and after a period of familiarization, speed and efficiency tend to rise. Changing jobs will incur costs of retraining. Thus hysteresis is another physical reality of this world. Hysteresis represents the reality that physical systems – the world we live in – depend on the facts of history. Yet this path-dependence is rarely reflected in economic models.

Together with the reality of imperfect information this has implications for how jobs are really obtained. Learning costs and economies of scale justify specialization and division of labour – irrespective of talent. When Peter Gabriel spoke to a group of young attendees of the World Economic Forum at Davos in 2004, his modesty was striking, especially when this talented artist declared: 'Talent is vastly overrated.' Perhaps this statement reflects his realization that although there are many talented artists, not all could make it into superstars, even though by talent many more may have been entitled to. Perhaps the allocators did not favour them ...

If most outcomes are due to anonymous market forces, we may more readily accept them – there is nothing we can do. They may thus appear 'fair'. If prices move until demand equals supply and one price applies to all, then this seems fair and transparent. But if reality is one of pervasive disequilibrium, where demand does not equal supply, then there may also be different effective prices for different people. Furthermore, some people will get the goods or the jobs, while equally qualified others won't. This becomes especially obvious when considering the types of jobs that many of us would like to have, thus where labour supply is significantly outstripping labour demand: movie actors, TV announcers, TV anchorpeople, singers, models, even successful painters, artists in general, writers and journalists. The majority to whom such jobs are not available and who may have less rewarding jobs will find it easier to accept if such jobs are said to have been determined by market forces. The incumbents are simply the best, and thus the market has efficiently allocated the jobs to them. But the fact is that excess demand for such jobs means that the labour market in these industries does not clear. It is rationed, and rationed markets are determined by allocation. Somebody has the power to pick and choose who will be given a chance in the form of a contract with a music company or a book deal – and who will be promoted sufficiently to reach prominence in a world characterized by imperfect information and lack of knowledge about whose works are truly valuable. The job of news reader on TV can probably be efficiently and effectively performed by thousands, if not tens of thousands of people. But there are far fewer such jobs available. It is thus not market forces that fill these desirable posts. Similarly, are the programmes offered on TV necessarily the best possible programmes that one could produce? Are all the important news items reported? Or are markets rationed, and a powerful executive has simply decided that certain types of programmes should be broadcast, while other information is withheld?

Thus it cannot be said that the market mechanism is unimportant. On the contrary, it appears to be playing an important role in our society – but that seems largely confined to the world of rhetoric and public relations: the rhetoric of the free market mechanism serves to hide the reality of pervasive rationing, untransparent allocation decisions and the power by the allocators to control resources. It therefore may serve to render reality more acceptable, without too much political resistance or demands for fairness, transparency and social justice. Ironically, the true role of the free market may be based on the reality of imperfect information and the consequent scope for manipulating information about reality.

Keeping up with the Joneses

In line with the deductive methodology, many economic models employ a theory of individual behaviour that is not founded on empirical observation. Once again the function of auctions – considered the stronghold of the market clearing paradigm – serves to illustrate this. The neoclassical model of human nature assumes that each individual only maximizes his/her own utility, without being influenced by what others do. Psychologies have long disproven this behavioural model of *Homo oeconomicus*, for instance in their recognition of the phenomenon of social facilitation. Herd behaviour has long been recognized in the literature, but this has not led to a revision of the model of individual utility maximization. It is true that as social beings, we humans do care about what others think of us, and often what others do and say can have profound effects on our behaviour beyond the mere transmission of information.

Thus competitive behaviour often dominates the dynamics of auctions: bidders may end up bidding much more than they had rationally decided an object was worth, just because a rival was trying to outbid them. This may still be rational: the level of interest shown by others may indeed be an important signalling device in a world of imperfect information. However, the status orientation and hierarchical competition that characterizes human nature also plays an important role. We may thus get more interested in an item purely because others are interested in it.

Once economists adopt the inductive method, a reality-based economics can be quickly assembled, because it can draw on the rich findings of other scientific disciplines, such as psychology, psychiatry, sociology, management science and biology, to name a few. Their results about human behaviour can be utilized to improve our models of individual action. So far, citations of these disciplines are rare in economics journals, perhaps because of the large number of 'anomalies' they yield (Thaler, 1992).[7]

According to the United States Declaration of Independence – the other document published in 1776 – it is a self-evident truth that the 'pursuit of happiness' is an 'unalienable right', comparable to life and liberty. Thus economics must also be about happiness. The assumption of deductive mainstream economics remains that the accumulation of material things (and money) makes us happy. But whether money and material things can make people happy is an empirical question, and one that is beginning to attract an increasing number of researchers. It was found that income may contribute to increased happiness, but only up to a point. Additional income does not increase happiness proportionately, and may even fail to increase it (Helliwell, 2001, cited in Frey and Stutzer, 2002). Income differences only explain a low proportion of differences in happiness among people (Easterlin, 2001). So far, empirical evidence seems to suggest that happiness is derived from interaction with other humans, especially when the desire to love and be loved and respected is fulfilled. This means that human motivation is intrinsically interactive, and not, as mainstream economics assumes, individualistic. It was already written several thousand years ago by someone famous for his wisdom: 'all labour and all achievement spring from man's envy of his neighbour' (Ecclesiastes 4:4). Similarly, why might Proverbs exhort that 'A good name is more desirable than great riches; to be esteemed is better than silver or gold' (Proverbs 22:1)? This suggests an alternative model of individual behaviour, in which the desire to be respected and competition for ranking are important. It is a world in which a sense of fairness often motivates behaviour or determines value judgements.[8]

Economics cannot contribute to knowledge if it has a deeply flawed understanding of human beings and what makes them happy. The new reality-based economics will have to free itself from the blinkers imposed by mainstream theories.

The German and Japanese challenge

In many ways, all of these findings are not new. The new kind of economics has an old predecessor. So has neoclassical economics: The direct forerunner of modern mainstream economics, operating with similar assumptions and coming to similar conclusions, was British classical economics of the nineteenth century. It already operated according to the deductivist paradigm.[9] At the time Britain was the world's leading economic and political power, running a world empire and mass-producing advanced industrial output that required a market. Classical economics appeared to serve a useful purpose for the empire: it recommended that other countries did not need to develop competing industries, or use government intervention, but instead should open their markets, without charging any tariffs, to British exports. This would – said the British classical economics – improve their welfare. Not surprisingly, classical economics was used to advance British power worldwide.

Thus it came that German economists were also confronted with the British classical school of thought. The German economists, like scientists from other disciplines, at the time used the inductive methodology. So they decided to empirically evaluate the British classical theories and their claims. Friedrich List, one of the first and most influential development economists, decided to investigate the British claim that deregulation, liberalization and opening up to free trade and free markets was the path to prosperity and economic development (just like it has been the Washington claim for the past decades). He developed the testable hypothesis that, if this claim was true, the major episodes of successful national economic development should be somehow linked to free trade and free market policies.

Studying the facts by meticulously researching the historical record of economic development of the major economic powers over the centuries, List concluded that there was not one major economic power that owed its successful development to free trade and free market policies. His conclusion still stands – although we now have the benefit of 150 years of further, and better, data on the world economy. List is particularly insightful on British economic development. He found that although British leaders were loudest in propagating the free market paradigm, British economic development was due to trade restrictions, protectionism, government intervention, industrial policy and other 'visible hands'. Until about the fifteenth and early sixteenth centuries, Britain indeed followed the precepts of free market economics by allowing *laissez-faire* trade and focusing on its comparative advantage. As a result it remained primarily a nation of shepherds, selling raw wool to foreign merchants. Economic prosperity did not grow significantly. Britain remained poor and underdeveloped. Researchers on modern-day developing countries have identified the reason: focusing on low-value-added primary commodities will not enhance welfare. High-value-added items will be imported, but their relative prices rise over time, while that of commodities falls – thus resulting in a steady deterioration of the terms of trade. Balance of payments crises and indebtedness follow.

In Britain's case this took the form of the Crown jewels being pawned to the dominating German traders. When the British leadership realized that the invisible hand was not doing much for the country, free trade was abandoned; protectionist trade and industrial policies were adopted. The government intervened by importing foreign know-how in high-value-added textile manufacturing – through importing experts from Flanders (as the now common surname Fleming attests), banning the import of processed wool products, stimulating domestic wool production through industrial policy and building a fleet of ships to market its produce.

The British textile industry was established by government intervention. Its mechanization triggered the industrial revolution, rendering Britain the top economic and military power. To boost British mass exports, convincing public relations activities had to persuade the rest of the world to open their markets. Classical economics served this purpose. Britain itself knew better: while British economists spoke of free trade and the theory of comparative advantage, the far superior and cheaper Indian textile produce was banned from Britain.

As List showed, the empirical facts are similar in the case of the US. The North American colonies were explicitly forbidden to manufacture anything for export and instead had to focus on their 'comparative advantage' in agriculture. The policy of suppressing the creation of indigenous industries in its American colonies while forcing them to purchase the fruits of the 'free markets' from Britain was identified by List as a factor in causing the War of Independence. The US started to develop rapidly when it replaced the 'free trade' regime imposed by Britain with protectionist trade barriers and government industrial policy to create high-value-added industries. At the same time, the British propaganda of free trade and free markets was copied in order to force world markets open for US exports. The rest is history.

Thus when German economists considered the virtues of classical economics over a hundred years ago, they rejected it as unrealistic and inapplicable to reality. Instead, they developed a different kind of economics that is based on realistic assumptions, such as that people care about others; that market imperfections are pervasive and that there is positive scope for fruitful government intervention – for instance in the purposeful designing of incentive structures and the allocation of resources to high-value-added industries, within a framework that aimed at social justice and was guided by both realistic and ethical considerations. These theories – dubbed variously the German empiricist approach, the German Historical School or the German ethical economics – had a profound impact on Japan and other East Asian countries, which studied them, adopted them and followed their policy advice.

The leaders, having read their German economists well, realized that the *laissez-faire* policy suggested by Britain would relegate developing countries to raw material exporter status and hence low growth. To achieve high growth, comparative advantage had to be created, through the visible intervention of government policy, primarily in the form of clever institutional design, but also in the measured allocation of resources. The Germans and East Asians used economic regulation to foster technological development and the development and competitiveness of targeted high-value-added industries. Furthermore, growth in itself was not considered the main goal of an economy. For a stable society, economic justice was also important – and again this would not come about without a visible hand.

As a result, the Germans and Japanese consciously created a different form of capitalism, which maintained market mechanisms, but ensured that not shareholders but society at large would be its main beneficiaries. Many aspects of the Japanese model were introduced in the successful East Asian economies. Instead of serving the few, a form of capitalism was born that succeeded in creating a decent quality of life for the many. By focusing on mutually beneficial cooperation and coordination, the designers of the German and Japanese systems managed to internalize externalities (costs and benefits not reflected in markets), minimize information costs, mobilize resources and motivate individuals. They recognized that people compete in hierarchical fashion and have a common desire for justice and fairness of organizational arrangements. They then succeeded in devising organizational forms that can reap benefits from cooperation in ways that all participants can consider fair. One such organizational form was the system of industry associations, which were a modern incarnation of the medieval guild structure. Due to their public goods character, resulting cartels often were welfare-enhancing. The cooperative orientation did not mean that there was no competition. That was encouraged in the form of competing for moving up ranks in hierarchies. Much more needs to be said on their approach, but this remains beyond the scope of the present book (see Werner, 2003c, 2003d, 2004c).

Reality-based economics, following the inductivist approach, was pioneered by German economists in the nineteenth century. Their writings emphasized credit and institutional design. This provides a final test of the validity of our approach: if their work was right, then those countries that followed their prescriptions, including the direction and allocation of credit and the shaping of overall institutions, should have performed well. These countries were Germany in the twentieth century, Japan, Korea and Taiwan since the late 1930s, and China since the 1980s, to name the most important examples. For many decades, their economic performance has been superior to that of most other countries. This, then, solves the final enigma, discussed in Chapter 5, namely that of the puzzlingly high economic growth of these countries.

24
A New Vision of
Macroeconomic Policy

... over the past decade or so, central banks have been made more independent and more accountable. The result has been the virtual elimination of the inflation bias problem that is caused by political interference in the monetary policy process, and better overall macroeconomic performance.

(Cecchetti, 2000)

We live in the Age of the Central Banker – an era in which Greenspan, Duisenberg, and Hayami are household words, in which monetary policy is generally believed to be so effective that it cannot safely be left in the hands of politicians who might use it to their advantage. Through much of the world, quasi-independent central banks are now entrusted with the job of steering economies between the rocks of inflation and the whirlpool of deflation. Their judgment is often questioned, but their power is not.

(Krugman, 2000)

The Fed, the European Central Bank and the Bank of Japan together set monetary policy for a zone that accounts for 80 per cent of the world's industrialized economic activity ... Rarely, if ever, can so much power have been wielded by such a small number of institutions sitting outside the direct democratic process.

(Goldman Sachs, quoted in Grant, 2000)

Neoclassical economics demonstrated that there is significant room for welfare-enhancing government intervention, because the conditions under which government intervention is inefficient are so unusual and exceptional that they do not apply anywhere in this world. Neoclassical economics showed that in the real world (as opposed to a theoretical dream-world), free markets cannot possibly lead to a social optimum. This means that there is a sound case for developing countries to oppose unmitigated free trade, for implementing suitable industrial policy to enhance growth and welfare, for organizing economies in a more cooperative fashion, for successfully establishing a more inclusive form of capitalism that provides social welfare for all and treats all people as valuable human beings.

Our specific findings concerning the credit creation process, a more realistic description of macroeconomics and the role played by the central bank leads us to the conclusion that in Japan the central bank has been excessively independent, lacking transparency in its policy implementation and unaccountable for its actions.

These findings remind us of just how powerful a central bank is. It can control the creation and allocation of claims on resources. It is thus in many ways more powerful than the government. Yet worldwide, central banks have become independent of and unaccountable to governments. Central bank independence has been one of the key demands made by the IMF in its dozens of adjustment policies all over the world. The US troops in Iraq quickly set up an 'independent' central bank as one of the policy priorities. What can be the meaning of democracy, if the most powerful function is not subject to any democratic checks and balances?

The Japanese case adds to the growing body of literature that finds economic arguments for removing central banks from control by democratically elected institutions neither compelling on theoretical nor empirical grounds (see, for instance, Forder, 1998a, 1998b, 1999, 2000). As long as we have a preference for a democratic institutional environment, political arguments for central bank independence are even less compelling. Milton Friedman, experienced in dealing with the world's central banks, recommends returning central banks to direct supervision by the government.

'The Fed is not subject to an effective budget constraint. It prints its own money to pay its expenses. The Federal Reserve does not have to face the voters' (Friedman, 1982, p. 114). Increased oversight by the parliament has not worked in the case of the Fed – concluded a Fed economist: 'It appears safe to conclude that increased Congressional oversight has not altered the conduct of monetary policy' (Pierce, 1978, p. 369). Pierce shows how the Fed has responded to any attempts at oversight with highly technical and obfuscating argumentation. That is why Friedman suggests

> either make the Federal Reserve a bureau in the Treasury under the secretary of the Treasury, or ... put the Federal Reserve under direct congressional control. Either involves terminating the so-called independence of the system. But either would establish a strong incentive for the Fed to produce a stabler monetary environment than we have had. (Friedman, 1982, p. 118)

Economists with conflicts of interest

Many economists have come to see deep flaws in studies that claim a link between more central bank independence and low inflation (see, for instance,

Forder, 1998b, 1999; Daunfeldt and de Luna, 2003). There is no sound empirical evidence that greater central bank independence leads to lower inflation. Furthermore, there is no evidence that more central bank independence leads to better macroeconomic performance, in terms of higher growth and less unemployment.

There are many economists who do claim that more central bank independence is desirable. However, empirical research, based on fieldwork and interviews with central bankers, has indicated that the relationship between the media and central bankers as well as between economists and central bankers may be more problematic than commonly assumed in the economics literature (Werner, 2004c). Further research is needed concerning the ways in which media information may be influenced by interested parties. Similarly, the question whether economists may be interested parties themselves cannot be avoided.

The issue of conflicts of interest in financial markets has received much media attention, especially since the fraud, accounting scandals and illegal activities involving large financial institutions were highlighted by New York Attorney General Elliot Spitzer. Spitzer scrutinized and publicly criticized the established practices of many large financial institutions. Today, equity analysts, for instance, announce their personal financial interests when they publish their analyses and recommendations. However, the same is not yet true for economists and academic researchers. Ironically, many economists assume in their models that agents rationally maximize their own self-interest, even if this neglects social or ethical norms or is of detriment to society at large. Given such publicly stated beliefs in the importance of such behaviour, it is surprising that economists themselves have not yet been subjected to greater scrutiny concerning possible conflicts of interest.

Recent findings suggest that there could be multiple motivations for the central bank in paying academics to act as consultants, advisers and presenters and to join central banks on lucrative 'advisory' contracts (see Werner, 2004c). Further research is needed concerning the degree of involvement of central banks in academia, whether in the form of sponsorship, invitations, publishing papers of academics in their journals and sending staff to attend international academic conferences.[1]

Meanwhile, the ECB announced in July 2004 that, together with other central banks, it will found a new journal that will cover 'central bank theory and practice'. The 'International Journal of Central Banking' will 'disseminate widely the best policy-relevant and applied research on central banking and to promote communication among researchers both inside and outside of central banks' (ECB, 2004). So far, the journals and publications produced by central banks have been almost exclusively based on deductive neoclassical economic theories, with little grounding in empiricism. Further, they have failed to cover all relevant aspects of central bank 'practice' or economic reality, and thus cannot be considered a forum for the objective discussion of central banking. To the contrary, there is evidence that central banks are interested parties, and thus the onus is on them to demonstrate that their publications are not merely tools to further their political goals.

Democratic macroeconomic policy

Having gained some insights into the actual goals of monetary policy in Japan, we can now briefly consider what monetary policy, as well as fiscal and structural policies *should* aim at.

Fiscal policy is growth neutral, and hence should be used sparingly and with the awareness that it is purely a redistributional policy. To avoid inefficient deadweight losses to society through needless government debt issuance and wasteful interest payments, the principle of a balanced budget should apply.

Structural and regulatory policy is important, since in a world of imperfect information the government has the important task of designing institutional and organizational settings of society in such a way that individuals are given the right incentives to work towards the overall goals of society, with maximum freedom for their individual action and the least amount of direct intervention necessary. This requires much more research on the topic of clever institutional design and incentive structure design – a topic of utmost importance in public policy. Beyond the shaping of institutional settings via formal and informal rules and regulations, structural policy can also be implemented through a reallocation of resources towards the type of society that is desired. The key tool for such intervention is monetary policy, which thus has functions beyond mere cyclical policy.

Monetary policy is the most powerful macroeconomic policy, since it not only affects economic growth, but can also reshape society. Given the power of monetary policy to control and allocate resources in the economy, it should be directly operated by an institution that is part of the democratic process, such as the ministry of finance or Treasury. Its operation should be transparent and accountable so that the overall goals of society can be reflected and deviations towards vested interest groups can be prevented or stopped early.

The fundamental principles of monetary policy in an institutional setting that allows for private credit-creating banks are not difficult: to minimize inflation and maximize real economic growth, credit should be created and allocated primarily for productive purposes. Consumer credit and speculative credit will result in consumer price or asset price inflation and hence should be avoided.

The specific type of mechanism most suitable to allocate credit for productive purposes requires further research. Historically, since the pioneering work of the Reichsbank, these have centred on credit controls of the type witnessed in Japan in the form of 'window guidance' (see Werner, 2003c,

2003d). Such credit controls have been used by almost all central banks in the past, and they operated by central bankers instructing banks to follow quotas for credit growth and prescribed sectoral allocation of loan extension. They should, however, not be decided in a non-transparent way by institutions that are not directly accountable for their actions and not directly part of the political process. Allowing privately-owned central banks, for instance, is unlikely to be the right type of incentive structure to ensure alignment of sectarian and overall interests. But even publicly-owned central banks will not be sufficient, if they can obtain a large degree of *de facto* independence.

Once the facts of credit creation and its potential are more widely known, democratic processes can be used to decide upon the goals that should be achieved and the most suitable mechanism to achieve them. A clever use of institutional design and credit allocation will allow far more ambitious goals to be implemented than has so far been the case. Not only recessions, unemployment and boom-bust cycles, but also poverty and destitution can in principle be eliminated.

As an example, an improved form of macroeconomic management can thus take the following form: through democratic institutions, society decides upon overall goals that the economy should fulfil. This may for instance be environmentally sustainable, stable economic growth which gives highest priority to quality of life of present and future generations. To achieve this goal, the democratically accountable credit control mechanism would openly discuss and decide upon a priority ranking for the issuance of credit. Thus research into new environmentally friendly energy sources may be given priority, as well as the creation of green urban spaces and leisure areas. Credit would then be created to fund such research or investment in such projects. Meanwhile, purely wasteful or environmentally destructive type of activities or activities that affect the well being of the people negatively would not receive newly created purchasing power. The decisions would have to be made in the open and subject to debates and voting.

Other societies may still be in a phase of development where fast economic growth is necessary. In that case, the goals and implementation of the credit allocation mechanism can be set similar to those of Japan in the 1960s. For instance, the role of shareholders could be restricted and managers given more influence over company policy. If a society decides that its population is not growing fast enough – as is the case in many industrialized countries – it could use the credit creating institutions to provide monetary incentives to childbearing families. Every childbearing family could, for instance, be paid $100,000 for each child born, perhaps administered such that withdrawals are only allowed for specific purposes, and then society would most likely be able to achieve its goal of increasing population. Such a policy would not be inflationary: among all inputs into the production function, human resources are by far the most important. Therefore this is the best example of productive credit creation, as long as resources are also spent on a high level of education.

Empirically, humans value low levels of inequality. Such goals can also be made explicit and achieved through institutional design. Interest rates could be kept at very low levels, or abolished entirely, since they create deadweight losses and lead to an inefficient concentration of wealth in the hands of a few.

Each time such intervention is decided upon, however, the details of the incentive structure must be well-designed, weighing the benefits and disadvantages or potential abuses of intervention, to achieve a simple and robust set-up. Also, from the start there should already be explicit exit mechanisms concerning the phasing out of the programme.

Some immediate goals

The implementation of such goals may be impractical in the short term, especially since vested interests that have benefited from the traditional set-up (with private credit creation used for sectarian interests) are unlikely to relinquish their influence easily.

Thus a more pragmatic and immediate goal may be to make legal changes so as to enable the government to impose a nominal GDP growth target that the central bank will be required to meet within a given time period (within a predetermined error margin and with severe, credible penalties on all senior staff for non-compliance) (Werner, 1997b, 1999d, 1999j, 2001a, 2002b).[2] Further, the government should ensure that its authority to supervise banks is used to monitor the allocation of credit and intervene when necessary in order to avoid unproductive credit creation.

Better still would be to ensure that the status of central banks, which are at the centre of the credit creation and allocation mechanism, is changed again. While it is commonly believed that central banks have not been independent enough, research shows that central banks have *de facto* had a high degree of independence and lacked any accountability concerning the monetary policy tool that matters most – the quantity and allocation of credit. Thus a change in the status of central banks is needed. This is especially true for central banks such as the ECB, whose legal status is somewhat of an anomaly: the ECB is independent not only of governments, but also of parliaments. The mere attempt at influencing the ECB – for instance through democratic debate and discussion – is forbidden according to the Maastricht Treaty (see Werner, 2003c). Given this surprising reality, those countries that have so far refused to join the euro system appear to have taken the wiser decision.

Subjecting the decision-making power over credit growth and its allocation in society to democratic controls must be the first step towards applying the new paradigm in economics and realizing the kind of economic policy that delivers better, more equitable results than the current mainstream approach.

Notes

Prologue

1 Roland Berger, Making Germany fit for the future, *Financial Times*, 8 July 2002.
2 Ibid.
3 Paul A. Samuelson, Free market key to prosperity, *Daily Yomiuri*, 24 June 2002.
4 See, for instance, Sim (2004). See also Philip Coggan, Fundamentalism explored, *Financial Times*, 8 April 2004.
5 An important, eloquent and influential early contribution was made by Chalmers Johnson, for instance, in Johnson (1982).
6 There is a tendency for economists, knowing *a priori* that only free markets can lead to success, therefore also to 'know' that Chinese economic success must have been due to free markets – without the need to back up this claim with empirical evidence. However, there can be little doubt that the Chinese economy relies heavily on government regulation and intervention, far more so than, for instance, economies in Europe. Even the *Financial Times*, usually among those prone to claim the Chinese success as evidence of the superiority of free markets, has occasionally conceded that the Chinese economy is 'Essentially a command economy' (*Financial Times*, Lex Column, 3 May 2004).
7 For a recent overview of his thinking and further references to his extensive work, see Stiglitz and Greenwald (2003).
8 The actual number is likely to be much larger, since many temporary and part-time staff have withdrawn from the workforce and are therefore not officially counted among the unemployed.
9 In the case of Russia, this is now recognized and documented to some extent by the World Bank, previously a major proponent of privatization in developing countries. See Andrew Jack, Oligarchs: A map of Russia's new empires, *Financial Times*, 7 April 2004.
10 As recently acknowledged by the IMF deputy managing director, neoclassical economist Anne Krueger; see Anne Krueger, Educating globalization's Luddites, *Financial Times*, 16 April 2004.
11 Bob Sherwood, Super-rich get richer as their fortunes grow 30%, *Financial Times*, 19 April 2004.
12 'Russia is dominated by a small number of business groups that are less efficient than other private sector owners and have captured a big slice of investment flows', says a World Bank report released today. After sampling more than 1,300 companies, the study concludes Russia's 23 largest business groups control more than a third of its industry by sales and at least a sixth of its jobs. The politically influential business "oligarchs" built their vast wealth from the privatisation of the 1990s', writes the *Financial Times* (Andrew Jack, Russia's oligarchs not efficient says World Bank, *Financial Times*, 7 April 2004).
13 There are now many studies in the field of happiness research. That money does not make one happy is a consistent result. See, for instance, the recent study by MORI, the opinion research firm: Life satisfaction and trust in other people, 2004, www.mori.com.

14 Even an otherwise mainstream economist such as Samuel Brittan appears to agree. See Samuel Brittan, There's more to life than growth, *Financial Times*, 26 March 2004.
15 Jon Boone, Debt fears make students depressed, *Financial Times*, 17/18 April 2004.
16 This is increasingly recognized even in the mainstream financial media; see Richard Tomkins, All we needed was love. Instead we got pornography, *Financial Times*, 26 March 2004.
17 Nicholas Timmins, CBI head calls for academy to teach community skills, *Financial Times*, 19 April 2004.
18 See Post-Autistic Economics Review at www.paecon.net.
19 For instance, research by the *Sunday Times* found that Tesco and Safeway, as well as Sainsbury's, Waitrose and Asda, all charged more for products purchased in bulk than for the same products purchased in smaller quantities or individually. See Jack Grimston and Andrew White, Bulk buys cost more than single items, *Sunday Times*, 27 June 2004.
20 Inductivism also requires the use of deductive logic. However, the analysis starts with empirical facts, and ends with testing and reformulating theories on the basis of constant empirical checking. Deductivism, by contrast, can be and often is wholly divorced from empirical reality.
21 For a concise exposé of inductivism and deductivism, including a cogent criticism of the latter, see Hay (1989). For the seminal work on the topic, see John Stuart Mill (1834).
22 On this topic, see the growing literature on the 'rhetoric' of neoclassical economics. For instance, McCloskey (1987, 1994).
23 Recent studies of British World War I propaganda have given a glimpse of the extent of misinformation used in democratic societies to motivate populations for war – a success noticed and subsequently utilized by numerous undemocratic regimes.
24 See, for instance, Philip Coggan, Fundamentalism explored, *Financial Times*, 8 April 2004. See also Martin Wolf, How managing growth can consign poverty to history, *Financial Times*, 5 May 2004.

Chapter 1

1 Philip Coggan, Will the US economy soar or belly-flop?, *Financial Times*, 26/27 July 2003.
2 Speech at the University of Wuerzburg in Germany on 7 February 2001 (Matsuda, 2001).
3 Takatoshi Ito (2000): 'The usual counter-cyclical macroeconomic policies have not worked in Japan in the second half of the 1990s, or at least not well enough' (p. 85). Paul Krugman (1998b): 'And the usual remedies for inadequate demand aren't working. Interest rates have been pushed down almost as far as they can go…The big public spending projects the Japanese government launches every now and then do create some jobs, but they never seem to yield enough bang for the yen: The economy keeps relapsing, while government debt keeps mounting' (p. 2).
4 See Mikitani (2000) for estimates of the cumulative output gap from 1992 through 1998.
5 Bank of Japan Governor Hayami (2002) put it this way: 'Strong monetary easing and large-scale fiscal spending were employed continuously during the 1990s.

Reflecting such monetary easing, monetary base and money stock continued to increase at a fairly rapid pace compared to the level of economic activity. Japan's economy, however, failed to return to a sustainable growth path. This clearly demonstrates that monetary easing cannot change banks' lending attitude, economic activity, and prices when there are various structural problems ...' (p. 4).

6 The former is from Hoshi and Patrick (2000, p. xi), the latter borrows partly from Dore (2000).

7 See, for instance, the widely-noted IMF paper by Kumar et al. (2003), or Krugman (2003).

Chapter 2

1 See Werner (2003c) for an introduction to the political economy of the decision-making process leading to the issuance of bonds, and the role played by the Bank of Japan in promoting the amendment of the Finance Law.

2 For an overview of the movement of fiscal deficits in the 1970s and 1980s, see Asako et al. (1991). See also Ihori et al. (2000).

3 See the official statements at the announcement of stimulation packages. For instance: 'Keikyū keizai taisaku (yōshi)', 16 November 1999, Economic Planning Agency (available at: www5.cao.go.jp/98/b/19981116b-taisakuyousi.html).

4 The overstatement could be due to double-counting items that had already been part of previous packages or budgets (for instance, when previous budget targets had not been fully met).

5 There were important tax reductions in 1994 and 1998. However, at other times, fiscal policy tightened. Hoshi and Patrick (2000) estimate that the 1997 ending of income tax rebates and the rise of the consumption tax from 3% to 5% increased government revenues by about 2 percentage points of GDP.

6 Dornbusch and Fischer (1987) emphasize that 'the distinction between selling debt to the public and selling it to the central bank is essential. The distinction between money and debt financing can be further clarified by noting that Treasury sales of securities to the central bank are referred to as *monetizing the debt*, meaning that the central bank creates (high-powered) money to finance the debt purchases' (p. 584).

7 The central bank can purchase government bonds in the secondary market one year after issuance. Economically, this is equivalent to primary market purchase. The political circumstances are different, since the government may not be able to determine the extent to which bonds are purchased by the central bank. Despite legal lack of independence, since the 1970s the central bank has independently made this decision.

8 Indeed, the government's borrowing is another measure of the stance of fiscal policy.

9 This suggestion was made by Werner (1994b, 1995a, 1995c, 1998c, 1998f, 2002b, 2000d, 2003a, 2003b, 2003c) and will be revisited in Part III.

10 The list has perhaps become shorter due to the apparent inability of fiscal stimulation to create a recovery. Supporters of fiscal spending programmes had at least become less vocal towards the end of the decade.

11 'Fiscal expansion under a liquidity trap will not increase the interest rate, and thus will not crowd out private investment' (Ito, 2000, p. 101).

12 'So far, a straight Keynesian prescription applies' (ibid., p. 102).

13 This was the most common calculation, used by Japanese private sector research institutions, as well as key government agencies. See, for instance, the Economic Planning Agency's Nagatani (1996), who argues in favour of fiscal stimulation on the basis of the argument that 'Even when the ripple-on effect is zero, fiscal stimulation policy will still at least have the "direct effect", which is that ¥1 trillion of increase in public investment will result in a ¥1 trillion in GDP increase.'

14 Posen follows a calculation common in financial markets in Tokyo, namely to distinguish between investment that 'adds to demand' – so-called *mamizu* – and that which does not. The *mamizu* is defined as including increased public spending and tax cuts. Loan programmes offered by government-affiliated institutions to the private sector and funded by postal savings deposits investment is deemed not to add to demand, but merely reallocating funding among various projects. The important insight from this distinction is the necessity to distinguish between government spending that increases net purchasing power in the economy, and government spending that merely reallocates existing purchasing power. However, the way this is attempted by the *mamizu* calculation is flawed. A meaningful distinction must focus on the credit creation process and include the central bank and the banking system, rendering true *mamizu* the monetized part of fiscal policy (see Part III).

15 Ito follows Posen's (1998) recommendations and suggests further stimulation in the form of lasting income tax cuts and tax incentives to stimulate private housing investment (Ito, 2000, pp. 103ff.). As Dirk Bezemer pointed out, there is a parallel to the proponents of privatization and liberalization who argue that those countries where these policies failed did not do enough of it.

16 Ito recognizes this, but leaves the questions raised unanswered. 'The question remains as to what prevented the economy from getting back on a self-sustained growth path. Was it the series of bad shocks? Or has the dynamic spill-over effect of fiscal packages become smaller in the 1990s? Or was the amount of actual stimulus smaller than generally recognized?' (Ito, 2000, p. 102). No attempts at answers follow, thus rendering the efficacy of fiscal expenditure an axiomatic assumption.

17 This line of reasoning falls far short of Popper's methodological principles. It may well be in the tradition of deductivist economics, which takes little interest in empirical evidence and concludes from any gap between theory and reality that the latter needs changing, not the former. However, it defies common sense. Nevertheless, even in the absence of omniscience concerning exogenous shocks, it is possible to test hypotheses concerning the *cause* of potential fiscal policy *in*effectiveness (see below).

18 While proto-monetarist formulations did not rely on interest rates, but the equation of exchange, as outlined below, and early monetarists (wisely?) said little about the precise transmission mechanism between money and the economy, later monetarist models (such as Friedman, 1956, Brunner and Meltzer, 1976) accepted the Keynesian interest-elasticity of the demand for money and thus argued that the ineffectiveness of fiscal policy relies on perverse wealth effects associated with bond-financed government spending, operating via interest rates (see Blinder and Solow, 1973). Since interest rates failed to rise during the 1990s, such later monetarist models are not suitable to explain the Japanese experience and will not be discussed further.

19 See Christ (1968), Friedman (1978), Blinder and Solow (1973), Ludvigson (1996). Those who argued that 'portfolio crowding in' may offset 'transactions crowding

out' and thus produce either a positive or ambiguous effect of debt-funded fiscal stimulation (such as Friedman, 1978) do not contribute towards finding an answer to the phenomenon observed in Japan during the 1990s, namely no significant rises in interest rates, but also no significant effect of fiscal stimulation.

20 Other proponents could especially be found among current or former Ministry of Finance officials, who had a tendency to oppose fiscal stimulation and argue in favour of monetary stimulation, while the Japanese central bank argued the opposite. In Part III we will see whose view has been more in line with the empirical facts.

21 Examples of empirical studies of the link between fiscal policy and interest rates in the US are Hutchison and Pyle (1984) and Hoelscher (1986). For examples and reviews of empirical work on the influence of fiscal policy on aggregate demand, see, for instance, Aschauer (1985) and Tatom (1985).

22 The annual average of the prime lending rate has declined every single year during the 1990s.

23 Proponents of interest rate crowding out could argue that the fall in interest rates happened *despite* the crowding out. Then, either interest rates would have fallen further without the fiscal spending, or they would have risen due to it, but other exogenous factors pushed them back down. But again, this argument stretches credulity. It seems that it has therefore in practice become accepted – in this case – to adopt a *mutatis mutandis* definition of crowding out.

24 McKibbin (1996) engages in this difficult exercise, making use of a multi-country structural model to endogenize shocks to the Japanese economy. Pointing out the anticipated nature of the fiscal spending packages (and their partial overstatement), he concludes: 'Rather than stimulating the economy, these fiscal measures acted to further slow economic activity as well as appreciate the real exchange rate' (p. 37). In McKibbin's model, the announcement effect of fiscal stimulation occurs immediately, appreciating the exchange rate and real long-term interest rates, while the positive effect occurs later, or to a lesser extent than announced (due to overstatement of the package). However, only data through 1995 is used, thus missing much of the 400 basis point drop in long-term interest rates over three and a half years, from about 4.7% in February 1995 to 0.7% in October 1998, not to mention the further drop to 0.43% by June 2003.

25 Walker (2002), for instance, says: 'The possibility of a crowding-out effect of government spending on investment is dismissed *ex ante*, given Japan's low real interest rates in recent years' (p. 286).

26 The argument that debt could be paid for by non-inflationary money creation cannot be handled by the type of models Krugman refers to, because due to further assumptions, including perfect information, they do not usually allow for the possibility of less than full employment output. With record-high unemployment and a ten-year recession in Japan, the relevance of such models is not entirely obvious.

27 If the fiscal stimulus takes the form of tax reductions for individuals and not increased government spending, then savings increase, while consumption remains unchanged – as the higher disposable income is not used for spending. If the fiscal stimulus takes the form of increased government spending on investment projects, incomes will not necessarily rise, thus consumption may not necessarily rise. But savings would rise. Since fiscal stimulation took the form of a combination of government spending and income tax changes (with the emphasis being clearly on government spending, though), the expected movement of consumption would be ambiguous with Barro-Ricardian equivalence. But the

behaviour of savings would unambiguously have to be counter-directional to the movement of government borrowing.

28 Walker (2002) also fails to test Ricardian equivalence directly. Instead, noting the low fiscal multipliers for Japan in the 1990s, he proposes a theory according to which the fiscal multiplier declines the larger the *level* of the budget deficit. He argues that government spending does exert a wealth effect on consumption, but one that is 'proportionate to the amount of waste in the budget'. Without providing empirical evidence, Walker assumes that 'the average quality of public spending decreases with the level of spending'. Walker finds a positive fiscal multiplier, contradicting Ricardian equivalence. Making a number of auxiliary assumptions, Walker defines as a large fiscal deficit one that amounts to more than 6–7% of output and finds that 'there is a threshold beyond which the effectiveness of fiscal spending falls off sharply' (p. 298). There is no test for robustness of these findings over different time periods or in other countries. Further, Walker says nothing about the mechanism by which the effectiveness of fiscal spending is reduced. Walker really argues that since fiscal policy was ineffective in Japan in the 1990s, and since it was large, it must have been *too large to be effective*. Thus the main question of concern, namely why steady and significant fiscal stimulation during the 1990s failed to trigger a significant and sustained economic recovery, remains unanswered: by arguing that fiscal policy was too large to be effective, Walker neglects to explain why fiscal policy, when it was not too large (and not too small), also failed to produce the desired results. Finally, Walker fails to address previous literature that discussed the issue of the absolute size of fiscal deficits and government debts. Most previous theories failed to attach much significance to the size of the fiscal deficit or national debt. One early example is Lerner's (1943) case that 'the absolute size of the national debt does not matter at all' (p. 47).

Chapter 3

1 The new Bank of Japan Law is available at www.boj.or.jp. Unlike the provisions of the Maastricht Treaty, in Japan democratically elected institutions will not breach laws or agreements by the mere attempt to influence the central bank's policies.

2 Cargill et al. (2000) summarize their argument as follows: 'There may be a significant difference between practical and legal independence. The Bank of Japan during the two decades prior to the 1998 revision [of the Bank of Japan Law] is a clear example of this difference. Starting in the mid-1970s, the Bank of Japan secured meaningful practical independence (Cargill, Hutchison and Ito, 1997), but lacked the legal basis because it continued to operate under the 1942 Law' (p. 111).

3 The starting shot was fired by then Vice Minister of Finance for International Affairs, Makoto Utsumi, in 1990. He vigorously criticized Bank of Japan governor Yasushi Mieno for excessive monetary tightening. Leading LDP politician Shin Kanemaru demanded Mieno's resignation. Mieno eventually lowered interest rates in 1991, which relieved political pressure on the central bank. However, as we will see, monetary policy remained tight. The subsequent recession severely damaged the standing of Ōkurashō, the old Ministry of Finance. Consequently, the Ministry failed to utter significant further public critique of monetary policy until its unceremonious end in January 2001. The other outstanding period of serious policy disagreement between the government and the central bank therefore had

to wait until the end of the decade. Since late 1998, critique of the central bank's policies has become a frequent theme of leading LDP politicians and members of the government (for instance, Chief Cabinet Secretary Hiromu Nonaka and Economic Planning Agency chief Taiichi Sakaiya in early 1999).

4 The research organs of the central bank produce regular, usually monthly and quarterly publications, in addition to irregular publications. In addition to the anonymous summaries of the Policy Board minutes, many Policy Board members give frequent speeches and lectures that inform us of their views. The spokesmen of the Bank of Japan include central bankers who must be considered 'practitioners', as well as many trained economists, who are employed by the central bank either in its economic and statistical research department, its Institute for Monetary and Economic Studies, or as members of the Policy Board, which *de jure* is designated as the highest decision-making body of the central bank. Cargill et al. (2000) make the point that the Policy Board, despite its strong legal powers, 'failed to assume this power and instead generally approved whatever the Bank staff through the Executive Board recommended' (p. 134). They then assert that the legal changes of 1998 have 'reinstated' the Policy Board 'as the primary policy-making body of the Bank of Japan ...' (p. 134). There has, however, so far been no empirical evidence that the actual function of the Policy Board has changed substantially, compared to the pre-1998 period.

5 Okina (1999) argued that already at that time monetary policy was 'historically unprecedented'.

6 The downward trend of nominal interest rates continued after the observation period of the 1990s, most dramatically in June 2003, when the ten-year benchmark government bond yield briefly dropped to 0.4%.

7 According to this definition there would also be other examples of a liquidity trap. For instance, the US in the 1940s also recorded near-zero interest rates, though productive capacity was arguably more fully employed.

8 In correspondence, Keynes explicitly disagreed with the Hicksian IS-LM interpretation of his liquidity trap (see Kregel, 2000). Consequently, in a strictly Keynesian sense the solution to a strictly Keynesian definition of a liquidity trap would be to peg long-term interest rates (as was done in the US during World War II; see Friedman, 1982). Kregel (2000), adopting Keynes' definition, thus argues that instead of being in a liquidity trap, Japan is in an underemployment equilibrium with deficient aggregate demand.

9 One-period bonds are traded at the beginning of each period.

10 'The problem is ... that the full-employment real interest rate is negative. And monetary policy therefore cannot get the economy to full employment unless the central bank can convince the public that the future inflation rate will be sufficiently high to permit the negative real interest rate. That's all there is to it' (Krugman, 1998d).

11 High powered money rose 25% from 1994 to 1997, while M2 + CD grew only 11%; as quoted by Cargill et al. (2000), p. 116.

12 Structural reform is defined by Krugman to include a clean-up of the banking system, a definition borrowed by the Koizumi administration in 2001.

13 'Unless one can make a convincing case that structural reform or fiscal expansion will provide the necessary demand, the only way to expand the economy is to reduce the real interest rate; and the only way to do that is to create expectations of inflation' (Krugman, 1998a, p. 12).

14 As evidence for their argument, they cite surveys conducted by the Bank of Japan, asking firms about their perception of the lending attitude of banks. They support

inflation targeting on the following grounds: (1) it would enhance transparency and accountability (indeed, Werner, 1998d, 1999a, 2002a, found evidence of severe lack of transparency and accountability); (2) the task of explaining monetary policy would become easier and policy changes could be explained without loss of credibility; (3) the parameters of the central bank's independence would be well-defined: it would have operational or instrument independence, though not goal independence; (4) the imposition of an inflation target 'likely would have a positive impact on financial markets and the economy as a whole' by helping to 'dispel the deflationary uncertainties that prevailed at the end of the 1990s' (Cargill et al., 2000, p. 133).

15 Short-term interbank rates were briefly pushed into negative territory by the Swiss central bank in early 1997. See Kugler and Rich (2001). A part of the overnight call market also temporarily recorded negative nominal interest rates in January and again in June 2003.

16 See also Krugman (2000), in which he concludes: 'No matter how much the monetary base increases, as long as expectations are not affected it will simply be a swap of one zero-interest asset for another, with no real effects' (p. 234).

17 See Itoh and Shimoi (2000), for instance, for a reiteration of Krugman's case.

18 The Bank of Japan stated in 1999 that it will maintain near-zero interest rates until 'deflationary fears subside', and in 2001 it said that it will maintain them until there is no more deflation.

19 'With severe limitations on instruments to ease monetary policy, however, I fear that an announcement of the target date by which to achieve, say, zero percent inflation, would have either no effects on the market or be counterproductive. The market may lose confidence in a central bank announcing a hard-to-hit target' (Ueda, 2001a). It is hard to conceive, however, how investors could lose any more confidence in the ability of the Bank of Japan.

20 'The BoJ's helplessness is particularly evident in the liquidity trap with a zero interest rate and unchanged foreign exchange expectations. Thus, Dr. Okina is perfectly right in saying that simply announcing a high inflation target (as called for by Krugman [1998a, 1998b]) would not be credible as long as the BoJ has not the means to implement it' (MacKinnon, 1999, pp. 185ff.).

21 'Moreover, further expansion of liquidity would weaken the yen, and yen depreciation further depresses Asian economies. Yen depreciation combined with an export drive is not a solution because it would create political conflict with the United States and would not help the Asian economies recover, something that is important for a Japanese economic recovery' (Ito, 2000, p. 99).

22 However, it is not clear that many proponents of money neutrality would follow Koo's advice of fiscal stimulation, since the type of assumptions that in theoretical models produce money neutrality also tend to produce fiscal policy neutrality.

23 For an overview of the key issues in the literature, see Blanchard (1990). For recent empirical work on the monetary determinants of nominal GDP in the Japanese case, see, for instance, Werner (1997d).

24 See, for instance, Moore (1988), Goodhart (1989d, 1994), Wray (1990, 2001), Arestis and Sawyer (2003b). For a survey of the money supply exogeneity-endogeneity debate, see Jao (1989).

25 As we will see, this view includes the claim that the central bank cannot influence the quantity of money or credit supplied to the economy, because otherwise financial sector stability would be endangered. Not unrelated to the rising worries about financial sector stability resulting from this stance, the central bank made a 180-degree about-turn in its policy with its 19 March 2001 decision to target

indicators of the quantity of money. There is no evidence that there were obstacles to the implementation of the bond purchase targets, nor that these bond purchases increased financial sector instability. The central bank has abandoned this view, thereby delivering the empirical evidence proving it counterfactual.

26   Granger causality is necessary but not sufficient to establish strong exogeneity.

27   In the short-run, the story is different. Here Okina recognizes that broad deposit aggregates are in no fixed link with short-term interest rates, so that 'the controllability of the money supply is not something the Bank of Japan's short-term money market operations can guarantee' (Okina, 1993b, p. 172). Indeed, there seems little the central bank can guarantee.

28   This view has a long tradition, including, among others, Friedman (1982), Poole (1982), Brunner and Meltzer (1983).

29   Iwata (1992a) also argues that the Bank of Japan is responsible for the asset price bubble of the 1980s – not because of its interest rate policy, but because of its excessive supply of high powered money.

30   Iwata also predicted that 'if the Bank of Japan does not discard its "BoJ Theory", then even if it does not make errors in assessing the business cycle, it is apparent that the risk is large that henceforth there will also be economic dislocation caused by monetary policy of the type that caused the great inflation of 1973/4, or the asset price surge and collapse this time' (Iwata, 1992b, p. 124).

31   More recently, Meltzer (2003) has argued that the transmission of monetary policy runs from an expansion of the monetary base and the money supply to a reduction in long-term interest rates, which would change the relative prices of assets and output. As will be tested more formally below, there is no evidence for the operation of such a chain of causation.

32   The Federal Reserve 'de-emphasized' M1 targeting in 1982 and abandoned formal targeting altogether in 1987 (Board of Governors of the Federal Reserve System, 1988).

33   Meltzer (2001) feels compelled to argue that the culprit has been the lack of independence by the Bank of Japan concerning its exchange rate policy, which is based on the observation that the Ministry of Finance remains in charge of official foreign exchange intervention. This argument, however, neglects the well-documented finding that sterilized exchange rate intervention lacks in effectiveness, that the Bank of Japan in principle sterilized the Ministry's official intervention and that there is no evidence that the central bank could not decide its sterilization policy autonomously.

34   'In a nutshell, the credit view asserts that in addition to affecting short-term interest rates, monetary policy affects aggregate demand by affecting the availability or terms of new bank loans' (Bernanke, 1993, p. 56).

35   'If banks merely satisfied their loan demand by issuing publicly held debt, there would be nothing unique about bank credit. Nothing would be fundamentally different from a bank making a loan with funds obtained from the sale of large, negotiable certificates of deposit, and a finance company making a loan with funds obtained from the sale of commercial paper. Monetary policy actions would have a similar effect on bank and other credit – there would be no separate bank lending channel for monetary policy' (Thornton, 1994, p. 39).

36   'Consequently, an open market operation that increases the quantity of reserves and bank deposits means that, other things being the same, banks have more funds to make more loans' (Thornton, 1994, p. 33).

37 Bernanke and Blinder (1992) found that banks first responded by shifting securities, rather than bank loans (which are longer-term contracts), but after a lag (of two years) also reduce bank loans.

38 Kakes et al. (2001) find that banks tend to shield their loan portfolios from the impact of monetary policy and instead adjust their securities portfolios.

39 It has been argued in theory that banks, unlike stock markets, may be able to engage in closer monitoring of companies (Sheard, 1989; Aoki and Dore, 1994; Aoki and Patrick, 1994; Okazaki and Okuno-Fujiwara, 1999). Interlocking shareholdings are seen in theory as a method to share risk (Sheard, 1994). However, Agarwal and Elston (2001) and Fohlin (1999) failed to find empirical support for this argument in the case of Germany. Caves and Uekusa (1976) found that in the Japanese case mainly group banks benefit from the *keiretsu* business groupings, not the individual firms. They tend to have a lower profit rate than non-group firms.

40 They argue that as long as their open market liabilities are imperfectly substitutable with managed liabilities, a credit effect remains. They find that during tight-money periods, when open-market interest rates rise, the prime rate rises by more. They note that this is difficult to distinguish from a balance sheet channel, where a tightening of monetary policy leads to a simultaneous worsening of both banks' and borrowers' balance sheets.

41 In addition, Morsink and Bayoumi (2000) reported the VAR findings that 'bank loans and securities respond in similar ways to monetary shocks, which is not consistent with the idea that banks use their relatively liquid assets (securities) as a temporary shock absorber and adjust their loans over the long run' (p. 155).

42 Woo (1999), examining the correlation between bank capital and lending growth, finds that there was no credit crunch before 1997, but that one occurred that year. Motonishi and Yoshikawa (1998) find that real shocks to the economy explain weak investment until 1997. Only in that year was there evidence that reduced lending, mainly to small firms, became a factor, though even then only a partial one. Morsink and Bayoumi (2000), using a VAR model, found that both monetary policy and banks' balances have been important sources of shocks, especially since 1996, and that firms and households have been unable to substitute borrowing from other sources for a shortfall in bank borrowing.

43 Moreover, there appears to be an overlap between these two categories, as borrowing by the corporate sector is a subset of both the liabilities of the corporate sector and borrowing by the private sector. The procedure to deflate loans by the GDP deflator to obtain 'real loans' is also debatable (as loans are also used for non-GDP transactions, but are not deflated by non-GDP prices, such as asset prices).

44 Total loans to large firms have been declining since the 1980s, which has been attributed to disintermediation and the greater possibilities for firms to raise funds from other financial intermediaries. As Meltzer (2001) points out, this makes the credit rationing argument dubious: it is known that large firms, the main customers of banks, have been abandoning the banks, to raise their funds directly in the markets. As a result, banks were then said to have lent excessively to small firms in the 1980s. If their lending is reduced during the 1990s, this would merely reverse the excessive lending of the 1980s. Moreover, large firms continue to be able to raise funds from elsewhere.

45 He argues that banks with non-performing loans should be expected to engage in excessive lending, rather than a credit contraction, as they gamble on high-risk projects to restore solvency.

46 The number of victims of loan sharks and illegal usury rose to 166,000 in the first half of 2003, already surpassing the annual high of 2002 by more than 40,000 (National Policy Agency, Tokyo). These statistics are often illustrated by gruesome reports about threats and pressure by loan enforcers, usually linked to organized crime, to get the borrower to sell internal organs or commit suicide in a way that feigns a fatal accident, to obtain the life insurance money.

47 Ministry of Finance, Survey of Incorporated Businesses, various issues. The figure is calculated by taking the average of quarterly data over the five-year period from 1996 to 2001. Small firms are defined, as usual, as firms with paid-in capital of less than ¥100 million.

48 If a bank credit crunch was said to be due to bad debts at banks, then this argument does not apply to other forms of funding, such as insurers (which only accumulated bad debts of 2% of loans as of 2002, 70% of which were already reserved against).

49 Mateut et al. (2003) note that trade credit had so far been neglected in the analysis of the role of bank lending in monetary policy transmission. Using evidence on 16,000 manufacturing firms, they show empirically that trade credit rises when bank lending falls.

50 The Bank of Japan's definition of the flow of funds items follows the IMF manual on flow of funds statistics.

51 In addition, the firms that are credit rationed tend to possess little land; the main landholders are larger firms.

52 Ogawa actually frames his findings in terms of the 'credit view', arguing that if a fall in land prices reduces bank lending irrespective of the call rate, this is supportive of the 'credit view'. In fact, it contradicts the argument of the credit view, and should instead be construed as support for the balance sheet view.

53 Nevertheless, Ogawa reports that in his empirical study 'a shock to the call rate has a long-lasting effect on investment, irrespective of the firm size'. This is surprising, given the well-known observation (the topic of this chapter) that interest rates (including call rates) declined significantly during the 1990s, without a sustained increase in investment and economic activity. It is due to the long observation period, from 1975 to 1998. In order to tackle directly the 'puzzle' of the ineffectiveness of interest rate reductions, Ogawa uses estimates of the relationships between variables in the 1975–90 period to estimate by how much investment of firms would have increased in the 1990s and by how much the ownership of land would have increased, if the same relationships as in the pre-1990s period had prevailed. Not surprisingly, Ogawa records that investment and land prices rose by less than what would have been expected if there had not been a puzzle. This, however, is merely restating the problem that Ogawa is supposed to solve. Then the fact that investment and land prices did not rise by as much as they should have is used by Ogawa to conclude that 'the land stock played an important role in affecting investment downturns of the 1990s when the land price fell sharply', which in turn is considered empirical support of the balance sheet channel. In actual fact, all Ogawa has been saying is that land ownership and investment did not increase by as much in the 1990s as they should have. He is using this known observation as evidence that a balance sheet channel has been at work. Since VAR analysis assumes that the underlying responses are linear and have not changed over time, the apparently different responses of the 1990s could not be explained by his model, even if he did actually set out to explain them.

54 For instance, Ogawa, citing Ueda (1993), uses the call rate as the sole measure of monetary policy, since he believes that the call rate has been 'the direct target of

monetary policy by the BoJ for most of the postwar period' (p. 394). As we will see, there is little evidence to support this assumption. Window guidance bank credit controls were the main tool of monetary policy by the Bank of Japan for most of the postwar period. Another surprise is that Ogawa then argues that 'the evidence of the negative effects of the call rate shock on investment does not necessarily support the monetary channel', since 'an increase in the call rate decreases the land price, which in turn aggravates the external finance premium and exerts a negative effect on investment under the credit channel' (p. 397). We are left at a loss about what, then, would constitute empirical support of the monetary channel in Ogawa's model. Perhaps the testing procedure is not suitable to distinguish between the alternative hypotheses?

Chapter 4

1 For detailed suggestions of US structural reform demands, see, for instance, the reports by the bilateral Structural Impediments Initiative (SII), which was launched in July 1989, with a final report released on 28 July 1990.
2 *The Economist*, Special report: American productivity, 13 September 2003.
3 For a discussion of some of these issues and a survey of some data sources, see Smith (2003).
4 Figures as quoted by Ed Crooks and Tony Major (2003).
5 See also Richard Donkin, Here is the art of achieving more for less, *Financial Times*, 19 September 2003.
6 See also Lydia Adetunji, US widens global gap in productivity, *Financial Times*, 1 September 2003.
7 Lou Dobbs, The high cost of productivity in U.S., *Daily Yomiuri*, 28 October 2003.
8 'It's time to begin questioning the current demands on our workforce, and time to talk straight about what higher productivity really means to the standard of living in the country', demands Lou Dobbs (2003).
9 *The Economist*, Economics Focus: Europe's work in progress, 16 November 2002.
10 *The Economist*, Charlemagne: a holiday from history, 9 August 2003.

Chapter 5

1 This view was formulated in Werner (1991, 1992, 1994b, 1995a, 1995c and later publications).
2 This argument has also been made by the IMF, the World Bank and the Asian Development Bank in the context of the Asian crisis. See, for instance, Kawai and Takayasu (2000). Please also note Werner (2000b, 2000c), contradicting this argument and providing an alternative explanation of the Asian crisis.
3 For a more complete description of the 'typical' Japanese firm, see, for instance, Aoki and Dore (1994); for a description of the historical roots and macroeconomic implications of the Japanese institutional design, see, for instance, Werner (2003c).
4 Ōkurashō formally ceased to exist in January 2001. The supervisory and regulatory functions over the financial sector were transferred to the predecessor of the current Financial Services Agency in 1998.
5 In 1996, a package with over 1000 deregulation reforms was announced by the government. Deregulation programmes had earlier targeted the telecommunications

sector (early 1990s), interest rates (mid-1980s), international capital flows (1980), the automobile sector (1980s), the steel and textile industries (1970s and 1960s), among others. Privatization had become a main concern of government policy in the mid-1980s. The number of foreign firms and financial institutions, though initially small, showed signs of increases already before the 1990s. For a list of structural reforms, see Ministry of Foreign Affairs (1999).

6 Hoshi and Patrick (2000) state: 'The magnitude of the transformation is remarkable. During most of the postwar period, Japan's financial system was characterized by the dominance of bank financing, close relations between banks and their corporate clients, and heavy regulation by the government. That is now becoming what seems to be the opposite: a system where financial institutions compete in capital and other financial markets without heavy intervention from the government' (p. 1).

7 I am mainly referring to German theories. For more on this topic, see Werner (1993, 2003d, 2004e).

Chapter 6

1 Speech given by Masaru Hayami, Governor of the Bank of Japan, at Kisaragi-kai in Tokyo, 30 May 2002 ('The Economy: Recent Developments and Challenges'), website of the Bank of Japan.

2 For details on the 2002 recovery, see Liquidity Watch, Profit Research Center Ltd. For forecasts of the 1996 recovery, see Werner (1994c, 1995c, 1995d); for details on the forecast of stronger than expected growth in 1999, see Werner (1998c).

3 Speech by Japanese Prime Minister Junichiro Koizumi delivered Wednesday 1 May 2002 at an Asia Society dinner in Sydney titled 'Japan and Australia Toward a Creative Partnership', as quoted by the *Japan Times* at http://www.japantimes.co.jp/cgi-bin/getarticle.pl5?np20020502b7.htm on 2 May 2002.

4 Ibid.

5 Koizumi made a feeble and hardly credible attempt to credit his reforms for the nascent recovery of 2002 in his Sydney speech, by claiming that they had indeed begun already: 'Reforms are already underway, and I believe we can see indications that the economy is moving toward bottoming out.' He fails to mention what these reforms were that had already been sufficiently implemented to have an impact on economic growth. There is no evidence that there were any.

6 Average quarterly call rates calculated from daily data; growth measured by seasonal differencing of logarithms.

7 Quarterly data, with bond yields being average yields calculated from daily data.

Chapter 7

1 See Acheson and Chant (1973a, 1973b), and Forder (2002), who applied their approach to the ECB. Milton Friedman (1982) identified this motivation in the case of the US Federal Reserve.

2 A quick glance at textbooks suggests that this seems to be one of the pastimes of economists. The notable exception is Goodhart (1989b), one of the very few books in monetary economics that explicitly points out the lack of meaning of such multiplier 'analysis'.

3 On the velocity decline in Japan, see, for instance, Ishida (1984), Bank of Japan (1988a), Miyao (1996), Yamada (2000), Kimura (2001a).
4 See Bank of Japan (1988a, 1988b) for such an argument about the Japanese case, or Burger (1988), Rasche (1986), Mankiw and Summers (1986), Tatom (1983), Taylor (1986), Siegel and Strongin (1986) about other countries.
5 See Engle and Granger (1987) and Miller (1988) for the US and Hendry and Ericsson (1983), Ireland and Wren-Lewis (1988) and Hall et al. (1988) for the UK.
6 See Board of Governors of the Federal Reserve System (1988).
7 Alan Greenspan, 2 March 2001, House Budget Committee, as quoted by DeRosa (2001).

Chapter 8

1 As some warned many years ago. See, for instance, Werner (1991).
2 Land prices, due to their lower degree of liquidity, tend to lag movements in stock markets by almost two years. A bottoming and eventual rise is likely soon, as we shall see in Part III.
3 On the UK, see Muellbauer and Murphy (1989) and Muellbauer (1992); on the Asian asset bubbles and their link to the Asian crisis, see Mera and Renaud (2000) and Werner (2003c).

Chapter 9

1 Capital outflows are a negative item in the balance of payments, but are represented as positive in the graph for expositional purposes.
2 The basic balance is the difference between the current account and net long-term capital flows.
3 The difference, made up by short-term capital flows, is largely the result of inter-office bank flows. During the 1980s, Japanese banks borrowed foreign currency to enable Japanese investors to conduct long-term foreign investment in excess of the current account surplus. During the 1990s, as the demand for overseas long-term investment collapsed, Japanese banks repaid these short-term loans from the rest of the world.
4 For further details on Japanese foreign investment in the 1980s and early 1990s, see Werner (1994a, 1997d, 2003c).

Chapter 10

1 Shimizu (2000) fails to make reference to any previous studies on Japanese bank lending and its determinants. He reports on his findings: 'For all types of loans, there are highly significant univariate causal relationships from either land price index to bank loans... No causality was found for any types of bank loans to land prices. In general, changes in land prices preceded changes in bank loans by about a year.' This is in contradiction to earlier findings by Werner (1992, 1997d), Ito and Iwaisako (1996), where disaggregated bank lending (to the real estate sector) explains land prices, often with a lead time of more than one year. A reason for Shimizu's different findings may possibly lie in the procedure used by him to create

monthly data for land prices out of what is originally only a biannual time series. By doing so, he used one piece of data to create six. Such procedures introduce arbitrary assumptions that may not hold and are thus suspect.

2   Shimizu even argues: 'Our evidence suggests that monetary policy did not directly and specifically affect land prices' (2000, p. 86). But if he dismisses the possibility that monetary policy has been the cause of either bank lending or land price movements, then there seem few candidates left to cause his otherwise open-ended model and explain just what determines land prices.

Chapter 11

1   Papers that have addressed the issue, however, according to Kashyap et al. (1999), without adequate rationale why banks cannot be replaced by non-bank intermediaries, are Diamond (1984) and Gorton and Pennacchi (1990). Their own model, like most of the recent literature on the topic, neglects a key institutional feature of banks, as discussed in the next chapter.

2   See, for instance, the speech by then Japanese Finance Minister Kiichi Miyazawa (1999), who blamed the Asian crisis partly on such a 'mismatch', or the International Finance Corporation's Endo (2001), the World Bank's Rojas-Suarez (2001), the Asian Development Bank Institute's Yoshitomi (2000) or Park (2001).

3   We are therefore not primarily concerned with banking reform that occurs due to different reasons, such as the transition from a socialist to a capitalist economy.

4   Empirical evidence is supportive of the argument that banks are 'special' in this sense, such as James (1987) and Hoshi et al. (1991).

5   Hoshi and Kashyap (2000), as we saw, advise Japan to 'fully open the markets now, most importantly to foreign financial institutions' in order to solve its problems.

Chapter 12

1   This was echoed over 70 years later by Stiglitz and Weiss (1988) in their paper on 'Banks as social accountants and screening devices for the allocation of credit'.

2   Bank of Japan governor Matsushita explains: 'A large part of the daily transactions of households, firms and investors are settled by means of funds transfers and remittances between banks. In turn, banks' balances are settled across their accounts held with the Bank of Japan. In other words, the majority of transactions conducted throughout the country is eventually concentrated and settled at the Bank [of Japan]. As a result, the amount settled across the current accounts at the Bank [of Japan] totals more than ¥300 trillion per day. This means that an amount equivalent to approximately 70 percent of Japan's annual GDP is transferred each day through the accounts at the Bank [of Japan]' (Matsushita, 1996, p. 7).

3   The figure is the average annual outstanding balance between 1996 and 2001, the second half of the 1990s.

4   For an accurate calculation, the actual transaction velocity of cash and coins is required. Normally, the income velocity is calculated by the ratio of annual nominal GDP to cash, which would be 8.3. Moreover, most writers argue that the trend of velocity has been declining since the 1980s. But even if we assume an unlikely high transaction velocity ten times as large, that is, 83 per year, we find that less than 5% of all transactions can possibly have been undertaken using notes and coins. This seems, if anything, an overestimate, since the cash transactions tend to

cover mainly small amounts each. For larger transactions, most agents prefer transfers through the banking system. The majority of transactions in value terms (dominated by the large transfers made by and between corporations, the government and various organizations) is in non-cash form.

5   The model of a pure credit economy postulated by Wicksell (1898) may be closer to reality than is usually recognized.

6   The historical fact of this sequence may indicate the recognition of problems with the banking standard – as we will see below. It is therefore possible to argue that the introduction of precious metal coinage by the Lydians may have been intended as an improvement upon the older, almost purely banking-based financial systems. In that case, the modern, banking-based systems might also represent a regressive development.

7   There is even some evidence that writing was developed there for the keeping of accounts related to banking transactions.

8   'Heichelheim has listed a number of distinct banking services such as deposit banking, "foreign exchange", giro, secured and unsecured lending not only internally but also externally, and is satisfied that "almost all these forms of banking business existed already as early as the third millennium BC … we have unmistakably clear records of such transactions between Babylonians, Assyrians and other nations of Asia Minor" (1958, II, 134)', writes Davies (1994, pp. 53ff.).

9   As recorded on Hammurabi's stele, now standing in the Louvre in Paris.

10 Grammar was used for this purpose: names were written in genitive case to record credits, while debits were recorded in dative. Davies (1994, p. 53).

11 However, coined money played a much larger role in Rome than in Babylon or Ptolemaic Egypt – perhaps another indication of reverse sequencing (see note 6 above).

12 It was cut into two, one for the creditor, while the smaller 'foil' was for the debtor – the 'counterfoil'. Both could be compared to see if they 'tally'. See Davies (1994, pp. 147–52).

13 Notable exceptions are cited below. Wicksell (1898) postulated a pure credit economy, and despite the clear dominance of credit transactions today, his approach remains neglected.

14 Schumpeter (1954) continues: 'In other words: practically and analytically, a credit theory of money is possibly preferable to a monetary theory of credit' (p. 717). Schumpeter credits Thornton and others with this idea. I am grateful to Messori (2002) for reminding me of this passage which I had underlined heavily in my copy of Schumpeter's *History* in 1993.

15 Meanwhile, despite the example of exponential revenue streams, most neoclassical economists assume that firms suffer from fixed or increasing costs per unit of output.

16 According to the UK Council of Mortgage Lenders, more than 250,000 households have interest-only loans that are not linked to investment policies designed to repay the loans. 14,000 of the households said in a survey they 'did not know how they would repay their loans'. In case of default, the banker repossesses the collateral, which may lead to evictions from homes in the case of mortgages. See Alexander Jolliffe, Regulator warns over interest-only home loans, *Financial Times*, 6 July 2004. If monthly payments of interest and principal are made, a 30-year mortgage of GBP 100,000 with a fixed interest rate of 10% will require 'only' an aggregate repayment of GBP 315,926, that is, interest payments of GBP 215,926.

17   Alternatively the fiction could be maintained that the customer borrowed gold, if it is agreed that this gold would immediately be deposited with the goldsmith, so that the customer could conduct purchases using the deposit receipts.

18   The solution of the goldsmiths – soon to be known as bankers – to the latter problem was to obtain a government charter to establish a bank whose paper issuance was either backed by the government or made legal tender to pay taxes. This institution, owned by the bankers, could then act as 'lender of last resort' and prevent bank runs or support the bankers if they did occur.

19   This had implications that affected the course of history, for it meant that the allocation of new purchasing power was not under the control of the government. Europe's monarchs believed that the bankers had large amounts of gold. When governments needed money and could not raise taxes further, they believed they had no choice but to borrow from bankers. But of course the bankers were doing nothing the kings and rulers could not have done themselves. The Old Testament says that the borrower is servant to the lender. Empirically, there seems indeed a certain degree of control and influence that can be exerted by the lender over the borrower. In the case of lending to kings, this meant that bankers could exert influence on national policies. Bankers were the masters who created and allocated purchasing power. See Werner (2003c, chapter 4).

20   Ironically, historians of Babylon, ancient Greece and Rome often show deeper insight about banking than many modern economists.

21   'Intermediation is the process by which banks and other financial institutions tailor the maturity, terms and types of financial claims to meet the demands of households and businesses' (Meltzer, 1995, p. 62).

22   The exception are the endogenous money and Austrian economics schools of thought, which recognize credit creation.

23   'The bank multiplier shows only that if you can observe the change in the monetary base between two occasions, and can predict the two relevant ratios, then you will be able to predict the change in the money stock with a high degree of confidence. This allows very little to be deduced about the process of adjustment. Indeed, most of the accounts of the dynamic process of adjustment which are derived from the multiplier approach are at best misleading and often wrong' (1989b, p. 136). Goodhart also explains that virtually any multiplier can be construed in order to link a larger aggregate to one of its smaller components. He gives the hypothetical example of the 'potato multiplier' of total consumer expenditure to argue eloquently that such exercises do not illuminate behavioural, let alone causal relationships.

24   Evidence for this can be found in the works of Law (1705), Thornton (1802), Mueller (1816), Rau (1826, 1832), Wagner (1857, 1872), Knies (1873), Macleod (1855/56), Wicksell (1898), Spiethoff (1905), Schumpeter (1912) and Hahn (1920). A number of economists also continued to recognize this in the postwar era, though their influence remained limited. For instance, Trescott (1960) points out that to grant a loan of US$1000 to a customer, 'a bank needs only to credit his account with $1000.00 in its books by a stroke of the pen ... The process of creating deposits is obviously a simple and painless one for the banks ... ' (p. 55).

25   As bank loans increase by US$9900, so do bank deposits. The initial deposit becomes reserve R of US$100, which allows deposits D of US$10,000. Thus the reserve requirement (R/D) of 1% is met.

26   It could even be said that the bank just 'pretends' it has the money, and nobody realizes. Such action could easily be construed as fraudulent. Historically, the

lending of gold that was promised to be on deposit with the goldsmiths, as well as the issuance of deposit receipts without any deposits having taken place (note issuance) could possibly be considered illegal at the time. Today, banking legislation has legalized this process. Nevertheless, there is an academic tradition, the 'Austrian School' of economics, which argues that bank credit creation remains illegal, since claims on the same resources are simultaneously issued by banks to different customers (see Hoppe et al., 1998).

27 The exception is the US government. The authors of the US Constitution ensured that the government has the right to issue money, a prerogative last used by President John F. Kennedy in one of his last executive orders (No. 11,110) on 4 June 1963.

Chapter 13

1 Humphrey (1997) mentions that other writers had formulated it before Newcomb, namely Joseph Land, Karl Rau, John Lubbock and E. Lavasseur.

2 More precisely: total volume of transactions = $P_T T = \Sigma p_{Ti} t_i$.

3 Pigou also formulated the money demand function M = kPY, with k representing a constant.

4 Some parts of real estate transactions are picked up by the housing investment statistics, but by no means the majority.

5 As Keynes (1930) points out, the quantity equation originally was a summation of transaction prices and quantities. Here we use the following notation: The value of transaction is $p_i q_i$ and the total value of transactions during a given time period (t_0) is PQ, given by

$$PQ = \Sigma_{ipiqi}^{n} p_i q_i = p_1 q_1 + \ldots + p_n q_n.$$

6 This was recognized and utilized by Fisher and Brown (1911), Keynes (1930) and Milton Friedman, who writes in his entry on 'Quantity Theory' in the *Encyclopaedia Britannica* that with MV = PT 'Each side of this equation can be broken into subcategories: the right-hand side into different categories of transactions and the left-hand side into payments in different form' (p. 435).

7 As has been suggested by Werner (1992, 1994b, 1994c, 1995a, 1995b, 1995c, 1996a, 1996b, 1996c, 1996d, 1996e, 1997a, 1997b, 1997c, 1997d, 1997e, 2002b, 2003c). See also Economics Focus, *The Economist*, 19 June 1993, p. 74.

8 Knut Wicksell (1898, 1906) presented a model of a pure credit economy, emphasizing the important function of banks as creators of new purchasing power. In his model, all transactions are settled by bank transfer or cheque drawn on cheque accounts with banks. He assumed that all saving is deposited with banks, banks do not hold reserves and can issue any amount of loans without risk of insolvency, all investment is bank-financed, banks lend solely to finance investment, and the economy is at full employment. For a lucid discussion of the role of bank credit in the theories of Steuart, Smith and Hilferding, see Lapavitsas (2004).

9 The Radcliffe report argued as follows: 'A decision to spend depends not simply on whether the would-be spender has cash or "money in the bank", although that maximum liquidity is obviously the most favourable springboard. There is the alternative of raising funds either by selling an asset or by borrowing … The ease with which money can be raised depends on the one hand upon the composition

of the spender's assets and on his borrowing power and on the other hand upon the methods, moods and resources of financial institutions and other firms which are prepared (on terms) to finance other people's spending level ... An analysis of liquidity ... directs attention to the behaviour and decisions that do directly influence the level of total demand' (1959, p. 132).

10 Benjamin Friedman (1981) has demonstrated that credit is at least as useful as money as an instrument that can be controlled by the central bank and to forecast movements in nominal GNP. Bernanke (1983) demonstrates how the Great Depression of the 1930s can be traced to credit market failure, not, as argued by Milton Friedman, a decline in money. King and Plosser (1984) report in a real business cycle model that the explanatory power of inside money for output was significantly better than money. Foster (1992) has successfully estimated a stable money demand function of sterling M3 by reliance on loan aggregates instead of deposits. Kashyap et al. (1992) demonstrated that banks view loans and securities as imperfect substitutes (so that monetary policy does affect credit availability) and that bank and non-bank sources of borrowing are imperfect substitutes (so that shifts in the financing structure affect investment).

11 In a pure credit economy there is no 'velocity' of circulation, since this concept originally came about when a narrow measure of 'cash', such as precious metals or central bank notes was used to represent M in the equation of exchange – since GNP (and its growth) was usually larger than the stock of cash (and its growth), it appeared as if one unit of 'cash' was used for multiple transactions, a number measured *ex post* by the ratio of GNP to cash (or, later, broader measures of 'money'). A credit economy, on the other hand, settles all transactions on banks' balance sheets. The velocity is always 1 or, more accurately, irrelevant. However, any empirical measure of credit is unlikely to be perfect, thus the inclusion of a constant, such as velocity, serves to formulate a less stringent empirical requirement, where credit creation is expected to be at least proportional to the relevant transaction values.

12 Proponents of the deposit view sometimes argue that it should not matter whether deposits or loans are being analysed, as both tend to be equal in the long run. This is not true, due to the main problems with deposit aggregates, including the problem of defining them. Werner (1996c) has shown that in the Japanese case, a broad credit measure and M2 + CD, the traditional deposit measure, diverged greatly in the 1990s. While significant growth of M2 + CD seemed to suggest an economic recovery in 1995, the credit aggregate suggested a contraction of nominal GDP growth – for the first time since 1931. The latter is what happened. Conversely, while M2 + CD growth remained stable from mid-1995, the credit aggregate suggested a sudden economic recovery from the fourth quarter of 1995, which again materialized.

13 Nevertheless, the accounting identities that national income equals consumption plus investment and also savings plus consumption and hence investment equals savings are always true *ex post*. However, they express no behavioural relationships and hence it should not be concluded from them that money is neutral or the banking sector does not need to be studied. Bank loans do not rise due to an increase in personal savings, reflected by higher deposits. The chain of causation starts with the creation of purchasing power by banks. Once purchasing power has been created, it then circulates, perhaps from an investor to a firm and from there on to the firm's employees. The employees may then save the money and hence pay it in as bank deposits. But the money would have ended up as bank deposits anyway. People can only save purchasing power that has previously been

created by the banking system. Savings also do not provide a direct limit for credit extension, as that is determined by the banking sector. This, however, does not diminish the importance of savings in general. Savings are necessary in order to keep the balance between purchasing power and the amount of goods that can be purchased: if banks create additional purchasing power by extending loans and national output remains the same, then as long as people do not increase their savings, by which they would reduce purchasing power, prices may rise. Investment is limited by the internal purchasing power of firms, the amounts of purchasing power firms can divert from other parts of the economy and the amount of newly created purchasing power by banks.

14 With the exception of the US, few countries can expect their created money to be accepted abroad. Thus, especially for developing countries, a shortage of foreign exchange can become a problem. However, this should only restrict imports of needed foreign produce or technology. Foreign investment is not necessary to support domestic growth, as that can be done on the basis of domestic credit creation. See Werner (2000b, 2000c) on India and Thailand.

15 It is somewhat inconsistent how some economists propose models that assume perfect information, on the one hand, and then wonder how they could integrate money in these models, on the other.

16 Williamson (1986) also proposes a model of credit rationing due to monitoring costs.

17 As Schumpeter (1912) said, money is different from all other goods and services, because money, as well as the right to money, can fulfil its function. This is not true for other goods and services: you cannot ride on the ownership right of a horse. This special feature of money places it in great demand. Thus the assumption that the demand for money is limited is unrealistic. While specific borrowers may wish to pay back their loans, whether this is true in aggregate is questionable.

18 The argument mentioned by Trautwein (2000) is, of course, derived from a different model of bank behaviour, where banks are assumed to be in need of deposits ('loanable funds') in order to be able to lend. This ignores the reality of credit creation, which is due to the fact that banks are still considered only 'financial intermediaries' but not creators of new purchasing power. Moreover, the likely scenario of a constant excess demand for loans is not considered.

19 For a survey on the credit crunch literature relevant to Japan and empirical evidence, see Werner (1996d) and Woo (1999). See also Yoshikawa et al. (1994) and Matsui (1996). Werner (1996d) provides some evidence that bad debts rendered banks more risk averse, thus reducing their credit supply.

Chapter 14

1 For details on the historical background of the Bank of Japan's disaggregated credit statistics, how this ties in with its credit controls, and on the historical origin of those controls, see Werner (2003d).

2 The Durbin-Watson statistic is not surprisingly very low for both equations, indicating that significance tests cannot be taken at face value; the main information value of these tests derives from the comparative figures and the correlation between the time trend and the velocities. Here, the message is unambiguous.

Chapter 15

1 One version of the real bills doctrine says that the creation of paper or credit money will not cause inflation as long as the money is issued in exchange for sufficient security, which would not follow from our framework. A version consistent with our model would be to state that the creation of credit will not cause inflation as long as the new purchasing power is used to produce new goods and services that find a market.

2 Credit creation mobilizes idle resources that have voluntarily been left idle, thus the term 'forced saving' for this process is perhaps not entirely accurate. It is true in the sense that those who unwittingly temporarily waive their claims on resources had not been asked beforehand.

3 Schumpeter was of course Austrian by nationality, although his early writings were more in the spirit of his German colleagues at the German universities, where he worked between 1925 and 1932, than that of the Austrian school.

4 This is in line with the work on financial repression, especially in East Asia, by Hellmann et al. (1997).

5 The subsequent dismal performance in many countries should not detract from this success. See Werner (2003c) on the causes of the crises in East Asia.

6 The entire model is kept in differences, because (a) breaks in the credit series can only accurately be adjusted when in differences, (b) credit creation is fundamentally a flow concept, (c) capital flows, which we will analyse below, are a flow variable on which accurate levels are unavailable, (d) the calculation of year-on-year absolute changes (or percentage changes) elegantly adjusts for pervasive seasonality, (e) differencing reduces the chance of spurious correlations.

7 I am grateful to Grayham Mizon for making the suggestion of this test and explaining its power to me.

8 As the tests presented in Werner (1997d) testify.

9 Engle et al. (1983) distinguish between weak, strong and superexogeneity. The latter means that the Lucas critique does not apply and the relationship remains invariant to policy changes.

10 See the quarterly *Liquidity Watch* and *Economic Quarterly* reports, Jardine Fleming Securities (Asia) Ltd, Tokyo, 1994–97.

Chapter 16

1 To provide a less well-known example from Asia, we may quote Marshall (1945), in his description of the Karen people of Myanmar: 'In the early 1900's many Karens who had cleared immense tracts of land raised large crops of paddy and became well-to-do. It was then that they employed many Burman and Indian coolies to work for them. They built substantial houses, often of teak, or in a few instances of brick. Some of them were able to add field to field and became really wealthy. It was at this time that money-lenders became very active and going about the villages imposed loans of easy money on the unsuspecting cultivators. These loans were then allowed to lie idle for a year or two until the interest, set at exporbitant rates, mounted to nearly double the original loans, when a sudden demand for full payment could not be met; and the results were that the lending sharks foreclosed on the rich paddy-fields. In this way many a Karen who was once a prosperous cultivator became a tenant on land that he had previously owned. This process continued until near the time of the invasion and the property, land, houses and cattle of the Karens as well as of Burman cultivators, were largely in

the hands of absentee landlords. The Indian Tamil Chettiars were the most numerous class of money-lenders and most exacting in demanding their pounds of flesh.'
2 For empirical evidence of the credit crunch problem in Japan see, for instance, Matsui (1996). On the US see, for instance, Gertler and Gilchrist (1994).
3 The Thai central bank used its 'Credit Planning Scheme' to control commercial bank credit. The Korean central bank, just as the Japanese one, used its 'Window Guidance'. See Werner (2000c) on Thailand, and Werner (1998d, 1999a, 2002a, 2003c) on how the Bank of Japan used its 'window guidance' credit control mechanism to force banks to increase speculative loans.
4 For details on the mechanism designed and commonly employed to prevent such 'speculative lending', see Werner (2002c, 2003d). For details on how this was applied in Thailand, see Werner (2000c); in India, see Werner (2000b); and Japan, see Werner (2002a) as well as chapter 20.
5 Sheng (1992) points out that as a rule of thumb financial distress is likely to become systemic when non-performing loans, net of provisions, reach 15% of total loans (assuming the average ratio of loan/loss provisions to be 50%, then a capital base of 8% would be totally eroded by loan loss provisions).
6 See Werner, 1991, 1992, 1994b, 1995a, 1995b, 1995c, 1995d, 1997a, 1997c, 1997d, 1997f, 1998f.
7 Hutchison (1994) uses a general test framework that models monetary factors as one of the possible shocks to aggregate demand and finds little explanatory power for land price rises. He finds, however, that unspecified supply shocks in the land market, such as tax laws, land-use policies, and so on, are of importance. To him the experience of the 1980s, when, after all, 'monetary factors may have played a large role in land price movements', is but an 'isolated episode' (p. 81). Ito and Iwaisako (1996) have found statistical support for the argument presented already in earlier versions of the present model (Werner, 1992) that land-related credit creation is the cause of land price rises in Japan (although their paper considers many variables in an *ad hoc* fashion and does not attempt to produce a generally applicable theoretical model).

Chapter 17

1 As in other studies on Japanese foreign investment, the focus is on long-term capital flows, which dominated the capital account and seem to have been the autonomous force, with short-term capital flows behaving more like a residual in order to balance the balance of payments identity between the capital and current accounts.
2 See the book by Jean-Jacques Servan-Schreiber with this title, which stirred French emotions, and may have contributed to the French raid of Fort Knox that triggered the end of the Bretton Woods system.
3 Ruffin and Rassekh (1986) discuss why in an international macroeconomic model, portfolio and 'direct' foreign investment should be considered in aggregate, rather than individually. They provide empirical evidence for the substitutability of both forms of long-term investment for the US case. Werner (1994a) provides explicit empirical evidence in support of the substitutability hypothesis in the case of Japan in the 1980s.
4 Testing without any lags over a longer time period (from 1974:1 to 1991:1), the close link between ΔF and ΔC_F was confirmed in the following simple regression (t values in parentheses):

$$\Delta F = 1142.204 + 2.118\ \Delta C_F$$
$$(0.754) \quad (15.2) \quad R^2 = 0.7725 \quad D.W. = 1.79$$

Chapter 18

1   As a result, 'Friedman stands out in arguing that fiscal policy does not have strong effects on the economy ...' (Dornbusch and Fischer, 1987, p. 671). 'Fisher comes close to asserting that *only* changes in the quantity of money affect the price level; Friedman is more clear in arguing that other factors can affect the price level, but that these other factors are of secondary importance' (Dornbusch and Fischer, 1987, p. 241; italics in original).

2   Milton Friedman, in his entry under 'Money: quantity theory' in the *Encyclopaedia Britannica*, p. 476.

3   Wray (2001) frames his argument in terms of high powered money, which however does not necessarily translate to greater effective spending: '... when demand is low, the private sector will not create money endogenously, hence, the government must expand the supply of HPM through fiscal policy.'

4   Hayashi (1998) argues that the central bank is essentially an agency that certain functions have been delegated to by the government. In this case it does not make sense for the government to issue bonds and pay interest for its borrowing, if it could instead ask the central bank to print money and pay for fiscal policy through costless, interest-free money creation. Hence the government could 'exchange interest-bearing government bonds with interest free reserves through the central bank's purchase of government bonds', as paraphrased by Okina (1999, p. 172).

5   Independence is not necessarily an obstacle, since a central bank can voluntarily cooperate to support the government's policy. As Bernanke (2000) pointed out, 'Cooperation with the fiscal authorities in pursuit of a common goal is not the same as subservience' (p. 163). Unfortunately, there are few examples of such cooperation by independent central banks.

6   It is not made explicit who had launched this 'radical idea'. However, there is some evidence that it may have emerged from the German credit school of economists. It is noteworthy that this 'radical' idea was successfully implemented in Germany in the 1930s. On this, see Werner (2004e).

7   This argument is in line with Goodhart's (1989b) description of the link between funding fiscal policy and the money supply.

8   This is effectively the policy combination adopted by the Reichsbank from 1933 to 1937. Its President, Hjalmar Schacht, appeared to have been well aware of the quantity crowding out problem of unmonetized fiscal policy. In addition to stepping up the credit creation of the Reichsbank (by purchasing various forms of assets, including government bonds and bonds of other government institutions), Schacht instructed the establishment of government institutions that implemented fiscal spending programmes and were funded by the issuance of bills of exchange that were purchased by the banks and the central bank. Funding fiscal expenditure with credit creation, as opposed to public bond auctions, is called 'silent funding' (*geraeuschlose Finanzierung*) in the German tradition. See Werner (2002c, 2003d).

9   This proposal has found several supporters since, such as Smithers (2001), Congdon (2001) and the *Financial Times'* Martin Wolf (2002).

10 In addition, even if banks were to hit their 'ceiling' imposed by the reserve requirements, the central bank would be forced to inject any necessary amount of liquidity in order to maintain its targeted call rate, as Goodhart (1989c) and Okina (1992a, 1993a, 1993b) have pointed out.

11 Dornbusch and Fischer (1987) emphasize that 'the distinction between selling debt to the public and selling it to the central bank is essential. The distinction between money and debt financing can be further clarified by noting that Treasury sales of securities to the central bank are referred to as *monetizing the debt*, meaning that the central bank creates (high-powered) money to finance the debt purchases' (p. 584).

12 An example is Ludvigson (1996), who reflects money-financed fiscal policy. In the case of Japan, money-financed fiscal expenditure is possible. Although the Finance Law does not allow the central bank to directly underwrite government bonds, it can purchase them in the secondary market one year after issuance. Economically, this is equivalent to primary market purchase. The political circumstances are different, however, since the government may not be able to determine the extent to which bonds are purchased by the central bank.

13 For details of Executive Order 11.110, see the US government website: www.archives.gov/federal_register/executive_orders/Kennedy.html

14 Reuters, Weaker yen may help Japan deflation fight – Stiglitz, 14 April 2003. Nikkei Net Interactive, In Search of a Prescription for the Japanese Economy: Summary of keynote speech by Joseph E. Stiglitz Monday, 14 April 2003, available at: www.nni.nikkei.co.jp/FR/TNKS/TNKSHM/20030414_stiglitz.html

15 Friedman also argued that such a bureau could work with only a small number of staff, since the Fed's net open market operations could be conducted by one person at one desk.

Chapter 19

1 See Werner (1992, 1994b, 1995a, 1995b, 1995c, 1996b).

2 See Werner (1992, 1994b, 1994c, 1995a, 1995b, 1995c, 1996a, 1996c, 1996d, 1996e, 1997a, 1997b, 1997c, 1997d, 1997e).

3 The Bank of Japan used to refer to its extra-legal window guidance credit controls as 'quantitative policy' (see the interview with Bank of Japan executive director Toshihiko Fukui, in Kinyū fukyō wo kataru (4): Nihon ginkō riji Fukui Toshihiko Shi, *Nihon Keizai Shinbun*, 26 December 1992, p. 5. The term has since become more broadly used, initially in Japanese and then, with a few years' lag, also in its English translation, most frequently by the Bank of Japan in rebuttals of proposals to ease monetary policy not by lowering interest rates, but by expanding some kind of monetary aggregate.

4 The Bank of Japan's argument is also seconded by Cargill, et al. (2000), who concede that there is demand for bank loans, but argue that a credit crunch implies that injections of liquidity (base and narrow money expansion) do not increase credit and aggregate lending, despite the existence of demand for bank loans by corporations at prevailing interest rates (p. 121). They thereby neglect the possibility that the central bank, just like a private bank, can also extent credit and hence alleviate any credit crunch, if it so wishes, as Werner (1994b, 1995a, 1995b, 1995c) has pointed out.

5 Iwata (1999, 2000a) supports this argument.

6 The central bank has engaged in most of these transactions in the past, demonstrating that they are all technically feasible and also deliver the desired positive impact on the economy. Note the experience of the Bank of Japan in the early postwar era, when the banking system was faced with an even larger

non-performing loan problem than during the 1990s. Purchasing currently idle real estate and turning it into parks for public use would support the real estate market, help the banks (that use real estate as collateral), increase credit in the economy (and hence boost economic activity) and, finally, improve the quality of life in Tokyo, a city which has the lowest per capita park surface area of the major world cities. And all this at zero cost to anyone.

7   McCallum (2001b) agrees that 'it is important to recognize that purchase of non-traditional assets is necessary for monetary policy to be helpfully stimulative'. Meltzer (1998) and Hayashi (1998) recommend abandoning call rates as operating target and substitution with high powered money. Similar to Krugman (1998a), Hayashi argues that an inflation target should also be introduced – suggesting to use 1% growth of the CPI. However, the transmission mechanism envisaged by Hayashi is also similar to Krugman's, namely not via direct quantity effects but inflation expectations, triggered by the inflation target, which will lower real interest rates, which in turn will stimulate the economy. Hamada (1999) advocates that the central bank expands bond purchases. Fukao (1999) rejects using high powered money as an operational target due to its large seasonal adjustment fluctuation, and instead suggests to target banks' excess reserves, calculated by subtracting required reserves from total reserves. It remains unclear, though, why seasonally adjusted high powered money cannot be used. Moreover, the proposals that aim at increasing banks' reserve holdings do not explain how exactly increased reserve holdings by the banks affect the economy positively. Allan Meltzer (1999) and McCallum (2001b) recommend that the Bank of Japan attempt to weaken the currency by substantial open-market sales of yen and purchases of foreign government bonds (thus presumably arguing less for direct quantity effects, but indirect stimulation of the economy via the – small – net exports). Bernanke (2000) argues that there is still much the central bank can do to stimulate the economy, even with zero interest rates. 'Far from being powerless, the BoJ could achieve a great deal if it were willing to abandon its excessive caution and its defensive response to criticism' (p. 151). 'Contrary to the claims of at least some Japanese central bankers, monetary policy is far from impotent today in Japan ... First – despite the apparent liquidity trap – monetary policymakers retain the power to increase nominal aggregate demand and the price level. Second, increased nominal spending and rising prices will lead to increases in real economic activity' (pp. 157ff.). Bernanke reminds us of the fact that the central bank can issue as much money as it likes. 'Hence, if the price level were truly independent of money issuance, then the monetary authorities could use the money they create to acquire indefinite quantities of goods and assets. This is manifestly impossible in equilibrium. Therefore money issuance must ultimately raise the price level, even if nominal interest rates are bounded at zero. This is an elementary argument, but ... it is quite corrosive of claims of monetary impotence' (p. 158). Since there is imperfect substitutability between assets, any policy to increase purchases of assets by the central bank, mainly government bonds, would ultimately affect asset prices by pushing them up. Bernanke concludes that the recession of the 1990s is a 'self-induced paralysis', with the monetary authorities carrying most of the blame.

8   Technically, this could easily be done through the same channels used to settle income and corporate taxes – only in reverse direction.

9   McCallum (1985) shows that this would be possible without inducing extreme volatility of short-term interest rates, especially if the intermediate target is the path of nominal GDP, and not money stock. This is in line with a number of

authors who have favoured the same nominal GDP target of monetary policy, including Meade (1978), Tobin (1980) and Bean (1983). Werner (1995b, 1995c, 2001a) favours nominal GDP growth as the target, because it represents the variable that the government, consumers, investors and businesses care about. Moreover, it does not suffer from as many measurement problems as other potential targets (such as prices, or real variables). As mentioned above, many proponents of the 'special case' of interest rate policy ineffectiveness support the imposition of an inflation target. By contrast, Svensson (1999), echoing Friedman's (1982) advice, argues in favour of a price level target.

10 See Werner (1996a, 1996b, 1996c, 1996e, 1997e, 1999d, 1999f, 1999i).

11 Technically, this would be extremely simple, since all banks settle online with the central bank. The transaction could take place in one morning.

Chapter 20

1 On the historical origin of Japanese credit controls as well as their origin internationally, see Werner (2002c, 2003d).

2 The more formal expression for it is *kashidashi zōkagaku kisei*, which means 'regulation of the loan increase amount'.

3 For instance, the official English-language book of 1973 by the Bank of Japan about its monetary policy emphasized that the Bank really followed orthodox central banking policies. It claimed: 'Window guidance is, in its nature, a supplementary tool of orthodox instruments of monetary policy – that is, Bank rate, open-market operations and reserve deposit requirements. It is used more as a weapon of monetary restraint than otherwise ... It must be stressed that it is a form of moral suasion, so that it presupposes co-operation on the part of financial institutions' (Bank of Japan, 1973, p. 159).

4 In October 1958 window guidance was officially replaced by supervision of bank reserve positions. But this so-called 'position guidance' was actually fixed such that it was essentially a continuation of window guidance. Original window guidance was re-established in January 1964, and its scope broadened to include trust, regional and mutual banks. It was again officially abolished in July 1965, as Japan's entry into the OECD required steps to deregulate financial markets and reduce direct controls. It was reintroduced in September 1967 and guidance was broadened to include the credit associations and the Central Cooperative Bank of Agriculture and Forestry (*Nōrin Chūkin*). After another brief termination in September 1968, window guidance was reintroduced in October 1969 and expanded to include 'guidance' on banks' security investment. Since 1973 it has included all client institutions of the Bank of Japan, including the Shinkin Banks (that is all deposit-taking financial institutions with reserves at the Bank of Japan and hence the power to create credit). The game of 'abolition' and reintroduction continued in the 1970s: in April 1975 the Bank of Japan suggested that window guidance had *de facto* been 'abolished', as all bank lending plans were seemingly sanctioned without interference (Nikkei, 1975). In June 1977, the Bank of Japan announced the introduction of a 'new procedure', whereby the banks could make their own loan growth plans, which would be accepted by the Bank of Japan. In June 1978, window guidance reappeared in the form of tight credit growth ceilings (Nikkei, 1978a). In December 1978, the Bank of Japan declared that tighter quantitative monetary control was necessary, because stock prices 'continue to rise rapidly, city centre land prices have risen sharply and there is too much money

[*kane amari*] circulating in the private sector'. It therefore informed the banks that it would tighten the loan increase quota drastically (Nikkei, 1978b, 1978c). In March 1979, the 'new procedure' was officially abolished again (Horiuchi, 1980). Later in 1979, it was re-established, targeting a reduction in housing loans and real estate-related lending (Nikkei, 1979). In 1980, continued tight window guidance forced banks to ask firms to pay back loans earlier than initially agreed (Nikkei, 1980a). With liberalization of capital flows from December 1980, the Bank of Japan considered expanding the scope of window guidance to include impact loans (foreign-denominated loans by Japanese institutions to domestic borrowers, usually swapped back into yen) (Nikkei, 1980b), but eventually only required banks to report about their impact loans at the monthly window guidance hearings with the banks.

5   Nevertheless, the literature is in disagreement whether and to what extent private sector firms managed to effectively 'evade' credit controls on bank loans by simply borrowing from non-bank financial institutions that were not subject to window guidance credit ceilings. Horiuchi (1977, 1978, 1980) argues that to the extent that this happens, window guidance is not effective. Others disagree (Eguchi, 1977, 1978; Teranishi, 1982; Shinohara and Fukuda, 1982). Hoshi et al. (1991) agree with Horiuchi that 'the imposition of window guidance on a subset of the creditors of manufacturing firms will lead to the substitution of loans from unrestricted sources for those from restricted banks'. However, they argue that alternative sources of funding are not perfect substitutes for all potential borrowers and find evidence in support of this. However, this debate about 'effectiveness' cannot be fruitful as long as no distinction is made between credit-creating financial institutions and financial intermediaries that have no power to create credit (such as life insurance companies and non-banks). Only loans by credit-creating institutions are of macroeconomic importance. If loans of non-credit-creating institutions rise in response to tighter credit controls, then this does not increase net new purchasing power in the economy (it merely represents a 'diversion' of already existing purchasing power). Therefore, necessary and sufficient condition for 'effectiveness' of window guidance is whether it succeeds in controlling the loan extension of the credit-creating institutions. All credit-creating institutions were subject to window guidance. The literature agrees that the Bank of Japan was successful in controlling the credit growth of those financial institutions that were subject to window guidance. Window guidance therefore was effective.

6   The study argued that the relationship between the economy (nominal GDP) and credit aggregates has 'weakened remarkably' compared to traditional money supply indicators, like M2 + CD. It claimed that for policy purposes, M2 + CD had been preferable (Bank of Japan, 1988b). This is despite the fact that elsewhere (Bank of Japan, 1988a), the central bank argued that M2 + CD was also not reliable as intermediary policy tool. Bank of Japan (1988b) suffers from two problems, which may explain why in this study credit fails to explain nominal GDP: firstly, credit is not disaggregated as in Werner (1997d). The second reason is an apparently inappropriate definition of 'credit' itself. In the study, the Bank of Japan chose to include loans by financial institutions that do not create credit in the definition of its 'broad' credit aggregates. This seems surprising, because the Bank of Japan has never made them subject to window guidance for this very reason.

7   Yet even the Bank of Japan's official pronouncements about the role of window guidance in the 1980s have been contradictory (usually depending on whether the report is issued in English or Japanese). A 1992 booklet, published only in Japanese, stated that 'although window guidance ... is merely a supplementary tool, during

times of monetary tightening it had the effect of directly controlling the loan increase amounts of financial institutions' (Bank of Japan, 1992b, p. 31).

8 A reason why many researchers have accepted the official view without subjecting it to more rigorous scrutiny may be that they recognize that in the specific institutional setting of early postwar Japan the use of credit controls was meaningful (because in an environment of regulated interest rates, credit would become rationed; interest rates could not be used as monetary policy tool; most investors relied on bank lending for fundraising, as both stock market and especially debt and money markets were underdeveloped; finally, capital flows were tightly regulated). However, in the 1980s, all these conditions changed and thus the economic rationale for continued window guidance weakened: liberalization of capital flows in December 1980, gradual deregulation of deposit interest rates from October 1985, increased creation of debt markets, the introduction of more short-term money market and general open market operations by the central bank all meant that other monetary policy tools could be used by the central bank, while there was the possibility that window guidance itself would become less effective in such an environment. This was often pointed out by the Bank of Japan. Needless to say, while the standard economic rationale for using window guidance may have weakened, economic, as well as other, for instance, political considerations (such as the informal and secret nature of the tool) may still have provided a reason for its existence.

9 No wonder Bank of Japan Banking Department Chief Tamura had to emphasize in 1991 to the press that 'this time', the abolition was for real and that 'in the future, window guidance will under no circumstances be re-instituted' (Nikkei, 1991).

10 Horiuchi (1993) describes how the Bank of Japan deliberately misled the public in the 1970s and early 1980s by making it believe that its main policy tool was interest rate control, and its main policy regime was monetarism. In 1978, the Bank of Japan officially introduced monetary targeting, a procedure by which the central bank selects a certain measure of the so-called money supply, such as M2 + CD, and at the same time announces a specific target for its growth rate that was to be attained in the next time period, such as the coming six months. Horiuchi reveals, however, that in actual fact the Bank of Japan did not use any monetarist principles, but simply controlled economy and money supply aggregates through its window guidance credit controls. The point of monetarism was to act as a smokescreen. Monetarism, Horiuchi explained, 'makes a strong case for the independence of the central bank. It is small wonder then that central bankers should use monetarism as a shield with which to defend themselves against the multifarious political pressures that may undermine their autonomy. BoJ officials pay serious attention to monetarism not because they believe in the veracity of the doctrine but because it may help them keep external pressures from intruding on the autonomy of their monetary control. In short, the BoJ's monetarism is a political tactic. The Bank's autonomy was greatly enhanced during the latter half of the 1970s ... The "monetarism" that the BoJ emphasized after the mid-1970s should be regarded as the Bankers' ploy to guard their own autonomy in the face of such political pressures' (Horiuchi, 1993, p. 114).

11 Indeed, a large part of what is known about pre-1980 window guidance is based on testimonies to a parliamentary subcommittee of the Diet (Jittai Chōsa Shōiinkai, 1959).

12 Unfortunately, it appears greatly underutilized. This may be due to the language barrier. However, even Japanese authors seem to make little use of it. This is despite the fact that, especially until the early 1990s, these papers have often been relied upon by the government and the bureaucracy to publish semi-official

statements. Often economic data are released by ministries or bureaucrats exclusively in the Nikkei. Moreover, the press club system prevalent in Japan enables officials to exert some influence over journalists. This may bias the press reporting towards being too conservative and rather too close to the official view. However, for our purposes this means that officials (whether they are named or simply referred to as 'sources') are unlikely to be misquoted in these papers. Therefore, if in these press sources testimonies by central bank officials who are involved with window guidance suggest a significant role of window guidance in the 1980, then this must be considered reliable.

13 The department where window guidance has been executed changed its English name several times during our observation period – although its Japanese name remained unchanged until 1997 (*Eigyō Kyoku*, which in Japanese firms denotes the department that is in contact with the clients, and hence would normally be translated as 'Sales' or 'Business Bureau'). From 1976 to February 1981, the English name was 'Banking Department'. Until May 1990, it was called 'Market Operations Department'. Then it was called 'Credit and Market Management Department'. Several additional changes and reorganizations took place in the late 1990s, further covering the tracks. Since these name changes could cause confusion and understate the high degree of institutional continuity (apparent when using the Japanese name, which has remained unchanged for most of the post-war era), for our purposes we simply stick to the original English name, the Banking Department.

14 Further quotes can be found in Werner (1998d).

15 One of the most useful interviews (tape-recorded) was with two Bank of Japan officials (referred to as nos 5 and 6) at the same time. It was not only an extremely frank and detailed interview, but the fact that two central bank eye-witnesses were present simultaneously provided an immediate second-witness consistency check. Other interviews were also in agreement.

16 This was a time when the far-reaching implications of the excessive loan growth during the 1980s were not yet fully apparent and the topic was not as controversial as it is now. This is likely to have minimized reporting bias and maximized the objectivity of interviewees.

17 A more detailed description of the fieldwork findings can be found in Werner (1998d).

18 The banks of the official 'all banks' definition, namely city banks, long-term credit banks, trust banks, regional banks, second-tier regional banks and shinkin banks; plus the *Nōrin chūkin*. For most of the time direct credit controls were imposed on yen-denominated loans, although banks also reported their 'impact loan' plans. Only from 1987 were credit controls also imposed for non-yen ('impact') loans.

19 There were three divisions in the Banking Department dealing with the banks: the first section dealt with the city banks, the second with the regional banks and the third with foreign banks. One official of the first section was in charge of one or two city banks. The Bank of Japan headquarters provided the regional offices with an overall loan allocation quota for the various types of banks under their supervision and the local officials then split this up into individual bank loan quotas. While outstanding loans of city banks were monitored daily, regional banks were only controlled once a month.

20 'In the monthly meetings, important questions are how much non-performing assets, how many loans to organised crime ("*yakuza*-company"), etc.' (Bank of Japan official 5).

21 Bank of Japan officials then used spreadsheets such as Lotus 123 and Multiplan to calculate for all the different bank types and banks how much their loans should increase in order to meet exactly the overall total loan increase target for the entire economy (Bank of Japan official 7). There was no official, firm rule for making this decision. Some general rules of thumb were: 'The loan increase quota was always proportional to the previous actual loans. Big banks can increase loans a lot, small [banks] little. We do it so that bank rankings won't change. Thus no matter how much a bank does in terms of competition, bank rankings do not change at all ... There was no free competition' (Bank of Japan officers, 5, 6). The quotas were determined according to the ranking of the banks. 'For this the BoJ used the following formula: for the main four city banks, for which the volume is similar (Sumitomo, Fuji, Mitsubishi, Sanwa), it was decided first. If they are 100, then from here it was certain how much the others would get: DKB would be 120, Mitsui and Tokai would get 80. Thus the order is preserved' (bank officer 4). Then the long-term banks and other bank types are decided proportionately ('Maybe 100 for IBJ, 50 for LTCB and 30 for NCB', bank officer 4). However, the Bank of Japan had far-reaching discretionary power to vary the quotas at will and favour some banks over others. So in practice, the precise loan increase quota usually differed for each bank and for each type of bank. Loans for some banks did not increase, even when others did. Once the window guidance loan growth quotas had been decided, the Bank of Japan would announce the aggregates of the main bank types to the press (the Nikkei), while the individual bank loan growth quotas remained undisclosed.

22 This finding is in contrast to the accepted view (for example, Calder, 1993) that window guidance was not used for the allocation of funds or monitoring of the sectoral allocation.

23 Interviews with both high-ranking and lower-ranking Ministry of Finance officials revealed gaping ignorance about the role of window guidance and thus the actual conduct of the Bank of Japan's monetary policy implementation. All officials appeared to have been well-briefed by none other than Bank of Japan staff who presented to them only the 'official version' that was also supplied to the public – namely that interest rates are the main monetary policy tool. This explains the otherwise surprising lack of Ministry involvement in window guidance: since the Ministry had some influence over interest rates, the Bank of Japan's misrepresentation that its main monetary policy tool are interest rates kept the Ministry in the erroneous belief that it was in charge of monetary policy (as the law also provided for).

24 The informal control of window guidance was also used to punish banks for other forms of 'misbehaviour' such as when a regional bank in the Nagoya area sacked a Bank of Japan *'amakudari'* ('descent from heaven' – an ex-bureaucrat who has obtained a high-ranking position in the private sector). The punishment can take the form of reduced loan quotas (Bank of Japan official 1).

25 While the quarter-end loan growth ceilings were strictly observed, banks increased loans by higher growth rates during the quarter (*fukumigashi* or *fukumi kashidashi*, also referred to as *'kamaboko'*, that is, 'fishroll', as charts of bank loan growth would show curves that bulge out within quarters, before declining again at the end of the quarter). Since the quarterly allocation was only checked on the last working day of the quarter, as long as banks managed to reduce their loan books again by the time of the quarter end booking, the Bank of Japan would not object. The Bank of Japan was fully aware of this phenomenon and tolerated it (Bank of

Japan officials 5, 6). City banks were usually subject to tighter window guidance controls, as they were given loan growth increments on both quarter-end and quarter-average basis (the latter not published). Together with daily monitoring this means that they could not even evade window guidance in between monitoring intervals. Thus *fukumigashi* occurred among other bank types, especially the regional banks (Bank of Japan official 7). In the words of a bank officer, 'the official statistical loan figures are an understatement of the actual lending. In the bubble time this *fukumigashi* was huge. Statistically if you see a 15% lending increase, the actual lending was higher by another 5% or so. Thus one should look at the monthly average data. The Bank of Japan knows about everything, but they said that it is OK if you follow our official guidelines. You are a good boy then' (bank officer 2). We found that there also was a window guidance quota for impact loans, but it was a much more generous one. When banks seemed set to overshoot the loan quotas, they would simply increase impact loans (that is, book their loans to domestic clients through a foreign branch, for instance in London, denominate it in a foreign currency, but immediately swap it back into yen). There was no punishment for not using up the impact loan quota. This quota existed from 1980, when foreign transactions were deregulated, but it stayed very loose until the late 1980s. It was monitored together with the normal yen-denominated window guidance. Bank officers said that while they 'always used 100%' of the yen-based window guidance quota, they only used between 80% and 100% of the impact loan quota. Some banks, like Daiwa bank, had noticeable 'leftovers' (bank officer 4). A Bank of Japan official said that this practice encouraged impact loans. The result of the surge in impact loans was that overall net long-term capital outflows as recorded in the balance of payments were understated, because impact loans were only counted as capital inflows 'above the line' in the balance of payments statistics, but not when banks made the necessary inter-office transfer to the offshore branch (a 'below the line' transfer). As a result, the Japanese net long-term capital outflows as recorded in the balance of payments statistics in the 1980s are an understatement of the actual net foreign investment by Japan. See Kubota (1988).

26 Bank officer 5 continued with the words: 'On the other hand, if it was not for window guidance, we would compete until *harakiri*. This is not good.' Since in the 1980s interest rates on small lot deposits (the bulk of most banks' deposits) were still regulated, banks could increase profits by increasing loan volumes. Moreover, banks were competing with each other to maintain their ranking, which is common to oligopolistic large-scale Japanese firms whose managers enjoy great freedom to pursue their own objectives, namely scale-maximization, due to cross-shareholdings that reduce shareholder influence. See, for instance, Aoki and Dore (1994) and Werner (2001a and 2002a). Competing for ranking, even without punishment from the Bank of Japan for underutilizing their loan quota, the banks all had an incentive to use up their quotas fully.

27 In addition to direct credit controls, during the 1980s the Bank of Japan also used a second quantitative policy tool – its control over its loans at the official discount rate to the banks (called 'BoJ loans' or *nichigin kashidashi*) in order to support the window guidance policy. These direct Bank of Japan loans to banks were also allocated in quotas, and are thus sometimes confused by observers with the 'window guidance' quotas that regulate the banks' total lending. Although the official reserve requirement was not used as an active monetary policy tool, banks had to meet it and when their window guidance loan quotas implied more

credit creation than was possible with current reserves, banks had to borrow reserves from the central bank, at the official discount rate. 'The quotas are secret, not published. But since banks actually go to the limit, one can take the actual figures [of bank borrowing from the central bank]' (Bank of Japan official 7). 'By how much banks can borrow from the Bank of Japan is decided monthly. This volume is decided by the RM1, the relational management one (the name has now changed). [It decides] by how much banks can obtain Bank of Japan loans ... These loans can be used for reserves [to meet the official reserve requirement]' (Bank of Japan official 7). In the late 1990s the inter-bank call rate fell below the official discount rate, indicating that such 'BoJ loans' were no longer the main avenue for direct lending to banks, which had shifted to open market operations.

28 Indeed, Bank of Japan officials said that window guidance was abolished at such short notice that it took the window guidance officers themselves by surprise. Hearings still took place in June, and Bank of Japan officials were preparing the window guidance quotas as usual, when the announcement about the abolition occurred and they suddenly ceased their work.

29 We noticed that all Bank of Japan officials had a tendency to speak about window guidance in the present tense, although the interviews took place more than a year after the official abolition.

30 Apparently, the Bank of Japan would announce the window guidance quota data only in response to direct enquiries from the general public or the media. The media sometimes chose to cover it, as we have seen above (usually, when there was an anomaly or some kind of link to current events, and thus 'news value'). Many observers made it a custom to ring the Bank of Japan around the time of the announcement of the quota, which was at the end of the quarter, and receive the information over the telephone.

31 The actual number of banks changed over the observation period.

32 This method must be considered superior to the one used in Werner (2002a), which is why it is adopted here. As will be seen, however, the outcome does not differ much and the conclusions remain the same.

33 Since the data exhibit strong seasonality, we calculated the seasonally differenced logarithms of the data series (with the exception of interest rates). Next, we test for stationarity, employing the augmented Dickey Fuller test. Unit roots were detected in the seasonally differenced series, but not after further differencing. Both bank lending series (as well as those of other explanatory variables, to be introduced below) are found to be I(2), or, more precisely, SI(1,1). Visual inspection of the seasonally differenced logarithms suggests low probability of a spurious regression, as the trends do not seem to diverge. Formal tests for cointegration of the I(1) series ruled out spurious correlation entirely.

34 To test for robustness, other regressions were run that also included ten-year JGB yields, industrial production and corporate profits. The outcome was very similar.

35 Bank of Japan economists sometimes argue that the window guidance figures for the 1980s were so closely in line with the bank lending figures because window guidance was not strictly enforced any more, and instead constituted voluntary lending plans of banks. However, our research refutes this argument. All eye-witnesses involved with window guidance in the 1980s that we interviewed confirmed that it was a binding procedure imposed by the Bank of Japan. Moreover, if window guidance was voluntary in the 1980s, it would be difficult to explain why the gap between actual lending and the quota, announced three

months in advance, shrank in the 1980s. If it was a non-binding, voluntary procedure, banks would not have to fear either overshooting or undershooting the
quota, and hence larger error margins should be expected than in the pre-1982
period. But our eye-witnesses have already told us why: banks did not act voluntarily. Non-compliance and non-fulfilment of the quota remained punishable by
the Bank of Japan. Moreover, the quota itself was not determined by banks, but
it was set by decision-makers at the central bank.

36 Rhodes and Yoshino's (1999) interpretation of data suffers from the following
main problems: (a) a general-to-specific empirical methodology is not applied and
the usual set of diagnostic tests are not cited; (b) it is erroneously assumed that
window guidance mainly concerned city banks (which in fact account for only
about half of all lending subject to window guidance); (c) it is incorrectly argued
that 'Data on the guidance given to other banks is not available' (p. 168), and city
bank lending is hence used as proxy for all window guidance; (d) no distinction
is made between financial institutions that create credit (and hence were subject
to central bank guidance) and those that do not; (e) without empirical justification it is claimed that window guidance 'was used as a tool for constraining loan
growth' (p. 167) as 'the BoJ's intention was to dictate the maximum allowable
expansion in bank lending, rather than to push banks to lend beyond their
desired levels' (p. 167). The latter assumption could bias an interpretation of an
unstable window guidance coefficient during periods when the Bank of Japan did
in fact encourage loan growth increases, such as the late 1980s. In any case, our
estimations, using aggregate window guidance of all four major bank types (thus
testing a loan volume twice as large as in Rhodes and Yoshino), found no structural break in the period from 1988 to 1991, as claimed by Rhodes and Yoshino's
study of city bank window guidance.

37 Patrick (1962) found that 'the "excessive" competition of city banks in extending
loans resulting in an overly rapid expansion of credit is a misplacing of the
responsibility for credit control. It is the duty of the Bank of Japan to control
the amount of credit creation by commercial banks ... The excess lending [of the
1950s] was the fault not of the banks trying to maximise profits, but of the Bank
of Japan for allowing such credit expansion to take place' (p. 182).

38 One senior Bank of Japan official even stated on the record to the Nikkei newspaper that the bubble was created by the Bank of Japan through its window guidance credit controls. See Nikkei (1992).

39 On 1 April 1998, the revised Bank of Japan Law became effective. With this, monetary policy was removed from democratic controls and entrusted to the Bank of
Japan's discretion. Since then, the central bank has refused to listen to the wishes
of the Prime Minister, the minister of Finance and other members of government
and parliament to implement a more stimulatory monetary policy.

Chapter 21

1 For details of the creation and propagation of the Asian crisis in the case of
Thailand, see Werner (2000c). For a comparison with the less-affected India, see
Werner (2000b). For a general discussion of the cause and effect of the Asian crisis,
see Werner (2003c).

2 Central banks often argue that they should not expand their credit creation
through the purchase of assets during times of crisis, as they would make a loss
and/or their balance sheets would deteriorate. This argument has no merit for

several reasons. First of all, even if central banks' balance sheets were to deteriorate, there are no negative consequences. Loss of reputation cannot be an argument, since not adopting the right policies, as has occurred in the case of the Bank of Japan, would cause a more severe loss of reputation. Further, if central banks were not to engage in such transactions in times of crisis, then when should they engage in such transactions? They certainly would not be necessary in times of financial boom. Most of all, the argument that central banks' balance sheets and thus reputations would suffer is based on the assumption that the balance sheet of the central bank is of the same nature as the balance sheet of a private sector corporation or bank. However, a central bank is special. Take the case of a central bank purchasing bad loans from banks at book value (say, for ¥100 trillion), although their market value is lower (say, only ¥20 trillion). It may superficially appear as if a loss of ¥80 trillion is made. This would be true in the case of agents other than the central bank. The central bank, however, in this case will make a profit of (at least) ¥20 trillion (since it creates money at zero cost and obtains something worth ¥20 trillion with it). While it is *possible* to represent this transaction on the central bank balance sheet such that the false impression of a loss of ¥80 trillion is created, there is no logically compelling reason why one might wish to do so. The habit of treating note issuance as a liability is only a bookkeeping convention due to the historic experience when cash was to be exchanged into gold on demand, and today does not imply that the central bank has any costs or actual liabilities when issuing new money.

Another misunderstanding may arise if one assumes that the economy always operates at the full employment level. As discussed above, in our model the necessary restrictive assumptions are not made and the very nature of a credit crunch recession suggests that the economy will be below full employment. Thus monetary stimulation will not lead to inflation and does not operate via an 'inflation tax' or the like.

3 BBC, IMF repents over Malaysian criticism, Wednesday 11 December 2002, 06:58 GMT.
4 This echoed the forced closures that were imposed on German companies by the US lenders in the early 1930s.
5 Anil Kashyap, Size is not the anwer for Japan's banks, *Financial Times*, 19 April 2004. See also Kashyap (2002) and its critical discussion in Werner (2004d).
6 As Standard & Poor's argues about Korea and Japan; see David Pilling, Tokyo urged to improve corporate governance, *Financial Times*, 16 October 2002.
7 In Japan in the 1980s, this took the form of US pressure to stimulate the domestic economy. In Thailand and other countries it took the form of US and IMF pressure to deregulate the capital account and establish offshore banking facilities. In both cases, the local central banks supported both theoretical arguments and policy action.

Chapter 22

1 Nichigin sōsai, kuni ya chihō no zeikin no tsukaikata 'hontōni heta', *Nikkei Net*, 18 September 2004, obtained at: www.nikkei.co.jp/news/keizai/20040918AT1F 1800E18092004.html
2 This finding is supported by theoretical and empirical research produced beyond the ranks of hard-core monetarists. Bernanke and Gertler's (1999) econometric

analysis attributes 'much of Japan's current dilemma to exceptionally poor monetary policymaking' (Bernanke, 2000, p. 150). Bernanke (2000) speaks of Japan's recession as being 'self-induced' by monetary policy. McKibbin's (1996) multi-country model comes to the same conclusions as our framework, namely that monetary tightening (together with fiscal expansion that crowded out the private sector) explains much of Japan's downturn.

3 Having followed the debate closely for a decade, a clear pattern has emerged: a set of often legalistic, technical or contradictory arguments is proposed by Bank of Japan spokesmen. As soon as the flaws and contradictions of one argument are pointed out in public, central bank spokesmen have reacted not by correcting their mistakes and their policy, but by correcting their line of argument and simply deploying an entirely different, usually unrelated argument that happens to come to the same conclusion. This environment of ever shifting explanations and counter-arguments by the central bank has hopelessly entangled the central bank in contradictions, which are happily ignored by the next spokesperson. While the arguments frequently change, the conclusion has always followed a common script, no matter which spokesman expresses his personal opinion: the central bank has throughout the 1990s done all it could. This is suggestive of a predetermined policy that spokesmen are required to market to the public. A useful summary of some arguments until 1999 is Okina (1999). His arguments have since been countered, and were subsequently upgraded by central bank spokesmen such as Yamaguchi (2001a, 2001b, 2001c).

4 He is referring to well-rehearsed Bank of Japan staples, such as: they cannot buy foreign assets, as this would encroach onto the territory of the Ministry of Finance, and they would never wish to take away any of the powers of the Ministry (although the Fed is not known to have held back on foreign bond purchases when needed, despite the fact that foreign exchange policy is the domain of the Treasury, as Bernanke, 2000, p. 161, points out); setting an inflation target will be counterproductive, as it may not be achievable and hence not credible; any further monetary easing will weaken the yen more than is desirable for Japan's trading partners; foreign exchange intervention will not work, because the liquidity trap makes monetary policy ineffective, and hence results in sterilized foreign exchange intervention – a particularly disingenuous argument, since sterilizing is precisely what the Bank of Japan usually does to negate any effect of foreign exchange intervention policies ordered by the Ministry of Finance; further monetary easing will not affect demand; it will create uncontrollable inflation (two contradictory claims that are sometimes uttered in one breath); the list could continue. It is intriguing how charming new variants seem to emerge from the Bank of Japan on a regular basis. One sometimes wonders whether the Bank of Japan awards internal prizes for a new technical or legalistic excuse that can be employed to avoid monetary stimulation. Ueda must have won one prize, since Governor Hayami has often borrowed from his 1999 rebuttal of the idea to purchase 'non-traditional assets': 'suggestions have been made to go beyond traditional tools of operations. The list is very long-term government bonds, stocks, consumer durables, real estate, foreign exchanges, and so on ... Whether central banks can systematically affect the prices of these assets is an old question to which no one has a satisfactory answer ... outright purchases of nontraditional assets ... generate various types of costs for the central bank and for the economy, some of which we may not be aware of and most of which are not explicitly dealt with in formal models economists use. These costs certainly ought to be weighed against possible benefits of the operations

before any decision is made. I hope we will not be the one to make such a risky decision' (Ueda, 1999, as quoted by Posen, 2000, pp. 198ff.). Perhaps the 'costs' Ueda refers to are an economic recovery, a decline in unemployment and fewer suicide cases? Perhaps not something the central bank is willing to risk.

5 This sentiment echoes the earlier finding by another famous expert on central bank policy, based on his experience in the US: 'I attended many such meetings of so-called academic consultants ... However, I finally concluded that the meetings were called purely for window-dressing purposes ...' (Friedman, 1982). The quote continues: 'I was unable to detect any influence whatsoever exerted by the consultants' comments on the system's actions. Indeed, the choice of the particular consultants invited to attend seemed designed to guarantee offsetting and contradictory advice, leaving the Fed free to pursue its own devices. However, even on those rare occasions when something approaching a consensus emerged, I could detect no subsequent effect on policy' (Friedman, 1982, p. 105).

6 An insightful journalist asked a key Bank of Japan official the question in 1992, whether the central bank should not complement its interest rate reductions with 'quantitative easing' or expansions in the money supply. The official responded: 'It used to be our common sense approach to watch both the interest rate side and the quantity side, and then take decisions, while quite widely employing methods of imposing limits, such as window guidance. Now the liberalization has moved forward and also the Bank of Japan has abolished window guidance. Now, to decide whether easing is sufficient or not, it is enough to see whether interest rates have fallen enough or not. Completely unrelated to that, I think that in the future the question will become important whether in a situation where financial institutions hold non-performing assets, bank behaviour will start to change completely, compared to the past – in other words, whether the behaviour of banks will differ from the past, when the Bank of Japan implements the same interest rate reductions as monetary policy, and whether the transmission mechanism of monetary policy is changing or not.' The interview was with Toshihiko Fukui, at the time Executive Director of the Bank of Japan. His familiarity with the 'window guidance' credit controls – the central bank's most important monetary policy tool of the postwar era – was not accidental: from 1986 to 1989 he had been director of the banking department, where he was responsible for the setting of the excessive bank loan quotas that the commercial banks were forced to fulfil by lending to the real estate sector (see Werner, 2002a). Moreover, Mr Fukui did not exactly lose touch with the central bank after his interview in 1992. To the contrary, from 1994 to 1998, as senior Deputy Governor of the Bank of Japan, he was the highest internal Bank of Japan member of staff (since the governor had been appointed from the outside). During the latter time period, Fukui oversaw the quantitative tightening of the central bank's credit creation policy, despite the sharp reduction in bank credit creation. The interview is reported in Kinyū fukyō wo kataru (4): Nihon ginkou riji Fukui Toshihiko Shi, *Nihon Keizai Shinbun*, 26 December 1992, p. 5.

7 The full quote is: 'By and large, it might be true that, if a central bank continues purchasing all kinds of assets, almost by definition, inflation can be created in the end. However, our goal is not to cause inflation but to realize a sustainable growth. As can be seen in the past experience of Japan's economy, it is not correct to assume that inflation comes first followed by an economic upturn or an increase in growth rate. What happened in the past was opposite: an economic upturn and a rise in growth rate came first and inflation followed with a lag. Therefore, the focus should be how to stimulate economic activities or, in other

words, how to make corporations invest more and households spend more' (Yamaguchi, 2001b, p. 9).

8   M. Hayami (2000b), The role of Japan amid the changing international environment, speech at the Meeting of the Executive Board of Directors of the Japan foreign Trade council, 7 June 2000, p. 4, available from Bank of Japan's website: www.boj.or.jp/en/press.

9   Maekawa was the chairman of a research group that reported to Prime Minister Nakasone and delivered its report on 7 April 1986. Another two reports followed, one a year later, and another in June 1988. See Werner (2002b).

10 While structural reforms proceeded, the central bankers simply shifted the goalposts. Ultimately, Hoshi and Patrick's (2000) definition appears accurate that the goal of structural reform is the introduction of a US-style economy. Having achieved 'remarkable structural reforms' already, Toshihiko Fukui (2001) had further structural change demands up his sleeve: 'The tasks that cannot be neglected include a sharp reduction in public works projects, drastic reforms of universities and promotion of academic-industry cooperation, corporate reorganization, creation of a society valuing individual achievement, and improvement of the social safety net.'

11 Almost verbatim, see also Deputy Governor Yamaguchi (2001c): 'In this environment, structural policies are important ... Expectations for future growth may well be enhanced as structural adjustments take hold' (p. 6).

12 Furthermore, the same view that cyclical policies cannot help, while for a recovery structural change is necessary, has also been expressed by various former Bank of Japan staff, including Saitō (1996, 2000), Inoue (2000), Kimura (2001b); Fukao (1999) is a notable exception.

13 'Nichigin fukusōsaikaiken', *Nikkei Kinyū Shinbun*, 24 November 1995, p. 7.

14 The structural reform agenda always included the change in the central bank law to make the Bank of Japan independent and unaccountable, until this goal was achieved in 1998. Mieno explained: 'In many countries today ... monetary policy making is entrusted to an independent central bank. This reflects the human wisdom that has been nurtured by history' (Mieno, 1994, p. 11). On later reform goals, see, for instance, Deputy Governor Yamaguchi: 'The role that the government should play in this is also quite large ... it is important to deregulate, to review the taxation system drastically, and to ensure that reform of public corporations progresses steadily. Another important challenge is to relieve the anxiety of households about the future by reviewing the social security system, including pension benefits' (Yamaguchi, 2001c, p. 11).

15 Y. Yamaguchi (1999), Monetary policy and structural policy: a Japanese perspective, speech by Yutaka Yamaguchi, Deputy Governor of the Bank of Japan, before Colloque Monetaire International at Banque de France, 8–9 October 1999, p. 5, available from the Bank of Japan's website: www.boj.or.jp/en/press.

16 Ex-BoJ Fukui negative on further monetary easing, Dow Jones, Tokyo, Thursday, 13 December 2001.

17 Often the reporters approve of the good intentions of the central bank. The article continues: 'In a political sense, this seems a reasonable suspicion. Virtually the only thing that has ever prompted Japanese politicians or business leaders to implement reform in recent years has been a market crisis or shortage of cash.' Gillian Tett, A hard choice for Japan, *Financial Times*, 2 December 2001.

18 For several Fukui quotes on this, see, for instance, Werner (2003e).

19   Nichigin sōsai, kuni ya chihō no zeikin no tsukaikata 'hontōni heta', *Nikkei Net*, 18 September 2004, obtained at: www.nikkei.co.jp/news/kcizai/20040918ATI F18092004.html.

20   Indeed, until April 1998, the Bank of Japan Law in Article 1 required the central bank to support government policy objectives. For most of the 1990s, governments made it clear, and backed their words with action, that their goal was to implement cyclical stimulation of the economy. To conform with the law, the Bank of Japan was therefore legally obliged to implement stimulatory monetary policies. However, it has failed to do so.

21   There does remain a case in defence of the Bank of Japan. It is built on the same argument that also supports the view that central banks should be made independent from democratically elected institutions. The argument is that, as objective technical experts, central bankers are more capable of implementing policies that are in the long run beneficial to the people. While it is understandable that the people and their governments might want to create quick recoveries, this is short-term thinking, akin to children wanting to have too many sweets or not wanting to go to school: for lack of knowledge, or lack of ability or discipline to focus on long-run goals, the children are making decisions that will hurt them in the long run. Therefore they do not get a choice: they are not legally entitled to make these decisions – their parents and the government through legislation make the decision for them. Similarly, the population of a country may lack discipline or understanding concerning economic policies. Therefore it could similarly be argued that they should not get a choice. So laws are promulgated that take away their influence over those economic policies that affect them most – namely monetary policy decisions. Instead, these decisions are now made by objective, highly trained technical experts who are disciplined to pursue long-term goals. There may be pain in the short run, but it will be good for the population in the long run. Essentially, the argument for central bank independence follows this line of reasoning. Therefore citizens' rights need to be taken away and highly trained experts should make the decisions for them. Anyone who follows this line of argument and agrees that people should not be given democratic rights, key decisions should be made by unelected technocrats, will have difficulty in drawing a distinction with the views on which totalitarian governments, like Hitler's Nazi regime, are based. The latter's view of euthanasia, eugenics and other issues was justified by the heartfelt belief that 'objective experts' should make decisions for the sake of what they knew to be the 'greater good' and the long-term 'benefit of the people'. Most of all, there is nothing in economic theory or empirical evidence to conclude that structural changes are actually necessary or beneficial (see Werner, 2004a).

22   Question by author to Jean-Claude Trichet at the World Economic Forum in Davos in January 2004. Answer: 'The monetary policy of the ECB is conducted through interest rates. I do not know what you mean by "credit creation".'

23   For more empirical work on the ECB and the Bank of Japan, see Werner (2003c).

Chapter 23

1   Quoted from Wikipedia, the free online encyclopedia, obtained at: http://en.wikipedia.org/wiki/Occam%27s_Razor.

2   Quoted from Wikipedia, obtained at: http://en.wikipedia.org/wiki/Occam% 27s_Razor.
3   Ockham (1979), p. 290 (*Sent.* I, dist. 30, q. 1): 'For nothing ought to be posited without a reason given, unless it is self-evident [*literally*, known through itself] or known by experience or proved by the authority of Sacred Scripture.' Even logicians not accepting the latter will agree with the former two necessary conditions.
4   With 'at the market' orders, executions are more likely. But prices will not be known. Again, due to market imperfections this means that buyers or sellers are not likely to receive fair value. Thus many fund managers insist on limit orders or first agree prices with their broker and/or the counter-party. In this case, the outcome is also likely to depend on order size and differ for different types of investors. Thus the executions are discrete cases that differ each time and there cannot be talk of continuous demand or supply functions or market equilibrium.
5   Muellbauer and Portes (1978) have shown that rationing of one market implies rationing of others.
6   Cube: surface area = $6l^2$; volume = l^3
    Sphere: surface area = $4\pi r^2$; volume = $4/3\pi r^3$.
7   For a survey of economic implications of happiness research, see Frey and Stutzer (2002).
8   Laboratory findings showed the importance of relative judgements of happiness (Smith et al., 1989; Tversky and Griffin, 1991).
9   On how it rather unscientifically introduced concepts from now outdated nineteenth-century energy physics to model consumer behaviour, see Mirowski (1989).

Chapter 24

1   The sponsorship of the Bank of Sweden Prize in Economic Sciences – by journalists erroneously but consistently called a 'Nobel Prize in Economics' – is another topic worthy of closer scientific examination. However, here it is not suggested that the views of an economist who supports central bank independence, such as Stephen Cecchetti who is quoted at the opening of this chapter, are in any way influenced by his close employment ties with central banks. His website does disclose the fact that he is 'consultant to central banks around the world ... From August 1997 to September 1999, he was Executive Vice President and Director of Research at the Federal Reserve Bank of New York, as well as Associate Economist of the Federal Open Market Committee' (http://people.brandeis.edu/~cecchett/ bio.shtml).
2   It is interesting to note that the Bank of Japan Law was changed subsequently to these proposals, such that the implementation of several of the 'quantitative easing' proposals became legally more difficult. The substance of the new Bank of Japan Law was drafted by the Bank of Japan itself and passed with only minor modifications in 1997 (effective from 1998).

Bibliography

Acheson, K. and J. Chant (1973a), Bureaucratic theory and the choice of central bank goals, *Journal of Money, Credit and Banking*, vol. 5, pp. 637–55.

Acheson, K. and J. Chant (1973b), Mythology and central banking, *Kyklos*, vol. 26, pp. 362–79.

Agarwal, Rajshree, and Julie Ann Elston (2001), Bank–firm relationships: financing and firm performance in Germany, *Economics Letters*, vol. 72, pp. 225–32.

Agenor, Pierre-Richard, Joshua Aizenman and A. Hoffmaister (2000), The credit crunch in East Asia: what can bank excess liquid assets tell us?, World Bank Working Paper 2483, IBRD, Washington, DC: World Bank.

Akabane, Takao (1997), *Nihon keizai tanteijutsu*, Tokyo: Toyo Keizai Shinpo Sha.

Allen, Franklin, and Anthony M. Santomero (1997), The theory of financial intermediation, *Journal of Banking and Finance*, vol. 21, nos 11–12, pp. 1461–86.

Allen, Roy E. (1989), Globalization of the U.S. financial markets: the new structure for monetary policy, in Richard O'Brien and Tapan Datta (eds), *International Economics and Financial Markets*, Oxford: Oxford University Press, pp. 266–86.

Allen, Roy E. (1994), *Financial Crises and Recession in the Global Economy*, Aldershot: Edward Elgar Publishing.

Allsopp, Christopher, and Colin Mayer (eds) (1994), Money and Banking, *Oxford Review of Economic Policy*, vol. 10, no. 4, Winter.

Andersen, Leonall C., and Keith M. Carlson (1970), A monetarist model for economic stabilization, *Federal Reserve Bank of St. Louis Review*, vol. 52, April, pp. 7–25.

Andersen, Leonall C, and Jerry L. Jordan (1968), Monetary and fiscal actions: a test of their relative importance in economic stabilization, *Federal Reserve Bank of St. Louis Review*, vol. 50, November, pp. 11–23.

Andreau, Jean (1999), *Banking and Business in the Roman World*, Cambridge: Cambridge University Press.

Aoki, Masahiko (1994), The Japanese firm as a system of attributes: a survey and research agenda, in Masahiko Aoki and Ronald Dore (eds), *The Japanese Firm: The Sources of Competitive Strength*, Oxford: Oxford University Press.

Aoki, Masahiko, and Ronald Dore (1994) (eds), *The Japanese Firm: The Sources of Competitive Strength*, Oxford: Oxford University Press.

Aoki, Masahiko, Hyung-Ki Kim and Masahiro Okuno-Fujiwara (1997), *The Role of Government in East Asian Economic Development: Comparative Institutional Analysis*, Oxford: Oxford University Press.

Aoki, Masahiko, and Hugh Patrick (eds) (1994), *The Japanese Main Bank System: Its Relevance for Developing and Transforming Economies*, Oxford: Oxford University Press.

Appleyard, Dennis R., and Alfred J. Field (1998), *International Economics*, 2nd edn, Boston: Irwin/McGraw-Hill.

Arestis, Philip, and Peter G. A. Howells (1996), Theoretical reflections on endogenous money: the problem with 'convenience lending', *Cambridge Journal of Economics*, vol. 20, pp. 539–51.

Arestis, Philip, Machiko Nissanke and Howard Stein (2003), Finance and development: institutional and policy alternatives to financial liberalisation, Working Paper 377, Annandale-on-Hudson: Levy Economics Institute of Bard College.

Arestis, Philip, and Malcolm C. Sawyer (2002), The Bank of England macroeconomic model: its nature and implications, *Journal of Post Keynesian Economics*, vol. 24, no. 4, pp. 529–45.

Arestis, Philip, and Malcolm C. Sawyer (2003a), Can monetary policy affect the real economy? The dubious effectiveness of interest rate policy, *Public Policy Brief*, no. 71, Annandale-on-Hudson: Levy Economics Institute of Bard College.

Arestis, Philip, and Malcolm C. Sawyer (2003b), The nature and role of monetary policy when money is endogenous, Working Paper 374, Annandale-on-Hudson: Levy Economics Institute of Bard College.

Arrow, Kenneth J. (1959), Towards a theory of price adjustment, in M. Abramowitz et al. (eds), *The Allocation of Economic Resources*, Stanford: Stanford University Press.

Asako, Kazumi (1991), The land price bubble in Japan, *Ricerche Economiche*, vol. XLV, nos 2–3, pp. 451–68.

Asako, Kazumi, T. Ito and K. Sakamoto (1991), The rise and fall of the deficit in Japan, *Journal of Japanese and International Economies*, vol. 5, pp. 451–72.

Aschauer, David (1985), Fiscal policy and aggregate demand, *American Economic Review*, vol. 75, no. 1, March, pp. 117–27.

Astle, David (1975), *The Babylonian Woe*, Toronto (n.p.).

Baba, Naohiko (1996), Empirical studies on the recent decline in bank lending growth: an approach based on asymmetric information, February, Institute for Monetary and Economic Studies, Bank of Japan, Discussion Paper 96-E-10.

Backhouse, Roger (1985), *A History of Modern Economic Analysis*, Oxford: Basil Blackwell.

Balassa, Bela, and Marcus Noland (1988), *Japan in the World Economy*, Washington, DC: Institute for International Economics.

Bank for International Settlements (BIS) (2002), *BIS 72nd Annual Report*, Basel, Switzerland: BIS, 8 July.

Bank of England (1996), *Inflation Report*, Summer quarter.

Bank of Japan (1973), *Money and Banking in Japan*, translated by S. Nishimura, edited by L. S. Pressnell, London: Macmillan Press.

Bank of Japan (1975), Nihon ni okeru mane sapurai no jūyōsei ni tsuite, *Chōsa Geppō*, July, pp. 1–11.

Bank of Japan (1987), Waga kuni no kinyū seido, edited by Yoshio Suzuki, Institute for Monetary and Economic Studies, Bank of Japan, Tokyo.

Bank of Japan (1988a), Saikin no money supply dōkō ni tsuite (On the recent behaviour of money supply), *Chōsa Geppō*, Bank of Japan, February, pp. 1–24.

Bank of Japan (1988b), Shinyō shūkei ryō (Credit aggregates) ni tsuite, *Chōsa Geppō*, Bank of Japan, December, pp. 35–45.

Bank of Japan (1991a), Waga kuni no kinyū seido (Our country's financial system), 7th edn, Institute for Monetary and Economic Studies, Bank of Japan.

Bank of Japan (1991b), The process of decision-making and implementation of monetary policy in Japan, Research and Statistics Department, Bank of Japan, Special Paper no. 198, by Nakao Masaaki and Akinari Horii, March.

Bank of Japan (1992a), Speech by Governor Yasushi Mieno: Behaviour of finance and economy in the Year 3 of Heisei, *Bank of Japan Monthly Bulletin*, June.

Bank of Japan (1992b), Nihon ginkō no kinō to gyōmu, Institute for Monetary and Economic Studies, Bank of Japan, Tokyo.

Barber, Tony (2001), An independent spirit in Europe: the timing of the ECB's rate cut reflects not just its economic judgement but also its determination not to give in to outside pressure, *Financial Times*, 11 May.

Barran, F., V. Coudert and B. Mojon (1995), Transmission de la politique monetaire et credit bancaire. Une application a trois pays de l'OCDE, *Revue Economique*, vol. 46, no. 2, pp. 393–413.

Barro, Robert J. (1974), Are government bonds net wealth? *Journal of Political Economy*, vol. 82, November/December, pp. 1095–117.

Barro, Robert, and H. Grossman (1976), *Money, Employment and Inflation*, Cambridge: Cambridge University Press.

Basu, Susanto (1996), Pro-cyclical productivity: increasing returns or cyclical utilization?, *Quarterly Journal of Economics*, August, pp. 719–51.

Barth, James, George Iden and Frank Russek (1984), Do federal deficits really matter? *Contemporary Policy Issues*, Fall.

Bayoumi Tamim (1999), The morning after: explaining the slowdown in Japanese growth in the 1990s, IMF Working Paper no. 99/13, Washington, DC: IMF.

Bayoumi, Tamim (2000), The morning after: explaining the slowdown in Japanese growth in the 1990s, in Tamim Bayoumi and Charles Collyns, *Post-Bubble Blues: How Japan Responded to Asset Price Collapse*, Washington, DC: IMF, pp. 10–44.

Bayoumi, Tamim (2001), The morning after: explaining the slowdown in Japanese growth in the 1990s, *Journal of International Economics*, vol. 53, pp. 241–59.

Bean, Charles R. (1983), Targeting nominal income: an appraisal, *Economic Journal*, vol. 93, December, pp. 806–19.

Belongia, Michael T., and James A. Chalfant (1990), Alternative measures of money as indicators of inflation: a survey and some new evidence, *Federal Reserve Bank of St. Louis Review*, St. Louis: Federal Reserve Bank of St. Louis, November/December.

Benassy, Jean Pascal (1986), *Macroeconomics: An Introduction to the Non-Walrasian Approach*, London: Academic Press.

Berger, Allen, and Gregory Udell (1994), Did risk-based capital allocate credit and cause a 'credit crunch' in the United States?, *Journal of Money, Credit and Banking*, vol. 26, pp. 585–628.

Bernanke, Ben S. (1983), Nonmonetary effects of the financial collapse in the propagation of the great depression, *American Economic Review*, vol. 73, pp. 257–76.

Bernanke, Ben S. (1993), Credit and the macroeconomy, *FRBNY Quarterly Review*, vol. 18, no. 1, Spring, New York: Federal Reserve Bank of New York, pp. 50–70.

Bernanke, Ben S. (2000), Japanese monetary policy: a case of self-induced paralysis?, in Ryoichi Mikitani and Adam S. Posen (eds), *Japan's Financial Crisis and its Parallels to U.S. Experience*, Special Report no. 13, Washington, DC: Institute for International Economics, September.

Bernanke, Ben S., and Alan S. Blinder (1988), Credit, money and aggregate demand, *American Economic Review, Proceedings*, vol. 78, May, pp. 435–39.

Bernanke, Ben S., and Alan S. Blinder (1992), The federal funds rate and the channels of monetary transmission, *American Economic Review*, vol. 82, September, pp. 901–21.

Bernanke Ben S., and Mark Gertler (1995), Inside the black box: the credit channel of monetary policy transmission, *Journal of Economic Perspectives*, vol. 9, no. 4, Fall, pp. 27–48.

Bernanke, Ben S., and Mark Gertler (1999), Monetary policy and asset price volatility, in *1999 Symposium: New Challenges for Monetary Policy*, Kansas: Federal Reserve Bank of Kansas City, pp. 77–128.

Bernanke, Ben S., Mark Gertler and Simon Gilchrist (1996), The financial accelerator and the flight to quality, *Review of Economics and Statistics*, vol. 78, no. 1, pp. 1–15.

Bernanke, Ben S., and Cara S. Lown (1991), The credit crunch, *Brookings Papers on Economic Activity*, vol. 2, pp. 205–39.

Black, F. (1972), Active and passive monetary policy in a neoclassical model, *Journal of Finance*, vol. 27, pp. 801–14.

Blanchard, Olivier Jean (1990), Why does money affect output? A survey, in B. M. Friedman and F. H. Hahn (eds), *Handbook of Monetary Economics*, Volume II, Amsterdam: Elsevier Science Publishers, chapter 15.

Blanchard, Olivier, and Stanley Fischer (1989), *Lectures on Macroeconomics*, Cambridge, MA: MIT Press.

Blinder, Alan S., and Robert M. Solow (1973), Does fiscal policy matter?, *Journal of Public Economics*, vol. 2, pp. 319–37.

Board of Governors of the Federal Reserve System (1988), *Federal Reserve Bulletin*, pp. 419–29.

Boughton, James M. (1991), Long-run money demand in large industrial countries, *IMF Staff Papers*, vol. 38, no. 1, March, pp. 1–32.

Bradford, David F. (1990), What is national saving? Alternative measures in historical and international context, NBER Working Paper Series, no. 3341, April.

Branson, William F. (1968), *Financial Flows in the US Balance of Payments*, Amsterdam: North-Holland.

Bredemeier, Sonning (1972), *Erfahrungen mit der Kreditplafondierung*, Veroeffentlichungen des Instituts fuer Empirische Wirtschaftsforschung, Berlin: Duncker and Humblot.

Brunner, Karl, and Allan H. Meltzer (1968), Liquidity traps for money, bank credit and interest rates, *Journal of Political Economy*, vol. 76, January, pp. 1–37.

Brunner, Karl, and Allan Meltzer (1976), An aggregate theory for a closed economy, in Jerome Stein (ed.), *Monetarism*, Amsterdam: North-Holland.

Brunner, Karl, and Allan H. Meltzer (1983), Strategies and tactics for monetary control, in Karl Brunner and Allan H. Meltzer (eds), Money, Monetary Policy and Financial Institutions, *Carnegie-Rochester Conference Series on Public Policy*, vol. 18, Amsterdam: North-Holland, pp. 59–104.

Burger, Albert E. (1988), The puzzling growth of the monetary aggregates in the 1980s, *Review*, St. Louis: Federal Reserve Bank of St. Louis, September/October.

Burnside, Craig, Martin Eichenbaum and Sergio Rebelo (1995) Capital utilization and returns to scale, in Stanley Fischer and Julio J. Rotemberg (eds), *NBER Macroeconomics Annual*, Cambridge, MA: MIT Press, pp. 67–123.

Calder, Kent E. (1993), *Strategic Capitalism, Private Business and Public Purpose in Japanese Industrial Finance*, Princeton: Princeton University Press.

Calomiris, Charles W., Charles P. Himmelberg and Paul Wachtel (1995), Commercial paper, corporate finance, and the business cycle: a microeconomic perspective, *Carnegie-Rochester Conference Series on Public Policy*, vol. 42, pp. 203–50.

Caprio, Jerry, and Daniela Klingebiel (1999), Episodes of systemic and borderline financial crises, mimeo, Washington, DC: World Bank, October.

Cargill, Thomas F. (1989), *Central Bank Independence and Regulatory Responsibilities: The Bank of Japan and the Federal Reserve*, New York: Salomon Brothers Center for the Study of Financial Institutions, New York University.

Cargill, Thomas F., Michael M. Hutchison and Takatoshi Ito (1997), *The Political Economy of Japanese Monetary Policy*, Cambridge, MA: MIT Press.

Cargill, Thomas F., Michael M. Hutchison and Takatoshi Ito (2000), *Financial Policy and Central Banking in Japan*, Cambridge, MA: MIT Press.

Caves, R., and M. Uekusa (1976), *Industrial Organization in Japan*, Washington, DC: Brookings Institution.

Cecchetti, Steven G. (2000), Making monetary policy: objectives and rules, *Oxford Review of Economic Policy*, vol. 16, issue 4, pp. 43–59.

Central Statistical Office (CSO) (1986), *Financial Statistics Handbook*, London: CSO.

Cheung, Yin-Wong, and Eiji Fujii (1999), A note on the power of money-output causality tests, paper presented at the Western Economic Association 73rd Annual Conference, published in *Oxford Bulletin of Economics and Statistics*, vol. 63, issue 2, May, pp. 247–61, available at: http://econ.ucsc.edu/faculty/cheung/9908oxfb.pdf

Chow, Gregory, C. (1960), Tests of equality between sets of coefficients in two linear regressions, *Econometrica*, vol. 28, no. 3, pp. 591–605.

Christ, Carl F. (1968), A simple macroeconomic model with a government budget restraint, *Journal of Political Economy*, vol. 76, January, pp. 53–67.

Claessens, Stijn, Daniela Klingebiel and Luc Laeven (2001), Financial restructuring in banking and corporate sector crises – what policies to pursue?, NBER, April, available at www.nber.org/books/mgmtcrises/claessens4-24-01.pdf

Clower, R. (1965), The Keynesian counterrevolution, in F. Hahn and F. Brechling (eds), *The Theory of Interest Rates*, London: Macmillan.

Cohen, Edward E. (1992), *Athenian Economy and Society: A Banking Perspective*, Princeton: Princeton University Press.

Congdon, Tim (2001), Money and the Japanese economic crisis, *Lombard Street Research Monthly Economic Review*, August, as quoted by Guido Zimmermann, Deflation und Geldpolitik in Japan: Was laeuft falsch? *Japan Analysen Prognosen* Nr. 185, May 2002, Japan-Zentrum der Ludwig-Maximilian-Universitaet Muenchen, Munich.

Corsetti, Giancarlo, Paolo Pesenti and Nouriel Roubini (2001), Fundamental determinants of the Asian crisis: the role of financial fragility and external imbalances, in Takatoshi Ito and Anne O. Krueger (eds), *Regional Global Capital Flows: Macroeconomic Causes and Consequences*, East Asian Seminar on Economics, vol. 10, Chicago: University of Chicago Press; New York: Federal Reserve Bank of New York and NBER.

Cramer, J. S. (1986), The volume of transactions and the circulation of money in the United States, 1959–70, *Journal of Business and Economic Statistics*, vol. 4, no. 2, April, pp. 232–52.

Crooks, Ed, and Tony Major (2003), Comment and analysis: hopes are rising that the eurozone economy is at a turning-point. But can it ever catch up with America?, *Financial Times*, 1 September.

Dalziel, Paul (2000), On the evolution of money and its implications for price stability, *Journal of Economic Surveys*, vol. 14, no. 4, pp. 373–93.

Davies, Glyn (1994), *A History of Money*, Cardiff: University of Wales Press.

Davis, E. P. (1989), Instability in the euromarkets and the economic theory of financial crisis, Bank of England Discussion Paper, no. 43.

DeRosa, David (2001), Recent innovations in Japanese monetary policy, mimeo, Yale School of Management, available at: http://icf.som.yale.edu/Conference-Papers/Summer2001/DeRosa_BOJ.PDF

Detken, Carsten, and Frank Smets (2004), Asset price booms and monetary policy, Working Paper Series, no. 364, May, Frankfurt: European Central Bank.

Deutsche Bundesbank (1992), *Monthly Report*, vol. 44, no. 8, August, Frankfurt: Deutsche Bundesbank.

DeYoung, Robert, Lawrence G. Goldberg and Lawrence J. White (1999), Youth, adolescence and maturity of banks: credit availability to small business in an era of banking consolidation, *Journal of Banking and Finance*, vol. 23, nos 2–4, February, pp. 463–92.

Diamond, Douglas (1984), Financial intermediation and delegated monitoring, *Review of Economic Studies*, vol. 51, pp. 393–414.

Dimsdale, Nicholas (1994), Banks, capital markets, and the monetary transmission mechanism, *Oxford Review of Economic Policy*, vol. 10, no. 4, Winter issue on money and banking, pp. 34–48.

Dore, Ronald (2000), *Stock Market Capitalism: Welfare Capitalism: Japan and Germany versus the Anglo-Saxons*, Oxford: Oxford University Press.

Dornbusch, Rudiger, and Stanley Fischer (1987), *Macroeconomics*, International editions, 4th edn, New York: McGraw-Hill.

Dotsey, Michael (1986), Japanese monetary policy, a comparative analysis, *Bank of Japan Monetary and Economic Studies*, Bank of Japan, October.

Drayson, Stephen J. (1985), The housing finance market: recent growth in perspective, *Bank of England Quarterly Bulletin*, vol. 25, no. 1, pp. 80–91.

Driscoll, John C. (1994), Does bank lending affect output? Evidence from the U.S., Working Paper, Cambridge, MA: Harvard University, Department of Economics.

Dwyer, Gerald (1985), Federal deficits, interest rates and monetary policy, *Journal of Money, Credit and Banking*, vol. 17, no. 4, November, pp. 655–81.

Easterlin, Richard A. (2001), Income and happiness: towards a unified theory, *Economic Journal*, vol. 111, pp. 465–84.

Economic Planning Agency (1991), Kokumin Keizai Sotorihiki no Suikei, *Keizai Bunseki*, April.

Endo, Tadashi (2001), Linkage of corporate bond market to government bond market, presentation at Workshop on Developing Government Bond Markets in Latin America, 11 June, International Finance Corporation, Washington, DC: World Bank Group, currently available at: www1.worldbank.org/finance/assets/images/Presentation_061101_-_Endo.pdf

Engle, R. F., and C. W. J. Granger (1987), Cointegration and error correction: representation, estimation, and testing, *Econometrica*, vol. 55, pp. 251–76.

Engle, R. F., David F. Hendry and J. -F. Richard (1983), Exogeneity, *Econometrica*, vol. 51, pp. 277–304.

Eguchi, Hidekazu (1977), Comment: Horiuchi Akiyoshi 'madoguchi shidō' no yūkosei, *Keizai Kenkyū*, vol. 28, pp. 242–5.

Eguchi, Hidekazu (1978), Tanki kinyū shijō no working ni tsuite – Horiuchi Akiyoshi shi no rejoinder e no kotae mo kanete, *Keizai Kenkyū*, vol. 29, pp. 81–4.

Einzig, Paul (1948), *Primitive Money in its Ethnological, Historical and Economic Aspects*, London: Eyre and Spottiswoode.

European Central Bank (ECB) (2004), Press release: launch of new publication *International Journal of Central Banking*, 26 July 2004, currently available at: www.ecb.int/press/pr/date/2004/html/pr040726.en.html

European Union (EU) (2003), Testimony before the Committee on Economic and Monetary Affairs of the European Parliament with the President of the European Central Bank, in accordance with Article 113(3) of the Treaty on European Union, Introductory statement by Dr Willem F. Duisenberg, President of the European Central Bank, Brussels, 21 May 2002, obtained at: www.ecb.int/press/key/date/2002/html/sp020521.en.html

Fama, Eugene F. (1980), Banking in the theory of finance, *Journal of Monetary Economics*, vol. 6, no. 1, January, pp. 39–57.

Fama, Eugene F. (1985), What's different about banks?, *Journal of Monetary Economics*, vol. 15, pp. 29–39.

Faruqi, Shaki (1994), *Financial Sector Reforms, Economic Growth, and Stability: Experiences in Selected Asian and Latin American Countries*, Washington, DC: World Bank.

Ferri, Giovanni, and Tae Soo Kang (1998), The credit channel at work: lessons from the Republic of Korea's financial crisis, mimeo, IBRD, Washington, DC: World Bank.

Fisher, Irving (1926), *The Purchasing Power of Money: Its Determination and Relation to Credit, Interest and Crises*, 2nd edn, assisted by Harry G. Brown, New York: Macmillan.

Fisher, Irving, and Harry G. Brown (1911), *The Purchasing Power of Money: Its Determination and Relation to Credit, Interest and Crises*, New York: Macmillan.

Floyd, John E. (1969), International capital movements and monetary equilibrium, *American Economic Review*, vol. 59, no. 4, September, pp. 472–92.

Fohlin, Caroline (1999), The rise of interlocking directorates in imperial Germany, *Economic History Review*, vol. 52, no. 2, pp. 307–33.

Forder, James (1998a), Central bank independence – conceptual clarifications and interim assessment, *Oxford Economic Papers*, vol. 50, pp. 307–34.

Forder, James (1998b), The case for an independent European central bank: a reassessment of evidence and sources, *European Journal of Political Economy*, vol. 14, pp. 53–71.

Forder, James (1999), Central bank independence: reassessing the measurements, *Journal of Economic Issues*, vol. 33, no. 1, March, pp. 23–40.

Forder, James (2000), Book review: Central bank independence and credibility: is there a shred of evidence? *International Finance*, vol. 3, no. 1, pp. 167–85.

Forder, James (2002), Interests and 'independence': the European Central Bank and the theory of bureaucracy, *International Review of Applied Economics*, vol. 16, no. 1, pp. 51–69.

Foster, J. (1992), The determination of sterling M3, 1963–88: an evolutionary macroeconomic approach, *Economic Journal*, vol. 102, no. 412, May.

French, Kenneth R., and James M. Poterba (1991), Were Japanese stock prices too high? *Journal of Financial Economics*, vol. 29, pp. 337–63.

Frey, Bruno S., and Alois Stutzer (2002), What can economists learn from happiness research? *Journal of Economic Literature*, vol. 40, no. 2, pp. 402–35.

Friedman, Benjamin M. (1978), Crowding out or crowding in? Economic consequences of financing government deficits, *Brookings Papers on Economic Activity*, vol. 3, pp. 593–641.

Friedman, Benjamin M. (1981), The roles of money and credit in macroeconomic analysis, Working Paper no. 831, National Bureau of Economic Research.

Friedman, Benjamin M. (2000), Japan now and the United States then: lessons from the parallels, in Ryoichi Mikitani and Adam S. Posen (eds), *Japan's Financial Crisis and its Parallels to U.S. Experience*, Special Report no. 13, Washington, DC: Institute for International Economics, September.

Friedman, Benjamin M., and Kenneth N. Kuttner (1993), Economic activity and the short-term credit market: an analysis of prices and quantities, *Brookings Papers on Economic Activity*, vol. 2, pp. 1–4.

Friedman, Milton (1953), The methodology of positive economics, in Milton Friedman, *Essays in Positive Economics*, Chicago: University of Chicago Press.

Friedman, Milton (1956), The quantity theory of money – a restatement, in Milton Friedman (ed.), *Studies in the Quantity Theory of Money*, Chicago: University of Chicago Press.

Friedman, Milton (1968), The role of monetary policy, *American Economic Review*, vol. 58, no. 1, March, pp. 1–17.

Friedman, Milton (1970), A theoretical framework for monetary analysis, *Journal of Political Economy*, vol. 78, no. 2, pp. 193–238.

388   *New Paradigm in Macroeconomics*

Friedman, Milton (1982), Monetary policy, theory and practice, *Journal of Money, Credit and Banking*, vol. 14, no. 1, February, pp. 98–118.
Friedman, Milton (1984), Lessons from the 1979–82 monetary policy experiment, *American Economic Review*, vol. 74, May, pp. 497–9.
Friedman, Milton (1997), Rx for Japan: back to the future, *Wall Street Journal*, 17 December, p. A22.
Friedman, Milton, and Anna J. Schwartz (1963), *A Monetary History of the United States, 1867–1960*, Princeton: Princeton University Press.
Fry, Maxwell J. (1978), Money and capital or financial deepening in economic development, *Journal of Money, Credit and Banking*, vol. 10, no. 4, November, pp. 464–75.
Fry, Maxwell J. (1980), Saving, investment, growth and the cost of financial repression, *World Development*, vol. 8, no. 4, April, pp. 317–27.
Fry, Maxwell J. (1984), Saving, financial intermediation and economic growth in Asia, *Asian Development Review*, vol. 2, no. 1, pp. 82–91.
Fukao, Kyoji, Tomohiko Inui, Hiroki Kawai and Tsutomu Miyagawa (2003), Sectoral productivity and economic growth in Japan, 1970–98: an empirical analysis based on the JIP database, July, paper presented at the NBER Thirteenth Annual East Asian Seminar on Economics, Productivity, 20–22 June 2002, Melbourne, Australia, currently available at www.nber.org/books/ease13/fukao-et-al7-18-03.pdf
Fukao, Mitsuhiro (1999), Nichigin wa motto ryoteki kanwa wo subekida (The bank of Japan should conduct further quantitative easing), *Shūkan Touyou Keizai*, 6 March, (in Japanese).
Fukao, Mitsuhiro (2003), Financial sector profitability and double gearing, in Magnus Blomstrom, Jenny Corbett, Fumio Hayashi and Anil Kashyap (eds), *Structural Impediments to Growth in Japan*, Chicago: University of Chicago Press.
Fukui, Toshihiko (2001), Year of testing for Japan's economy, *Nikkei Weekly*, 5 March, p. 7.
Fukui, Toshihiko (2002), Japan's financial system in need of radical surgery, *Nikkei Weekly*, 5 March, p. 7.
Fukuyama, Francis (1992), *The End of History and the Last Man*, New York: Free Press.
Gertler, Mark (1988), Financial structure and aggregate economic activity: an overview, *Journal of Money, Credit and Banking*, vol. 20, no. 3, August.
Gertler, Mark, and Simon Gilchrist (1993), The role of credit market imperfections in the monetary transmission mechanism: arguments and evidence, *Scandinavian Journal of Economics*, vol. 109, May, pp. 309–40.
Gertler, Mark, and Simon Gilchrist (1994), Monetary policy, business cycles and the behavior of small manufacturing firms, *Quarterly Journal of Economics*, vol. 109, pp. 309–40.
Glasner, D. (1992), The real-bills doctrine in the light of the law of reflux, *History of Political Economy*, vol. 24, pp. 867–94.
Goldfeld, Stephen M. (1974), New measures of fiscal and monetary policy, 1958–1971, Princeton: Princeton University, Econometric Research Program.
Goldfeld, Stephen M. (1976), The case of the missing money, *Brookings Papers on Economic Activity*, vol. 3, pp. 683–730.
Goldfeld, Stephen M., and Daniel E. Sichel (1990), The demand for money, in B. M. Friedman and F. H. Hahn (eds), *Handbook of Monetary Economics*, Volume I, Amsterdam: Elsevier Science Publishers, pp. 300–56.
Goldsmith, Raymond W. (1969), *Financial Structure and Development*, New Haven: Yale University Press.

Goodhart, Charles A. E. (1973), Analysis of the determination of the stock of money, in J. M. Parkin and A. R. Nobay (eds), *Essays in Modern Economics*, London: Longman, reprinted in Charles A. E. Goodhart (ed.), *Monetary Theory and Practice*, London: Macmillan Press, 1984.

Goodhart, Charles A. E. (1989a), The conduct of monetary policy, *Economic Journal*, vol. 99, June, pp. 293–346.

Goodhart, Charles A. E. (1989b), *Money, Information and Uncertainty*, 2nd edn, London: Macmillan.

Goodhart, Charles A. E. (1989c), Has Moore become too horizontal? *Journal of Post-Keynesian Economics*, vol. 14, Fall, pp. 134–6.

Goodhart, Charles A. E. (1989d), What do central banks do? Issues in central banking, Supplement, Sydney: Reserve Bank of Australia, reprinted in Charles A. E. Goodhart (1995), *The Central Bank and the Financial System*, London: Macmillan.

Goodhart, Charles A. E. (1994), What should central banks do? What should be their macroeconomic objectives and operations? *Economic Journal*, vol. 104, pp. 1424–36.

Gordon, R. J (1977), The theory of domestic inflation, *American Economic Review*, vol. 67, February.

Gordon, R. J. (1984), The short-run demand for money, *Journal of Money, Credit and Banking*, vol. 16, pp. 403–34.

Gordon, R. J. (1999), Has the 'new economy' rendered the productivity slowdown obsolete?, mimeo, Evanston: Northwestern University; currently available at http://research.stlouisfed.org/conferences/workshop/gordon.pdf

Gorton, Gary, and George Pennacchi (1990), Financial intermediaries and liquidity creation, *Journal of Finance*, vol. 45, pp. 49–71.

Government of Korea (1997, 1998, 1999, 2000), Letter of Intent from the Republic of Korea to the Managing Director of the IMF, Seoul (the public parts of all letters from the first to the ninth are currently available on the IMF's website at: www.imf.org/external/country/kor/index.htm?type=23).

Government of Thailand (1997, 1998, 1999), Letter of Intent from the Kingdom of Thailand to the International Monetary Fund, Bangkok (the published parts of all letters from the first to the eighth are currently available on the IMF's website at: www.imf.org/external/country/tha/index.htm?type=23).

Gowland, D. (1985), *Money, Inflation and Unemployment*, Hemel Hempstead: Harvester Wheatsheaf.

Grant, James (2000), When money becomes a confidence trick, *Financial Times*, 10 July, p. 19.

Greenwald, Bruce C., and Stiglitz, Joseph E. (2003), *Towards a New Paradigm in Monetary Economics*, Cambridge: Cambridge University Press.

Guender, A., and M. Moersch (1997), On the existence of a credit channel of monetary policy in Germany, *Kredit und Kapital*, vol. 30, no. 2, pp. 173–85.

Gurley, J. G., and E. S. Shaw (1955), Financial aspects of economic development, *American Economic Review*, vol. 45, no. 4, September, pp. 515–38.

Gurley, J. G. and E. S. Shaw (1960), *Money in a Theory of Finance*, Washington, DC: Brookings Institution.

Hahn, Albert (1920), *Volkswirtschaftliche Theorie des Bankkredits*, Tuebingen: J. C. B. Mohr.

Hall, Steven, Brian Henry and Joe Wilcox (1988), The long-run determination of the UK monetary aggregates, mimeo, London: Bank of England.

Hamada, Koichi (1999), *Shūkan Tōyō Keizai*, 13 November, reprinted in Kikuo Iwata (ed.) (2000b), *Kinyū seisaku no ronten*, Tokyo: Toyo Keizai Shinpo Sha, chapter 1.

Hamada, Koichi (2002), Defure yōninronshani tou, Kokumin keizai wo kowashitemo yoinoka, *Chūou Kouron*, January 2002.

Hämäläinen, Sirkka (2003), How the European Central Bank manages the euro and what is in store for 2003, speech to the American Business Forum on Europe, New York, 14 January 2003, currently available at: www.ecb.int/press/key/date/2003/html/sp030114.en.html

Handa, Jagdish (2000), *Monetary Economics*, London and New York: Routledge.

Hansen, B. (1973), On the effects of fiscal and monetary policy: a taxonomic discussion, *American Economic Review*, vol. 63, no. 4, pp. 546–71.

Harada, Yutaka (1999), *Nihon no ushinawareta ju nen*, Tokyo: Nihon Keizai Shinbunsha.

Haubrich, Joseph G. (1990), Non-monetary effects of financial crises: lessons from the Great Depression in Canada, *Journal of Monetary Economics*, vol. 25, March, pp. 223–52.

Hay, Donald A. (1989), *Economics Today: A Christian Perspective*, Apollos, Leicester: Inter-Varsity Press.

Hayami, Masaru (1999), On recent monetary policy, excerpted and translated from a speech given by Masaru Hayami, Governor of the Bank of Japan, at the Japan National Press Club in Tokyo on 22 June, Tokyo: Bank of Japan, currently available from the Bank of Japan's website.

Hayami, Masaru (2000a), Revitalisation of Japan's Economy, speech given by Masuri Hayami, Governor of the Bank of Japan, at the Japanese Economic Research Center on 29 May, p. 8, currently available from Bank of Japan's website.

Hayami, Masaru (2000b), The role of Japan amid the changing international environment, speech at the Meeting of the Executive Board of Directors of the Japan Foreign Trade Council on 7 June, currently available at: www.boj.or.jp/en/press/press_f.htm

Hayami, Masaru (2000c), Challenges for Japan's economy: the central bank's perspective, speech given by Masaru Hayami, Governor of the Bank of Japan, at the Keizai Club, 22 December, available at: www.boj.or.jp/en/press/koen064.htm

Hayami, Masaru (2001), Recent economic developments and monetary policy, English translation of speech given by Masaru Hayami, Governor of the Bank of Japan, at Naigai Chousa Kai (the Research Institute of Japan), 7 March, available at: www.boj.or.jp

Hayami, Masaru (2002), Toward revitalization of Japan's economy, speech given by Masaru Hayami, Governor of the Bank of Japan, at the Keizai (Economic) Club, 29 January, available at: www.boj.or.jp/en/press/koen073.htm

Hayashi, Fumio (1998), Keizai Kyoshitsu – Nichigin, base money no mokuhyō wo (The Bank of Japan should set a base money target), *Nihon keizai Shinbun*, 29 December (in Japanese).

Hayashi, Fumio, and Edward C. Prescott (2002) The 1990s in Japan: a lost decade, *Review of Economic Dynamics*, vol. 5, no. 1, pp. 206–35.

Helliwell, John F. (2001), How's life? Combining individual and national variables to explain subjective well-being, mimeo, Vancouver: University of British Columbia, Department of Economics.

Hellmann, Thomas, Kevin Murdoch and Joseph E. Stiglitz (1997), Financial restraint: towards a new paradigm, in M. Aoki, M. Kim and H. Okuno-Fujiwara (eds), *The Role of Government in East Asian Economic Development*, New York: Oxford University Press.

Hendry, David F. (1979), Predictive failure and econometric modelling in macroeconomics: the transactions demand for money, in R. Ormerod (ed.), *Modelling the Economy*, London: Heinemann.

Hendry, David F. (1984), Econometric modelling of house prices in the UK, in David F. Hendry and K. F. Wallis (eds), *Econometrics and Quantitative Economics*, Oxford: Basil Blackwell.

Hendry, David F. (1986), Econometric modelling with cointegrated variables, *Oxford Bulletin of Economics and Statistics*, vol. 48, no. 3, special issue.

Hendry, David F. (1987), Econometric methodology: a personal perspective, in T. F. Bewley (ed.), *Advances in Econometrics*, Cambridge: Cambridge University Press, chapter 10.

Hendry, David F. (1995), *Dynamic Econometrics*, Oxford: Oxford University Press.

Hendry, David F. (2000), *Econometrics: Alchemy or Science?* New edn. Oxford: Oxford University Press.

Hendry, David F., and Neil R. Ericsson (1983), Assertion without empirical basis: an econometric appraisal of 'Monetary trends in the United Kingdom' by Milton Friedman and Anna Schwartz, Bank of England Panel of Academic Consultants, Panel Paper no. 22, October.

Hendry, David F., and G. E. Mizon (1978), Serial correlation as a convenient simplification, not nuisance: a comment, *Economic Journal*, vol. 88, pp. 549–63.

Hendry, David F., and J. -F. Richard (1983), The econometric analysis of economic time series, *International Statistical Review*, vol. 51, pp. 111–63.

Hetzel, Robert L. (1999), *Economic Quarterly*, Federal Reserve Bank of Richmond, vol. 85, no. 1, Winter.

Hildebrand, Philipp M. (2003), Monetary policy in a global context, speech by Philipp M. Hildebrand, member of the governing board, Swiss National Bank, to the Swiss-American Chamber of Commerce, Zurich, 8 October, obrained at: www.snb.ch/d/download/publikationen/ref_031008_pmh.pdf

Hinds, Manuel (1988), Economic effects of financial crises, Policy Research Working Paper no. 104, Washington, DC: World Bank, Washington.

Hoelscher, Gregory (1986), New evidence on deficits and interest rates, *Journal of Money, Credit and Banking*, vol. 17, February.

Hoover, Kevin D. (1988), *The New Classical Macroeconomics: A Sceptical Inquiry*, New York: Basil Blackwell Inc.

Hoppe, Hans-Hermann, Jörg Guido Hülsmann and Walter Block (1998), Against fiduciary media, *Quarterly Journal of Austrian Economics*, vol. 1, no. 1, pp. 19–50.

Horiuchi, Akiyoshi (1977), Madoguchi shidō no yūkōsei, *Keizai Kenkyū*, vol. 28, pp. 204–13.

Horiuchi, Akiyoshi (1978), Eguchi Hidekazushi no comment ni kotaeru – madoguchi kisei no yūkōsei ni tsuite, *Keizai Kenkyū*, vol. 29, pp. 78–80.

Horiuchi, Akiyoshi (1980), *Nihon no kinyū seisaku – kinyū mechanism no jisshōbunseki*, Tokyo: Toyo Keizai Shinpo Sha.

Horiuchi, Akiyoshi (1993), Japan, in Haruhiro Fukui, Peter H. Merkl, Hubertus Mueller-Groeling and Akio Watanabe (eds), *The Politics of Economic Change in Postwar Japan and West Germany, Volume 1, Macroeconomic Conditions and Responses*, London: Macmillan, chapter 3.

Hoshi, Takeo (1994), The economic role of corporate grouping and the main bank system, in Masahiko Aoki and Ronald Dore (eds), *The Japanese Firm: The Sources of Competitive Strength*, Oxford: Oxford University Press.

Hoshi, Takeo, and Anil Kashyap (2000), Japan's Big Bang starts to whimper, *Asian Wall Street Journal*, 21 February.

Hoshi, Takeo, Anil K. Kashyap and David Scharfstein (1991), Corporate structure, liquidity and investment: evidence from Japanese industrial groups, *Quarterly Journal of Economics*, vol. 106, pp. 33–60.

Hoshi, Takeo, and Hugh Patrick (2000), The Japanese financial system: an introductory overview, in Takeo Hoshi and Hugh Patrick (eds), *Crisis and Change in the Japanese Financial System*, Norwell: Kluwer Academic Publishers.

Hoshi, Takeo, David Scharfstein and Kenneth J. Singleton (1991), Japanese corporate investment and Bank of Japan guidance of commercial bank lending, paper presented at the Conference on Japanese Monetary Policy, National Bureau of Economic Research, Tokyo, published in Kenneth Singleton (ed.) (1993), *Japanese Monetary Policy*, Chicago, IL: University of Chicago Press, pp. 63–94.

Howells, Peter, and Iris Biefang-Frisancho Mariscal (1992), An explanation for the recent behavior of income and transaction velocities in the United Kingdom, *Journal of Post-Keynesian Economics*, vol. 14, no. 3, Spring, pp. 367–88.

Hubbard, Glenn R. (1995), Is there a 'credit channel' for monetary policy? NBER Reprints 2013 (also Working Paper 4977, 1994), National Bureau of Economic Research.

Hume, David (1752), *Hume's Writings on Economics*, edited by E. Rotwein, Edinburgh: Nelson, 1955.

Humphrey, Thomas M. (1997), Fisher and Wicksell on the quantity theory, *Economic Quarterly*, Richmond: Federal Reserve Bank of Richmond, vol. 83, no. 4, Fall, pp. 71–90.

Hutchison, Michael M. (1994), Asset price fluctuations in Japan: what role for monetary policy? *Bank of Japan Monetary and Economic Studies*, vol. 12, no. 2, December.

Hutchison, Michael, and David Pyle (1984), The real interest rate/budget deficit link, *Review*, San Francisco: Federal Reserve Bank of San Francisco, Fall.

Ihori, Toshihiro, Takero Doi and Hiroki Kondo (2000), Japanese fiscal reform: fiscal reconstruction and fiscal policy, Discussion Paper CIRJE-F-83, Tokyo: University of Tokyo.

Ikeo, Kazuhito (2001), Keizai Kyōshitsu: Nihon, seisansei kōjōni zenryokuwo, *Nihon Keizai Shinbun*, 6 March.

International Bank for Reconstruction and Development (IBRD) (1993), *The East Asian Miracle, Economic Growth and Public Policy*, Oxford: Oxford University Press.

International Bank for Reconstruction and Development (IBRD) (2001), *Finance for Growth: Policy Choices in a Volatile World*, Oxford: Oxford University Press.

International Labour Office (ILO) (2003), *Key Indicators of the Labour Market, Third Edition*, Geneva: ILO.

International Monetary Fund (IMF) (1977), *The Monetary Approach to the Balance of Payments: A Collection of Research Papers by Members of the Staff of the International Monetary Fund*, Washington, DC: IMF.

International Monetary Fund (IMF) (2002), *Japan: Staff Report for 2002 Article IV Consultation*, Washington, DC: IMF.

Inoue, Kengo (2000), *Naniga tadashii keizaiseisakuka*, Tokyo: Nihon Keizai Shinbunsha.

Ireland, Jonathan, and Simon Wren-Lewis (1988), Buffer stock money and the company sector, paper presented at the Money Study Group Conference, Oxford, September, published in *Oxford Economic Papers* (1992), vol. 44, no. 2, pp. 209–31.

Ishida, K. (1984), Divisia monetary aggregates and demand for money: a Japanese case, *Bank of Japan Monetary and Economic Studies*, vol. 2, pp. 49–80.

Ito, Takatoshi (2000), The stagnant Japanese economy in the 1990s: the need for financial supervision to restore sustained growth, in Takeo Hoshi and Hugh Patrick (eds) (2000), *Crisis and Change in the Japanese Financial System*, Norwell: Kluwer Academic Publishers.

Ito, Takatoshi, and Tokuo Iwaisako (1996), Explaining asset bubbles in Japan, *Bank of Japan Monetary and Economic Studies*, vol. 14, no. 1, July.

Itoh, Motoshige, and Naoki Shimoi (2000), On the role of monetary policy in a deflationary economy: the case of Japan, Tokyo: University of Tokyo, Discussion Paper CIRJE-F-90, September.

Iwata, Kikuo (1992a), Iwayuru 'kaneamari' to chikakōtō ni tsuite, *Kinyū Keizai Kenkyū*, no. 2, January.

Iwata, Kikuo (1992b), 'Nichiginriron' wo hōki seyo, *Shūkan Tōyō Keizai*, 12 September, pp. 124–8.

Iwata, Kikuo (1992c), Keizai Kyōshitsu: base money kyōkyūzō wa kanō, Fukyō yobu nichiginseisaku, *Nihon Keizai Shinbun*, 24 December.

Iwata, Kikuo (1994), Keizai Kyōshitsu: Nichigin, tsūka kyōkyūryō no jūshiwo, *Nihon Keizai Shinbun*, 13 December.

Iwata, Kikuo (1999), Keizai Kyōshitsu – Ryōtekikanwa, hōhōshidai de kōka, *Nihon Keizai Shinbun*, 30 September.

Iwata, Kikuo (2000a), Choukikokusai kaikiri opewo zōgaku subeki, *Ronsō Tōyō Keizai*, January; reprinted in Kikuo Iwata (ed.) (2000b), *Kinyū seisaku no ronten*, Tokyo: Toyo Keizai Shinpo Sha, chapter 7.

Iwata, Kikuo (ed.) (2000b), *Kinyū seisaku no ronten*, Tokyo: Toyo Keizai Shinpo Sha.

Jaffee, Dwight M., and T. Russell (1976), Imperfect information, uncertainty and credit rationing, *Quarterly Journal of Economics*, vol. 90, no. 4, November, pp. 651–66.

Jaffee, Dwight, and Joseph Stiglitz (1990), Credit rationing, in B. M. Friedman and F. H. Hahn (eds), *Handbook of Monetary Economics*, vol. II, Amsterdam: Elsevier Science Publishers, pp. 1838–88.

James, Christopher (1987), Some evidence on the uniqueness of bank loans, *Journal of Financial Economics*, vol. 19, pp. 217–35.

Jao, Y. C. (1989), Money supply exogeneity and endogeneity: a review of the monetarist post-Keynesian debate, *Greek Economic Review*, vol. 11, no. 2.

Jittai Chōsa Shōiinkai (1959), Nihon ginko o chūshin to suru sengō kinyū no jittai chōsa, in Ministry of Finance, Banking Bureau (ed.), Chū ginkō seido, *Kinyūseido chōsakai kankei shiryō*, Tokyo: Printing Bureau of the Ministry of Finance.

Johnson, Chalmers (1982), *MITI and the Japanese Miracle: The Growth of Industrial Policy 1925-1975*, Stanford: Stanford University Press.

Jorgenson, Dale W., and Kazuyuki Motohashi (2003), The role of information technology in the economy: comparison between Japan and the United States, paper prepared for RIETI/KEIO Conference on Japanese Economy: Leading East Asia in the 21st Century?, Keio University, 30 May 30.

Judd, J. P., and J. L. Scadding (1982), The search for a stable money demand function: a survey of the post-1973 literature, *Journal of Economic Literature*, vol. 20, pp. 993–1023.

Kagin, Justin (2002), Flying money, mimeo, Tokyo: Sophia University.

Kakes, Jan, Philipp Maier and Jan-Egbert Sturm (2001), Monetary transmission and bank lending in Germany, *Kredit und Kapital*, vol. 34, no. 1, pp. 505–25.

Kaldor, Nicholas (1970), The new monetarism, *Lloyds Bank Review*, July.

Kashyap, Anil K. (2002), Sorting out Japan's financial crisis, *Economic Perspectives*, Q4, vol. 26, no. 4, Chicago: Federal Reserve Bank of Chicago, pp. 42–55, also published as NBER Working Paper no. 9384, National Bureau of Economic Research, December. The paper can be downloaded from: www.chicagofed.org/publications/economicperspectives/2002/4qepart4.pdf

Kashyap, Anil K., Raghuram Rajan and Jeremy C. Stein (1999), Banks as liquidity providers: an explanation for the coexistence of lending and deposit-taking, NBER Working Paper no. w6962.

Kashyap, Anil K., and Jeremy C. Stein (1993), Monetary policy and bank lending, NBER Working Paper no. 4317, National Bureau of Economic Research.

Kashyap, Anil K., and Jeremy C. Stein (1997), The role of banks in monetary policy: a survey with implications for the European Monetary Union, *Federal Reserve Bank of Chicago Economic Perspectives*, September/October, pp. 2–18.

Kashyap, Anil K., and Jeremy C. Stein (2000), What do a million observations on banks say about the transmission of monetary policy? *American Economic Review*, vol. 90, no. 3, pp. 407–28.

Kashyap, Anil K., Jeremy C. Stein and David W. Wilcox (1992), Monetary policy and credit conditions: evidence from the composition of external finance, National Bureau of Economic Research Working Paper Series, no. 4015.

Kashyap, Anil K., Jeremy C. Stein and David W. Wilcox (1993), Monetary policy and credit conditions: evidence from the composition of external finance, *American Economic Review*, vol. 83, no. 1, March, pp. 78–98.

Katz, Richard (2001), Curing Japan: monetary easing is no quick fix, *Financial Times*, 21 November.

Kawai, Masahiro (1987), The Japanese demand for long-term assets in the 1980s, Paper presented to the United States–Japan Consultative Group on International Monetary Affairs, Washington, DC, 2–3 October.

Kawai, Masahiro (1990), Japan's demand for foreign securities in the 1980s, Discussion Paper no. 240, Osaka University: Institute of Social and Economic Research.

Kawai, Masahiro (1991), *Japanese Investment in Foreign Securities in the 1980s*, Canberra: Australia–Japan Research Centre.

Kawai, Masahiro, and Ken-ichi Takayasu (2000), The economic crisis and banking sector restructuring in Thailand, in Ghon S. Rhee (ed.), *Rising to the Challenge in Asia: A Study of Financial Markets*, Volume 11, Thailand, Manila: Asian Development Bank, Manila, pp. 37–103.

Keeton, W. R. (1979), *Equilibirum Credit Rationing*, New York: Garland Publishing.

Keran, Michael W. (1969), Monetary and fiscal influences on economic activity – the historical evidence, *Federal Reserve Bank of St. Louis Review*, vol. 51, November, pp. 5–24.

Keran, Michael W. (1970), Monetary and fiscal influences on economic activity – the foreign evidence, *Federal Reserve Bank of St. Louis Review*, vol. 52, February, pp. 16–28.

Keynes, John Maynard (1930), *A Treatise on Money*, Volume 1, London: Macmillan.

Keynes, John Maynard (1932), *Essays in Persuasion*, New York: Harcourt, Brace and Company.

Keynes, John Maynard (1936), *The General Theory of Employment, Interest and Money*, London: Macmillan.

Kimura, T. (2001a), The impact of financial anxieties on money demand in Japan, in H. J. Klöckers and C. Willeke (eds), *European Central Bank, Seminar on Monetary Analysis: Tools and Applications*, Frankfurt: ECB, pp. 97–144.

Kimura, Takeshi (2001b), *Capital Flight*, Tokyo: Jitsugyou no nihonsha.

Kindleberger, Charles P. (1966), Capital movements and international payments adjustment, *Konjunktur, Zeitschrift fuer angewandte Konjunkturforschung*, Volume 12, Part 1, pp. 10–27, reprinted in Charles P. Kindleberger, *International Money – A Collection of Essays*, London: George Allen and Unwin, 1981, pp. 209–24.

Kindleberger, Charles P. (1978), *Manias, Panics, and Crashes: History of Financial Crises*, New York: Basic Books.

King, Robert, and Charles Plosser (1984), Money, credit and prices in a real business cycle, *American Economic Review*, vol. 74, June, pp. 363–80.

King, Stephen R. (1986), Monetary transmission: through bank loans or bank liabilities?, *Journal of Money, Credit and Banking*, vol. 18, no. 3, pp. 290–303.

Kiyotaki, Nobuhiro, and John Moore (1997), Credit cycles, *Journal of Political Economy*, vol. 105, pp. 211–48.

Klein, Lawrence R. (1968), *The Keynesian Revolution*, London: Macmillan.

Knies, Carl (1873), *Das Geld: Darlegung der Grundlehren von dem Gelde, mit einer Voreroerterung uber das Kapital und die Uebertragung der Nutzungen*, Berlin: Weidmannsche Buchhandlung.

Koo, Richard (1991), Japan and international capital flows, mimeo, Tokyo: Nomura Research Institute, April.

Koo, Richard (1995), Keizai Kyōshitsu: Kōzōhenka taiō, teokurefusege, *Nihon Keizai Shinbun*, 11 January.

Koo, Richard (1996), *Tōki no enyasu jitsuju no endaka*, Tokyo: Toyo Keizai Shinpo Sha.

Koo, Richard (1998), *Kinnyū kiki kara no dasshutsu*, Tokyo: PHP Kenkyūjo.

Koo, Richard (1999), *Nihonkeizai kaifukue no aoshashin*, Tokyo: PHP Kenkyūjo.

Kormendi, Roger (1983), Government debt, government spending and private sector behaviour, *American Economic Review*, vol. 73, no. 5, December, pp. 994–1010.

Kouri, Pentti J. K., and Michael G. Porter (1974), International capital flows and portfolio equilibrium, *Journal of Political Economy*, vol. 82, May/June, pp. 443–67.

Kregel, Jan A. (2000), Krugman on the liquidity trap: why inflation won't bring recovery in Japan, Working Paper no. 298, Annandale-on-Hudson: Jerome Levy Economics Institute, Bard College, March.

Krugman, Paul (1998a), Japan's trap, May, available at: http://web.mit.edu/krugman/www/japtrap.html

Krugman, Paul (1998b), Setting sun – Japan: what went wrong?, 11 June, available at: http://web.mit.edu/krugman/www/japan.html

Krugman, Paul (1998c), It's baaack: Japan's slump and the return of the liquidity trap, *Brookings Papers on Economic Activity*, vol. 2, pp. 137–205.

Krugman, Paul (1998d), Japan: still trapped, mimeo, November, obtained at: http://web.mit.edu/krugman/www/japtrap2.html

Krugman, Paul (1999), A special page on Japan, currently available at: http://web.mit.edu/krugman/www/jpage.html

Krugman, Paul (2000), Thinking about the liquidity trap, *Journal of the Japanese and International Economies*, vol. 14, pp. 221–37; old version obtained at: www.wws.princeton.edu/~pkrugman/trioshrt.html

Krugman, Paul (2003), Is the world stumbling into an economic quagmire?, reprinted in the *International Herald Tribune*, 27 May.

Kubota, Isao (1988), *Seikai o ugokasu nihon*, Tokyo: Zaikei yōhōsha.

Kubota, Isao (2001), On 'Princes of the yen', GLOCOM Global Communications Platform, Tokyo, October, available online at: www.glocom.org/debates/200109_kubota_on_princes/index.html

Kugler, Peter, and Georg Rich (2001), Monetary policy under low interest rates: the experience of Switzerland in the late 1970s, paper presented at the 32nd meeting of the Ausschuss fuer Geldtheorie und Geldpolitik – Verein fuer Socialpolitik, Frankfurt, 16–17 February; available at: www.snb.ch/d/downloand/publikationen/ref_010411_ri.pdf

Kuhn, Thomas S. (1962), *The Structure of Scientific Revolutions*, Chicago: University of Chicago Press.

Kumar, Manmohan S., Taimur Baig, Jörg Decressin, Chris Faulkner-MacDonagh and Tarhan Feyziogùlu (2003), Deflation: determinants, risks and policy options, IMF Occasional Paper no. 221, 30 April, Washington, DC: IMF.

Kure, Bunji (1973), *Kinyū seisaku – nihon ginkō no seisaku unei*, Tokyo: Toyo Keizai Shinpo Sha.

Kure, Bunji (1975), Nihon ginkō no madoguchi shidō, *Shikan Gendai Keizai*, vol. 17, March.

Laidler, David (1985), Comment on 'Money demand predictability', *Journal of Money, Credit and Banking*, vol. 17, no. 4, part 2, pp. 647–53.

Laidler, David (1986), What do we really know about monetary policy?, *Australian Economic Papers*, vol. 25, no. 46, pp. 1–16.

Lakatos, I. (1970), Falsification and the methodology of scientific research programmes, in I. Lakatos and A. Musgrave (eds), *Criticism and the Growth of Knowledge*, Cambridge: Cambridge University Press.

Lapavitsas, Costas (2004), Hilferding's theory of banking in the light of Steuart and Smith, *Research in Political Economy*, vol. 21, pp. 161–80.

Law, John (1705), *Money and Trade Consider'd with a Proposal for Suppllying the Nation with Money*, Edinburgh.

Law, John (1720), *Money and Trade Consider'd with a Proposal for Suppllying the Nation with Money. By Mr. John Law, now Director of the Royal Bank at Paris*, London.

Leeper, E. M., and D. B. Gordon (1992), In search of the liquidity effect, *Journal of Monetary Economics*, vol. 29, pp. 341–69.

Lein, Lawrence R. (1968), *The Keynesian Revolution*, London: Macmillan.

Lenormant, François (1878), *La Monnaie dans l'Antiquite*, Paris.

Lerner, Abba P. (1943), Functional finance and the federal debt, *Social Research*, vol. 10, no. 1, February, pp. 38–52.

Leventakis, John A. and Sophocles N. Brissimis (1991), Instability of the US money demand function, *Journal of Economic Surveys*, vol. 2, pp. 131–61.

Levine, Ross (1997), Financial development and economic growth: views and agenda, *Journal of Economic Literature*, vol. 35, June, pp. 688–726.

Levine, Ross, and David Renelt (1992), A sensitivity analysis of cross-country growth regressions, *American Economic Review*, vol. 82, no. 4, pp. 942–63.

Lucas, Robert E. (1972), Expectations and the neutrality of money, *Journal of Economic Theory*, vol. 4, pp. 103–24.

Ludvigson, Sydney (1996), The macroeconomic effects of government debt in a stochastic growth model, *Journal of Monetary Economics*, vol. 38, pp. 25–45.

Ludvigson, Sydney (1999), The channel of monetary transmission to demand: evidence from the market for automobile credit, New York: Federal Reserve Bank of New York, Working Paper no. 9625.

Macleod, Henry Dunning (1855/56), *The Theory and Practice of Banking: With the Elementary Principles of Currency, Prices, Credit and Exchanges*, London: Longman, Brown, Green and Longman, Volumes 1 and 2.

Macpherson, D. (1805), *Annals of Commerce*, 4 Volumes, London.

Malinvaud, E. (1977), *The Theory of Unemployment Reconsidered*, Oxford: Basil Blackwell.

Mankiw, N. Gregory, and Lawrence H. Summers (1986), Money demand and the effects of fiscal policies, *Journal of Money, Credit and Banking*, November, pp. 415–29.

Marshall, Harry I. (1945), The Karens of Burma, Burma Pamphlets no. 8, London: Longman.

Mateut, Simona, Spiros Bougheas and Paul Mizen (2003), Trade credit, bank lending and monetary policy transmission, Economics Working Papers ECO2003/02, Florence: European University Institute.

Matsuda, Kunio (2001), Chief representative in Frankfurt, Bank of Japan, speech at the University of Wuerzburg in Germany, 7 February, Working Paper Series from Overseas Representative Offices, Bank of Japan.

Matsui, Kyoshi (1996), Kinnen ni okeru ginkō no kashidashi kyōkyū to jittai keizai katsudō no kankei ni tsuite – Credit crunchron ni kan suru kōsatsu, Institute for Monetary and Economic Studies, IMES Discussion Paper 96-J-17, October, Bank of Japan, Tokyo.

Matsushita, Yasuo (1996), Speech given by Yasuo Matsushita, Governor of the Bank of Japan, to the Japan National Press Club in Tokyo, 14 June, available at: www.boj.or.jp/en/press/koen002.htm

McCallum, Bennett, T. (1985), On consequences and criticisms of monetary targeting, *Journal of Money, Credit and Banking*, vol. 17, no. 4, part 22, pp. 570–97.

McCallum, Bennett T. (1993), Reply to Comments by Kunio Okina, *Bank of Japan Monetary and Economic Studies*, vol. 11, no. 2, November.

McCallum, Bennett, T. (2000), Theoretical analysis regarding a zero lower bound on nominal interest rates, *Journal of Money, Credit and Banking*, vol. 32, part 2, November, pp. 870–904.

McCallum, Bennett T. (2001a), Inflation targeting and the liquidity trap, NBER Working Paper no. 8225, April.

McCallum, Bennett T. (2001b), Japanese monetary policy again, Shadow Open Market Committee, 15 October, mimeo.

McCloskey, Deirdre (1987), *The Rhetoric of Economics*, Wisconsin: University of Wisconsin Press.

McCloskey, Deirdre (1994), *Knowledge and Persuasion in Economics*, Cambridge: University of Cambridge Press.

McKibbin, Warwick J. (1996), The macroeconomic experience of Japan since 1990: an empirical investigation, mimeo, Canberra: Economics Department, Research School of Pacific and Asian Studies, Australian National University.

McKinnon, Ronald I. (1973), *Money and Capital in Economic Development*, Washington, DC: Brookings Institution.

McKinnon, Ronald (1999), Comments on 'Monetary policy under zero inflation', *Monetary and Economic Studies*, December, Bank of Japan.

Meade, J. E. (1978), The meaning of internal balance, *Economic Journal*, vol. 88, pp. 423–35.

Meltzer, A. H. (1995), Monetary, credit (and other) transmission processes: a monetarist perspective, *Journal of Economic Perspectives*, vol. 9, Fall, pp. 49–72.

Meltzer, Allan (1998), Time to print money, *Financial Times*, 17 July.

Meltzer, Allan (1999), The transmission process. Paper prepared for a conference on the Monetary Transmission Process: Recent Developments and Lessons for Europe, sponsored by Deutsche Bundesbank, Frankfurt, 25–27 March.

Meltzer, Allan H. (2001), Monetary transmission at low inflation, Carnegie Mellon University and American Enterprise Institute, published in Bank of Japan, *Post-Bubble Kinyū Seisaku*, Tokyo: Daiyamond Sha (in Japanese).

Meltzer, Allan H. (2003), A reality check for the conventional wisdom, *Financial Times*, 18 August.

Mera, Koichi, and Bertrand Renaud (eds) (2000), *Asia's Financial Crisis and the Role of Real Estate*, Armonk, NY: M. E. Sharpe.

Messori, Marcello (2002), Credit and money in Schumpeter's theory, Departmental Working Papers, Rome: Tor Vergata University, CEIS.

Mieno, Yasushi (1993), Current economic developments in Japan and abroad, Special Paper no. 227, May, Bank of Japan. Transcript of speech given by Yasushi Mieno to the Economics Club in Tokyo on 20 April.

Mieno, Yasushi (1994), The conduct of monetary policy by the Bank of Japan, *Bank of Japan Quarterly Bulletin*, August, Tokyo: Bank of Japan.

Mikitani, Ryoichi (2000), The facts of the Japanese financial crisis, in Ryoichi Mikitani and Adam Posen (eds), *Japan's Financial Crisis and its Parallels to U.S. Experience*, Special Report no. 13, Washington, DC: Institute for International Economics, September.

Miles, David K., and Joe Wilcox (1991), The money transmission mechanism, in Chistopher J. Green and David T. Llewellyn (eds), *Surveys in Monetary Economics*, Volume I, *Monetary Theory and Policy*, Oxford: Basil Blackwell.

Mill, John Stuart (1834), *A System of Logic, Ratiocinative and Inductive: Being a Connected View of the Principles of Evidence, and the Methods of Scientific Investigation*, London: John W. Parker.

Miller, Roger L., and David D. VanHoose (1993), *Modern Money and Banking*, International Editions, 3rd edn, New York: McGraw-Hill.

Miller, Stephen M. (1988), Long-run and short-run money demands: an application of co-integration and error-correction modeling, mimeo, June [no other details avialable].

Ministry of Finance (1993), The mechanism and economic effects of asset price fluctuations: a report of the Research Committee, Tokyo: Institute of Fiscal and Monetary Policy, April.

Ministry of Foreign Affairs (1999), Japan's approach to deregulation to the present, Tokyo: Government of Japan, Ministry of Foreign Affairs, available at: www.mofa.go.jp/j_info/japan/regulate/approach9904.html

Minsky, Hyman, P. (1982), The potential for financial crises, Working Paper no. 46, St. Louis: Washington University, Department of Economics.

Mirowski, Philip (1989), *More Heat Than Light: Economics as Social Physics, Physics as Nature's Economics*, Cambridge: Cambridge University Press.

Miyao, R. (1996), Does a cointegrating M2 demand relation really exist in Japan?, *Journal of the Japanese and International Economies*, vol. 10, pp. 1–10.

Miyazawa, Kiichi (1999), Beyond the Asian crisis, speech on the occasion of the APEC Finance Ministers' Meeting in Langkawi, Malaysia, 15 May, available at: www.mof.go.jp/english/if/e1b068.htm

Mommsen, Theodor, and Joachim Marquardt (1887/88), *Handbuch der roemischen Alterthuemer*, Leipzig: Hirzel.

Moore, Basil J. (1988), *Horizontalists and Verticalists: The Macroeconomics of Credit Money*, Cambridge: Cambridge University Press.

Moore, Basil J., and Andrew R. Threadgold (1980), Bank lending and the money supply, Bank of England Discussion Paper no. 10, London: Bank of England.

Moore, Basil J., and Andrew R. Threadgold (1985), Corporate bank borrowing in the UK, 1965–81, *Economica*, vol. 52, pp. 65–78.

Morgan, Peter (1994a), Liquidity factor won't prevent recovery, *Nikkei Weekly*, 13 June, Tokyo: Nihon Keizai Shinbunsha.

Morgan, Peter (1994b), Kashidashi fushiwa kaifuku no samatage ni naranu, *Nikkei Business*, 18 July, Tokyo: Nihon Keizai Shinbunsha.

Morsink, James, and Tamim Bayoumi (2000), Monetary policy transmission in Japan, in Tamim Bayoumi and Charles Collyns (eds), *Post-Bubble Blues: How Japan Responded to Asset Price Collapse*, Washington, DC: IMF, pp. 143–63; previously published as A peek inside the black box: the monetary transmission mechanism in Japan, IMF Working Paper WP/99/137, Washington, DC: IMF.

Motonishi, Taizo, and Hiroshi Yoshikawa (1998), Causes of the long stagnation of Japan in the 1990s: financial or real?, paper presented at the NBER Tokyo Conference, 29–30 October.

Muellbauer, John (1992), Anglo-German differences in housing market dynamics, *European Economic Review*, vol. 36, nos 2–3, April, pp. 539–48.

Muellbauer, John, and A. Murphy (1989), Why has the UK savings rate collapsed?, Working Paper, London: Credit Suisse First Boston, July.

Muellbauer, John, and Richard Portes (1978), Macroeconomic models with quantity rationing, *Economic Journal*, vol. 88, pp. 788–821.

Mueller, Adam (1816), *Versuch einer neuen Theorie des Geldes, mit besonderer Rücksicht auf Grossbritannien*, Leipzig.

Murphy, Antoin E. (1997), *John Law, Economic Theorist and Policy-Maker*, Oxford: Clarendon Press.

Nagatani, Yasutaka (1996), Keizai Kyoushitsu: Yakuwari hatashita 'keiki taisaku', *Nihon Keizai Shinbun*, 16 February.

National Land Agency (1990), *Tochihakusho*, Japan (in Japanese).

Nelson, Robert H. (2001), *Economics as Religion, from Samuelson to Chicago and Beyond*, University Park: Pennsylvania State University Press.

Newcomb, S. (1885), *Principles of Political Economy*, New York: Harper.

Niehans, J. (1984), *International Monetary Economics*, Baltimore: Johns Hopkins University Press.

Niggle, C. J. (1988), The increasing importance of financial capital in the US economy, *Journal of Economic Issues*, June.

Nikkei (1975), Nichigin, chi sogin no madoguchi kisei 'haishi', 3–4–75, p. 1.

Nikkei (1978a), Nichigin no Hōjin e no madoguchi shidō waku, 7–9gatsu wa zennenhi 8%gen no mitōshi, 23–6–78, p. 3.

Nikkei (1978b), Nichigin, kinyū o 'ryōteki yokuseigata' ni – kabu, tochi kōtō o keikai; 15–12–78, p. 1.

Nikkei (1978c), Nichigin, 1–3gatsu no madoguchi shidō waku o 20% herasu, 23–12–78, p. 1.

Nikkei (1979), Togin chūshin ni jūtaku loan no kashishiburi medatsu, 23–7–79, p. 3.

Nikkei (1980a), Kinyū kikan, kigyō ni kigenmae hensai yōkyū, 23–3–80, p. 1.

Nikkei (1980b), Nichigin, gaitameginkō no impact loan yokusei e 'madoguchi' shidō o kentō, 31–12–80, p. 1.

Nikkei (1981), Nichigin, madoguchi shidō o jijitsujō teppai, 26–12–81, p. 3.

Nikkei (1982a), Ginkō yokonarabi ni ihen, 22–9–82, p. 3.

Nikkei (1982b), 10–12gatsu no madoguchishidō, dokoni kieta 650oku en, 7–10–82, p. 5.

Nikkei (1984a), Kinyū chōsetsu shijō kinrisōsa wo jūshi, madoguchi shidō kara tenkan, 26–4–84, p. 3.

Nikkei (1984b), Madoguchi kisei o ōhaba kanwa kashidashi ni tsuikawaku, 18–9–84, p. 3.

Nikkei (1985), 4–6gatsu no madoguchi kisei, togin 35.5%zō, 30–3–85, p. 3.

Nikkei (1986), Nihon shiki Kinyū seisaku wa 'madoguchi shidō' ni ari – Beirengin economist bunseki, 7–10–86, p. 3.

Nikkei (1988), Tokushū: Nichigin no kinyū chōsetsu, madoguchi shidō jiyūka susumi isondo wa teika, 5–4–88, p. 10.

Nikkei (1990), Nichigin ryōtekihikishime kyōka togin no kashidashi zōkagaku 10–12 gatsu 2warigenmo, 13–9–90, p. 5.

Nikkei (1991), Nichigin, madoguchi shidō haishi o seishiki kettei, jikkosekinin ginkō ni hatasu, 28–6–91, p. 7.

Nikkei (1992), Nagoya shitenchō ga keiken, zaitech trouble nichigin nimo sekinin, 26–12–92, p. 7.

Nikkei Kinyū (1987), Nichigin kinyū suji kansoku, inpakuto rōn madoguchi shidō no taishō ni, 1–10–87, p. 1.

Nikkei Kinyū (1988a), Chōshingin 2.4% shintakugin 2% zō shuyōkō 4–6 gatsuki kashidashi, 25–3–88, p. 1.

Nikkei Kinyū (1988b), Nichigin, impakuto rōn wo yokusei – togin 13% zō 4–6 gatsu, zōkagaku 25% sakugen, 30–3–88, p. 1.

Nikkei Kinyū (1989), Tsūka kyōkyūryō to kinri – Nezuyoi kashidashi iyoku, nichigin, kane amari yokusei, 13–6–89, p. 2.

Nikkei Kinyū (1991a), Nichigin, madoguchi shidō o seishiki ni haishi – soredemo nokoru?, 28–6–91, p. 3.

Nikkei Kinyū (1991b), Togin ni aratana nayami, nuchigin no madoguchi shidō haishi, 11–7–91, p. 3.

Nikkei Koshasai Joho (1991), Nonbank kenkyukai jokosho – sanko setsumei shiryo, *Nihon Koshasai Kenkyujo*, no. 772.

Nishimura, Kiyohiko G., and Yuko Kawamoto (2003), Why does the problem persist? 'Rational rigidity' and the plight of Japanese banks, *World Economy*, vol. 26, no. 3, March, pp. 301–24.

Noguchi, Yukio (1990), Japan's land problem, *Japanese Economic Studies*, Summer.

Noguchi, Yukio (1992), *Baburu no Keizaigaku*, Tokyo: Nihon Keizai Shinbunsha.

Ockham, William of (1979), *Scriptum in librum primum Sententiarum (Ordinatio)*, Distinctiones XIX–XLVIII, in *Opera Theologica*, vol. IV, ed. by Girard Etzkorn and Francis Kelly, St. Bonaventure, New York: St. Bonaventure University, 1979.

Ogawa, Kazuo (2000), Monetary policy, credit and real activity: evidence from the balance sheet of Japanese firms, *Journal of the Japanese and International Economies*, vol. 14, pp. 385–407.

Okazaki, Tetsuji, and Masahiro Okuno-Fujiwara (eds) (1999), *The Japanese Economic System and its Historical Origins*, Oxford: Oxford University Press.

Okina, Kunio (1991), Nihon ni okeru kinyū chōsetsu, *Kinyū Kenkyū*, vol. 10, no. 2, July, Tokyo: Bank of Japan.

Okina, Kunio (1992a), 'Nichiginriron' wa machigatte inai, *Shūkan Tōyō Keizai*, 10 October, pp. 106–10.

Okina, Kunio (1992b), Seisakurongi wo konran saseru jitsumu e no gokai, *Shūkan Tōyō Keizai*, 26 December, pp. 142–6.

Okina, Kunio (1993a), Comments on 'Specification and analysis of a monetary policy rule for Japan: a central banker's view', Bank of Japan, *Monetary and Economic Studies*, vol. 11, no. 2, November.

Okina, Kunio (1993b), *Kinyū seisaku, Chū ginkō no shiten to sentaku*, Tokyo: Toyo Keizai Shinpo Sha (in Japanese).

Okina, Kunio (1999), Monetary policy under zero inflation: a response to criticisms and questions regarding monetary policy, *Monetary and Economic Studies*, December, Tokyo: Bank of Japan.

Park, Jae-Ha (2001), Invitation to Workshop on 'Development of Domestic and Regional Capital Markets' at the Asian Development Bank Institute, 13/14 June, Tokyo, currently available at: www.worldbank.org/html/extdr/offrep/eap/eapprem/capitalmktworkshopagenda.pdf

Patrick, Hugh T. (1962), *Monetary Policy and Central Banking in Contemporary Japan*, Bombay: University of Bombay.

Patrick, Hugh T. (1964), *Nihon ni okeru kinyū seisaku*, Tokyo: Toyo Keizai Shinpo Sha ~~e translation of Patrick 1962).

ston (ed.) (1965), *Harpers Dictionary of Classical Literature and* / York: Cooper Square Publishers.

(2002), Monetary policy does matter: control causality and superex- *rd Bulletin of Economics and Statistics*, vol. 64, no. 5, pp. 473–86.

Phillips, Chester A. (1920), *Bank Credit*, New York: Macmillan.

Pierce, James L. (1978), The myth of congressional supervision of monetary policy, *Journal of Monetary Economics*, vol. 4, pp. 363–70.

Pigou, Alfred C. (1917), The value of money, *Quarterly Journal of Economics*, vol. 32, November, pp. 38–65.

Pilat, Dirk (1993), The sectoral productivity performance of Japan and the US, 1885–1990, *Journal of Income and Wealth*, vol. 39, no. 4, December, pp. 357–75.

Polak, Jacques J. (1997), The IMF monetary model at forty, IMF Working Paper WP/97/49, April, Washington, DC: IMF.

Polak, Jacques, and Argy, Victor (1977), Credit policy and the balance of payments, in IMF, *The Monetary Approach to the Balance of Payments: A Collection of Research Papers by Members of the Staff of the International Monetary Fund*, Washington, DC: IMF, pp. 205–26.

Pollexfen, John (1697), *A Discourse of Trade, Coyn, and Paper Credits: and of Ways and Means to Gain, and Retain Riches*, London: Brabazon Aylmer.

Polo, Marco (1987), *The Travels of Marco Polo*, translated and with an introduction by Ronald Latham, London: Penguin Books.

Poole, William (1982), Federal Reserve operating procedures: a survey and evaluation of the historical record since October 1979, *Journal of Money, Credit and Banking*, vol. 14, part 2, November, pp. 575–96.

Posen, Adam (1998), *Restoring Japan's Economic Growth*, Washington, DC: Institute for International Economics.

Posen, Adam S. (2000), The political economy of deflationary monetary policy, in Ryoichi Mikitani and Adam S. Posen (eds), *Japan's Financial Crisis and its Parallels to U.S. Experience*, Special Report no. 13, Washington, DC: Institute for International Economics, September.

Przeworski, Adam, and James Raymond Vreeland (2000), The effect of IMF programs on economic growth, *Journal of Development Economics*, vol. 62, no. 2, August, pp. 385–421.

Quandt, Richard E., and Harvey S. Rosen (1986), Unemployment, disequilibrium and the short run Phillips curve: an econometric approach, *Journal of Applied Econometrics*, vol. 1, pp. 235–53.

Radcliffe, Lord (Chairman) (1959), Committee on the working of the monetary system, *Report*, Cmnd 827, London: HMSO.

Ramey, Valerie A. (1993), How important is the credit channel in the transmission of monetary policy?, *Carnegie-Rochester Conference Series on Public Policy*, vol. 39, no. 0, pp. 1–45.

Rasche, Robert H. (1986), M1-velocity and money demand functions: do stable relationships exist?, *Journal of Monetary Economics*, vol. 27, pp. 70–2.

Rau, Karl Heinrich (1826), Grundsatze der Volkswirthschaftslehre, Lehrbuch der politischen Oekonomie, Bd. 1, Winter, Heidelberg.

Rau, Karl Heinrich (1832), Grundsatze der Finanzwissenschaft, Lehrbuch der politischen Oekonomie, Bd. 3, Winter, Heidelberg.

Rhodes, James R., and Naoyuki Yoshino (1999), Window guidance by the Bank of Japan: was lending controlled?, *Contemporary Economic Policy*, vol. 17, no. 2, April, pp. 166–76.

Rojas-Suarez, Juliana (2001), From Basel I to Basel II: implications for emerging markets, Washington, DC: World Bank Institute, presentation obtained at: www.worldbank.org/wbi/banking/finsecpolicy/financeforum2002/pdf/rojassuarez.ppt

Roley, V. (1985), Money demand predictability, *Journal of Money, Credit and Banking*, vol. 17, pp. 611–41.

Romer, Christina D., and David H. Romer (1990), New evidence on the monetary transmission mechanism, *Brookings Papers on Economic Activity*, vol. 1, pp. 149–213.

Romer, C. D., and D. H. Romer (1994), Monetary policy matters, *Journal of Monetary Economics*, vol. 34, pp. 75–88.

Romer, Paul (1990), Endogenous technological change, *Journal of Political Economy*, vol. 98, pp. 71–102.

Rostovtzeff, M. (1941), *The Social and Economic History of the Hellenistic World*, Oxford: Clarendon Press.

Ruffin, Roy J., and Farhad Rassekh (1986), The role of foreign direct investment in US capital outflows, *American Economic Review*, vol. 76, pp. 1126–30.

Saitō, Seiichirō (1996), Keizai Kyōshitsu: Kinyū Shisutemu, shijōgenrini, *Nihon Keizai Shinbun*, 23 August.

Saitō, Seiichirō (2000), Keizai Kyōshitsu: Stockjūshi no riron, seisaku wo, *Nihon Keizai Shinbun*, 23 August.

Santoni, G. J. (1987), Changes in wealth and the velocity of money, *Review*, St. Louis: Federal Reserve Bank of St. Louis, March, pp. 16–26.

Sawamoto, Kuniho, and Nobuyuki Ichikawa (1994), Implementation of monetary policy in Japan, in Tomas J. T. Balino and Carlo Cottarelli (eds), *Frameworks for Monetary Stability*, Washington, DC: IMF.

Schumpeter, Joseph A. (1912), *Theorie der wirtschaftlichen Entwicklung*, Leipzig: Duncker and Humblot.

Schumpeter, Joseph A. (1917–18), Das Sozialprodukt und die Rechenpfennige: Glossen und Beitraege zur Geldtheorie von heute, *Archiv fuer Sozialwissenschaften und Sozialpolitik*, vol. 44, pp. 627–715.

Schumpeter, Joseph A. (1934), The theory of economic development, *Harvard Economic Studies*, Volume 46, Cambridge, MA: Harvard University Press.

Schumpeter, Joseph A. (1954), *History of Economic Analysis*, New York: Oxford University Press.

Selden, R. T. (1956), Monetary velocity in the United States, in Milton Friedman (ed.), *Studies in the Quantity Theory of Money*, Chicago: University of Chicago Press.

Seyffert, Oskar (1904), *Dictionary of Classical Antiquities*, translated, revised and edited, with additions, by Henry Nettleship and J. E. Sandys, New York.

Shaw, Edward S. (1973), *Financial Deepening and Economic Development*, New York: Oxford University Press.

Sheard, Paul (1989), The main bank system and corporate monitoring and control in Japan, *Journal of Economic Behaviour and Organisation*, vol. 11, pp. 399–422.

Sheard, Paul (1994), Interlocking shareholdings and corporate governance in Japan, in Masahiko Aoki and Ronald Dore (eds), *The Japanese Firm: The Sources of Competitive Strength*, Oxford: Oxford University Press, pp. 310–49.

Sheng, Andrew (1992), *Bad Debts in Transitional Socialist Economies*, Washington, DC: World Bank, Financial Policy and Systems Division.

Sheng, Andrew (1996), Banking fragility in the 1980s: an overview, in Andrew Sheng (ed.), *Bank Restructuring – Lessons from the 1980s*, Washington, DC: World Bank.

Shibuya, Hiroshi (1991), Dogakuteki tsuka kachi no antei to kinyu seisaku – kinri, shisan kakaku, infre shihyo, mimeo, Riron Keizei Gakkai (Conference of the Japanese Association of Economic Theory).

Shigemi, Yosuke (1995), Asset inflation in selected countries, *Bank of Japan Monetary and Economic Studies*, vol. 13, no. 2, December.

Shimizu, Yoshinori (2000), Convoy regulation, bank management, and the financial crisis in Japan, in Ryoichi Mikitani and Adam S. Posen (eds), *Japan's Financial Crisis and its Parallels to U.S. Experience*, Special Report no. 13, Washington, DC: Institute for International Economics, September.

Shinohara, Soichi, and Mitsuo Fukuda (1982), Nichigin kashidashi to madoguchi shidō no yūkosei, *Keizai Kenkyū*, vol. 33, pp. 259–62.

Shinpo, Seiji (1996), Keizai Kyōshitsu: Sairyōseisaku yori, chūchōkijūshini, *Nihon Keizai Shinbun*, 10 April.

Shirakawa, Masaaki (2001), Monetary policy under the zero interest rate constraint and balance sheet adjustment, *Economics*, May, Tokyo: Toyo Keizai Shinpo Sha.

Siegel, Diane F., and Steven Strongin (1986), Can the monetary models be fixed?, *Economic Perspectives*, Chicago: Federal Reserve Bank of Chicago, November/December, pp. 3–14.

Sim, Stuart (2004), *Fundamentalist World: The New Age of Dogma*, Cambridge: Icon Books.

Sims, C. A. (1972), Money, income and causality, *American Economic Review*, vol. 62, pp. 540–52.

Skidelsky, Robert (2000), *John Maynard Keynes, Fighting for Freedom, 1937–1946*, London: Penguin.

Smith, Jeremy (2003), International productivity comparisons: an examination of data sources, *International Productivity Monitor*, Spring.

Smith, Richard H., Ed Diener and Douglas H. Wedell (1989), Intrapersonal and social comparison determinants of happiness: a range-frequency analysis, *Journal of Personality and Social Psychology*, vol. 56, no. 3, pp. 317–25.

Smithers, Andrew (2001), The importance of funding policy for Japan's recovery, Smithers & Co., 29 September; as quoted by Guido Zimmermann, Deflation und Geldpolitik in Japan: Was laeuft falsch? Japan Analysen Prognosen Nr. 185, May 2002, Japan-Zentrum der Ludwig-Maximilian-Universitaet Muenchen, Munich.

Solow, Robert M. (1957) Technical change and the aggregate production function, *Review of Economics and Statistics*, vol. 39, pp. 312–20.

Sparks, Christopher, and Mary Greiner (1997), US and foreign productivity and unit labor costs, *Monthly Labor Review*, Bureau of Labor Statistics, February, pp. 26–49.

Spencer, Roger W. and William P. Yohe (1970), The 'crowding out' of private expenditure by fiscal policy actions, *Federal Reserve Bank of St. Louis Review*, vol. 52, October, pp. 12– .

Spiethoff, Arthur (1905), *Beitraege zur Analyse und Theorie der allgemeinen Wirtschaftskrisen*, Berlin: Duncker und Humblot.

Spindt, Paul A. (1985), Money is what money does: monetary aggregation and the equation of exchange, *Journal of Political Economy*, vol. 93, pp. 175–204.

Spindt, P. A. (1987), On the supply of the demand for money, Special Studies Paper, no. 215, Washington, DC: Board of Governors of the Federal Reserve System.

Stiglitz, Joseph E. (2001), Information and the change in the paradigm in Economics, Prize Lecture, given on the occasion of the award of the Bank of Sweden Prize in Economic Sciences, 8 December, currently available at: www.nobel.se/economics/laureates/2001/stiglitz-lecture.pdf

Stiglitz, Joseph E. (2002), *Globalisation and its Discontents*, New York: W. W. Norton.

Stiglitz, Joseph E., and Bruce Greenwald (2003), *Towards a New Paradigm in Monetary Economics*, Cambridge: Cambridge University Press.

Stiglitz, Joseph E., and Andrew Weiss (1981), Credit rationing in markets with imperfect information, *American Economic Review*, vol. 71, no. 3, pp. 393–410.

Stiglitz, Joseph E., and Andrew Weiss (1988), Banks as social accountants and screening devices for the allocation of credit, NBER Working Paper no. 2710, National Bureau of Economic Research.

Stiglitz, Joseph E., and Andrew Weiss (1992), Asymmetric information in credit markets and its implications for macro-economics, *Oxford Economic Papers*, vol. 44, no. 4, October, pp. 694–724.

Stock, J. H. and M. W. Watson (1989), New indexes of coincident and leading economic indicators, *NBER Macroeconomics Annual*, Cambridge, MA: MIT Press, pp. 351–93.

Stone, Courtenay C., and Daniel L. Thornton (1987), Solving the 1980s' velocity puzzle: a progress report, *Review*, St. Louis: Federal Reserve Bank of St. Louis, August/September, pp. 5–23.

Sundararajan, Vasudevan, and Tomas Balino (eds) (1991), *Banking Crises: Cases and Issues*, Washington, DC: IMF.

Suzuki, Yoshio (1974), *Gendai Nihon kinyūron*, Tokyo: Toyo Keizai Shinpo Sha.

Svensson, L. O. (1999), Price-level targeting versus inflation targeting: a free lunch?, *Journal of Money, Credit and Banking*, vol. 31, pp. 277–95.

Takenaka, Heizo (1996), Keizai Kyōshitsu: Seisaku kettei e no michisuji minaose, *Nihon Keizai Shinbun*, 15 May.

Tatom, John A. (1983), Was the 1982 velocity decline unusual?, *Review*, St. Louis: Federal Reserve Bank of St. Louis, August/September, pp. 5–15.

Tatom, John A. (1985), Two views of the effects of government budget deficits in the 1980s, *Review*, St. Louis: Federal Reserve Bank of St. Louis, October.

Taylor, Herb (1986), What has happened to M1?, *Business Review*, Philadelphia: Federal Reserve Bank of Philadelphia, September/October, pp. 3–14.

Taylor, J. B. (2000), Alternative views of the money transmission mechanism: what difference do they make for monetary policy?, *Oxford Review of Economic Policy*, vol. 16, pp. 60–73.

Teranishi, Juro (1982), *Nihon no keizai hatten to kinyūron*, Tokyo: Iwanami Shoten.

Tett, Gillian (1998), A bang or a whimper? An inefficient system for allocating capital is the issue at the heart of Japan's decision to launch today's Big Bang, *Financial Times*, 31 March.

Tett, Gillian (2001), Japan set for delay in dealing with bad loans, *Financial Times*, 7 June.

Thaler, Richard H. (1992), *The Winner's Curse: Paradoxes and Anomalies of Economic Life*, New York: Free Press.

Thomas, R. Leighton (1997), *Modern Econometrics*, Harlow: Pearson Education Ltd.

Thornton, Daniel L. (1994), Financial innovation, deregulation and the 'credit view' of monetary policy, *Review*, St. Louis: Federal Reserve Bank of St. Louis, no. 1, January/February, pp. 31–49.

Thornton, Henry (1802), *An Enquiry into the Nature and Effects of the Paper Credit of Great Britain*, London: Hatchard.

Tobin, James (1963), Commercial banks as creators of 'money', in D. Carson (ed.), *Banking and Monetary Studies*, Irwin: Homewood; reprinted in *Essays in Economics*, Volume I, *Macroeconomics*, Amsterdam: North-Holland.

Tobin, James (1969), A general equilibrium approach to monetary theory, *Journal of Money, Credit and Banking*, vol. 1, pp. 15–29.

Tobin, James (1980), Stabilisation policy ten years after, *Brookings Papers on Economic Activity*, vol. 1, pp. 19–72.

Trautwein, Hans-Michael (2000), The credit view, old and new, *Journal of Economic Surveys*, vol. 14, no. 2, pp. 155–89.

Trescott, Paul B. (1960), *Money, Banking and Economic Welfare*, New York: McGraw-Hill.

Trichet, Jean-Claude (2004a), The challenges for the European economy in 2004, speech by Jean-Claude Trichet, President of the European Central Bank, Conference organized by Foro de la Nueva Economia and The Wall Street Journal, Madrid, 29 January 2004, obtained at: www.ecb.int/press/key/date/2004/html/sp040129.en.html

Trichet, Jean-Claude (2004b), Structural reforms and growth, as highlighted by the Irish case Keynote Address by Jean-Claude Trichet, President of the European Central Bank, delivered at the Whitaker Lecture organized by the Central Bank and Financial Services Authority of Ireland, Dublin, 31 May 2004, obtained at: www.ecb.int/press/key/date/2004/html/sp040531.en.html

Trichet, Jean-Claude (2004c), Supply side economics and monetary policy, speech by Jean-Claude Trichet, President of the European Central Bank, at the Institut der Deutschen Wirtschaft, Köln, 22 June 2004, obtained at: www.ecb.int/press/key/date/2004/html/sp040622_1.en.html

Trichet, Jean-Claude (2004d), The current state of the European economy and the ECB's monetary policy concept, speech by Jean-Claude Trichet, President of the European Central Bank, delivered at the International Financial Forum, Paris Europlace, Paris, 9 July 2004, obtained at: www.ecb.int/press/key/date/2004/html/sp040709.en.html

Tullock, Gordon (1957), Paper money – a cycle in Cathay, *Economic History Review*, new series, vol. 9, issue 3, pp. 393–407.

Tversky, Amos, and Dale Griffin (1991), Endowment and contrast in judgments of well-being, in Richard J. Zeckhauser (ed.), *Strategy and Choice*, Cambridge, MA, and London: MIT Press, pp. 297–318.

Ueda, Kazuo (1987), Japanese capital outflows: 1970 to 1986, unpublished paper, Osaka University, August.

Ueda, Kazuo (1990), Japanese capital outflows, *Journal of Banking and Finance*, vol. 14, pp. 1079–101.

Ueda, Kazuo (1993), A comparative perspective on Japanese monetary policy: short run monetary control and the transmission mechanism, in K. Singleton (ed.), *Japanese Monetary Policy*, Chicago: University of Chicago Press.

Ueda, Kazuo (1999), Remarks presented at a Federal Reserve Bank of Boston conference on monetary policy in a low-inflation environment, Woodstock, Vermont, 20 October, currently available at: www.boj.or.jp/en/press/04/press_f.htm

Ueda, Kazuo (2001a), Speech given at the Council on Foreign Relations in New York, 11 May, currently available at: www.boj.or.jp/en/press/04/press_f.htm

Ueda, Kazuo (2001b), Japan's liquidity trap and monetary policy, paper based on a speech given to the Japan Society of Monetary Economics held at Fukushima University, 29 September, currently available at: www.boj.or.jp/en/press/04/press_f.htm

Vilar, P. (1976), *A History of Gold and Money 1450–1920*, English edn, London: NLB.

Vittas, Dimitri, Gerard Caprio and Patrick Honohan (eds) (2002), *Financial Sector Policy for Developing Countries: A Reader*, Oxford: Oxford University Press; World Bank.

von Glahn, Richard (1996), *Fountain of Fortune: Money and Monetary Policy in China, 1000–1700*, Berkeley and Los Angeles: University of California Press.

Wagner, Adolph (1857), *Beitrage zur Lehre von den Banken*, Leipzig: L. Voss.

Wagner, Adolph (ed.) (1872), Karl Heinrich Rau's Lehrbuch der Finanzwissenschaft, 6. Ausg., vielfach verandert und theilweise vollig neu bearbeitet von Adolph Wagner, Leipzig: C. F. Winter.

Walker, W. Christopher (2002), Ricardian equivalence and fiscal policy effectiveness in Japan, Asian Economic Journal, vol. 16, no. 3, pp. 285–302.

Walsh, Carl E. (2003), *Monetary Theory and Policy*, Second Edition, Cambridge: MIT Press.

Weberpals, Isabelle (1997), The liquidity trap: evidence from Japan, Working Paper 97–4, Bank of Canada, February.

Werner, Richard A. (1991), The great yen illusion: Japanese capital flows and the role of land, Oxford, Institute of Economics and Statistics, *Applied Economics Discussion Paper Series*, no. 129, December.

Werner, Richard A. (1992), Towards a quantity theorem of disaggregated credit and international capital flows, paper presented at the Royal Economic Society Annual Conference, York, April 1993, and at the Fifth Annual PACAP Conference on Pacific-Asian Capital Markets in Kuala Lumpur, June 1993.

Werner, Richard A. (1993), Japanese-style capitalism: the new collectivist challenge? An analysis of the nature and origin of Japan's political economy and social order, paper presented at the Fifth Annual International Conference of the Society for the Advancement of Socio-Economics (SASE), 26–28 March, New School for Social Research, New York.

Werner, Richard A. (1994a), Japanese foreign investment and the 'land bubble', *Review of International Economics*, Oxford: Blackwell, vol. 2, issue 2, June, pp. 166–78.

Werner, Richard A. (1994b), *Liquidity Watch*, Jardine Fleming Securities, Tokyo, May.

Werner, Richard A. (1994c), Q4CY94, *Economic Quarterly*, Jardine Fleming Securities, Tokyo, October.

Werner, Richard A. (1995a), Bank of Japan: start the presses!, *Asian Wall Street Journal*, 13 June.

Werner, Richard A. (1995b), *Liquidity Watch*, Jardine Fleming Securities, Tokyo, June.

Werner, Richard A. (1995c), Keiki kaifuku, ryōteki kinyū kanwa kara, *Nihon Keizai Shinbun*, Keizai Kyoshitsu, 2 September.

Werner, Richard A. (1995d), Q3 1995: Japan at the crossroads, *Economic Quarterly*, Jardine Fleming Securities, Tokyo, September.

Werner, Richard A. (1996a), Liquidity no nobi, kasoku, *Nikkei Kinyū Shinbun*, 28 February.

Werner, Richard A. (1996b), The BoJ prolonged Japan's recession, *Asian Wall Street Journal*, 13 June.

Werner, Richard A. (1996c), Nichigin manipulation, *Ronso Toyokeizai*, Part I: July, pp. 64–73; Part II: September, pp. 130–9; Part III: November, pp. 190–5, Tokyo: Toyo Keizai Shinpo Sha (in Japanese).

Werner, Richard A. (1996d), Has there been a 'credit crunch' in Japan?, paper presented at the Fifth Convention of the East Asian Economic Association (EAEA), Bangkok, October.

Werner, Richard A. (1996e), How the Bank of Japan won, *Asian Wall Street Journal*, 11 November.

Werner, Richard A. (1997a), Ryoteki kinyū kanwa de keikikaifuku, *Nihon Keizai Shinbun*, Keizai Kyoshitsu, 26 February.

Werner, Richard A. (1997b), Dokuritsusei yorimo kokumin no kanshi kyoka o isoge, *Shukan Toyo Keizai*, 31 May.

Werner, Richard A. (1997c), 'Shinyō sōzōryō' ga seichō no kagi, *Nihon Keizai Shinbun*, Keizai Kyoshitsu, 16 July.

Werner, Richard A. (1997d), Towards a new monetary paradigm: a quantity theorem of disaggregated credit, with evidence from Japan, *Kredit und Kapital*, vol. 30, no. 2, pp. 276–309, Berlin: Duncker und Humblot.

Werner, Richard A. (1997e), Kawase retowa shinyōsōzōryōkakusa de kimaru, *Shūkan Economist*, 26 August, Mainichi Shinbunsha, Tokyo.

Werner, Richard A. (1997f), Zaiseihikishimewa keikino purasuzairyōda, *Shūkan Economist*, 23 September, Mainichi Shinbunsha, Tokyo.

Werner, Richard A. (1998a), Ginkōno riagewa keikikaifuku no zenchōda, *Shūkan Economist*, 16 June, Mainichi Shinbunsha, Tokyo.

Werner, Richard A. (1998b), Minkan ginkō kara no kariire de, keikitaisaku wo okonaeba 'issekinichō', *Shūkan Economist*, 14 July, Mainichi Shinbunsha, Tokyo.

Werner, Richard A. (1998c), Keiki handan wo ayamaraseru nichigin no jōhōdokusen, *Shūkan Economist*, 18 August, Mainichi Shinbunsha, Tokyo.

Werner, Richard A. (1998d), Bank of Japan window guidance and the creation of the bubble, in Florentino Rodao and Antonio Lopez Santos (eds), *El Japon Contemporaneo*, Salamanca: University of Salamanca Press, 1998.

Werner, Richard A. (1998e), Shinyōsōzō wa fuetekita 99nendowa josōgai no seichōka, *Shūkan Economist*, 10 November, Mainichi Shinbunsha, Tokyo.

Werner, Richard A. (1998f), Keikiwa zaiseiseisaku dewanaku, kinyūseisaku no tenkande kaifuku ni mukau, *Shūkan Economist*, 8 December, Mainichi Shinbunsha, Tokyo.

Werner, Richard A. (1998g), BIS kara tettai, beikokusaimo baikyakuwo, *Jitsugyō no nihon*, October.

Werner, Richard A. (1999a), Nihon ni okeru madoguchi shidō to 'bubble' no keisei, *Gendai Finance*, MPT Forum, Tokyo: Toyo Keizai Shinpo Sha, March (in Japanese).

Werner, Richard A. (1999b), Chōkikinri no jōshō wa 99nenkeikifaifuku no shōka, *Shūkan Economist*, 12 January, Mainichi Shinbunsha, Tokyo.

Werner, Richard A. (1999c), Krugmankyojūni hanron, nichiginwa ōhaba ni tsū kakyōkyūwo fuyashiteiru, *Shūkan Economist*, 9 February, Mainichi Shinbunsha, Tokyo.

Werner, Richard A. (1999d), Why the Bank of Japan is responsible for creating, prolonging the recession, *Nikkei Weekly*, 12 July.

Werner, Richard A. (1999e), Bubble no yōinwo tsukuttanowa nichigin no madoguchi shidō data, *Shūkan Economist*, 13 April, Mainichi Shinbunsha, Tokyo.

Werner, Richard A. (1999f), Kōkanonai nichigin no kawase shijōkainyū, *Shūkan Economist*, 13 July, Mainichi Shinbunsha, Tokyo.

Werner, Richard A. (1999g), Japans Wirtschaftsreformen der neunziger Jahre: back to the future, in Werner Schaumann (ed.), *Japans Kultur der Reformen, Referate des 6. Japanologentages der OAG in Tokyo*, Iudicium, Munich (in German).

Werner, Richard A. (1999h), Soundness of financial systems: bank restructuring and its impact on the economy, paper presented at the International Conference on Central Banking Policies, 14–15 May, Macau Cultural Centre.

Werner, Richard A. (1999i), Nichiginwa futatabi keikikaifuku no me wo tsundeiru, *Shūkan Economist*, 10 August, Mainichi Shinbunsha, Tokyo.

Werner, Richard A. (1999j), Keizaitaisaku ni hitsuyōnanowa nichiginhōno saikaiseida, *Shūkan Economist*, 12 October, Mainichi Shinbunsha, Tokyo.

Werner, Richard A. (2000a), Seifu no minkanginkō kara no kariireseisaku wo kangei suru, *Shūkan Economist*, 7 March, Mainichi Shinbunsha, Tokyo.

Werner, Richard A. (2000b), Indian macroeconomic management: at the crossroads between government and markets, in Ghon S. Rhee (ed.), *Rising to the Challenge in Asia: A Study of Financial Markets*, Volume 5: India, Manila: Asian Development Bank.

Werner, Richard A. (2000c), Macroeconomic management in Thailand: the policy-induced crisis, in Ghon S. Rhee (ed.), *Rising to the Challenge in Asia: A Study of Financial Markets*, Volume 11: Thailand, Manila: Asian Development Bank, September, also available on the internet at: www.profitresearch.co.jp

Werner, Richard A. (2000d), Japan's plan to borrow from banks deserves praise, *Financial Times*, 9 February.

Werner, Richard A. (2001a), *En no Shihaisha*, Soshisha, Tokyo.

Werner, Richard A. (2001b), Rejoinder to book review by Mr Isao Kubota of Princes of the Yen, GLOCOM Global Communications Platform (online available online at: www.glocom.org/debates/200110_werner_rejoinder/index.html and in GLOCOM Monthly Newsletter), Tokyo, October.

Werner, Richard A. (2001c), Chū ginkō wa kaheikyōkyū ni yotte keizaiseichō wo tsukuridasu kotoga dekiru, *Kinyuzaisei Jijō (Finance Review)*, 15 October, pp. 26–30.

Werner, Richard A. (2002a), Monetary policy implementation in Japan: what they say vs. what they do, *Asian Economic Journal*, vol. 16, no. 2, Oxford: Blackwell, June, pp. 111–51.

Werner, Richard A. (2002b), The 'enigma' of Japanese policy ineffectiveness in the 1990s, *The Japanese Economy*, vol. 30, no. 1, Armonk, NY: M. E. Sharpe.

Werner, Richard A. (2002c), The impact of German development economics on modern Japanese society, paper presented at the Sixth Conference on Social Change and Economic Development in the History of Economic Thought, European Society for the History of Economic Thought (ESHET) 2002, 14–17 March, Rethymno, University of Crete; short version in Yiorgios Stathakis and Gianni Vaggi (eds) (2003), *Perspectives on the History of Economic Thought*, Cheltenham: Edward Elgar.

Werner, Richard A. (2002d), How to get growth in Japan, *Central Banking*, vol. XIII, no. 2, November, pp. 48–54.

Werner, Richard A. (2002e), Rezession aus Frankfurt, *Financial Times Deutschland*, 22 August.

Werner, Richard A. (2003a), *Kyokō no Shūen, Makurokeizai Shin Paradaimu no Makuake*, Tokyo: PHP Kenkyūjo.

Werner, Richard A. (2003b), *Nazo Toki – Heisei Daifukyō*, Tokyo: PHP Kenkyūjo.

Werner, Richard A. (2003c), *Princes of the Yen: Japan's Central Bankers and the Transformation of the Economy*, Armonk, NY: M. E. Sharpe.

Werner, Richard A. (2003d), A reconsideration of the rationale for bank-centered economic systems and the effectiveness of directed credit policies in the light of Japanese evidence, *The Japanese Economy*, vol. 30, no. 6, November–December 2002, pp. 3–37.

Werner, Richard (2003e), *Fukyō ga owaranai hontō no riyū* (Central Banking and Structural Change) (in Japanese), Tokyo: Soshisha.

Werner, Richard A. (2004a), No recovery without reform? An empirical evaluation of the structural reform argument in Japan, *Asian Business and Management*, vol. 3, no. 1, London: Palgrave Macmillan.

Werner, Richard A. (2004b), Post-crisis banking sector restructuring and its impact on economic growth, *The Japanese Economy*, vol. 30, no. 6, November–December 2002, pp. 3–37.

Werner, Richard A. (2004c), Aspects of career development and information management policies at the Bank of Japan. A frank interview with a fomer central banker, *The Japanese Economy*, vol. 30, no. 6, November–December 2002, pp. 38–60.

Werner, Richard A. (2004d), A discussion of Anil K. Kashyap's paper 'Sorting out Japan's financial crisis', *The Japanese Economy*, vol. 30, no. 6, November–December 2002, pp. 61–87.

Werner, Richard A. (2004e), The credit creation process in the German 'Credit School' and its impact on the design of financial markets in Germany and Japan, paper presented at the Eighth Annual Conference of the European Society for the History of Economic Thought (ESHET), 'Money and Markets', Venezia and Treviso, February.

Werner, Richard A. (2004f), Why has fiscal policy disappointed in Japan? Revisiting the pre-Keynesian view on the ineffectiveness of fiscal policy, paper presented at the International Conference in Macroeconomic Analysis and International Finance 2004, Rethymno, University of Crete, May, and the 21st Symposium on Banking and Monetary Economics, University of Nice – Sophia Antipolis, June.

Whyte, William Foote (1988), *Learning from the Field: A Guide from Experience*, Beverly Hills, CA: Sage Publications.

Wicksell, Knut (1898), *Geldzins und Gueterpreise*, Jena: Fisher.

Wicksell, Knut (1906), *Lectures on Political Economy*, London: Routledge & Kegan Paul Ltd.

Wicksell, Knut (1907), The influence of the rate of interest on prices, *Economic Journal*, vol. 17, pp. 213–20.

Willett, Thomas D., and Francesco Forte (1969), Interest rate policy and external balance, *Quarterly Journal of Economics*, vol. 78, pp. 242–62.

Williamson, S. D. (1986), Costly monitoring, financial intermediation and equilibrium credit rationing, *Journal of Monetary Economics*, vol. 18, no. 1, pp. 159–79.

Wilson, D. (2000), Japan's slow-down: monetary versus real explanations, *Oxford Review of Economic Policy*, vol. 16, pp. 18–33.

Withers, Hartley (1909), *The Meaning of Money*, London: Smith, Elder.

Wolf, Martin (2002), How to avert a ratings disaster, *Financial Times*, 27 March.

Woo, David (1999), In search of a 'capital crunch': supply factors behind the credit slowdown in Japan, IMF Working Paper no. 99/3, Washington, DC: IMF.

Woolley, Charles Leonard (1936), *Abraham, Recent Discoveries and Hebrew Origins*, London: Faber and Faber.

Wray, Randall L. (1990), *Money and Credit in Capitalist Economies: The Endogenous Money Approach*, Aldershot: Edward Elgar.

Wray, Randall (2001), The endogenous money approach, Center for Full Employment and Price Stability, Working Paper no. 17, August.

Yamada, H. (2000), M2 demand relation and effective exchange rate in Japan: a cointegration analysis, *Applied Economic Letters*, vol. 7, pp. 229–32.

Yamaguchi, Yutaka (1999), Monetary policy and structural policy: a Japanese perspective, speech by Yutaka Yamaguchi, Deputy Governor of the Bank of Japan, before Colloque Monetaire International at Banque de France, 8–9 October, available at: www.boj.or.jp

Yamaguchi, Yutaka (2001a), Remarks by Yutaka Yamaguchi, Deputy Governor of the Bank of Japan, at the Edinburgh Finance and Investment Seminar, 22 June, available at: www.boj.or.jp/en/press/koen068.htm

Yamaguchi, Yutaka (2001b), Remarks by Yutaka Yamaguchi, Deputy Governor of the Bank of Japan, at the JCIF International Finance Seminar, 17 October (English translation by the Bank of Japan, 22 October), available at: www. boj.or.jp/en/press/

Yamaguchi, Yutaka (2001c), The economic situation and monetary policy in Japan, speech given by Yutaka Yamaguchi, Deputy Governor of the Bank of Japan, at the Economic Seminar of the Japan Research Institute, 26 November, available at: www.boj.or.jp

Yoshida, Kazuo (1996), Keizai Kyōshitsu: Mato hazure data 'keiki taisaku', *Nihon Keizai Shinbun*, 25 January.

Yoshikawa, Hiroshi (1993), Monetary policy and the real economy in Japan, in Kenneth Singleton (ed.), *Japanese Monetary Policy*, Chicago: University of Chicago Press, pp. 121–59.

Yoshikawa H., E. Eto and T. Ike (1994), Chusho kigyo ni taisuru ginko ni yoru 'kashishiburi' ni tsuite keizai bunseki: seisaku kenkyu no shiten, Tokyo: Economic Planning Agency.

Yoshino, Naoyuki (1991), Nonbank no yushi to chika, *Jutaku Tochi Keizai*, Summer.

Yoshino, Toshihiko (1962), *Waga Kuni no Kinyūseido to Kinyūseisaku*, Tokyo: Shiseido.

Yoshitomi, Masaru (1996), Keizai Kyōshitsu: Zaisei, kōzōakaji no teichaku fusege, *Nihon Keizai Shinbun*, 26 February.

Yoshitomi, Masaru (2000), Policy prescriptions for East Asia, in Eric S. Rosengren and John S. Jordan (eds), *Building an Infrastructure for Financial Stability*, Federal Reserve Bank of Boston Conference Series no. 44, Boston: Federal Reserve Bank of Boston, June, currently available at: www.bos.frb.org/economic/conf/conf44/cf44_20.pdf

Index of Authors

Compiled by Sue Carlton

Index of Subjects

Compiled by Sue Carlton

Printed in Great Britain
by Amazon